Meaning and Power in the Language of Law

Legal practitioners, linguists, anthropologists, philosophers and others have all explored fundamental challenges presented by language in formulating, interpreting and applying laws. Building on centuries of interaction between legal practice and jurisprudence, the modern field of 'law and language', or 'forensic linguistics', brings insights in linguistics and related fields to bear on topics including legal drafting and translation, statutory interpretation, expert evidence on language use and dynamics of courtroom interaction. This volume presents an interlocking series of research studies engaged with different legal jurisdictions and sociopolitical contexts as well as with the more abstract notion of 'law'. Together the chapters, written by international leaders in their fields, highlight recent directions in research and investigate in particular how law expresses yet also conceals power relations in its crafted use of words and in the gaps and silence between those words.

JANNY HC LEUNG is Associate Professor of English and Programme Director of Law and Literary Studies at the University of Hong Kong. She co-authored the book *Language and Law: A Resource Book for Students* with Alan Durant (2016); her monograph, titled *Shallow Equality and Symbolic Jurisprudence in Multilingual Legal Orders*, is forthcoming.

ALAN DURANT is Professor of Communication in the School of Law at Middlesex University, London. His recent books include *Language and Law*, co-authored with Janny HC Leung (2016), *Language and Media*, co-authored with Marina Lambrou (2009) and *Meaning in the Media: Discourse, Controversy and Debate* (2010).

Meaning and Power in the Language of Law

Edited by

Janny HC Leung

University of Hong Kong

Alan Durant

Middlesex University, London

CAMBRIDGE
UNIVERSITY PRESS

CAMBRIDGE
UNIVERSITY PRESS

University Printing House, Cambridge CB2 8BS, United Kingdom

One Liberty Plaza, 20th Floor, New York, NY 10006, USA

477 Williamstown Road, Port Melbourne, VIC 3207, Australia

314–321, 3rd Floor, Plot 3, Splendor Forum, Jasola District Centre, New Delhi - 110025, India

79 Anson Road, #06-04/06, Singapore 079906

Cambridge University Press is part of the University of Cambridge.

It furthers the University's mission by disseminating knowledge in the pursuit of education, learning, and research at the highest international levels of excellence.

www.cambridge.org
Information on this title: www.cambridge.org/9781107112841
DOI: 10.1017/9781316285756

First published 2018

Printed in the United Kingdom by Clays, St Ives plc

A catalogue record for this publication is available from the British Library

ISBN 978-1-107-11284-1 Hardback

Contents

Contributors

JANET AINSWORTH is the John D. Eshelman Professor of Law at Seattle University. Before joining the law school faculty in 1988, she practiced law at the Seattle-King County Public Defender Association. Her research interests lie at the intersection of law, language and culture. Author of more than thirty articles and book chapters, she has published in law reviews such as the *Yale Law Journal* and the *Cornell Law Review* as well as in linguistics journals; her articles have been reprinted or excerpted in six anthologies. Her most recent publications include *Speaking of Language and Law*, with Roger Shuy and Lawrence Solan, published in 2015, and *Discursive Constructions of Consent in the Legal Process*, with Susan Ehrlich and Diana Eades, published in 2016. She serves on the editorial boards of several international journals and, with Lawrence Solan, is co-editor of the Oxford University Press series, *Studies on Language and the Law*. In 2016, she was awarded a Lifetime Achievement Award by the Germanic Society for Forensic Linguistics. Her *pro bono* legal activities include authoring *amicus curiae* briefs to appellate courts, including the US Supreme Court, serving as a member of Washington State Supreme Court Committee on Pattern Jury Instructions and volunteering as appellate consultant to the National Association of Criminal Defense Lawyers, from which she received its Outstanding Service Award in recognition of her contributions.

SILVIA DAHMEN teaches phonetics and linguistics at the English department of Cologne University in Germany. Prior to this position, she taught at the German department of Cologne University. She holds a PhD in phonetics, an MA in English Linguistics and Literature and in Scandinavian Languages, and a degree in Intercultural Education. Her main fields of research are the influence of first-language phonetics and phonology on the pronunciation of German and English as a second language, effectiveness of pronunciation training methods for second-language learners and the role of phonetics in the field of language and law.

ALAN DURANT is Professor of Communication in the School of Law at Middlesex University, London. Before transferring into law, he was Professor of Communication at Middlesex University Business School, and earlier Professor and Head of the School of English, Cultural and Communication Studies, also at Middlesex. Previous posts include Professor and Head of English at Goldsmiths' College, University of London (1990–93) and Director of the Programme in Literary Linguistics, University of Strathclyde, Glasgow (1986–90). Among his earlier books, *Meaning in the Media: Discourse, Controversy and Debate* was published in 2010 and *Language and Media*, co-authored with Marina Lambrou, was published in 2009. With Janny HC Leung, he is co-author of *Language and Law: a Resource Book for Students* (2016).

KRISTIN ENOLA GILBERT is a PhD candidate in the Department of Criminology, Law & Justice at the University of Illinois at Chicago. She is the author of peer-reviewed articles in *Gesture* and *Multimodal Communication*. She studied gesture with Susan Goldin-Meadow at the University of Chicago and is completing a dissertation on multimodal conduct in focus groups evaluating community policing training in the United States.

PETER GOODRICH was the founding Dean of the Department of Law, Birkbeck College, University of London, where he was Corporation of London Professor of Law before he moved to Cardozo School of Law, New York, in 1999. In the expansive domains of international legal education, Goodrich teaches and researches law, aesthetics and film, and, not afraid of medieval-length titles, recently published *Legal Emblems and the Art of Law:* Obiter depicta *as the Vision of Governance* (2014). He co-authored and co-produced the feature documentary *Auf Wiedersehen: 'Til We Meet Again* (2011) and is the artistic director of the short documentary *Of Many* (2014). Currently completing a book on Judge Daniel Paul Schreber, titled *Schreber's Law: Jurisprudence and Judgment*, he is Director of the Program in Law and Humanities at Cardozo School of Law and Affiliate Professor of Law in the School of Social Science at New York University, Abu Dhabi.

CHRIS HEFFER is Director of MA Programmes, including the MA in Forensic Linguistics, in the Centre for Language and Communication Research at Cardiff University, and co-founder of Cardiff Language and Law (CaLL). He has published articles in linguistic and legal journals on various theoretical and communicational aspects of the trial process and jury instruction and is the author of *The Language of Jury Trial: A Corpus-aided Analysis of Legal-Lay Discourse* (2005) and co-editor of *Legal-Lay Communication: Textual Travels in the Law* (2013). He has a particular interest in communication breakdown between judge and jury and has advised judicial studies boards on this. Heffer is currently completing a book on untruthfulness, *Lying and Bullshit in Life and Law: The Untruthfulness Framework*, and has also been working for several years on a monograph, *Rhetoric and Rights: A Theory of Forensic Discourse*. He sits on the editorial board of the Oxford University Press Language and Law series and is possibly the only forensic linguist to have testified in a trademark case in the United Kingdom.

CHRISTOPHER HUTTON is Chair Professor in the School of English at the University of Hong Kong. He taught Yiddish Studies as an assistant professor in the Department of Germanic Languages at the University of Texas at Austin from 1987 to 1989 before moving to Hong Kong. His research concerns the history of linguistics, in particular the relationship between linguistics and race theory, linguistics and colonialism, and linguistics and fascism. In the last decade he has been working on the politics of language and interpretation in the context of the law. His publications include *Linguistics and the Third Reich* (1999), *Race and the Third Reich* (2005), *Language, Law and Definition* (with Roy Harris, 2007), *Language, Meaning and the Law* (2009), *Word Meaning and Legal Interpretation* (2014), and *Signs, Meaning and Experience* (with Adrian Pablé, 2015).

JANNY HC LEUNG is Associate Professor of English at the University of Hong Kong. She has an LLM from Yale and a PhD in applied linguistics from Cambridge, and currently coordinates a double degree programme in Law and Literary Studies at the University of Hong Kong. Her research interest lies in the interdisciplinary area of language and law, with a particular focus on bilingual and multilingual jurisdictions. Her articles have appeared in journals including *Semiotica, International Journal of Speech, Language and Law, Journal of Legal Pluralism, Journal of Multilingual and Multicultural Development* and *International Journal of the Semiotics of Law.* She was a Visiting Scholar at the Harvard-Yenching Institute, Harvard University, in 2013–14, and, with Alan Durant, is co-author of *Language and Law: A Resource Book for Students* (2016). Her monograph, titled *Shallow Equality and Symbolic Jurisprudence in Multilingual Legal Orders*, is forthcoming.

MEIZHEN LIAO obtained his PhD in linguistics from the Chinese Academy of Social Sciences. He is currently Professor of Linguistics of the School of Foreign Languages, Central China Normal University. His academic interests include forensic linguistics, pragmatics and discourse metaphor. Among his publications are 'Metaphor as a Textual Strategy in English' (*Text*, 1999); 'A Study of Interruption in Chinese Criminal Courtroom Discourse' (*Text & Talk*, 2009); *A Study of Courtroom Questions, Responses and their Interaction* (2003); 'The Goal-Driven Principle of Communication' (*Journal of Foreign Languages*, 2009); and 'Courtroom Discourse in China' (in *Handbook of Language and Law*, 2012).

GREGORY MATOESIAN is a professor in the Department of Criminology, Law & Justice at the University of Illinois at Chicago. He is a formally trained linguist and social theorist. His main interest is multimodal conduct in the construction and co-construction of legal context. He is the author of *Reproducing Rape: Domination through Talk in the Courtroom* (1993) and *Law & the Language of Identity: Discourse in the William Kennedy Smith Rape Trial* (2001), and co-editor (along with Elizabeth Mertz and David Ford) of *Translating the Social World for Law* (2016).

LAURA NADER is Professor of Anthropology at the University of California, Berkeley. Her current work focuses on how central dogmas are made and how they work. *Energy Choices in a Democratic Society* (1980) is a multidisciplinary collaborative effort of the National Academy of Sciences. *Harmony Ideology – Justice and Control in a Zapotec Mountain Village* (1990) and *Essays in Controlling Processes* (1994, 1996, 2002) emerge from a theoretical perspective that crosses disciplinary boundaries. *Naked Science – Anthropological Inquiry into Boundaries, Power and Knowledge* (1996) provides a framework for understanding power arrangements in global science. *The Life of the Law* (2002) is about the interface between law and anthropology with an argument that the plaintiff is the life of the law. Her films *To Make the Balance* and a later PBS film *Little Injustices* are widely disseminated, as is the book (with Ugo Mattei) *Plunder – When the Rule of Law is Illegal* (2008). Her most recent publication is *What the Rest Think of the West – Since 600 AD*, published 2015. In 1995 the Law and Society Association awarded her the Kalven Prize for distinguished research on law and society. Nader is a member of the American Academy of Arts and Sciences.

SIDDHARTH NARRAIN is a lawyer and legal researcher based in Delhi. He is currently a Visiting Faculty at the School of Law, Governance & Citizenship, Ambedkar University Delhi and an Honorary Visiting Fellow at The Sarai Programme, Centre for the Study of Developing Societies (CSDS), Delhi. His research focuses on legal issues arising around the circulation of excitable speech on social media during communal and ethnic violence in India. He follows and contributes to debates around freedom of speech and expression and gender and sexuality rights in India. Narrain has previously worked with the Alternative Law Forum, Bangalore, and as a journalist with *The Hindu* Group of publications in Delhi. He is co-editor of *The Shifting Scales of Justice: The Supreme Court in Neo-liberal India* (2014), a collection of essays on the politics of the Indian Supreme Court. His work has been published in a number of journals, magazines and websites including the *Economic and Political Weekly, Seminar, The Indian Express, The Asian Age, The New Indian Express, Kafila, The Hoot, The Wire, Scroll.In,*

Yahoo News, The Alternative, Infochange India, Himal Southasian and Time Out Bengaluru. Narrain studied at the National Law School of India University, Bangalore; the Asian College of Journalism, Chennai; and Harvard Law School.

KATSUO NAWA is Professor of Cultural Anthropology, Institute for Advanced Studies on Asia, the University of Tokyo. He was Research Scholar at the Centre of Nepal and Asian Studies, Tribhuvan University, Nepal (1992–95), Visiting Fellow, Clare Hall, the University of Cambridge (2002–03), and Visiting Scholar, Harvard-Yenching Institute (2013–14). Largely based on his ethnographic fieldwork in Far Western Nepal, he has written extensively on interethnic and inter-caste relations, the sococultural transformation and ritual process, and language use and its objectification. His current research interests include ethnohistory of a Himalayan village, politics and poetics of 'ethnic' movements and literacy, translation and language ideologies in Nepal. His major publication includes *Nepal, Byans oyobi Shuhen Chiiki niokeru Girei to Shakai Hanchu ni kansuru Minzokushiteki Kenkyu: Mouhitotu no 'Kindai' no Fuchi (An Ethnographic Study on Rituals and Social Categories of Byans, Nepal and Adjacent Regions: Another Constellation of 'Modernity')* (2002), which won the 30th Shibusawa prizes from the Shibusawa Fund for Ethnological Studies in 2004; and two volumes of books co-edited with Hiroshi Ishii and David N. Gellner, *Nepalis Inside and Outside Nepal: Social Dynamics in Northern South Asia* vol. 1, and *Political and Social Transformations in North India and Nepal: Social Dynamics in Northern South Asia* vol. 2 (2007). He is a co-editor of *Asian Anthropology*.

LAWRENCE M. SOLAN is the Don Forchelli Professor of Law and Director of the Center for the Study of Law, Language and Cognition at Brooklyn Law School. He holds a PhD in Linguistics from the University of Massachusetts and a JD from Harvard Law School. Much of his writing concerns the interpretation of statutes and contracts. His books include *The Language of Judges* (1993), *Speaking of Crime* (2005, with Peter Tiersma) and *The Language of Statutes: Laws and Their Interpretation* (2010). Solan and Peter Tiersma co-edited *The Oxford Handbook of Language and Law* (2012), and, with Janet Ainsworth and Roger Shuy, Solan is co-editor of *Speaking of Language and Law: Conversations on the Work of Peter Tiersma* (2015). Solan has been a visiting professor at Yale Law School, as well as in the Psychology Department and Humanities Council at Princeton University.

MARCO WAN is Associate Professor of Law and Honorary Associate Professor of English at the University of Hong Kong, where he directs the programme in Law and Literary Studies. He has published widely in law and the humanities. He edited *The Legal Case: Cross Currents between Law and the*

Humanities (2012) and is the author of *Masculinity and the Trials of Modern Fiction* (2016). He is Managing Editor of *Law and Literature*. He received his PhD and law degree from the University of Cambridge, where he was an Evan-Lewis Thomas Law Scholar and Sir Edward Youde Memorial Fellow. He also holds a BA from Yale University and an LLM from Harvard Law School. He is currently working on a monograph on law and Hong Kong cinema.

Acknowledgements

This volume would not have been possible without an event that provided its initial focus: an international roundtable held at Harvard in 2014, from which further discussion of the topics, critical exchanges and new and fundamentally revised contributions followed. The editors gratefully acknowledge the generous support of the Harvard-Yenching Institute in funding that scholarly meeting, during a period when Leung was a visiting scholar (academic year 2013–14). Not all the discussants at the roundtable were able to contribute to this volume, and not all contributors to the volume could attend the initial roundtable. But the 2014 sessions have remained an essential reference point in guiding the book's aims and significantly helped to shape its final content.

At Cambridge University Press the editors would like to thank Helen Barton for her encouragement of and continuing support to work at the intersection between linguistics and law, and Stephanie Taylor and Bethany Johnson for assistance in preparing the final version of the book from our manuscript.

Editors' Introduction

Janny HC Leung and Alan Durant

It is hardly a new observation that language is central to law. Such a claim seems self-evident: legal documents, as well as their interpretation and application, consist of words, and legal proceedings in courts and other tribunals take place primarily through language, in a combination of spoken and written forms. But sometimes a stronger claim is made: that language is not just central to but 'constitutive' of law. How far this further claim, which is debated from many different perspectives in this book, is supportable depends a lot on what speakers or writers intend by 'constitutive'. Even allowing for the performative capability of legal discourse discussed at various points in this volume (e.g. in bringing entities or relations between parties into being, or altering such relations), the force of law must always be recognised as also having non-verbal means of expression. Water cannons, firing squads and imprisonment have all played their part alongside speech in establishing and preserving 'law's authority' in various circumstances. But while linguistic operations and processes may not fully 'constitute' law, it is fair to say they contribute substantially to how laws are brought into being, how law operates as a system of general rules applied to particular sets of facts, and how law maintains its legitimacy among those subject to it.

Within the wider, open-ended enterprise of understanding what constitutes law and the interaction that takes place between law and various aspects of social behaviour, an expanding field of 'law and language' has emerged over the past fifty years, a period we date here from publication in 1963 of *The Language of the Law* by UCLA law professor David Mellinkoff. This volume is a contribution to that field. The extent and rapidity of growth of the field in recent decades can be seen in a short quotation from a work by one of the field's other early authors, Harold Berman's *Law and Language: Effective Symbols of Community*. The first draft of Berman's short but wide-ranging book was completed in 1964, only a year after Mellinkoff's. Nearly fifty years passed, however, before it was published in 2013, because the manuscript had been mislaid when Berman moved in 1985 from Harvard Law School, where he taught, to Emory. A great deal changed between Berman's composition and the book's publication as regards the impact of linguistic analysis on law. By 2013, it appeared quaintly anachronistic to say, as Berman had put it a generation earlier,

> Surely one of the most important types of language spoken by a community is the language of law. Yet the language of law has been almost totally neglected by most writers on language and either totally neglected or badly mistreated by most writers on law. (Berman 2013: 64)[1]

Interdisciplinary Approaches to 'Law and Language'

With the emergence in recent decades of this relatively distinct field of 'law and language', there is now a specialized area of study concerned with the intersection between these two important domains. Before going on to engage with perspectives and findings in this newly established field, however, it is worth pointing out that, in broader terms, the field of enquiry is far less recent than such a description would suggest.

Many of the questions and unresolved problems of present investigations of language and law are posed in new forms and in contemporary terminology, but they draw significantly on approaches to issues developed in different terms and contexts throughout the history of a cluster of related disciplines: in political and moral philosophy; in nineteenth- and twentieth-century sociology; in literary criticism of successive periods; and in hermeneutics, rhetoric and anthropology – as well as in those publications generally described as jurisprudence. In the Introduction to a book which will take up many of these same topics, it is worth recalling at the outset some of the main features of that history.

For more than two millennia in Western traditions, and for a similar period in a number of other cultural traditions, language has been acknowledged as the essential medium, but also as a significant obstacle, in formulating general rules to govern social relationships and behaviour (for critical discussion, see Goodrich 1986). How laws should be formulated was a topic, for example, among philosophers from Plato and Aristotle onwards, through St Augustine, Aquinas, Gratian, Herder, Savigny and Bentham, leading into modern jurisprudence (most notably the work of H. L. A. Hart).[2] In a second major stream of discussion – now a distinct category but in classical and mediaeval scholarship part of a different overall configuration of disciplines (the classical

1 Different reference points could complicate this picture. One alternative starting point, for example, might have been an earlier source: the series of *Law Quarterly Review* articles on language in law written in 1945 by the British jurist Glanville Williams (1945). And doubt could be cast on the present position by a more equivocal view expressed as recently as 2011 by Freeman and Smith in their edited collection of essays: that 'the relationship between law and language studies remains relatively unexplored in the British legal academy' (Freeman and Smith 2011: 6).

2 An accessible, eloquent and chronologically narrated account of legal theory and its relation both to philosophy and politics is Kelly (1992).

quadrivium and trivium) – sustained discussion also took place of the aims, techniques and effects of legal rhetoric. That strand of thinking shows a similar and often interwoven lineage: from Isocrates in ancient Greece and the contrasting positions of Plato and Aristotle, through Cicero and other Roman orators on legal and political rhetoric into changing religious conceptions of how human language should be related to truth and belief in the Middle Ages. Rhetoric then flourished in increasingly secular forms in Early Modern European humanism (Vickers 1989), until a period of critique and loss of influence set in during the seventeenth century, under pressure from simpler forms of expression deemed more suited to emergent scientific reasoning and experiment. Interest in rhetoric then revived once more, gaining ground in law in two modern directions: one shown by the stylistic achievements of nineteenth- and early twentieth-century courtroom advocacy, before a renewed period of reaction against legal oratory which continues; the other more concerned with forms of reasoning and evident in 'legal realist' arguments (i.e. arguments put forward most influentially by late nineteenth- and early twentieth-century U.S. judges and legal philosophers, challenging whether legal judgments are or can be arrived at based solely on reasons articulated verbally, or whether unspoken moral, pragmatic and other considerations play an essential part). From this historical strand associated with rhetoric emerges a prominent theme in modern legal theory, especially in the United States: focus on 'rhetoricity' as a proxy for power in discourse, as for instance in the critical legal studies movement (e.g. Goodrich), in neo-pragmatism (e.g. Fish) and in forms of literary jurisprudence (e.g. White). In each of these approaches, scholars have drawn attention to law as a persuasive or rhetorical practice as much as a moral or formal system – either to celebrate that characteristic or remonstrate against it.

Building on these deep historical foundations, what is now typically thought of as 'law and language' scholarship reflects a number of important further inputs. The field was energized, for example, by developments in twentieth-century social scientific and humanities disciplines, including anthropology, sociology and especially linguistics. Contemporary work is accordingly best understood – perhaps because of the variety of influences on it – as a cluster of intersecting approaches rather than as a unified research programme.

Within the intersecting approaches, a number of contributory streams may be identified. Continuing with a primarily historical approach, for example, some scholars have traced the development of legal discourse within the more general emergence of literacy, first in handwritten forms (Danet and Bogoch 1992; Clanchy 1993), then later in print, describing a changing political economy of printing that over time created an established legal literature (Harvey 2015). Another strand, of philologically inspired research, describes and critiques the historical development and contemporary manifestations of the terminology and discourse styles used in law (Mellinkoff 1963; Tiersma 1999;

Mattila 2016). Other scholars working in philosophy of language have pursued implications of the work of Wittgenstein, Grice, Searle and others in examining the philosophical foundations of language in law, exploring topics including vagueness, intentionalism and textualism in legal interpretation, as well as how far legislation should be understood as communication (Kurzon 1986; Kevelson 1988; Marmor and Soames 2011). Sociolegal scholars and linguistic anthropologists have conducted fieldwork examining uses of language and their associated ideologies, meanings and values, in sites including U.S. law schools (Mertz 2007), tribal courts (Richland 2008) and American small claims courts (Conley and O'Barr 1990). The more visible emergence of a 'forensic linguistic' branch of the field is often said to have begun with applied linguistic work by Enkvist in the early 1960s, but then grew in ways particularly inspired by courtroom evidence given by Coulthard and French in the United Kingdom and by Shuy, Butters and other researchers in the United States. This forensic linguistic approach – now perhaps the most widely known version of 'law and language' – frequently analyses linguistic data relevant to legal investigations or litigation (e.g. utterances, wiretaps, e-mails) in ways that can result in submission of expert evidence where deemed admissible at trial. Other linguists have drawn on contrastive linguistics and translation theory in examining the practice of interpreting and the wider bilingual and multilingual legal contexts in which it takes place (Berk-Seligson 2002; Šarčević 1997). Similarly concerned with questions of language policy, especially where those questions engage 'access to justice' issues, other linguists (e.g. Eades 2010) have sought to mitigate linguistic barriers created in legal proceedings by distinctive styles of language use, often among regional or ethnic groups including indigenous populations. Other researchers again compare approaches to meaning in legal interpretation with sometimes rather different understandings of how language works that have developed in linguistics and related fields (Hutton 2009).

Across this range of approaches, 'law and language' has become a notable recent entrant among what are sometimes called 'law and' subjects (law and literature, law and society, law and economics, etc.). But whether referred to as 'law and language', 'forensic linguistics', 'legal linguistics' or by some other name – and whether applying linguistic expertise or probing long-recognised jurisprudential problems from new angles – today the field is well established. It can boast two international professional associations: the International Association of Forensic Linguists (IAFL) and the International Language and Law Association (ILLA). It has no fewer than seven international journals dedicated to its various strands of research (notably the *International Journal of Speech Language and the Law*, the *International Journal for the Semiotics of Law* and the recently launched biannual journal *Language and Law*). The field has been shaped by pioneering monographs (Mellinkoff 1963; Goodrich 1987; Bix 1993; Solan 1993, 2010; Tiersma 1999; Schane 2006; Hutton 2009, 2014; Mattila

2016; Berman 2013; Marmor 2014), and publishers have brought work together in a number of handbooks and edited collections, including some prompted by conferences or other events (Schauer 1993; Gibbons 2003; Coulthard and Johnson 2007; Gibbons and Turrell 2008; Freeman and Smith 2011; Solan and Tiersma 2012; Solan, Ainsworth and Shuy 2015; Visconti 2018). There is also at least one practical student textbook which introduces topics across the subject area range described earlier (Durant and Leung 2016).

This Volume

This collection of essays addresses many of the intersections between law and language previously described. Building on an international roundtable held at the Harvard-Yenching Institute at Harvard University in 2014, after which further discussion and critical exchanges took place, the book brings together writing by scholars working in several different disciplines including law, linguistics and anthropology. Many of the contributors are international leaders in the field of 'law and language'; some are emergent scholars (though in several cases prominent in related fields). All share a concern with fostering dialogue in what Tiersma (2009: 11) called, in a cautious formulation based on observations we have made earlier about the subject's formation, a 'relatively fractured' field.

The roundtable which inspired the book was organised around a theme to which speakers directed their thoughts based on their respective expertise and interests: 'Law as living language', a theme evoking the symbolic interface provided for law by verbal discourse that Berman, from whom the phrase was taken, also liked to call 'communification' (Berman 2013). That theme, taken forward in contributions to this book, explores law and language as each a fundamental attribute of the human condition which serves to articulate profound and general human needs or tendencies – in this way a theme inviting consideration of deep-seated questions that are easily overtaken by abstractions of legal theory or the specifics of legislation and case law. Contributions to the volume point to a sense, cutting across particular case studies they examine, that many features and problems of language in law can only be understood as disconnects, mismatches, or awkward silences – as failures of clarity or certainty which are somehow resolved by their idealisation as special characteristics of legal discourse. Prominent in such lines of thinking is concern with tacit assumptions behind many aspects of verbal expression in law, including how words create – through their presuppositions and implications – a kind of 'unspoken language of the law'.

We should comment on the word 'meaning' in the book's title. Understood in broad terms and at different levels, the term 'meaning' signals the concern described earlier with what may be inferred (or fail to be inferred) from legal discourse, especially among mixed professional and lay audiences. The book contains discussion of the semantics of particular words (e.g. in statutory interpretation; as regards law's doctrine of 'plain meaning'; or in seeking to define what law is). Some chapters examine complications presented by utterance meaning (e.g. in courtroom questioning and interpreting, where difficulties of testimony and evidence are inevitably entwined with problems of word meaning). Other chapters extend discussion to the wider significance attributed to stretches of verbal discourse (e.g. in the politics of hate speech). Across and between what might be thought of as these different levels of language or analysis of language, emphasis on meaning in most chapters is concerned with how norms are articulated (and implicit relations of power created) in ways that include not only verbal choices, ambiguity, and other audible or visible evidence of linguistic signs but also through omission and silence.

A second key concept throughout the volume is power. In conjunction with the book's exploration of meaning, we seek to shed light on how power relations expressed in language play a part in law's exercise of legitimate (as well as sometimes illegitimate) authority. By including the word 'power' in the book's title, we draw attention to a cluster of issues which confront the field under discussion but which are rarely addressed directly. Thirty years ago, not drawing attention to the issue of power in 'law and language' studies might have appeared unsurprising; but such an omission now – though still common – would call for comment. For example, while discussion of the concept of power may be more central in social theory than in law or linguistics, even in a 'social theory' context such discussion overlaps with legal topics wherever law is viewed as being one among various social institutions rather than as an abstract system of rules. Further, over the last thirty years or so power has become a more important topic in linguistics, as well as in anthropology; and power is also an important theme in legal theory, ranging across topics such as sovereignty, command and recognition understandings of legal obedience, and coercion. It is to be expected therefore that questions to do with power will surface in interdisciplinary discussion of law and language, even if the frameworks of reference available for addressing such questions depend substantially on researchers' particular background disciplines.

As a way into the approaches to power that contributors to this volume may be making reference to, in what follows we outline briefly some of the main considerations that need to be taken into account.

The history of the concept of power is most easily traceable in overlapping but sometimes contrasting political and philosophical positions on topics including government, social order, class and inequality. Major thinkers on these matters include Machiavelli, Hobbes, Locke, Kant, Weber and Marx, as well as twentieth-century writers such as Habermas, Gramsci, Foucault and Hayek (for critical discussion, see Hindess 1996, whom we follow in our outline later here but who would also include Lukes among such thinkers). In the resulting multidimensional debate about what 'power' is, a number of major issues surface when writers about law and language invoke concepts of power in explaining the significance of their research.

Commonly in the social sciences, as well as in everyday conversation, the word *power* is used to signal ability to directly control (coerce) people's behaviour. Such power may be viewed as unjust or even as evil; or alternatively it may be viewed as necessary in given circumstances, as in Hobbes. But exercise of power in this sense is assumed to be endemic to humans as social beings. Traced in particular situations, power of this kind can appear as a quantitative phenomenon: a variable amount of generalised capacity to act successfully in imposing a specific will on others. But imposition of power by force or threat of force of this kind is often contrasted with another conception: power as a kind of authority. This contrasting notion is commonly invoked where the sorts of power in question are perceived as legitimate in relation to an established social structure, or exercised in a 'soft' form (e.g. by influence including after consultation or encouragement by incentives). In such contexts, what we understand as power serves to make social actions possible, as much as constraining or preventing them. This second conception then becomes more complicated by its frequent combination of capacity to act with some kind of claimed legitimation in the form of a right, entitlement or even responsibility to act – with these characteristics resting ultimately on the consent of those over whom power is exercised and to whom power may be held accountable.

These widely recognised contrasts show power to be an ambivalent concept. Beyond such foundational distinctions, too, power also needs to be assessed in other respects. Some conceptions of political power, for example, are monolithic; they presume ultimate control over resources of all kinds (whether such power is concentrated in one person, such as a sovereign or tyrant, or is embodied in state institutions and other bodies). Other conceptions, in contrast, conceive power as something dispersed in a pluralistic way across many civil society organisations, divided up in localised pockets of delegated and legitimised power – 'powers' – exercised by bodies as their respective 'jurisdictions' (for wider discussion, see Edwards 2004). In such pluralistic social structures, interpretation of the overall nature and effects of power has to proceed differently. A given power regime might illustrate, for instance, a highly structured Gramscian pattern of hegemony: there is an alignment of more than one social group rather than a unified social elite, and it is those groups functioning together which secures a political settlement. Alternatively, the same regime might (following Foucault) be thought more difficult to analyse: its power structure could appear not to be easily compartmentalized but instead diffused across a very large number of social factions and actors, all of them disenfranchised and unwitting to some extent.

As might be expected, much of the difficulty in such 'social theory' debates is echoed in appeals made to notions of power in linguistics and textual analysis. The basic idea that language expresses 'power' is itself rarely doubted, because language is one of or perhaps *the* major symbolic means of encoding and mediating social relationships. But exactly what is meant by power beyond this general proposition is harder to say, and seems likely to vary between different linguistic settings including whole linguistic cultures. Bourdieu, among others, has emphasized how, as speakers of a language, we tend to be aware of many ways in which linguistic exchanges reflect different positions in a social hierarchy and so can express relations of domination, subordination and exclusion. Some of the mechanisms for doing this are obvious (e.g. variation in accent, intonation, vocabulary differences and honorifics); others are less clear, such as varying forms of command and different kinds of rhetoric, varying between vernacular, professional/educated and traditional elite forms. Other linguistic mechanisms again express authority or control by means of general verbal behaviour (including selective allusiveness, domination of conversational turn-taking, or use of language to intimidate or show condescension or contempt).

Despite the pervasiveness of power relations, it is only relatively recently that power has emerged as an explicit research theme in linguistics. It did so perhaps particularly in opposition to myths of the social homogeneity of language-using communities and the assumed detachment of language as a system (e.g. in concepts such as Saussure's *langue* or Chomsky's *competence*) from fields of social relations in which language use is embedded (for discussion, see Bourdieu 1977). Earlier, the value-neutral description of contemporary language systems as pioneered by Saussure had itself been a major intellectual shift and a defining achievement in the development of modern linguistics: a move away from nineteenth-century philology in theory and prescriptive approaches to language use in instruction manuals and classrooms. Part of what was sacrificed in this formation of modern linguistics, however, was attention to the way in which, where situational variation in language use occurs, what is at stake is not only whether usage is contextually appropriate (in the sense of being matched to a given situation) but how far and in what ways such usage is governed by social and historical stratification.

Developing in, among other sources, important insights in educational linguistics (e.g. in Bernstein's [1975] work on correlation between social class, linguistic performance and what he called control), power emerges as a research topic especially in critical discourse analysis, or CDA (e.g. in work during the 1970s by Fowler, later in widely influential publications by Fairclough, Wodak, Van Dijk and others). The main aim of the investigation in such work on different institutional settings (ranging from media discourse and doctor-patient interaction through to more visibly political communications) has been to show

how unequal power relations and concealed ideological meanings are embedded in discourse and how they affect its interpretation, perceived status and other effects.

Discussion of power in law is for obvious reasons rather different. Not only is law the main public institution charged with dispensing, constraining and accounting for power in society, but it is transparently hierarchical in multiple ways: in its overall purpose (social ordering and control); in its institutional structure (authority expressed through a hierarchy of courts and law reports, as well as by symbolism and ritual); and linguistically (through rules stipulating the right to speak or not speak in given situations; whether what is said by someone will be presumed true, authoritative, or even admissible; and what actions follow from what someone in any given legal capacity says or writes). Questions about power in law are as a result less to do with whether power relations exist, or can be exposed, or even what the regime creating such power relations is, to the extent that the system of authority is prescribed and explicit rather than hidden. Instead, the important issues concern the merits of those stated rules as regards their capability to deliver justice rather than inflict injustice (in whatever way the legal system conceives justice); and how far the rules governing use of power in legal procedures adequately characterise what actually happens.

What follows from this unique social status of law is arguably that critical work in the field needs to be especially vigilant in specifying the aims and scope of criticism: whether, for example, an analysis is claiming systemic critique or failure, for instance that some or all of the legal system is flawed; or whether the study in question is not challenging the validity or legitimacy of the legal system or of a particular legal measure but rather seeking to expose flaws in the application of law in a given case or set of circumstances (e.g. as a result of conflict of interest, judicial or procedural error, or individual corruption). Individual studies may involve a mix of these two kinds of critique. But levels of analysis and the precise relationship between them will be crucial, especially because persuasive criticisms will imply different lines of response: for example, application for judicial review or its equivalent (testing whether administrative procedures were followed); campaigns for justice in a particular case (possibly through reversal of a decision, retrial or even posthumous pardon); agitation for wider law reform; or still wider civil disobedience or generalised political opposition.

As is evident from these thumbnail accounts, a number of different streams in thinking about power converge in discussions of law and language and, as might be expected, have been responded to in different ways in leading studies. Applying linguistic techniques to recognised issues in law and criminology, for example, focusing on legal proceedings including courtroom trials, mediation and small-claims tribunals, a series of publications by Conley and O'Barr has looked at class and power relations (see O'Barr 1982; Conley and O'Barr 1990, 1998). Tackling 'access to justice' issues, linguists have analysed verbal strategies employed in the courtroom (Cotterill 2003), especially coercive aspects of courtroom questioning (Danet and Kermish 1978; Dunstan 1980). Feminist scholars have sought to unmask patriarchal power in law, including its perpetuation through language (a particularly detailed analysis of how patriarchy persists in the law on domestic violence is Siegel 1996). Other studies have examined linguistic disadvantage faced by vulnerable populations such as children (Brennan 1995) and second-language speakers and speakers of non-standard varieties of language (Eades 2003). The scope of court interpreters to influence the outcome of trials has been investigated from the perspective of use and potential misuse of delegated powers (Berk-Seligson 2002); and Angermeyer (2015) has shown how institutional language practices affected the ability of minority litigants in New York City to participate in interpreter-mediated small-claims hearings.

In such legal-linguistic studies, which cut across topics and disciplines, it is inevitably a challenge to find common principles or unified research goals and method. Distinctions of the kind previously outlined regarding what 'power' is, for example, are far easier to explore in theoretical abstraction than when articulated in the course of detailed arguments in which power is identified in some more specific topic or issue, typically in relation to perceived injustice. Understanding exactly how language contributes to power in law, and what the linguistic analysis of power in law can contribute to social change, will accordingly continue to be a challenge as well as an ambition for the field of law and language, alongside other challenges such as the ever-present need to negotiate fundamental differences between descriptive and normative approaches to language associated with the two respective fields. The chapters in this volume unsurprisingly reflect different intellectual traditions and values in relation to such issues. As they are presented together here, however, we are confident that they offer new ways to see important directions in which future (including critical) accounts of language in the law are likely to develop.

The Chapters

We conclude this Introduction with an overview of the individual chapters. In addition to the short summaries which follow, a longer headnote is provided immediately before each chapter, to expand such description and offer an indication of the chapter's scope and main arguments. To make it easier to use references, a separate list of references for cited works is given at the end of each chapter rather than in a consolidated bibliography for the whole book at the end.

Part I, concerning the character of legal language, begins with anthropologist Laura Nader's critical reflection on political effects she associates with core legal terms (Chapter 1). Nader argues that such terms are both idealised and abused in the United States. She describes how people's ability to perceive injustice is hindered by repeated exposure to a cluster of positive abstract words (not only directly law-related terms such as *justice* or the phrase *the rule of law* but also value terms including *consensus, harmony* and *equality*). The cumulative effect of such terms, Nader argues, is damaging where the words in question denote concepts that should help to prevent injustice. Rather than doing so, she suggests, such words convey unexamined ideological values, obscure their related negatives and perpetuate the political status quo. Law, Nader concludes – which is concerned as much with unspoken realities as with expressly articulated values – can be reduced by such language to merely an elaborate means of social control.

Alan Durant's essay (Chapter 2) looks at the history, current meaning and controversies surrounding the core expressions we use to describe law, including words such as *law, justice, rights, authority* and *legitimacy*. Drawing on an oddity noticed by the British jurist Glanville Williams, that law's 'moderately precise technical language' is 'least precise in its most fundamental parts' (Williams 1945: 113), Durant shows how the words he examines convey varying and sometimes contradictory notions of what law is, even as they play a major role in creating law's legitimacy and in building sometimes fragile consensus around the relationship between law, public policy and changing social values.

Christopher Hutton (Chapter 3) scrutinises the seemingly transparent term 'ordinary language', which is frequently used in the course of judicial interpretation of the law to convey the idea of plain or commonsense, everyday meaning. Through an analysis of the wider intellectual history underpinning debates about what ordinary language is, Hutton shows why this phrase is anything but straightforward, and draws attention to interpretive practices it is used to describe and sometimes conceal. To illustrate his theoretical arguments, Hutton presents a case study in which he discusses appeals to the ordinary language categories of 'man', 'woman' and 'sex' in case law related to transgender marriage in several jurisdictions.

The two essays in Part II explore conflicts between legal authority and social and cultural forces in specific jurisdictions.

Tracing the practice of including a eulogy in published laws in Nepal, Katsuo Nawa (Chapter 4) raises geopolitical as well as national questions about where the authority of law comes from. He tackles such issues by highlighting a clash between western notions of constitutionalism and the power exercised by the Nepalese monarchy until 2006. Interlingual indeterminacy, Nawa shows (i.e. slippage and uncertainty when concepts are transferred between languages) can lead to an unforeseen renegotiation of power relations – potentially serving new political or religious interests – where (usually smaller) jurisdictions transplant legal concepts from other, usually globally more influential legal systems.

Rather than examining circumstances in which legal authority is directly exercised, Marco Wan (Chapter 5) shows how tensions subjectively experienced by legal subjects may be expressed in the language of cinema, especially in settings where law is undergoing major change, is under political pressure or engenders social conflict. Combining theoretical and textual analysis, Wan develops a close reading of a vampire film produced in postcolonial Hong Kong. He shows how 'legal subjectivity' may be conveyed in socially important ways and at different levels by the language of film, not only in more explicitly articulated legal and political discourse.

The three chapters in Part III focus on legal meaning conveyed by silence and omission, simultaneously highlighting different methodological approaches.

Greg Matoesian and Kristin Enola Gilbert (Chapter 6) show the rhetorical power of gesture in legal advocacy. They present a set of analytical tools for describing non-verbal communication that is readily perceived but whose mechanisms are not generally well understood. Through their analysis of closing courtroom argument, Matoesian and Gilbert show how courtroom lawyers are able to synchronize speech, gesture and gaze in putting forward a case, using multiple parallel channels of forceful but largely unnoticed emphasis and reinforcement.

Liao Meizhen (Chapter 7) presents a comparative analysis of courtroom questioning in China and the United States. In doing so, he directs attention towards background assumptions about the nature of law, which are not obvious when any given jurisdiction is examined in isolation. Liao contrasts several aspects of questioning: when questions are asked, to whom, and why. He also describes the types of question asked. Viewed in a larger context, Liao's findings probe wider questions related to practical truth-finding, presumption of guilt, evidentiary requirements, participant roles and the overall purpose served by trials.

Through historical analysis, Siddharth Narrain (Chapter 8) explores hate speech as an increasingly contested terrain. When the phenomenon is considered globally, Narrain argues, entrenched positions are found both for regulating hate speech and for permitting it. He goes on to present a critical reading of the history of hate speech regulation in India, tracing it to circumstances under colonial rule which led to enactment of laws calculated to protect 'wounded community sentiment', especially in the area of religion. Narrain then charts the history forward from that point, taking his discussion into contemporary tensions triggered, he argues, by politicized use – even hijacking – of relevant legislation when mobilised by political or religious interest groups as a vehicle for suppressing minority voices rather than protecting them.

Part IV discusses the form and manner of legal communication in different legal domains, linking questions of the linguistic form of discourse to underlying ideologies.

Building on his earlier monograph examining multiple audiences for courtroom discourse (Heffer 2005), Chris Heffer (Chapter 9) introduces a model he has developed to account for courtroom miscommunication (the Voice Projection Framework). Heffer then applies his model to a legally minor but controversial recent British case. He explains why communication breakdown can easily occur between judges and jurors and links such breakdown in part to the institutional design of courtroom interaction. Heffer's analysis builds into a critique of courtroom discourse, which he tests against the complexity of the multiple purposes trials need to serve in a common law system.

Janny HC Leung (Chapter 10) analyses the political significance of different methods used in legal translation. Ethnocentrism and ideology, she shows, have an impact on lexical and other choices made in translating. While processes of legal translation are rarely subject to public scrutiny, Leung argues, it is possible to show how particular approaches to legal translation reflect power relations and to assess the role different approaches play in maintaining or potentially challenging aspects of social structure. Opposing the common perception that law is an abstract formal system beyond the reach of such considerations, Leung critiques continuing lack of attention paid to power asymmetry in theories of legal translation.

The final section of the book exposes tensions between what language is used in law to achieve and the constraints on doing so that can be exposed by linguistic analysis and commentary.

Janet Ainsworth (Chapter 11) draws attention to inherent difficulties in cross-cultural communication. She suggests that such difficulties create problems both for linguistic minorities in a given jurisdiction and for legal practitioners seeking to understand legal systems other than their own. Ainsworth asks how far the reasoning processes relied on in legal procedures are affected by variation in the grammatical and other structures of different natural languages. Revisiting the idea of 'linguistic relativity', or structural variation between languages that gives distinctive shape to concept formation by the speakers of any given language, Ainsworth concludes that such linguistic differences should be taken into account in bilingual courtrooms.

Lawrence Solan and Sandra Dahmen (Chapter 12) outline challenges associated with using spoken language as legal evidence. They highlight dangers that extend beyond the kinds of semantic indeterminacy associated with interpretation of legal documents. Solan and Dahmen review how courts have dealt with disputed transcription and illustrate how linguists can sometimes assist the courts in resolving speech perception difficulties. Although their chapter focuses on the English language, many of Solan and Dahmen's insights are generalisable to spoken communication in other languages.

The book ends with an 'Afterword' by Peter Goodrich (Chapter 13). Goodrich's work over three decades has explored many of the kinds of gaps and silences in approaches to the analysis of legal language that have been outlined earlier in this Introduction. In his concluding chapter, he uses the 'unspoken words' trope offered by the conceptualisation of this book as a route into dissecting the relation in law between the said and the unsaid. Rather than viewing the two as a dichotomy, Goodrich addresses their dependency on each other. Linking his comments about particular features of legal language with wider issues about the nature of law, Goodrich points to the conundrum that, in legal discourse as elsewhere, the unsaid can only be accessed through what is said – but the said can only be understood in context of what remains unsaid.

REFERENCES

Angermeyer, P. (2015). *Speak English or What?: Codeswitching and Interpreter Use in New York City Courts*. New York: Oxford University Press.

Berk-Seligson, S. (2002 [1990]). *The Bilingual Courtroom: Court Interpreters in the Judicial Process* (2nd ed.). Chicago and London: University of Chicago Press.

Berman, H. (2013). *Law and Language: Effective Symbols of Community*. Cambridge: Cambridge University Press.

Bernstein, B. (1975). *Class, Codes and Control*. 4 vols. London: Routledge.

Bix, B. (1993). *Language and Legal Indeterminacy*. Oxford: The Clarendon Press.

Bourdieu, P. (1977). *Language and Symbolic Power*. Translated by J. B. Thompson. Cambridge: Polity.

Brennan, M. (1995). The Discourse of Denial: Cross-Examining Child Victim Witnesses. *Journal of Pragmatics* 23: 71–91.

Clanchy, M. (1993). *From Memory to Written Record*. Oxford: Blackwell.

Conley, J. M. and O'Barr, W. (1990). *Rules versus Relationships: The Ethnography of Legal Discourse*. Chicago: University of Chicago Press.

Conley, J. M. and O'Barr, W. (1998). *Just Words: Law, Language and Power*. Chicago: University of Chicago Press.

Cotterill, J. (2003). *Language and Power in Court: A Linguistic Analysis of the OJ Simpson Trial*. Basingstoke: Palgrave Macmillan.

Coulthard, M. and Johnson, A. (2007). *An Introduction to Forensic Linguistics: Language in Evidence*. London: Routledge.

Danet, B. and Bogoch, B. (1992). From Oral Ceremony to Written Document: The Transitional Language of Anglo-Saxon Wills. *Language and Communication* 12(2): 95–122.

Danet, B. and Kermish, N. (1978). Courtroom Questioning: A Sociolinguistic Perspective. In L. Massery II (ed.) *Psychology and Persuasion in Advocacy*. Washington, DC: The Association of Trial Lawyers of America, 413–441.

Dunstan, R. (1980). Context for Coercion: Analyzing Properties of Courtroom 'Questions'. *British Journal of Law and Society* 7(1): 61–77.

Durant, A. and Leung, J. (2016). *Language and Law*. London and New York: Routledge.

Eades, D. (2003). Participation of Second Language and Second Dialect Speakers in the Legal System. *Annual Review of Applied Linguistics* 23: 113–133.
Eades, D. (2010). *Sociolinguistics and the Legal Process*. London: Multilingual Matters.
Edwards, M. (2004). *Civil Society*. Cambridge: Polity.
Freeman, M. and Smith, F. (eds.) (2011). *Law and Language: Current Legal Issues 2011*, Vol. 15. Oxford: Oxford University Press.
Gibbons, J. (2003). *Forensic Linguistics: An Introduction to Language in the Justice System*. Oxford/Malden, MA: Blackwell Publishing.
Gibbons, J. and Turrell, M. (2008). *Dimensions of Forensic Linguistics*, Amsterdam: John Benjamins.
Goodrich, P. (1986). *Reading the Law: A Critical Introduction to Legal Method and Techniques*. Oxford: Blackwell.
Goodrich, P. (1987). *Legal Discourse: Studies in Linguistics, Rhetoric and Legal Analysis*. London: Macmillan.
Harvey, D. (2015). *The Law Emprynted and Englysshed: The Printing Press as an Agent of Change in Law and Legal Culture, 1475–1642*. London: Hart.
Heffer, C. (2005). *The Language of Jury Trial: A Corpus-Aided Analysis of Legal-Lay Discourse*. Basingstoke: Palgrave.
Hindess, B. (1996). *Discourses of Power: From Hobbes to Foucault*. London: Wiley and Sons.
Hutton, C. (2009). *Language, Meaning and the Law*. Edinburgh: Edinburgh University Press.
Hutton, C. (2014). *Word Meaning and Legal Interpretation: An Introductory Guide*. Basingstoke: Palgrave.
Kelly, J. (1992). *A Short History of Western Legal Theory*. Oxford: Clarendon Press.
Kevelson, R. (1988). *The Law as a System of Signs*. New York: Plenum Press.
Kurzon, D. (1986). *It Is Hereby Performed . . . : Explorations in Legal Speech Acts*. Amsterdam/Philadelphia: John Benjamins.
Marmor, A. (2014). *The Language of Law*. Oxford: Oxford University Press.
Marmor, A. and Soames, S. (eds.) (2011). *Philosophical Foundations of Language in the Law*. Oxford: Oxford University Press.
Mattila, H. (2016). *Comparative Legal Linguistics*. Surrey: Ashgate.
Mellinkoff, D. (1963). *The Language of the Law*. Eugene, OR: Resource Publications.
Mertz, E. (2007). *The Language of Law School: Learning to "Think Like a Lawyer"*. New York: Oxford University Press.
O'Barr, W. (1982). *Linguistic Evidence: Language, Power, and Strategy in the Courtroom*. New York: Academic Press.
Richland, J. (2008). *Arguing with Tradition: The Language of Law in Hopi Tribal Court*. Chicago: University of Chicago Press.
Šarčević, S. (1997). *New Approach to Legal Translation*. The Hague: Kluwer Law International.
Schane, S. (2006). *Language and the Law*. London: Continuum.
Schauer, F. (ed.) (1993). *Law and Language*. Aldershot: Dartmouth Press.
Siegel, R. (1996). "The Rule of Love": Wife Beating as Prerogative and Privacy. *Yale Law Journal* 105: 2117–2207.
Solan, L. (1993). *The Language of Judges*. Chicago: University of Chicago Press.

Solan, L. (2010). *The Language of Statutes: Laws and Their Interpretation*. Chicago: University of Chicago Press.
Solan, L., Ainsworth, J. and Shuy, R. (2015). *Speaking of Language and Law*. New York: Oxford University Press.
Solan, L. and Tiersma, P. (eds.) (2012). *The Oxford Handbook of Language and Law* Oxford: Oxford University Press.
Tiersma, P. (1999). *Legal Language*. Chicago: University of Chicago Press.
Tiersma, P. (2009). What Is Language and Law? And Does Anyone Care? In F. Olsen, A. Lorz and D. Stein (eds.) *Law and Language: Theory and Society*, 2008. Loyola–LA Legal Studies Paper No. 2009-11, available at https://ssrn.com/abstract=1352075
Vickers. B. (1989). *In Defence of Rhetoric*. Oxford: The Clarendon Press.
Visconti, J. (ed.) (2018). *A Handbook of Communication in the Legal Sphere*, Berlin: de Gruyter.
Williams, G. (1945). 'Language and the Law', 61 *Law Quarterly Review*, in 4 sections, at 71, 179, 293, 384, reprinted in Schauer, F. (ed.) (1993). *Law and Language*. Aldershot: Dartmouth Press, 71–183.

Part I

Sui generis or Socially Problematic: The Character of Legal Language

1 The Unspoken Language of the Law

Laura Nader

EDITORS' NOTE TO CHAPTER 1

Laura Nader draws attention in this chapter to how voices that could contribute to a genuine achievement of social justice may be drowned out by the influence of an idealized terminology of which a great deal of legal discourse consists. Discourse about law, she argues, has been dominated by core terms which are abstract, highly positive in connotation, and (or but) idealistic. Among such terms Nader focuses especially on the word *justice*, which she suggests conjures up imagery of well-functioning social institutions, an orderly and properly scrutinized system, and efficient procedures – all in contrast with its antonym *injustice*, which evokes a sense of immediacy, exclusion, and urgent need for further action. It is not coincidence, she contends, that the word *justice* attracts far more attention, and has in fact been consistently used more frequently (at least in published writing) than its opposite.

Widening an argument prefigured in this respect in the thinking of General Semanticists such as Chase (1938) and Hayakawa (1939), Nader argues that people's ability to perceive injustice is hindered by the familiarity of abstract words used to convey legal concepts that should help prevent such injustice. Familiar words, she suggests, carry unexamined ideological meaning, suppress the scope of our imagination, and perpetuate the status quo. In claiming that there is to this extent a risk of deception inherent in the core terminology of legal discourse, Nader's opening essay to the volume argues that justice is denied on numerous occasions in the United States because what needs to be said is left unsaid. Developing this claim, she suggests that actual justice may be frustrated by the use of key legal terminology, including the word *justice* itself, or the phrase *the rule of law*, as well as by the use of highly valorized terms such as *harmony*. Through the use of such language, she says, law can be turned into merely a means of social control.

Challenging conventional assumptions surrounding core legal values, she asks: what is it that makes alternative dispute resolution (ADR) more "harmonious" than litigation, and whose interest does that apparent "harmony" serve? Is *the rule of law*, as actually practised, always legal? Why is it often possible to litigate corporate crimes as "civil" rather than "criminal" cases? What in detail is the difference between a *terrorist* and a *criminal*? By questioning complacency surrounding familiar but difficult words that mix legal content with political symbolism, Nader presents a vigorous critique of double standards in the behaviour of those in power.

REFERENCES

Chase, S. (1938). *The Tyranny of Words*. New York: Harvest Books.
Hayakawa, S. I. (1939). *Language in Thought and Action*. New York: Harvest Books.

The Unspoken Language of the Law

Writing this essay made me realize that I have been writing on law and language for many years but have not had the opportunity to pull my thoughts together. Having studied the spoken language of the law elsewhere for many years, what I present here is a brief synthesis of my current position on what might be called in contrast the "unspokenness" of law in the United States. Anthropological experience in more than one locale commonly inspires comparison with one's home country, whether implicit or explicit.

In researching law here and elsewhere, comparison of the language of law in different places commonly directs attention to process in courts as opposed to more generalized contexts like moots or informal settings, although a few anthropologists have dealt specifically with law or litigation and language. One non-Western example is Charles Frake's "Litigation in Lipay: A study in Subanum Law," in which Frake describes litigation as a contest of skill, "in this case of verbal skill, accompanied by social merry-making, in which the loser pays a forfeit . . . along with drinking, feasting, and ceremonializing" (ibid.: 221). The Subanum, he notes, had a view of litigation centered on verbal performance. Robert Hayden in writing on the style of speaking in an Indian caste panchayat (or council), comments on the disorderly style of overlapping speech as contrasted with the ordering of speaking turns in Western legal settings. Language takes central place in my PBS film on *Little Injustices* in Mexican Zapotec courts where, as with the Indian situation Hayden describes, there is little turn-taking and much overlap. In these examples we are describing settings which have evolved *without* writing and *without* the institutional and written formality of, for example, Western courts.

When anthropologists find themselves in their own society, however, the focus in studies of language and the law may shift from spontaneous speech to written texts. Elizabeth Mertz, for example, analyzes "social voices" by examining the U.S. Supreme Court's decisions in two famous cases in order to understand "the semiotic features of these narratives. Legal opinions are analysed as narratives" (1988). William O'Barr and John Conley, an anthropologist and a law professor respectively, analyze transcripts of small claims court sessions in six U.S. cities (1990), identifying contrasting types of legal discourse within the context of sociolinguistic variables. But if you don't broaden your scope, if you don't study up, down, and sideways at the same time, law and language studies get focused too narrowly on linguistic details without looking at the social context, which would normally include the victims of law or the defendants. James Spradley however, did focus on what he called "urban nomads" in his book *You Owe Yourself a Drunk*, in which he quoted verbatim the observations and reflections of the people jailed for drunkenness. His analysis suggests that, after being arrested for drunkenness and used as free jail labor, when you are free you feel like you owe yourself a drink and so the cycle continues, and once again you are arrested on charges of drunkenness.

Thus, as I think about future studies I am not inclined to pursue narrow avenues of law and language because they have the color of "done deals" rather than the discovery of broader social contexts of law language which lend themselves to understanding root causes. What interests me now is what is *not* said and why: the unspoken language of the law, a subject I have been publishing on for some time. In what follows, I describe the use and abuse of key words such as *justice* and *injustice*, crime as a category, key beliefs like the concept of lack, legal concepts such as *terra nullius* (empty lands) to create rule of law after the fact, selective uses of courts in The Hague, and the abuse of words like *harmony* or *terrorism* that shatter any notions of evolution of the law from barbarism to civilization as proposed by the likes of Oliver Wendell Holmes, Jr. in 1881. All of my efforts, although inspired by comparison with non-state society materials, focus on American law in its broadest context.

During the fall of 1981, while teaching at the Yale Law School I received a letter from a Canadian social scientist inviting me to a conference on injustice; not justice, but injustice. That was intriguing, for in the back of my mind I remembered Edmund Cahn's seminal work *The Sense of Injustice* (1964 [1949]). Injustice for Cahn is "live with movement and warmth in the human organism" (ibid.: 13–14). In contrast, Cahn notes that the concept of justice is contemplative and "contemplation bakes no loaves." Cahn was not really interested in concepts themselves. Rather, he was interested in the consequence of concepts: that justice is static and injustice is active. Imagine a Department of Injustice rather than a Department of Justice. I published an article (Nader 2010) about the bias in favor of the concept of justice over injustice. In our library at UC Berkeley we found something like 667 titles using the word *injustice* as compared with 8,800 items using the word *justice*. Anthropology titles were no different: 44 items for *injustice*, 912 *justice* entries. Needless to say, Cahn's work did not spawn an academic industry of those who wanted to do something about injustice.

In 1999 John Rawls published his book *A Theory of Justice*. Unlike Cahn, his book garnered much attention and spawned an industry. The words we use tell a good deal about both ideology and priorities. Rawls is a philosopher and his influence was primarily intellectual and academic. In a word, he was abstract and contemplative; but as Cahn said, "contemplation bakes no loaves." I must confess that upon first reading Rawls I felt repulsion. Where are the concrete instances? Only "realistic utopias"? Apparently academic interest in justice provides hope for the present by celebrating an ideal: justice. In this way, myths of a just society are perpetuated through abstract reason. But as Cahn argues, without emotion in addition to reason we never address injustices (Nader 2010). My article, "The Words We Use: Justice, Human Rights, and the Sense of Injustice," (Nader 2010) was itself a reaction to attending a conference on "Mirrors of Justice" during which the word *injustice* was rarely spoken. Justice is positivity, a mirage, while injustice is in the present reality.

My interests went further than the words we use to include the rhetoric to be found at the top of our legal hierarchy in relation to the Alternative Dispute Movement. The Alternative Dispute Resolution (ADR) explosion in the United States, which then extended globally, was launched at the Pound Revisited Conference in 1976 by the Chief Justice of the U.S. Supreme Court, Warren Burger. Chief Justice Burger, both at the conference I attended and many times after, launched the movement with rhetoric that made possible the shift from adversarial modes to ADR in the handling of disputes in America, from facts and legal rights to feelings and relationships (Nader 1989). It was a movement against lawyers and the legal rights movement, a movement against the contentious, a movement to control litigation spawned by the rights movements of the 1960s.

The Chief Justice delivered speeches all over the country, and because of his authoritative position he set the tone for the language that characterized the speeches and writings of others. He warned that adversarial modes of conflict resolution were tearing the society apart, and claimed that Americans were inherently litigious and that alternative forms were more civilized. He followed the peremptory style of assertive rhetoric: common sense was mingled with unsubstantiated statements about "a litigation explosion," lawsuits and war as opposed to arbitration and peace. In my analysis of his speeches I noted that major parts of his speech were unsubstantiated, and that he ignored scholarly arguments such as those of Professor Lon Fuller of Harvard Law School: arguments that distinguished ADR's psychotherapy-influenced forums from "traditional" legal mediations. However, in a brief time privatization and psychologisms took hold; and by 1985 Burger was attacking his critics, again with assertive rhetoric. His anti-litigation rhetoric took hold and became ubiquitous in news media, in the therapeutic community, in schools and universities, and in churches.

The Chief Justice had successfully set the tone in spite of excellent corrective analyses by Marc Galanter (1983) of Wisconsin Law in "Reading the Landscape of Disputes," Owen Fiss (1984 of Yale Law) in "Against Settlement," and others who questioned the veracity of the anti-law movement's claims. Private lawmaking makes it hard to get discovery, limits appeals, and precludes decisions from leading to precedents. However, the use of language in fueling a harmony ideology worked. A few of us began to examine the consequences of a movement to control the rights movements of the 1960s – civil rights, consumer rights, women's rights, environmental rights, Native American rights – "the garbage cases" as Robert Bork, a conservative judge, called them. Post-confrontational Democrats were emerging. Tort "deform" flourished to eviscerate the best tort system in the world; the civil justice system sank. And the ADR movement, now called by various names, went global, covering all but countries like those in Asia where harmony was already a mode of control. In Asia, by contrast, the U.S. pushed for Rule of Law courts. Rhetoric from the top is powerful; in the U.S. case rhetoric is a means to pacification, moving the country from legal process to mind processing, a movement to control the legal rights movement.

In 2008, my colleague Ugo Mattei and I published *Plunder – When the Rule of Law is Illegal*. In this work we examined the uses made of the phrase *Rule of Law*. Both of us had been attentive to the increasing use of the phrase to justify illegalities such as the war on Iraq, and had written papers independent of each other. In my case, I was alerted to *Rule of Law* as a controlling process, specifically when used as a justification for the invasion of Iraq once it was realized that Saddam Hussein's government did not have weapons of mass destruction (Nader 2009), the original excuse for invasion. *Plunder* was preceded by "Law and the Frontiers of Illegalities" (Nader 2009), an early analysis of rule of law discourse in the service of political, military, and economic power using Iraq as my primary example. I asked what if, under conditions of rapid change or rupture such as the war in Iraq, illegalities from above become the law? What if systems of legalities and systems of illegalities have come to be not two domains but one? In Iraq lawlessness and plunder appeared to be supported by "rule of law" and by democracy discourse both nationally and internationally. Two decades earlier John Gardner (1980) was among the first to document the use of legal development as a process that came to be exploited in his insightful book *Legal Imperialism*. Gardner saw firsthand that an instrumental, imported law can result in the undemocratic concentration of legal power in the state or in large multinational corporations. Patterns of law have been exported by colonial or imperial powers within a variety of contexts, in Gardner's case under the rubric of law and development that went mostly unnoticed as imperialism. Under colonialism and empire of the American sort, imported legal systems operate predominantly to subvert local law and universalize American legal concepts, thus enhancing the globalization of American law, whether it be Rule of Law or Alternative Dispute Resolution policies.

The example of the invasion of Iraq was a prime example of an old pattern among Western colonial powers, at least since the coming of Columbus to America (Mattei and Nader 2008). In the case of Iraq, an unelected Paul Bremer and his Governing Council passed edicts, closed newspapers, outlawed unions, destroyed Iraqi indigenous culture under "rule of law" discourse. What was interesting about this pattern were the headlines that began to appear simultaneously in U.S. newspapers (and on television, radio, etc.). Examples of such stories appeared in the *New York Times*, *Wall Street Journal*, *Washington Post*, plus of course many local newspapers such as the *San Francisco Chronicle*: IRAQ'S JUDICIAL SYSTEM LACKS PRACTITIONERS, SCHOLARS SAY; U.S. SEEKS SOLID CORE TO FIX IRAQ'S BROKEN LEGAL SYSTEM; TEAM TO REBUILD IRAQ'S COURTS INCLUDES THREE FEDERAL JUDGES; ISLAMIC JUSTICE TAKING HOLD IN BAGHDAD; AMERICAN WILL ADVISE IRAQIS ON WRITING NEW CONSTITUTION; IN IRAQ, A JUSTICE SYSTEM WORTH SAVING; WITH IRAQI COURTS GONE YOUNG CLERICS JUDGE; OCCUPIERS AND THE LAW; WOMEN IN IRAQ DECRY DECISION TO CURB RIGHTS, and so on. The invaders were going to civilize the Iraqis and spread democracy. Never mind that international law (both according to the Hague regulations of 1907 and under the 1949 Geneva Convention, both ratified by the United States) prohibits an occupying nation from transforming a defeated society into its own likeness. In fact, the Iraqis already had Rule of Law: "The Iraqi Civil Code of 1953 was one of the most innovative and meticulously systematic codes of the Middle East. Iraqi jurists [. . .] drafted a code that balanced and merged elements of Islamic and French law in one of the most successful attempts to preserve the best of both legal systems" (Abou El Fadl 2003).

According to Khaled Abou El Fadl (a professor at UCLA School of Law), when the Ba'ath Party came to power in 1968 Saddam declared a constant state of emergency and as a result was able to rule mostly by executive order. What Paul Bremer accomplished was the creation of an efficient neoliberal market that gave preference to U.S. corporations over the development of the Iraqi economy and that served to change Iraq from a centrally planned economy to a market economy. In this case rule of law was said to fulfill what was in fact a non-existent lack.

A Euro-American configuration of institutions and belief systems has normalized and powered a Euro-American use of "rule of law" and "lack": ideologies key to the colonial and imperial project whether it was being exercised by the British, French, Americans . . . in pursuit of their own enrichment (Nader 2005). My paper "Law and the Theory of Lack" (ibid.) was about rhetoric, about the rule of law or lack of it, as a form of ethnocentrism recently described as legal orientalism by law professor Teemu Ruskola (2002). Ruskola wants to challenge the historic claim by Western observers that China lacks an indigenous tradition of "law." After all, Ruskola notes, China boasts dynastic legal codes going back to the Tang dynasty. Despite much effort to debunk the view of China as lacking in law, we still have scholars arguing that Chinese law is not even worthy of the word *jurisprudence*. But beyond lacking law, the Chinese are now charged with ignoring the law they had. Many scholars exhibit an inability to make reference to Western law in anything but the most idealized representations.

So what may be called the "unspoken" language of the law includes positive words and phrases like *justice*, *rule of law*, or *harmony*, which stand in opposition to words like *lack*: and words that facilitate the take such as *terra nullius*, a concept related to lack indicating an emptiness, as in a land without people for people without lands. *Terra nullius* was elaborated by philosophers interested in property rights, most famously by John Locke in the eighteenth century, whose justifications for entitlement improvements led to alterations in legal administrative practices. Daniel Boorstin (1941) notes, "'Locke' became the pseudonym for everyman's theory of property" (ibid.: 165). Swiss philosopher Emmerich de Vattel was more explicit in his 1758 *The Law of Nations*. His arguments about land were congenial to the colonizing nations of the eighteenth century because he gave legal justification for the colonial appropriations of lands, thereby lending moral authority to what First North American Peoples might describe as theft:

> The earth belongs to all mankind.... All men have a natural right to inhabit it... all men have an equal right to things which have not yet come into the possession of anyone. When Therefore a Nation finds a country uninhabited and without an owner, it may forcefully take possession of it. In connection to the discovery of the new World, it is asked whether a nation may peacefully occupy any part of a vast territory in which are found only wandering tribes whose small numbers cannot populate the whole country. (see Williams 1986: 127–29)

Land that was occupied by indigenous nations was brushed aside since Native Americans were viewed as "lacking," for example, they were not legally capable of holding territorial title or property rights. The meaning of the term *terra nullius* was popular even though challenged by thinkers in and outside the legal profession. Along with the rights of conquest, John Locke's 1689 arguments in *Treatises of Government* were used to promote the idea that Native American properties could be appropriated by command of the Christian god – to make best use of land, something the pagans did not have the wherewithal to accomplish.

In the same vein, extant legal categories are often remade by powerful forces to fit new conditions. Labeling a case as civil or criminal goes mostly unnoticed, but has important effects (Nader 2001). One example is the effort made by wrongdoers to categorize criminogenic acts as civil cases. A nine-year legal saga began in 1982 in Woburn, Massachusetts. It dealt with a serious health problem that started with a series of childhood leukemia cases. The clustering of the cancer cases stimulated the search for the cause of the sickness and deaths of the children. The children's families suspected that two Woburn plants belonging to two corporations – W. R. Grace and Co. of New York and Beatrice Foods Company of Chicago – had contaminated two municipal drinking wells. The families retained a Boston personal injury attorney, and the story was chronicled in the context of the workings of toxic tort litigation by Jonathan Harr in his book, *A Civil Action* (1995), and later made into a Hollywood movie of the same name. The point here is that the families filed a *civil* suit against Grace and Beatrice. But why was this a civil complaint? There is an easier burden of proof than a criminal complaint under current law. It could have been criminal: an offense against the state of Massachusetts. Indeed in later cases, for example *Masschusetts v. Feingold* in 1997, the defendants were charged with the criminal act of exposing company employees to hazardous chemicals. And there was a string of such criminal toxic cases following Woburn. Occupational health and safety laws make it easier for employees to file a criminal complaint. Yet overall it has been observed that those who commit corporate misdeeds are commonly those who, unlike all other criminal groups in the United States, have the power to define the law under which they operate. In the Woburn case two powerful corporations got off, with Beatrice winning and W. R. Grace settling for 8 million dollars. Crime is a category that may be applied arbitrarily. In this case, a civil action, rather than a criminal action, only exacerbated the sense that Beatrice Foods and W. R. Grace had literally gotten away with murder.

Such corporate cases can also stimulate pushback, causing new words or concepts to be created. In the 1960s and 1970s there appeared the notion of "corporate crime," not used prior, and now we also have a weekly newsletter "Corporate Crime Reporter." *Terra nullius* cases eventually spawned an American Indian movement. The Native American rights movement wanted observance of existing laws, that is, their treaties. And the ADR movements, still in their heyday, are already stimulating response about the demise of the civil justice system for ordinary peoples. There is a dialogue happening between the powerful and the many although it is not always visible in public places.

Two more examples will suffice before I discuss the wider meaning of an unspoken language of law. The first deals with the metamorphoses of the word *criminal*. The Unabomber was a serial killer in the United States. Timothy McVeigh was a domestic criminal who saw himself as a patriot. Does it become easier to understand criminal behavior by using the term *terrorist* rather than *criminal*? The Italian mafia was composed of a network of criminals. They were not labeled terrorists even during World War II when the United States was at war with Italy. The Mexicans refer to the Mexican drug cartel as a criminal network even though it is part of an international cartel. What is a *terrorist* anyway, and how did the label become so ubiquitous and why?

Efforts to define what a terrorist is result in a series of dismal failures. Yesterday's terrorist is today's hero; Nelson Mandela is often cited as an example. The politics of labeling have infected academic reasoning, especially in the case of those who make a living in terrorism studies. The selectivity is staggering. An overt example of "terrorism" was the Israeli military attack on the USS Liberty – a Navy communications ship not a warship – in 1967, killing thirty-four Americans and wounding 171 others. The act was basically dealt with by our government by turning the other way, being complicit.

In *Terror and Taboo: The Follies, Fables, and Faces of Terrorism*, Joseba Zulaika and William Douglass make clear the arbitrariness in one of their many examples: "a Pentagon report in 1988 listed Mandela's African National Congress as one of the world's 'more notorious terrorist groups,' whereas pro-South African government RENAMO, which the same report admits killed over 100,000 civilians between 1986 and 1988, is identified merely as an 'indigenous insurgent group'" (1996: 12). The authors continued, citing CIA director William Casey, who stated that 109 definitions of "terrorist" were too narrow and ordered a new draft that "went whole hog, took every kind of national liberation movement, every left-wing movement that used violence, and called them terrorists." There were some protests because, under such a broad brush, George Washington and Simon Bolivar would be considered "terrorists"; but Zulaika and Douglass make the observation that reports of terrorist attacks are assembled based on the definitions used. In a 1979 CIA report the claim was made that 3,336 terrorist attacks had been reported since 1968, but in a 1980 report covering the same period the number was 6,714. The increase was definitional. Terrorism is a concept so open to abuse that the government can promote it at will; to wit, President Obama's drone wars, targeting terrorists while including civilians as collateral damage. It would seem that the politics of labeling might require minimally stable categories. Absent an agreed-upon meaning, however, terrorism is a subject taken seriously in everything from the media to university courses in political science. In search of meaning, specific targets receive ethnic labels: Muslims, Arabs, and so on. In this case linguistic categories have life and death consequences decided outside the law.

At this point it is important to return to a distinction increasingly made between state terrorism and non-state terrorism. World War II should be remembered as the war that violated the international laws that defined war as between enemy combatants. The attacks on Dresden civilians in Germany and Nagasaki and Hiroshima in Japan are often cited as violations of international law. It is now apparent that both armies and terrorists kill civilians. Nowhere to my knowledge of government definitions of *terrorism* or *terrorists* is the idea of state terrorism institutionalized. When 9/11 happened, we had a departmental meeting at Berkeley to discuss the events. I argued that what happened was criminal, and that the criminals should be found and tried. That was not to happen. Compare the War on Terror and the War on Crime. If we do so, we realize that when billions are spent on the National Security industry and terrorism deaths as opposed to deaths by homicide, the latter shrink in importance. Every day is 9/11 in Afghanistan, one Pakistani medical doctor noted. Both non-state and state terrorists see the world in black and white; they desire revenge, and the justification is the state of exception (Agamben 2005). In President Obama's address to the nation on June 23, 2011, he says the world should be reminded that "[w]e don't forget." After the targeted assassination of Osama Bin Laden, he declared that such killing was justice. Obama is a constitutional lawyer; so is Biden. They were aware of the legal ramifications of such killing, but the state of exception paradigm allows suspension of the law, a permanent state of emergency that erases the legal status of a person (ibid.: 3), resulting in "indefinite detention" and trial by "military commissions."

Since lawyers have a monopoly on law matters, in this country it is up to them to provide an education for all those law professionals who are determining the direction of law or lawlessness in our country. Language is key to understanding the fictions.

Courts protect the lawless with doctrines like "no standing to see," "state secrets" and "it's a political question." The United States portrays the War on Terror as rational, a permanent state of exception. If one accepts this portrayal, it becomes difficult to see connections between increasing centralization of power, a permanent war economy, causes of blowback, and other consequences of the controlling processes of empire. Countering the terrorism myth's false conceptions of cause, threat, and definition opens the possibilities for a more pragmatic reflection of the distinctions between barbarism, savagery, and civilization as defined by our most distinguished legal thinkers.

One last example, before I sum up, deals with the work of anthropologist Kamari Clarke on the International Criminal Court concerning African indictees (Clarke 2009). Clarke is interested in the meaning of the Court's arrest warrants – all African – in relation to colonialism, inequality, and violence. The politics of extradition is tied to the African Union's response to develop an African court with criminal jurisdiction. Clarke's subject is complex, and as we will see best summarized by her inclusion of the words used when referring to the International Court's apparent "targeting Africa and Africans": nineteen ICC cases, all in African countries. Jean Ping, then President of the African

Union Commission, notes that the "ICC always targets Africans. Does it mean that you have nothing on Gaza? Does it mean you have nothing [on the] Caucasus? Does it mean that you have nothing on the militants in Colombia? There is nothing on Iraq? We are raising this type of question because we don't want a double standard." Zimbabwean Robert Mugabe said in front of the General Assembly, "the leaders of the powerful Western states, guilty of international crimes, like Bush and Blair, are routinely given the blind eye. Such selective justice has eroded the credibility of the ICC on the African continent." In response the Court says "justice for victims through the application of the law defines the Court's work, not politics." A Gambian Prosecutor insists, "it's not about politics but the law. I will use the law to uphold justice . . . we should focus on, and listen to, the millions of victims who continue to suffer from massive crimes." – Justice as law, or law as justice.

Clarke argues that utterances of this kind involve a kind of affective retribution, linking historical injustices to technically unrelated contemporary concepts, thereby widening the lens of traditional understandings of "law" and "justice" and in the process moving beyond a punitive construct of individual aggressor to redress structural and affective dimensions of justice. Thus, according to Clarke, Africans would have been forced to take responsibility for transnational crimes committed on the African continent, which would include Africa's resource wars, linking them to histories of subordination. Africans are disputing the power of international law to intervene and are responding with regional solutions to regional problems. Clarke cites particular strategic rhetorical acts as examples of gaining traction in anti-ICC protests, and notes parallels between the resistance of the Mau Mau independence fighters and to the ICC as related to the same colonial armature of power. Clarke has her mind on tensions through which notions of justice compete. For this reason Clarke has defined her project with sufficient scope to understand the larger meanings and effects of verbal practices, or how language is used.

The preceding examples, and there could be many more, fall into two kinds of "unspokenness": the implicit meanings and assumptions behind the words that *are* used (e.g. *rule of law*, *terra nullius*, *terrorist*) and the fact that some terms are not used or are infrequently used (e.g. *injustice, corporate crime*). But, if such examples illustrate an unspoken language of the law, where are they unspoken?

In the United States unspoken terms are avoided by the mass media. They are also, for the most part, not probed by academic linguists, law professors, or even in departments of rhetoric. Academics prefer idealized or abstract law language, and some may turn into narrow specialists often making use of impenetrable jargon. The exceptions are there also, as with activist researchers focused on prisons and intent on the selectivity involved in deciding who goes to prison. But, in a larger sense, the consequences of words that are or are not used is a diminishment in lawful behavior, and invites retaliation and a gradual loss of legitimacy of law and the legal system overall.

Lawless World by Philippe Sands (2005) is one of a number of works on the diminishment of law's efficacy. These publications are scattered, but at some level Americans must realize, if they are not in denial, that *counterterrorism*, for example, is vengeance not justice. There are no charges, no due process, no verdict other than "we remember." Eventually, such trends could lead to increased authoritarian rule, loss of democracy, or fascism because the key virtue of law is its protection of our cultural values: political freedom and "we the people."

In 1935, the Eleventh Penal and Penitentiary Congress met in Berlin. Forty countries were represented. The Minister of Justice opened the meeting. He spoke about the idea of "justice" in the German Penal Reform. No mention was made of Dachau, a concentration camp where prisoners did not know why they had been arrested or when they would be charged or brought to trial. There is a lesson in the German example that should guide our research. We might regularly ask what aspects of law and language need to be given priority in our research? What are the key issues? By calling attention to unspokenness, this chapter (and the paper on which it is based) attempts to illustrate the shadowy underside, the features that escape formal analyses as in lack, *terra nullius*, terrorism, injustice, or double standards. The lack of scrutiny suits those in power. Part of our task as anthropologists is to call attention to social silences hidden in plain sight. Thus, one conclusion of my chapter is that language allows people in power to pick and choose which laws they want to impose, inflect, deflect, and avoid in favor of raw power: military, economic, or otherwise. "Self-defense" is used to justify blatant aggression by the perpetrators, and aggression or "terrorism" to condemn adversaries. Thus, lies about lawfulness are all about words. In a recent dispatch from Ferguson, Missouri, Jelani Cobb noted that President Obama's response to "unpunished racial injustices" constitutes "a genre unto themselves:" an unmitigated optimism, an urge for calm, faith in American institutions, even-handedness. The title of the piece was "Barack Obama, Ferguson and The Evidence of Things Unsaid."

REFERENCES

Abou El Fadl, K. (2003). "Rebuilding the Law." *Wall Street Journal*, 21 April.

Agamben, G. (2005). *State of Exception*. Chicago: University of Chicago Press.

Boorstin, D. (1941). *The Mysterious Science of the Law*. Cambridge, MA: Harvard University Press.

Cahn, E. (1964 [1949]). *The Sense of Injustice: An Anthropocentric View of the Law*. New York: New York University Press.

Clarke, K. (2009). *Fictions of Justice: The International Criminal Court and the Challenge of Legal Pluralism in Sub-Saharan Africa*. New York: Cambridge University Press.

Coates, T.-N. (2014). "Barack Obama, Ferguson, and the Evidence of Things Unsaid." *The Atlantic*. www.theatlantic.com/politics/archive/2014/11/barack-obama-ferguson-and-the-evidence-of-things-unsaid/383212/
Conley, J. and O'Barr, W. (1990). *Rules versus Relationships: The Ethnography of Legal Discourse*. Chicago: University of Chicago Press.
Fiss, O. (1984). "Against Settlement." *Yale Law Journal* 93: 1073.
Frake, C. (1963). "Litigation in Lipay: A study in Subanum Law," in *Proceedings of the Ninth Pacific Science Congress* 3: 217–222.
Galanter, M. (1983). "Reading the Landscape of Disputes: What We Know and Don't Know (and Think We Know) About Our Allegedly Contentious and Litigious Society." *UCLA Law Review* 31: 4.
Gardner, J. A. (1980). *Legal Imperialism: American Lawyers and Foreign Aid in Latin America*. Madison: University of Wisconsin Press.
Harr, J. (1995). *A Civil Action*. New York: Vintage Press.
Hayden, R. (1984). "A Note on Caste Panchayats and Government Courts in India: Different Kinds of Stages for Different Kinds of Performances." *Journal of Legal Pluralism* 22: 43–53.
Mattei, U. and Nader, L. (2008). *Plunder: When the Rule of Law Is Illegal*. Malden, MA: Wiley-Blackwell.
Mertz, E. (1988). "The Uses of History: Language, Ideology, and Law in the United States and South Africa." *Law & Society Review* 22: 661–685.
Nader, L. (1989). "The ADR Explosion – The Implications of Rhetoric in Legal Reform." In *Windsor Yearbook of Access to Justice*. Ontario, Canada: University of Windsor, 269–291.
Nader, L. (2001). "Crime as a Category." In J. Berreman (ed.) *Windsor Yearbook of Access to Justice*, 326–340.
Nader, L. (2005). "Law and the Theory of Lack." *Hastings International and Comparative Law Review* (Winter) 28(2): 191–204.
Nader, L. (2009). "Law and the Frontiers of Illegalities." In von Benda-Beckmann, F., von Benda-Beckmann, K. and Griffiths, A. (eds.) *The Power of Law in a Transnational World: Anthropological Inquiries*. New York: Berghahn Books, 54–73.
Nader, L. (2010). "Epilogue – The Words We Use: Justice, Human Rights, and the Sense of Injustice." In Clarke, K. M. and Goodale, M. (eds.) *Mirrors of Justice: Law and Power in the Post-Cold War Era*. Cambridge: Cambridge University Press, 316–331.
Rawls, J. (1999). *A Theory of Justice*. Cambridge, MA: Belknap Press.
Ruskola, T. (2002). "Legal Orientalism." *The Michigan Law Review*, 101(1): 179–234.
Sands, P. (2005). *Lawless World*. London: Penguin Press.
Spradley, J. (1988). *You Owe Yourself a Drunk: An Ethnography of Urban Nomads*. Washington, DC: University Press of America.
Williams, N. (1986). *The Yolngu and Their Land: A System of Land Tenure and the Fight for Its Recognition: A System of Land Tenure and the Fight for Its Recognition*. Stanford, CA: Stanford University Press.
Zulaika, J. and Douglass, W. (1996). *Terror and Taboo: The Follies, Fables, and Faces of Terrorism*. New York: Routledge Press.

2 Seeing Sense: The Complexity of Key Words That Tell Us What Law Is

Alan Durant

EDITORS' NOTE TO CHAPTER 2

One of the most persistent tropes in the field of language and law is the densely loaded expression that law is a 'profession of words'. The influence of that phrase stems from Mellinkoff's use of it at the beginning of *The Language of the Law* (1963); and its intricacies have been systematically explicated in Constable (1998). 'Words', when used in legal contexts, can mean anything from lexical items independent of context through to particular tokens in a given context; 'words' is also used, also vaguely, to mean part of a whole utterance or text. Ainsworth, this volume, also draws attention to how the 'profession of words' phrase may bear some responsibility for more attention being given in current research to legal vocabulary than to other linguistic structures such as syntactic organisation. Durant's chapter is a study of the established 'vocabulary' kind; but it goes beyond description of the legal lexicon into analysis of the potential impact of semantic variation in people's use of general legal terms on public understanding of and attitudes towards law.

Durant argues that words including *law* itself, *justice*, *authority*, *rights*, *rule*, *regulation, legitimacy*, and others form a loose but distinctive subfield within the English lexicon: a field made up of general words naming or describing law which together conceptualise what law is and how it fits into the wider field of social relations. Such words may on some occasions of use, he argues, be treated as legal terms of art. But even in their legal settings – especially across different jurisdictions – they show considerable indeterminacy of meaning, especially polysemy, vagueness, and contestability. Durant's chapter explores which words it is useful to think of as being in such a cluster of core, general terms of law. He then describes what is meant in this context by polysemy, vagueness, and contestability and, through an extended reading of the history, semantic development and current use in different meanings of the word *law*, shows how such considerations can affect what we understand as 'law' in legally and politically relevant ways.

In a recent volume celebrating the work of the late Peter Tiersma (along with Mellinkoff, perhaps the other most influential figure in modern linguistic work on legal language), the U.S. jurist Frederick Schauer assessed what has been accomplished in the study of legal vocabulary and what remains to be done. He concluded, 'The work that remains to be done, however, is that of analysing the relationship between the conventions of the technical and the conventions of the ordinary, and to do so in a way that recognises law's parallel needs to speak to itself and at the same time to speak to those outside it' (Schauer 2015: 38). Durant's chapter responds to the challenge posed by that assessment.

REFERENCES

Constable, M. (1998). 'Reflections on Law as a Profession of Words'. In B. Garth and A. Sarat (eds.) *Justice and Power in Sociolegal Research.* Northwestern University Press, 19–35. Available online at http://www.mcgill.ca/files/crclaw-discourse/Constable.pdf

Mellinkoff, D. (1963). *The Language of the Law.* Eugene, OR: Resource Publications.

Schauer, F. (2015). 'On the Relationship between Legal and Ordinary Language', in P. Tiersma, L. Solan, J. Ainsworth, and R. Shuy (eds.) (2015) *Speaking of Language and Law: Conversations on the Work of Peter Tiersma.* New York: Oxford University Press, 35–38.

Seeing Sense: The Complexity of Key Words That Tell Us What Law Is

The nature of law, the rule of law, legal order, law and order, rightful, basic human rights, rights and responsibilities, against natural justice, social justice, the interests of justice, just and equitable

There is an interesting group of English words and expressions – illustrated here by sample phrases clustered around *law*, *right(s)*, and *justice* – which are generally recognised as communicating important attributes of what we call 'law'. Those attributes (including authority, legitimacy, justness, etc.) are relevant whether we are thinking of law as an abstract entity (cf. *natural law* or *positive law*), as a body of doctrines or institutional system (cf. *the law, legal order*), or as a singular realisation (*a law*, *legislative act*). For centuries arguments about such attributes have complicated debates about what distinguishes 'law' from coercion and other forms of exertion of power, from custom and belief or retribution and revenge, and from moral judgement. So the existence of a cluster of 'key' expressions[1] which lexicalise those attributes can seem an elephant in the room in efforts to understand 'the language of law'.

[1] The phrase 'key expressions' here alludes to the established use of the term 'keywords'. Analysis of such keywords in English is usually associated with the work of Raymond Williams (1976/1983), who started to research such words by collecting usage of a cluster of five words (*industry, democracy, class, art*, and *culture*) that suggested themselves as 'key points' from which he could draw 'a map' of 'changes in life and thought' he was seeking to explain in *Culture*

What I will call in shorthand 'law-designating' words including *law*, *right(s)* and *justice*, as just mentioned (plus *equitable*, *authority*, *sovereignty*, *legitimate*, *rule*, *order* and *regulation*, and some others introduced later) are used in various ways in different contexts. Some are used in legal rules. Some combine with other words to form stable phrases, and among those phrases some lend their name to a legal principle, doctrine or ideal (e.g. *legitimate expectation*, *the rule of law*). Most can also be found in political, diplomatic, journalistic and scholarly comment on the place and significance of law in society. The same clustering of expressions surfaces in conversation among people subject to law but not professionally involved in making, applying or studying it. In the last-mentioned of these domains, general public usage or 'ordinary language', such words and phrases offer vernacular versions – frequently dismissed as bowdlerised versions – of what law is and what values it stands for.

In 'non-legal' settings among the situations just described, expressions which form the general terminology of law are commonly used with meanings or nuances that differ, sometimes markedly, from their conception in law. An *order* may be a meal, *authority* a generalised enemy, and *law* something Kafkaesque; *sovereignty* can become a vague political football; and *the rule of law* may be an established status or a continuously tested process or aspiration, or even taken to be something resembling *law and order*. Are such uses nothing more than misuse of technical terms and ignorance – hence 'bowdlerisation'? Lawyers mostly say so, emphasising the separation of law from other kinds of discourse as a specialist field with its own terminology, mode of reasoning, and rules. Many non-lawyers, on the other hand – and among them some philosophers – foreground how vague or ambiguous many of the core terms in and about law are. Is it possible that these two opposing views are not completely at odds with one another, and that the property of semantic indeterminacy – an incompleteness or failure of words to signify a particular meaning – is functional in some way analogous to how vagueness has been shown to play particular roles in legal drafting and statutory interpretation (Endicott 2000; Waldron 1994)? This essay considers the possibility.

The idea that a social purpose might be served by complexity, rather than precision, in words whose task it is to tell us what law is seems odd. But, if substantiated, the idea could be significant as regards the 'language of law', because the words and phrases in question are not generally considered to be uncertain but rather are viewed as having settled meanings, even when there is profound

and Society 1780–1950 (1958: 13). Williams planned to publish entries for these and other such words as an Appendix to that book but later published instead a separate book: a 'vocabulary of culture and society' consisting of over 100 words (for context and discussion, see Durant 2006). My involvement in research based on Williams's approach in the 'Keywords Project' (http://keywordsproject.pitt.edu) has shaped this chapter, though the specialised, normative treatment of meaning in law leads to substantially different lines of argument.

disagreement as regards what those meanings are. As is often pointed out, *law* has its etymological origins in something being 'fixed' or 'laid down'; adjectival *right* develops from 'movement in a straight line, direct, unswerving'; and *lex* and *legal* are traceable controversially either to 'something tied or bound', from Latin *ligare*, or 'something written down to be read', from Latin *legere* (Cassin 2014). In the absence of a prescriptive language Academy, however, by what authority could meanings for such words be prescribed for situations where they are not employed as specialised legal terms but rather, as most of the words to be discussed have been for centuries, used as active political and general expressions?

The relation between legal and other meanings associated with the same words in different contexts merits investigation, despite the significant difficulty that the questions which surface are interdisciplinary. The issues are linguistically interesting because of the questions about semantic variation and norms they raise; they are also legally interesting, in appearing to engage the principle of legal certainty. The 'public understanding' aspect of that principle requires words used in law to be definite and clear in telling us what the law is, so that citizens can organise their affairs in a way that does not break the law. Sensibly, but leaving important problems unresolved, the principle only expects such words to tell us what the law is, not what law is.

Proper analysis of semantic variation in the meaning of general legal words calls for investigation of each word, as well as of the semantic relationships between them. Here there is scarcely space even to mention them all. But there are general points worth making even if those points can only be illustrated by brief examples. Subject to these limitations, this chapter probes how the distinction used in dictionaries between 'general' and 'specialised' usage relates to law in a highly distinctive way. It examines aspects of semantic indeterminacy in some core legal expressions that follow from their polysemy, vagueness or contestability, and asks whether, on account of these characteristics, such expressions may in some way function as a conduit for, rather than as a blockage to, legal-lay communication. If so, the chapter concludes, questions arise regarding how (and how far) public participation in law is made possible by what is communicated, given the fundamental asymmetries of power and understanding of law involved.

Context: Language of Law, Theories of Law

It is counterintuitive that the most general words which name and describe law might not have been exhaustively discussed already. A substantial body of scholarship exists on legal concepts and their associated terminology, as well as on representation of legal words in specialist dictionaries (Mac Aodha 2014). Introductions to legal pedagogy, in English, often acknowledge the many meanings of *law* (though less often differences of meaning between *law* and cognate words in other languages). In this section I argue that, despite these considerations, not enough attention has been given to the meaning of general legal words. To develop this point, I comment first on two fields which might be expected to examine such meanings but seem not to in any detail: linguistic studies of legal vocabulary and discussion in Anglo-American philosophy of law on how word meaning contributes to legal concepts.

Linguistic Approaches to Legal Vocabulary

Work in linguistics is mostly descriptive, including studies concerned with vocabulary (lexis). Where analysis is *not* descriptive, linguistic studies are still only rarely prescriptive (prescriptive approaches typically fall outside the scope of linguistics as a discipline). Rather, linguistic studies that go beyond description generally aim to be explanatory (e.g. by accounting for aspects of language acquisition or, at a higher level, the human capacity that makes language acquisition possible). From the outset, therefore, there is typically a divergence of purpose between linguistic and legal approaches to what words mean.

The central descriptive task of linguistics consists in examining structures and patterns in language use as they actually occur rather than as they should be. Such features, including word meaning, can be described 'synchronically' (as contrasts within a given language system at a particular point in time) or 'diachronically' (concerned with historical change). Either approach can have a comparative dimension, examining contrasts between different languages or contact between them such as borrowing of loanwords.

Linguistic studies of 'the language of the law' often combine historical and synchronic perspectives, and tend to emphasise the distinctiveness, even peculiarity, of legal language as a variety (Mellinkoff 1963; Crystal and Davy 1969; Tiersma 1999). Peculiarities noted include complexity of sentence grammar in operative legal documents, minimal use historically of punctuation or structure mapping by means of paragraphs and sections, a preponderance of vocabulary of Romance origin, persistent archaism, and use of 'binomial pairs' (i.e. doubling of near-synonyms such as *aid and abet, cease and desist, last will and testament*, often collocating words with origins in different languages; sometimes also triples, such as *null, void and to no effect*). More recently, legal language has been shown to be a suitable topic for corpus linguistic investigation (Coulthard and Johnson 2007). Comparative studies are less common. But Mattila (2016) describes legal use of language in a number of European languages and assesses the legacy of Latin in legal systems developed in those languages. Cassin (2014) traces linguistic and conceptual interaction between languages and considers English expressions such as *authority, justice, law, liberty, power*, and *the rule of law* – along with their counterparts in other European languages – to be 'untranslatables': the words do have cognates, but those cognates are embedded in different formations of ideas as well as different institutions and legal systems. Also concerned with cross-linguistic comparison, Wierzbicka (1997, 2006) has mapped semantic overlap and differences for various cultural fields onto roughly sixty postulated semantic primitives of a 'natural semantic metalanguage', or NSM (her analysis of *reasonable* being the most relevant legal discussion; Wierzbicka 2006). As has been suggested earlier, however, comparative analysis is important within jurisdictions as well as between them, especially historically. Any account of legal English vocabulary, for example, must assess the changing role played in its development by different languages, including Norse, Anglo-Saxon, Anglo-Norman, and Latin.

Linguistic discussion that is concerned particularly with the meanings of words as used in law has directed its spotlight less on words naming or describing what law is than on challenges faced by judges in statutory construction: how meanings are attributed by courts in applying laws that use ordinary words to establish legal categories. Hutton (2014) analyses numerous cases. Solan (2010) and Carston (2011), in different ways, evaluate how judicial approaches to attributing meaning (for instance based on maxims, Scalia and Garner 2012) relate to natural language processing as understood in linguistics and psychology. Durant (2010) explores how courts interpret words used in utterances other than those found in the wording of legal rules: words which become the crux of a legal dispute because of their contested occurrence in media discourse or communication online.

The focus of the present topic, however, is on general terms for law which can bear varying meanings across different domains of use, and has received little attention. Central to the topic, as with statutory interpretation but with different emphasis, is the dichotomy with which this section began: between descriptive and normative purposes in both the use and analysis of language. 'Normative' purposes, in this context, must be clarified as operating at several levels. First, there is normative with respect to behavioural outcomes (since operative legal language confers rights, imposes obligations, and guides action, and so performs a socially directive function; linguistically, commands, use of modals such as *ought* or *should*, and implied meanings all play a part). Second, there is 'linguistically normative' (concerned with which words should be used, for example to comply with courtroom etiquette, and how words should be construed in legal cases). Both these senses need then to be distinguished from so-called normative legal theory, which is interested in what law could or should be and stands in contrast to two established 'analytical' approaches: descriptive legal theory (e.g. doctrinal studies investigating regularities in a particular legal system) and explanatory legal theory (e.g. Marxist accounts of how law serves an ideological function in social structure). Although in legal discourse different levels of normativity typically reinforce each other, linguists bring a descriptive and explanatory mind-set even to normative language. It is of course possible to examine linguistic normativity descriptively (Bartsch 1987); but understanding the normative constraints on language use in law requires a level of familiarity with legal concepts and procedures that can discourage linguistic researchers, especially if they feel unsympathetic in principle to normative linguistic judgement.

Words and Concepts in Jurisprudence

The possibility that core words for law have not been exhaustively examined in jurisprudence seems still less likely. But there are grounds for thinking it may be the case in works that treat explication of verbal meaning as largely irrelevant to conceptual analysis at the level required of general theories of law. As Finnis puts it in his account of legal theories, early in *Natural Law and Natural Rights*,

> Jurisprudence, like other social sciences, aspires to be more than a conjunction of lexicography with local history, or even than a juxtaposition of all lexicographies conjoined with all local histories. (Finnis 1979: 4)

Works of Anglo-American jurisprudence by theorists such as Dworkin or Raz, like Finnis, tend to construct their arguments through critique, use of hypothetical scenarios, and practical reasoning. In doing so, they show only passing interest in the meaning of words. Ultimately this is the case with Finnis, too, though his writing is often more attentive to verbal nuance – before dismissing it as irrelevant:

> I use the concept of justice with all the breadth that that concept has had in academic discussion since Aristotle first treated it as an academic topic. That is to say, I set aside all the special and limited shades of meaning that the word *justice* may have acquired in common parlance.... We must let our discussion be ruled by the substantive questions we have in mind (about what is reasonable and unreasonable in human conflict), not by the conventions and associations of our language. (Finnis 1979: 161–62)

In accounts of law that go beyond particular laws or legal systems – into arguments for instance about *natural law*, *the nature of law*, *the authority of law*, or *law as justice*, as works by the authors mentioned do – specific legal systems are treated as instantiations of a supposed more general legal form. At that level of abstraction complexities in the meaning of words get left behind except where some specific ambiguity hinders the argument.

Emphasis on concepts more than on how words convey them has not been an uninterrupted tradition in Anglo-American philosophy of law, however (let alone in the longer history of thinking about law, for instance among the Scholastics and Renaissance lawyers who were accustomed to grappling with philological problems). The contemporary emphasis I have mentioned involves to some extent a reaction against an earlier 'linguistic turn', including a period of influence of ordinary language philosophy on the jurisprudence of H. L. A.

Hart from the late 1940s onwards. In *The Concept of Law* (1994 [1961]), Hart acknowledges the influence on his thinking of Oxford philosopher J. L. Austin (a second John Austin, not the nineteenth-century jurist and author of *The Province of Jurisprudence Determined* (1861)). Hart praises Austin's insight that, as Hart glosses it in the Preface,

> Many important distinctions, which are not immediately obvious, between types of social situation or relationships may best be brought to light by an examination of the standard uses of the relevant expressions and of the way in which these depend on a social context, itself often left unstated. (Hart 1994 [1961]: vi)

Hart and other legal philosophers of the time were especially impressed by Austin's essay 'A Plea for Excuses' (1979 [1956]) and incorporated ideas into their thinking encapsulated in Hart's tribute to Austin: that it is possible to use 'a sharpened awareness of words to sharpen our perception of the phenomena' (Hart 1994 [1961]: vi). For a variety of reasons, nevertheless, *The Concept of Law* proved a high-water mark of influence of this kind of language-focused analysis.

The next generation of influential philosophers of law in the same tradition, especially Raz and Dworkin, thought differently. In Dworkin's *Law's Empire* (1986), references to 'semantic' characteristics are to something wider than verbal nuance. Dworkin uses 'semantic' to refer to what he calls 'semantic theories': theories which, as he describes them, are concerned with 'how all lawyers use the word *law*' (Dworkin 1986: 36). But 'use the word *law*' here is figurative (and note that Dworkin is only interested in how lawyers use the word, not how other language users do). He begins his analysis of law by contrasting 'semantic' with 'plain fact' accounts (i.e. accounts of particular laws which have been passed) and describes semantic theories as ones which call for 'digging out shared rules from a careful study of what lawyers say and do' (Dworkin 1986: 43), especially elucidation of rules and criteria supporting a 'common assumption, which is that we [*lawyers again*] do share some set of standards about how *law* is to be used' (Dworkin 1986: 32). Dworkin's interest in *law* is that it is the main word in English which conventionally triggers the concept; it is the concept accessible in some largely unexamined way beyond the word itself which is of main theoretical interest to him (see the final section of this chapter for further discussion).

In a similar vein, though steering towards a different theoretical position, Hart's former student Raz suggests (2009) that sometimes too much attention rather than too little is given to word meaning. At various points he maintains that there is no particular need in developing a general theory of law even to use the word *law* (or the phrase *the law*, which he treats as roughly equivalent). It would be possible, Raz maintains, to talk about law 'by talking of the system of courts and legislature and the rules they endorse in a state, or in other ways'. Law's essential features, in Raz's view, include claims to legitimate moral authority, being source-based, and claims to have peremptory force (2009: 97). Each of these features, however, is a broad concept whose verbal formulation seems to reprise the problem of verbal meaning he would prefer to circumvent; the words used might designate potentially very many different referents, or none at all, in different historical periods and social systems.

Explication of word meaning of a kind Hart, adapting Austin, had favoured was displaced in a shift that not only affected philosophy of law but the whole of analytical philosophy; and in continental philosophy discussion of words and their meanings set off in other directions. Fifty years on it is far less true than when Hart wrote it that, as he put it in his entry for 'Jurisprudence' in the first (1960) edition of the Unwin *Concise Encyclopaedia of Western Philosophy and Philosophers* (Urmson and Rée 1989: 155), 'the elucidation of the expression *law* and terms embodying fundamental legal concepts (e.g. rights and duties, legal personality, ownership, sources of law) is now regarded especially in England as an independent and important study'.

Legal Meaning

Two important considerations lose their urgency when less attention is paid to word meaning in the analysis of law. One is a procedural matter: how, largely through judicial decision, law controls verbal meaning not by one single means but in a number of related ways. The other is the fact that the most general words we use to name and describe law fit only very awkwardly into that combination of approaches. This section of the chapter outlines how courts rather than philosophers and linguists deal with legal meaning, which they do largely by distinguishing different interpretive categories which are subject to specific interpretive conventions. It also points out that, while a sophisticated, historically evolved strategy governs the interpretive culture of law, that interpretive culture exerts no direct authority over the meanings attributed to words in domains beyond law. As a result, words used concurrently both in legal and in other fields may retain or vary from understandings prescribed for them in their legal use in ways that are unpredictable and may be problematic.

Types of Vocabulary

Words which make up the lexicon of a language are commonly distinguished into types, classifiable on the basis of alternative properties. Word class (or part of speech) is an obvious classification, which plays a role both in grammar and semantics. The etymology or historical origin of words offers another significant basis for grouping. Words are also often grouped according to usage, including whether they feature generally in discourse or only in specific styles (e.g. technical, religious, legal). Categorising some vocabulary items as technical terms and defining the relation that should exist (rather than necessarily does exist) between them and other general or ordinary words plays an important role in shaping law as a field.

Many domains of language employ technical terminology (as 'terms of art'), domains including science, technology, and medicine; economics and professions such as law and business; and sport and leisure pursuits. Law is generally recognised among these as creating and controlling its terms of art in a distinctive way. In fields based on observation, measurement or experiment, for example, one or more starting points in a practice or field external to language can serve to anchor definitions. Further terms are added and defined reciprocally but ultimately in relation to one or more such external reference points. In more theoretically and discursively constituted fields, such as theology or philosophy, for most terms (since these will principally be abstract words) there will be nothing concrete to point to, and so no external, ostensive basis for naming or definition. Correct usage is stipulated by whatever forms of institutional authority are sanctioned. In this sense many legal terms, not only acknowledged legal fictions (Fuller 1967), involve 'deeming' or declaring something to be endowed with a particular scope or meaning: legal practice creates or adopts its terms and stipulates their meaning not by reference back to something fixed and external but forwards, for the purpose of application to something by required deference to established legal authority.

Categories of Words for Interpretive Purposes

Reflecting specific features of how terminological authority is created in general, four general types of expression can be distinguished in legal use.

- Some expressions are recognised legal terms of art (e.g. *assumpsit, rescission, derogation, best endeavours*). These have specialised meanings. Some are in Latin or of French origin (e.g. *mens rea, de minimis, lien, bailment*), and many have little or no circulation beyond law in other varieties of the language (e.g. *fee simple, estoppel*). Some have been called 'legal homonyms' (Tiersma 1999: 111–12), because one context for their use is legal while another is general, for example *consideration, conversion, detriment, liable*. But such expressions are not homonyms in the traditional sense, of different words etymologically which share the same form, such as *bank* of a river and *bank* as a financial institution. Rather, they are words whose senses are simply different enough that each occurs in a recognisably separate context. Potentially such terms could create ambiguity, but they tend not to because their alternative meanings are clear enough in a given context (and a reader or listener encountering an unclear use will recognise that some other meaning is intended which they have not grasped). Because terms of art become well established professionally, they do not need to be explained on each occasion among people who use or encounter them. Learning to understand and use such expressions is part of becoming a lawyer in the sense proposed by Mertz (2007).

- Alongside such terms of art there are words explicitly defined for the purpose of a particular law, contract, or other document and typically presented in its first section or alternatively in separate definition or interpretation clauses or an added schedule. For example, section 1 of the Addressing Bullying in Schools Act (Northern Ireland) 2016 defines 'bullying':

  (1) In this Act *'bullying'* includes (but is not limited to) the repeated use of
  (a) any verbal, written or electronic communication,
  (b) any other act, or
  (c) any combination of those, by a pupil or a group of pupils against another pupil or group of pupils, with the intention of causing physical or emotional harm to that pupil or group of pupils.

  In recent UK legislation, additional explanatory notes are provided alongside the main legislative text (in relation to the section quoted here, those notes give further specification of what a 'school' is). In some circumstances, definition can be the main subject matter of a set of regulations (e.g. the UK Capital Gains Tax [Definition of Permanent Interest Bearing Share] Regulations 1999/1953). Definitions formulated along such lines are confined to use for the purpose of the particular instrument.
- Other words again are recognised as being in need of judicial construction (legal interpretation), typically because they are vague and therefore unclear in the applicable legislation. These are instances of Hart's 'open texture', famously illustrated by his 'No vehicles in the park' example (1994 [1961]: 126–30). For Hart, there is a kind of gradience from core to peripheral or penumbral exemplars in relation to prototypical instances of a category (in this case, regarding what a 'vehicle' is [for discussion see Hutton 2014]). Vagueness in such 'category words' is resolved by judicial decision: seemingly fuzzy scope is judicially clarified so that a definite legal outcome, reflecting in or out of the relevant category, can be decided.
- There are also so-called ordinary words of English. These are not legally defined, and their meaning is presumed to be generally understood or can be 'taken on judicial notice' (i.e. the court does not require argument or evidence on the point). In a UK trademark registration application for the word mark LUV, for instance (*Elliot's Trade Mark Application* [2014] R.P.C.13), the judge could declare that 'the meanings of *love* are well known to anyone with a command of the English language', even though the application was for the mark to be used on goods including sex toys and aids. Other counterintuitive and problematic examples include the important phrase *beyond reasonable doubt* (for discussion of difficulties created by this example, see Heffer this volume).

For some words in these categories – most obviously the terms of art – a word is intended to be recognised as a member of its assigned category. This flags how it should be interpreted. With other words, context of use plays an important part in how a word is treated (e.g. a word used in a statute and construed by a judge primarily in relation to a given fact situation may have already been defined, potentially differently, or may be re-defined later in a different legal context). What matters overall is that the distinctions are governed in legislation either by definition or by judicial reference to interpretive aids in applying the legislation (see, within a massive literature on statutory interpretation, Barak 2005; Greenawalt 2013).

In the intricacies of this area of legal procedure it is easy to forget that the system of normative interpretation applies only to the legal use of words, even though many of the words used in law – notably the general terms discussed in this chapter – have a wide circulation in contexts where such normative rules do not apply. Unstipulated interpretation of *estoppel* is unlikely to raise problems, because the word is hardly used except where a legal context already exists. With legal homonyms like *consideration*, mostly it is clear when a non-legal meaning is intended; if *consideration* is introduced in a context where it could convey a contract-like meaning (while the other meanings, something like 'detail' or 'thoughtfulness', would be more likely), then the word will probably be interpreted as figurative or humorous. Vague terms are slightly different. The word *boat* might be defined or construed as a kind of building for a specified legal purpose; but this will have minimal impact on conceptualisation of boats generally (as well as no decisive impact on what a boat is in a different legal context). Importantly, beyond law's interpretive jurisdiction legal adjudications of word meaning may influence how people think but they are not binding. How serious or otherwise this characteristic of legal vocabulary is depends on the nature and significance of the word in question. It may not matter much with *estoppel, consideration*, or *boat.* But scope for variation in what is meant by terminology indicating legal principles and purposes raises the politically crucial question of how far public understanding matches legal understanding with respect to *justice*, *rights*, *authority*, or *the rule of law*.

Tension between Different Bases for Meaning

There is one further complication in this interpretive landscape that must be mentioned: what kind of meaning, for a given expression, will satisfy an expectation of being the right kind? Interwoven with extensively discussed theoretical topics such as attributing intention and choosing between a text's literal meaning or overall purpose, interpreters may relate the basis for a decided meaning to how language works in different ways.

Underpinning word meaning in legal settings, there are two major alternative emphases in this respect. Each happens to reflect an established perspective in linguistic thinking: one would be described as synchronic, the other as diachronic. Both ultimately prescribe interpretations, and so what language means, in that, within whatever range of alternative interpretations exists, a singular, correct construction will be imposed on a problematic expression. But the stereotypical view of law deciding meaning depends on more subtle interaction between two legal norms.

One of the two interpretive norms coincides fairly closely with the default position in modern linguistics. It presumes that speakers of a language internalise vocabulary as a network of contrasts, rather than as historical word stories (because a child acquires a contemporary state of the language system in which he or she is immersed and understands distinctions and nuance spontaneously, without reference to etymology or an expression's historical development). This view finds its first main expression in linguistics in the work of the early twentieth-century Swiss linguist Ferdinand de Saussure, and is then developed in several directions in structuralist semantics (for history and discussion, see Geeraerts 2010: 47–100). As regards semantic variation, the view typically takes for granted the homogeneity of a language community (in ideal form they are all users of the same common system of contrasts), subject to some qualification for dialectal or sociolectal, and potentially idiolectal terms. Law echoes these broad interpretive assumptions (in a common-sense rather than theoretical way) in its adoption of 'ordinary reader' and 'plain meaning' approaches to interpretation.

But there is another, contrasting historical-philological approach. That approach draws attention to how any expression has an origin in the language (either as a coining or borrowing from one or more other languages) and a traceable development of meanings that changes over time but which may cumulatively be relevant to a modern social concept (e.g. 'ethnic', 'family', 'work', 'worker', 'neighbour', 'torture', 'genocide', 'freedom', or 'justice'). This interpretive emphasis may also begin from contemporary use but accepts that reflection on meaning is deepened by familiarity with historical substrata, especially when interpreting documents or subject matter from or indebted to earlier periods (in practice, the view can range from conservative appeals to etymology as an ultimate standard through to historical reconstruction of a word's history as a way of tracing conceptual complexity).[2] Common law draws on such a historical conception in close reading of textual detail in precedential

[2] A number of important historical perspectives on meaning are bundled together here, though they differ in important respects. Among the most relevant here are these: Goodrich (1986) presents a historical and critical overview of hermeneutic approaches in 'reading the law'; Geeraerts (2010: 1–46) and Kay and Allan (2015) trace the background to philology and diachronic lexical semantics; Empson (1951) offers close readings of historically complex words in literature (e.g. *wit*,

judgments, both as regards difficult words under scrutiny in a given legal case and in interpreting the language used in previous judicial rulings.[3] This historical hermeneutic has however been specialised in a particular direction in common law reasoning, especially in higher courts. The repeated practice of judicial construction in so many cases has engaged successive generations of judges in seeking to resolve, or at least in commenting on, interpretive problems to do with words and phrases as they arose.

Arguably it is the combination of these nuanced ideas of meaning that creates law's (at least common law's) rich interpretive culture. Exactly how courts and other tribunals triangulate between different viewpoints outlined earlier is nevertheless not easy to describe, because interpretation is embedded in kinds of reasoning which are frequently articulated in other terms. Detailed reasoning about meaning may be presented as much by emphasising that the relevant authority is good as that the linguistic argument is good.

Cluster of 'Key' Words

With relevant contexts now in place – that is, the existence of a debate about what word meaning contributes to legal concepts and the use in law of a range of interpretive strategies that nevertheless do not govern word meaning beyond law – it is time to address more directly which words are worth investigating as the cluster of words I claim show significant semantic indeterminacy in their different uses.

Use of the term *cluster* here involves a commitment to the idea that words are not mere atoms of conceptual content but relate to other words as members

honest, sense); Skinner (1998) investigates conceptions of *liberty* in political circulation during the emergence of *liberalism*; Raymond Williams's 1976 'Preface' to *Keywords* (1976/1983) describes how the historical development of word meanings surfaces in conflicting efforts to understand present-day society and values.

3 The term *common law* is itself interesting in this respect. There is the clear modern meaning (a system of law applied by judges based on cases and precedent, in contrast with *civil law* or *civilian* systems); there is the historical meaning (the imposition on a previously regional legal system of a greater degree of standardisation, achieved in England from the twelfth century onwards by a unified system of courts combined with travelling judges, as introduced by Henry II); and there is a third meaning which combines historical reality with myth and can colour the other two: that of law 'shared or available to all', a use foregrounded especially when 'our' is placed in front: 'our common law'. This third use, combined with the historical sense, presents a glowing image of community ownership of law 'since time immemorial'. Any such image of 'time immemorial' is difficult to justify, however, either to mean 'always' or even in doctrinal use to indicate time before legal memory (i.e. any time before the accession of Richard I in 1189). The main political settlements that have shaped common law's relation to the modern population come later, in shifts from feudalism into capitalism and from the assumed divine right of kings into representative, Parliamentary democracy, by way of events including the Civil War, tyrannicide, Bill of Rights, colonial domination overseas and more recent independence movements and wars. For discussion of further difficulties with this expression regarding exactly what areas and aspects of law it applies to, see also Glanville Williams (1945: 302).

of lexical fields within the overall lexicon. The least committing version of this idea is hardly controversial, either intuitively or in structuralist linguistics from Saussure onwards. But the precise basis on which such groupings are decided has been subjected to considerable scrutiny and the most apt terminology for use in the present case cannot be presumed.[4] Whatever term is adopted, exact membership of what I will call simply a 'cluster' cannot be fixed definitively. Nor can an overall number of members. Word clusters are elastic networks, linking to adjacent semantic domains in different ways. This characteristic is especially notable where the words in question are abstract and polysemous, because patterns of similarity and contrast around them depend on which sense is activated in signaling a particular relation. So it is far more difficult to justify membership of words in a semantic field of abstract terms about law – where the main point to be made about such terms is that they are polysemous and vague – than to group concrete terms which form part of a recognisable schema (e.g. *table, chairs, knives and forks*, including *vase of flowers* while excluding *donkey, microscope*, and *serenity*).

Despite difficulties with word groups in general, there seem good reasons to want to think of the general terminology of law as a cluster. First, many words appear uncontroversial as prominent words naming or describing the social institution and values of law. Those words, it would seem, should occur frequently in jurisprudence and, if less prominently, in related fields including 'law and society', constitutional law, and political theory. Secondly – but in ways that turn out to be complicated – candidate words seem as if they should relate to each other according to an established taxonomy of sense relationships (such as synonymy, antonymy, or hyponymy).

This second expectation presents challenges as regards what the basis is of connections between prospective members of the cluster. *Order* and *rule* both seem obvious candidates for inclusion, for instance. In one of the senses of each, the two are near-synonyms for (and so might be grouped with) legally important *command*, despite awkwardness when separating out their meanings as nouns and as verbs. In another sense of each, though, the two words signify the abstract social purpose, state, or outcome of law as a system, not a single instruction; and in this sense they enter into different semantic relationships with surrounding words (e.g. they are closer to *regime* or *governance*). Or consider how *justice* invites being seen as a superordinate (or hyperonym) of *law*. Law is one among a number of ways of achieving justice (there are

[4] The concept of, and history of theories related to, lexical fields is traced in detail in Geeraerts (2010: 52–70). The loosest relationship is simply between words used in a general conceptual or thematic domain; but many such words may not be restricted to or specialised for use in that domain. A stronger requirement is that words should show a measured likelihood of co-occurrence; and a still stronger requirement might insist on semantic relationships such as synonymy, antonymy, and hyponymy between members. What is called a 'lexical set' is bound by interlocking semantic relationships (e.g. *mother, father, daughter, son, sister, brother*).

alternatives such as charity or political initiative) but 'being just' can appear a necessary feature or entailment of *law.* Such semantic relationships, when stated, can appear extremely reductive, however. The relation between the two words *law* and *justice* can be seen to be more complicated by considering the celebrated maxim sometimes held to encapsulate *natural law*: 'unjust law is no law' (or, switching the sense of *law* from abstract to concrete in both instances, 'an unjust law is not a law'). The meaning of this maxim, as translated from Latin *injusta lex non est lex*, has been debated from renderings of Aristotle onwards, through Saint Augustine and Aquinas, up to the present; and the semantic relationship between its main terms appears crucial to claims which surround it and their ramifications. Whether in Latin or English, the maxim seems to confirm that *law* entails 'justice', since law without justice is said not to be law. But it also affirms the opposite: that there is potentially a class of law (i.e. unjust law) which lacks justice. Arguably part of the maxim's memorable, self-contradictory effect results from tension created precisely by uncertainty regarding the semantic relationship between *law* and *justice.*

Word nets devised primarily on the basis of semantic relationships and applied to abstract semantic domains often seem crude and reductive in this way. Intersections of meaning between polysemous, abstract words do not fit easily into established semantic categories or neat tree diagrams. Rather, the meaning relations between them are a kaleidoscopic movement of facets and relations, criss-crossing in ways that invite but elude definitive description. A purely 'semantic relations' approach would simplify details of conceptualisation in a given context of use and cut off any given meaning from its relevant lexical history, textual tradition, or surrounding ideas.

It is important in selecting general 'law' words, however, not to allow difficulties of this kind to eclipse the value of describing relationships between words and concepts by considering them as a 'cluster'. But which words should be included? Here, as the outcome of an informal process combining introspection, general reading, and consulting dictionaries and thesauruses, is a provisional selection (based on apparent family resemblances, observed tendency to occur together, and in some cases to create an appearance of more systematic semantic relations).

1. A **minimal** list should include *law, justice*, and *right(s)*, as well as words based on *lex* and *leg-* (a formation etymologically unrelated to *law*) including *legal* and *the principle of legality*. Something is considered law or law-related if it is named or described by any of these words.[5] *Equity* may also

[5] The first chapter of Jeremy Bentham's *Of Laws in General* (first published 1780, but held back for nine years by the author during which time he claimed that half the printed sheets had been devoured by rats) is concerned with 'how a law may be considered in eight different respects' (each the subject of a separate later chapter). Bentham emphasises 'the necessity of these verbal discussions', and analyses why no other word than *law* in English 'would answer the purpose as well' in conveying the distinctive concept of law. Bentham examines the relative merits of

fit in this first group, as a further word indicating an area, type, or quality of law, though the word's development complicates that categorisation. Leaving aside financial meanings of *equity*, use of *Equity* with capital E in British English suggests a hyponym of *law*: a particular division within the English legal system, initially a route of direct appeal to the sovereign in the person of the Lord Chancellor, bypassing common law courts; then later, the distinct Courts of Equity until absorbed into the court system by the Judicature Acts of the 1870s. Alternatively, however, *equity* might be considered a meronym of *law* (a part or quality of what law is: its fairness and even-handedness, resulting in 'equitable' treatment). Other words here include *regulation*, bringing with it a distinction likely to problematise the scope of *law* in any discussion of that word's vagueness: between *hard law* and *soft law*. *Regulation* itself is both vague and contested among policymakers and professionals, cutting across earlier relations between state and market and between public and private actors in the delivery of law. This might also be the place for *jurisprudence*, whose meaning is both 'body of law including case law' (e.g. 'jurisprudence of the European court') and 'science of human laws in general; philosophy of law'.

2. Given the historical centrality of arguments between *positive* and *natural law* approaches to what law is, *morality* appears an important word in the variable synthesis of notions expressed in law. Modifying terms which combine with *law*, including *divine*, *natural*, and *positive* also warrant inclusion here. Note, however, that parallel expressions in form may not be symmetrical in meaning: *natural law* denotes a legal and philosophical tradition, from ancient Greek origins onwards, concerned with aspects of law including divine provenance, universals, and human reason; *natural rights*, important in political changes during the eighteenth century, denotes human rights considered inherent or inalienable but ridiculed by Bentham as 'nonsense upon stilts'; *natural justice* is a narrower, originally seventeenth-century doctrine, that anyone whose rights are affected by an official decision should be entitled to advance notice and a fair hearing before an unbiased judge (a principle now more often known, as expressed using other words within the same cluster of general terms, as *right to a fair hearing*).
3. Also to be added should be words which indicate the basis on which, or premises from which, general concepts of law are derived: *legitimate* and *authority* seem obvious here. Other related words include *impartiality* and *fair*, but these seem less particularly legal (they are arguably used mostly

other words that 'come into competition with' *law*, including *command, commandment, order, injunction, decree, precept, specialist, ordinance and edict, constitution, regulation, establishment, institutional*, and *mandate*. The modern Athlone Press edition of this work (1970) was edited by the legal philosopher H. L. A. Hart, discussed earlier as having been especially influential in emphasising the continuing importance of linguistic meaning in shaping legal concepts.

in a wider social context, in this respect similarly to the otherwise undoubtedly central terms *public/private, reason/reasonable*, and *interest*, including *public interest* and *best interest*). In the development of law generally and international law in particular, *customary* is also important.

4. Overlapping with the preceding group, next might be words concerned with values that law aspires to or protects, and desired social conditions that systems of law seem calculated to bring about: *order* (in its abstract, 'system' sense), *freedom, liberty, civil liberties, liberties of the subject* (plural but less, rather than more, than singular abstract *liberty* because restricted by being possessed by someone who is only a 'subject'), and similarly qualified *freedom under the law*. This grouping might also include *equality*, extending to *equality before the law* as well as, in litigation, *equality of arms*.
5. A further subgroup appears salient in showing how law is expressed and relates to other social values and structures, including power: *power* itself (including different meanings when shifted from abstract to concrete and when used in the plural: *delegated, discretionary*, and *special powers*); also, *coercion, command, obligation, binding, duty*, and *enforcement*. Inclusion of particular words here depends again on the particular sense in which they are understood: *power* is part of one semantic grouping when used to signify an abstract resource potentially monopolised or distributable by a (human, institutional, or symbolic) *sovereign*, but in another group when specifying some particular delegated jurisdiction or agency. In turn *jurisdiction* meshes with one grouping in its abstract meaning of 'authority' or 'competence', but another when specifying a place or institution in which a particular authority is exercised. In turn *authority*.... The potentially circular connections and definitions we embark on in such categorisation, with one expression glossed by surrounding terms in the same group, is of course not specific to this field but a general problem of definition; it may even strengthen a sense that the words should be viewed as a group rather than individually.
6. At a further remove from core 'naming' terms come expressions which denote general characteristics of a polity: *democracy* and *governance, representation* and *representative, constitution, separation of powers, policy, state*. These valuably foreground the constitutive (and *constitutional*) rather than coercive dimension of law; but as regards their place in this cluster they seem likely to appear primarily political rather than legal words.

A feeling may already have taken hold, at some point during this exercise, of beginning to deal with different kinds of word: some less abstract, or in a different field, possibly with less of a naming or descriptive role in relation to law. Perhaps some kind of limit should therefore be imposed, perhaps after group 5 or, if not there, after group 6? Or would it be better to reverse the process and think of words which should not be included? Reasons for exclusion of marginal cases might include not being used frequently enough, or having only a technical rather than also a general meaning, or seeming to be at the wrong level of generality. There is a group of words, for example, which all show some degree of relevant polysemy and vagueness but describe institutions more than they do law as a concept: *court*, *trial*, *case*, *hearing*, *tribunal*; and there are words with similar properties for legal actors including *judge*, *advocate*, *party*. And there are words which denote values or principles prominent in law but whose currency has not extended into general vocabulary: *habeas corpus* and *ultra vires*, as well as arguably *prerogative* and *proportionality*.

Given the informality of the process adopted for choosing words as members, what I am calling a 'cluster' of key terms cannot be more than an intuitive word web. Various methods could be adopted to refine the process, ranging from corpus linguistic frequency-of-occurrence measures to double-coding protocols using agreed criteria for decisions made by researcher readers.[6] Even as informally as this exercise has been conducted, however, an impulse to cluster does not stop easily: it is difficult to think about any one of the preceding words without cross-referring to others. In the most general sense, therefore, they *are* a cluster. Collectively, such words designate – they lexicalise as far as any words can, albeit in historically and culturally specific ways – some fundamental level of what law is. Yet for all that, the most general words of law, which Raz treats as mostly unproblematic because they form 'part of the common terminology of practical discourse in general' (Raz 2009: 30) remain elusive both in their meaning individually and in the semantic relationships they enter into with each other.

Polysemy, Vagueness, and Contestability

In the face of such classificatory difficulty, it is important to return to the reason for considering this open-ended group of words as a 'cluster'. This section develops in greater detail an account of how words of the general type included in the cluster behave in terms of their meaning. First I summarise aspects of meaning I consider significant. Concern here is no longer only with what the words mean in legal settings, but also with any given word's semantic footprint across all its different contexts of use. Then I take one word – *law* itself – for more detailed illustration. Looking closely at just one word, for reasons of space, restricts comparative discussion (though some reference is necessarily made to connections radiating out to other words). *Law* was chosen as my

[6] Approaches to using corpus linguistic techniques for identifying and analysing key words in given fields include Stubbs (2001), which presents case studies on particular words and phrases based on a combination of traditional concepts such as lexical field, sense relations, and collocation with more recent corpus techniques; and Baker and McEnery (2015), which uses and also reflects on methods for identifying words and phrases that are simultaneously marked in terms of relative frequency and thematic importance.

example because – as the word was shown earlier to be for some philosophers of law – *law* is emblematic in designating the conceptual domain signalled by words including *law, justice, rights*, and *regulation*. The word *law* also exemplifies fairly clearly the main points about meaning that would need to be highlighted equivalently in other words considered to be in the cluster.

Multiple Senses

One pronounced feature of words identified as members of the cluster I am describing (though also shown in a less marked way by many other words) is their polysemy. Polysemy occurs when a word has more than one distinct sense and where its multiple senses are felt by native speakers to be related (Cruse 1986). A textbook example is *mouth* (of a face) and *mouth* (of a river). The 'river mouth' sense appears a figurative extension from the form and function of a human mouth, and has become on this basis an additional, conventional meaning. Virtually all the words discussed in the previous section are polysemous in this way. Different relationships exist, however, between polysemous senses. These include hyponymy (where as mentioned earlier one sense denotes a type of the entity denoted by another sense) and meronymy (where one sense denotes a part of the entity denoted by another sense). Senses at different levels of concreteness or abstraction are also common. So is figurative extension by means of tropes such as metaphor and metonymy. Historically, polysemous senses arise from processes of semantic change including sense widening and narrowing, amelioration, and pejoration (see Kay and Allan 2015: 25–48). While it is unremarkable that words show polysemy in this way, the consequences for interpretation seem particularly significant in law because of the importance law attaches to the consistent use of words even if, beyond law, other meanings with different degrees of closeness to the legal meanings may be ascribed to the same word.

One effect of polysemy on interpretation can be ambiguity, which arises when more than one sense is activated for a word simultaneously, often intentionally. This can create uncertainty as to what was meant. For ambiguity to arise (which in most kinds of discourse is relatively uncommon, because one meaning will typically fit a given context better than another), two conditions need to apply: an expression must have more than one established meaning, and the interpreter must either entertain an extraneous or incorrect reading or alternatively find it difficult to decide what the intended meaning was. In poetry, religious discourse, jokes, and some other kinds of discourse, ambiguity can also work in another way. An interpreter may be encouraged to entertain the multiple meanings simultaneously. Ambiguity of this kind can be created either by lexical characteristics (alternative meanings for a particular word) or by syntax (alternative parsings of a grammatical structure). In legal drafting, major efforts are made to avoid ambiguity because it creates a kind of indeterminacy which calls not for acceptable 'filling in' of meaning by judges, as vagueness may, but instead an apparently additional interpretive decision that may be perceived as encroaching on the role of the legislature.

Another, under-acknowledged consequence of multiple senses is confusion of level between concrete and abstract meanings. Different senses related in this way exist for most words in the cluster, as can sometimes be seen in their grammatical behaviour, especially whether they can be preceded by an article *the/a*, and whether they also occur in the plural. As Chomsky cautions, however (1965: ii, 64), the relation between countable and mass words in grammar does not map directly onto the concrete/abstract distinction: in his example, *boy* is a count noun distinct both from the mass noun *butter* (which is still concrete but not countable) and from abstract *sincerity.* Some examples appear straightforward: 'a rule of law' (countable and concrete, a specific legal measure) as compared with 'the rule of law' (an abstract – as well as historically complex, culturally varying, and hotly disputed – political value). But other examples shift meaning in apparently minor yet sometimes important ways. The difference between concrete *order* ('command') and abstract *order* ('arrangement', 'system') has already been noted. But there is a further distinction within use of the second of those senses: *order* in one meaning is something that law should consistently uphold, while politically and socially it should not show itself to be partisan to a given *order* (in the first of these two uses *order* is abstract but not countable, while in the second it is both abstract and countable).[7]

In highlighting the importance of concrete and abstract senses, it is important not to lose sight of how this distinction within the senses of a polysemous word interacts with other facets of conceptualisation to produce intricate shadings of meaning far beyond easily enumerable senses. Staying with *order*, an array of philosophical and historical nuances opens up. Philosophical meanings of *order* have been described especially clearly in Finnis (1979: 136–39), who identifies four uses as aspects of one single general meaning: 'a set of unifying relationships'. The first kind, for Finnis, is 'natural order' that we do not ourselves bring about: 'the order studied by the natural sciences' (in describing this kind of order Finnis excludes the related, purposive 'watchmaker'

[7] The difference between these senses of *order* is emphasised in relation to the phrase *law-and-order* in Raymond Williams's final discussion of 'keywords' in his 1985 essay 'Mining the Meaning: Key Words in the Miners' Strike' (Williams 1989). Williams suggests that four words were crucial during this major industrial dispute, which Williams felt involved 'the dislocation of our habitual social order': *management*, *economic*, *community*, and *law-and-order*. Of the last of these words, he comments, 'I take this as a single word, as it is currently used. [...] For it is the arbitrary combination of what should be two quite different words and concepts that is the key to its contemporary ideological effects.... Listening to some ministers, it is easy to pick up their real sense of *order*, which is command: obedience to lawful authority; indeed, when combined with the 'right to manage', obedience to all authority.... What is at issue, in any conflict about a particular law, is the underlying definition of the desired social order (Williams 1989: 125).

alternative: 'divine order'). Finnis's second 'order' is what humans 'bring into understanding' in creating internally coherent knowledge and reason. Thirdly, there is 'order' imposed by humans onto whatever matter around them is subject to their powers (e.g. systematic use of inventions or the products of technology); and fourthly, there is the 'order' or state of unity brought about 'by intelligently deliberating and choosing', an order of social interaction, management, and communal organisation. For Finnis, what matters most about these recognised senses is how they pave the way for a notion of 'human community', and so require law to be understood in terms of interpersonal connections rather than purely at the level of an individual legal subject. But arguably what makes the four kinds of order (which postulate different origins, states of nature, and creative agency) more generally important is that they lend real or symbolic weight in different historical periods to more complex uses of the word (Foucault 2001, though note that the French title of this work – *Les mots et les choses* – does not contain the word *order*).[8] In a hierarchical extension of the basic meaning of 'series', *order* has been used to denote social or professional rank, status, or class (e.g. orders of monks or knights), as well as status in other social institutions or conventional arrangements (e.g. *order of wedlock*). It has also been used normatively to denote a harmonious condition of everything being 'correct', 'in a healthy state', and 'in its place', even 'normality' (in contrast with *out of order* and *disorder*). But complications follow, including whether a particular use of *order* is descriptive or ascriptive (or one of these dissembling the epistemological status of the other). An *order of plants* in biology may seem to fall in Finnis's first category, of 'order out there in the world' (though it might be better understood as combining properties of his first and second categories); *alphabetical order* may seem an example of Finnis's third kind (a human-made, technological convention). But what about abstract *religious order* or concrete 'a religious order'? Such order, or such an order, may lay claim to derivation from *divine order*, while being in obvious respects a human-made institution. And what, then, about *feudal order*, *legal order*, or *New World Order* (the last of these in all its various intellectual and political twentieth-century manifestations)? Such usages absorb several different, even potentially conflicting dimensions and resonances of what *order* means.

Vagueness

Vagueness is more significant in legal language than ambiguity although, like ambiguity, it combines with effects of polysemy where the vagueness in question is only of a particular sense rather than in an expression's overall meaning. The phenomenon has been extensively analysed, not only in philosophy of

[8] Foucault appears initially to have preferred the title 'L'ordre des choses', but that title had already been used by someone else.

language (e.g. in close connection with semantic indeterminacy more generally in Quine 1960: 125–29) but also in legal construction and adjudication, including how vagueness can be useful to lawmakers (Endicott 2000). It has also been examined in detail by Waldron in relation to the U.S. doctrine of 'void-for-vagueness' (Waldron 1994).

To summarise Waldron's impressive, formally set out description, an expression is vague if it is imprecise in the sense that there are: objects or instances within the domain of the expression's usual use where an interpreter will be unable to decide whether the object or instance falls within the meaning of the expression or not, and where the interpreter who finds herself or himself in such a position attributes that inability to decide to the expression's meaning rather than to a lack of further information (Waldron 1994: 513). Waldron's example is the colour term *blue*. Most people, he says, would hesitate when shown various colour patches in deciding whether some shade of turquoise or lavender is or is not blue, or whether it is borderline.

In *Word and Object*, Quine (1960: 126–27) points out that a general term for physical objects can in fact be vague in this way in more than one respect: the general term *mountain*, he notes, is vague in relation to how much terrain each indisputable mountain occupies, and it is vague in terms of what lesser eminences should count as a mountain at all. For many words, vagueness of these kinds raises questions about the different approaches to categories already alluded to: Aristotelian 'necessary and sufficient conditions' accounts; 'prototype and goodness-of-exemplar' understandings associated first with 'family resemblance concepts' in Wittgenstein, then with prototype theory in psychology; and legal 'open texture' as discussed in Hart.

Vagueness has tended to be a prominent topic in linguistic semantics but not in pragmatics, where it tends to be viewed as an aspect of contextual modulation of meaning by inference (e.g. Sperber and Wilson 1995). In law, the difference between meanings which are conventional aspects of a word and meanings which are constructed by inference is not consistently drawn. Vagueness of expressions is nevertheless discussed in law in many contexts, especially in relation to conceptual categories, as explained earlier; in relation to so-called trivial vagueness (where a general rather than precise expression has been used unadvisedly or as inappropriate hedging introduced into a legal document); in discussion of the boundary between vagueness and arbitrariness; and regarding the vagueness of general evaluative terms such as *reasonable* (Soames 2011).

Contestability

The third kind of indeterminacy of meaning that commonly arises with general legal terminology scarcely features in treatments of meaning in linguistics. But it is important across the range of uses of the 'law words' under discussion in this chapter.

The meaning of an expression can be said to be contestable if the expression communicates an evaluative (often called appraisive) force but at the same time exhibits incompatible characteristics or elements which offer alternative ways of satisfying that same evaluative judgement. The most well-known account of contestability in this sense is to be found in an article by the philosopher W. B. Gallie (1956) concerned with concepts rather than verbal expressions. In Gallie's account, controversially discussed under the description he coined of 'essentially contested concepts', for contestability to exist there must also be a history of struggle between alternative criteria involved in efforts to secure a 'proper' meaning for the expression/concept. Among Gallie's examples are concepts expressed by words including *art*, *democracy*, and *social justice* (as well as what he calls an 'artificial example', of *championship* and *champions*). Waldron's discussion (Waldron 1994) sifts carefully through Gallie's detailed criteria governing whether a concept satisfies the conditions of being 'essentially contested' ('essentially' meaning in its essence, rather than merely 'thoroughly or intensively'). The example Waldron then analyses in more detail (Waldron 1994: 529–34), based on Gallie's discussion, is that of *democracy*, which can be considered contestable because of three linked conditions:

1. *democracy* can be explicated in terms of political representation but it is not implausible alternatively to explicate the word's meaning in terms of direct participation in government;
2. *democracy* has a favourable evaluative meaning, such that people want to and feel democracy should be promoted; and
3. because of the two preceding conditions, a history has built up of using *democracy* to embody what nevertheless remain rival political principles (e.g. 'every political system should have a representative structure' and 'we ought to encourage direct popular participation in government').

By analogy with this illustration, it is easy to see that many expressions in the cluster of law-naming or law-designating words introduced earlier are contestable in this sense. Gallie mentions *liberty* and *social justice* in this context; and *the interests of justice*, *law and order*, *authority*, *legitimacy*, and *basic human rights* are all similarly amenable to such analysis (though their contestability can of course be overridden by normative interpretation in a legal setting). It should be noted, nevertheless, that, since contestability in this sense only applies to words which involve an appraisive force (i.e. they are evaluative and implicitly encourage pursuit of acclamation for a particular conception of the contested word or concept), this kind of semantic indeterminacy is unlikely to be found in many other words in the cluster identified previously.

The Word Law

In light of these fairly abstract distinctions about meaning and semantic indeterminacy, now consider the word *law* in more detail, taking this word as an example of the kinds of complexity I claim make general words for and about law difficult in legal-lay communication. As a way into examining *law*, the word, rather than slipping directly into the concept or concepts it is taken to convey, the *Oxford English Dictionary* (OED) is an obvious place to start (especially if read in conjunction with concise or pocket dictionaries and with dictionaries compiled on different lexicographical principles such as COBUILD publications).[9] This is not only because of the OED's acknowledged authority but because it is compiled on historical principles and offers a range of related resources.[10] First I offer an outline of what the OED says about *law*; then I address the significance of considering word meaning in ways the dictionary opens up in thinking about legal concepts.

The OED entry for *law* has not been fully revised since 1902 but contains draft additions up to 2004. Strictly there are five headword entries for *law*: four nouns and a verb. The four nouns cover meanings of: 'a body of rules' (the entry mainly discussed here), 'score, share of expense', 'round or conical hill', and an interjection sense conveying surprise or dismay, 'Oh law!'). The verb means roughly 'ordain' or 'render lawful' but is virtually obsolete.

The entry for *law* as 'a body of rules' begins with information about pronunciation, variant word forms, relative frequency of use (Band 7, among the top 1,000 words in English), and etymology. A pop-up gives a timeline of first attestation for each recorded sense (with peaks in the number of new senses in early seventeenth century and mid-nineteenth century), as well as a separate timeline of sense development (showing dates and duration for each). To represent the word's various senses, four Roman numeral major branches provide an overall structure, divided into twenty numbered principal senses (subdivided in turn into lettered senses making a total of fifty-one recorded senses). Each sense – it is conceivable that fewer or more could be distinguished by what lexicographers call further 'splitting' or 'lumping' together – is traced to its first attestation (and final date of recorded use, where obsolete); each is also annotated with usage information (e.g. 'rare' or 'archaic'). The senses are each also illustrated by quotations accompanied by the name of their author and the date of publication (578 in total, with a timeline of sources for the quotations provided in another pop-up). Following this detailed listing of the word's senses when it

9 All modern dictionaries base their headwords and entry content on computerised linguistic corpora. But some (including Collins COBUILD dictionaries) also adopt a policy of ordering meanings based on attested frequency in their corpus. For detailed analysis of the COBUILD project, see Sinclair (1987).

10 The OED is best now thought of as an online publication (www.oed.com). In print, it was first published in parts as *A New English Dictionary on Historical Principles*, eds., J. A. H. Murray, H. Bradley, W. A. Craigie & C. T. Onions (OUP, Oxford, 1884–1928); 2nd edition 1989; 3rd edition in progress. See the OED webpage for details of and articles about related resources including the *Historical Thesaurus of the Oxford English Dictionary* (HTOED).

is used as a separate form, equivalent information is provided for related compounds (e.g. *law enforcement*). All this semantic information can be combined with a thesaurus approach to meaning – in philological terms, an onamasiological rather than semasiological perspective – by cross-referencing to HTOED (the OED's historical thesaurus; Kay and Allan 2015: 92–112). Such cross-referencing makes it possible to connect with the semantic field in which *law* has been used by examining cognate terms for each sense at different points in the period during which English law developed (terms including *assize* (1303), *droit* (1480), *jure* (1496), and words for legal science including *juristics* (1837) and *nomology* (1880)).

Scaled back from such richness of evidence, in outline the modern word *law* might be described as follows. *Law* emerges from Late Old English *lagu* (circa 1000), a form derived in turn from Old Norse *lag*, 'something laid down or fixed'. The native word in Old English had been *ǽ*. The OED also notes that, 'as *law* is the usual English rendering of Latin *lex*, and to some extent of Latin *jus*, and of Greek *νόμος*, its development of senses has been in some degree affected by the uses of these words'. (Further discussion of the significance and legacy of these origins, with particular regard to European philosophy, law and politics, can be found in entries for the respective words in Cassin 2014.)

Three of the word's four main branches of meaning in the OED entry have titles: 'I. A rule of conduct imposed by authority'; 'II. Without reference to an external commanding authority'; and 'III. 'Scientific and philosophical uses'. The fourth, unnamed branch contains only one sense, s20: 'Allowance in time or distance made to an animal that is to be hunted, or to one of the competitors in a race, in order to ensure equal conditions.' It is the three named senses which give both the general concept of law and, in the relation between Branch 1 and Branch 3, show significant conflicts in social thinking that have complicated the word's development and current use.

The first branch ('rule of conduct imposed by authority') compresses into a single grouping senses covering two vast areas of law, 'human' and 'divine'. Within 'human', the dictionary also deals with both customary and positive law. Alongside the three other branches, this telescoping gives some idea of the scale and scope of this word that has been condensed into what is still a lengthy analysis. *Human law* (s1–8), from about 1100, covers 'the body of rules, whether proceeding from formal enactment or from custom, which a particular state or community recognizes as binding on its members or subjects'. As a whole it is this branch which distinguishes the most familiar meanings: 'legal system', a 'code or system of rules'; 'one of the individual rules which constitute the "law" of a state or polity'; and 'the condition of society characterized by the observance of the laws'. This branch also notes use of *law* to mean substantive area of law (law 'divided, according to the matter with which it is concerned'); and traces use of *law* 'in contradistinction to equity'. *Law* is also exemplified meaning 'legal profession', and to signify legal proceedings: 'action of the courts of law, as a means of procuring redress of grievances or enforcing claims; judicial remedy'.

Perhaps what is most striking, however, to a modern reader accustomed to the reach of administrative legal measures in securing policy or social engineering goals (e.g. specifying taxation details, correcting for market failure, or stipulating food standards), is the second prong of this first branch: the extent and variety of uses that signify 'divine law' (ss9–16). Some of these senses are not recorded after the sixteenth century but some remained current until the end of the nineteenth century. Such senses range from 'the body of commandments which express the will of God with regard to the conduct of His intelligent creatures' through divine law as 'implanted by nature in the human mind, or as capable of being demonstrated by reason', to 'the system of moral and ceremonial precepts contained in the Pentateuch', 'the law of Moses, the Mosaic or Jewish law'; and broadest of all, *law* meaning 'a religious system'.

Branch 2 (which traces uses 'without reference to an external commanding authority') is less relevant to legal discussion. It does, however, evoke how grounded in custom and convention other senses may be. Section 14, for instance, deals with 'custom, customary rule or usage; habit, practice', and later senses illustrate uses to mean 'rule of action or procedure; one of the rules defining correct procedure in an art or department of action, or in a game' (examples here include rules of the card game whist, rules for hospitality, codes of honour, and the *law of the jungle*). How far these are meanings 'without reference to an external commanding authority' must depend on the particular case but also inevitably to some extent on the meaning given to polysemous *authority* (itself a very substantial entry in the OED).

Branch 3 begins (in s17) with what law means in the 'sciences of observation' and in the 'physical sciences', broadly from the seventeenth century onwards. In sciences of observation, *law* (here as a count noun) signifies 'a theoretical principle deduced from particular facts, applicable to a defined group or class of phenomena, and expressible by the statement that a particular phenomenon always occurs if certain conditions be present'. This is the sense condensed in a less technical rendering as one of the meanings in Dr Johnson's *Dictionary* (1755): '*Law*, an established and constant mode or process; a fixed correspondence of cause and effect'. In the physical sciences, on the other hand, *law* is 'called more explicitly *law of nature* or *natural law*'; and some quotations here, selected prior to 1902, reflect a tension between divine origin, human perception, and reasoning. Illustrative quotations include Boyle's 'The Wisdome of God does . . . confine the Creatures to the establish'd Laws of Nature' (1665), and Locke's, 'A Law of Nature . . . something that we may attain to the knowledge of, by our natural Faculties' (1694). Further quotations indicate domains in which such laws obtain, including general laws of motion, the universal law of gravitation, laws of reasoning, and Grimm's law in philology.

Law *and Concepts of Law*

How much illumination can be expected from reading one OED entry in this way? This question is approached by considering the *law* entry itself first, and then in comments on my use of *law* as an example of complexity claimed to exist in most or all words in the cluster of legal 'key' words.

The OED entry for *law* illustrates a series of points made earlier. It shows legal and other uses of *law* across various fields and discourse types: law, religion, science, games, and hunting. Its four branches and fifty-one recorded senses confirm that *law* is highly polysemous in the view of lexicographers. The word's range of senses varies on a number of dimensions: different subject areas, degree of technicality (including in different fields), degree of generality and potential for vagueness, degree of concreteness and abstractness, and social register. On an assumption that meaning in at least some cases involves representation of the speaker's beliefs, the meanings also reflect significant differences between historical periods of thinking. Some views expressed in the various senses, and in accompanying quotations, are now to be found only in historical sources – part of a cultural substratum of modern legal thinking – whereas others remain current and amount to socially dominant current understandings. Others again are current but likely to be confined to the thinking of specialised, minority social or interest groups. Together, this range shows the social-semantic footprint of *law* as a word of English.

The dictionary makes no attempt to extend its encyclopaedic information, and does not comment on the relative spread, weight, uptake, or influence of ideas represented in the various senses. But by no means all the senses reported are in fields distant from what a lawyer or philosopher of law thinks of as 'law' or relevant to law; and many of the varying senses are not trivial in relation to a lawyer's or philosopher's concerns. Some, in fact, are expressions of major alternatives or lines of argument related to the general legal meaning of *law*. In this way, many of the senses reported chart uses of the word that a reader might expect to encounter in a legal or jurisprudential argument, and whose significance within such an argument he or she might wish to assess as precisely as possible.

The word's main complexities, however, are not in any one sense or in the word's range of senses. Rather, they concern unresolved blending, intersection, or interstices between senses of the kind introduced earlier in relation to *order*, including points at which meanings are positioned in relation to one another in an overall field. One major complication, which runs through the history of legal thinking as well as through debates about the legal systems of 'good' and 'bad' states, resembles the point made earlier by reference to the condensed natural law maxim 'unjust law is no law': how far *law* implies moral grounding for rules it articulates, in a manner analogous to *justice*. Historically this issue is central to religious and philosophical, as well as legal, debate about *natural law* and *positive law*. In OED s15, *law* does convey a 'justice' meaning: 'what is considered right or proper; justice or correctness of conduct'. But that meaning became obsolete in English around 1500. Unsurprisingly, the thesaurus link for s15 sense is to words with moral or ethical resonances: *right*, *justice*, and *rightfulness* (and may suggest semantic differentiation taking place between the two words during the period in the context of late Mediaeval reinterpretations of Classical legal thinking). How far *law* retains such an implied, residual meaning has now to be assessed based on a view taken of its relation to other words around it in different fields of contemporary discourse, particularly *rights* and *justice*.

The other main, unresolved issue associated with the word *law* concerns law's provenance, an issue highly germane to understanding what gives law its authority that surfaces in the relationship between the OED's first and third branches of meaning.[11] Branch 1 acknowledges such a complication in a note linked to s9c (the first sense in 'divine' meanings for *law*). Concerning the phrase *the law of nature*, it notes, 'now rarely, because of the frequency of that expression in sense 17' (i.e. the first sense of Branch 3, 'scientific and philosophical uses'). The OED comments on the relevant scientific sense in a note as follows:

> In the physical sciences, *law* is 'called more explicitly law of nature or natural law. The 'laws of nature', by those who first used the term in this sense, were viewed as commands imposed by the Deity upon matter, and even writers who do not accept this view often speak of them as 'obeyed' by the phenomena, or as agents by which the phenomena are produced'.

The physical science meaning of *law*, that is to say – the one conveying 'demonstrated general principle', and on one reading proclaiming the ambition and values of secular science – inherited an earlier, religious schema that was no longer completely believed by many users of the expression but which was

[11] The question of where law comes from and what gives it its authority is of course a major, if not the central, question for legal theory, with positions ranging historically and culturally across divine commandment or inspiration, customary cultural practice, the command of a sovereign and obligations created through 'recognition' by those subject to the law, and elaboration from a basic, grounding norm – among others. Kelly's (1992) chronologically narrated account of legal theory, from the Greeks through to the closing stages of the twentieth century, is particularly accessible and eloquent in its discussion of the relationship between arguments in jurisprudence and philosophical and political ideas. A thought-provoking recent historical and comparative discussion of the relationship between law's provenance and its social function is *The Fall of the Priests and the Rise of the Lawyers* (2016), written by the English international financial lawyer Philip Wood. Concerned with questions of the morality of law, past and present, as well as with international finance, Wood traces the changing balance between religions and legal systems in different places and periods, arguing for better understanding of the contemporary role of law in creating and preserving human values.

nevertheless retained by them and continues to be discernible as an implication at some indefinite level of possibility.

What is striking in these aspects of the development of *law* is that there is no neat compartmentalisation between concepts of natural law, positive law, and scientific law. Rather, the interrelation between these concepts appears as something that can on occasion morph into hybrid or qualified versions which give expression to what was (and for many people remains) an unresolved but fundamental question about the origin of orderliness in the world and its articulation or transformation into human order and law.

Acknowledging such messiness in ideas conveyed by *law* – ironically the prototypical term for universality of authority and application – conflicts with the aim of understanding *law* as an expression of 'univocal' concepts. Despite this, close reading of the word in the OED and beyond need not undermine efforts to formulate ideal-type concepts or develop arguments based on them. The value of the kind of verbal analysis offered here lies rather in the close-up it offers of processes of making meaning: a sharpened image of changing and sometimes conflicting local uses of words which create and explore what gradually becomes more generalised social thought, alongside uses of language which communicate as far as possible in already established categories.

But *law*, it might be queried, is hardly representative in this respect. Is it not an unusual or even unique word? Could it be an exception among the other expressions listed previously? It might be, but the points being made about *law* are echoed strongly in most of those other words. Even a brief reading of the OED entries for those other words shows complexity in number and range of senses, in the historical development of different branches of meaning, and as regards current polysemy. In most, there is one or more historical turning point, divergence, or conflict related to alternative conceptualisations. With some, a crux of meaning relates to one or more new fields in which the word begins to be used (in ways that result in coexisting technical and general uses); or there may be tension between meanings that emerges between concrete and abstract levels, or different conceptual fields stimulating new lines of figurative use. Further, because polysemy is often accompanied by vagueness (Mehl 2013), as well as sometimes by contestability, the words grouped earlier do all seem complex in the ways I have claimed *law* is. What was argued for *law* more generally can also be shown for the other words: that values, arguments, contradictions, and dilemmas are inscribed in a word's multiple, developing senses.[12] Although much about the meaning of such abstract legal terms could only be established by more systematic study, there seems an important watershed here in thinking

12 Although written in a different research context, my 'keyword' entries for *legitimate* and *rights* illustrate these features (http://keywordsproject.pitt.edu). Other relevant entries in the Keywords Project corpus include: *authority, freedom* and *liberty*, and *privilege*.

about legal vocabulary: between understanding legal 'key words' as materials in a historical process of negotiating ideas and values, and considering words as vehicles for concepts that can be detached from the history of their formulation and deployed in contexts where it is an overall argument, rather than a density of multiple ideas, interpretations, and attitudes embedded in particular words, which is expected to be communicated.

Conclusions

The account I have offered of this relatively unexplored topic in 'the language of law' remains highly schematic. My intention has been to show the potential interest of the topic and draw attention to possible lines of enquiry. In conclusion, however, it is important to comment on two areas of significant theoretical difficulty. One concerns a common reservation: that discussing philosophical concepts as if they resemble word meanings is misguided. The other concerns a claim I made at the beginning of the chapter: that semantic indeterminacy in general legal terminology might serve a social purpose in communication between the legal sphere and public discourse at large.

Concepts and Conceptions

It is not incompatible with the criticisms developed earlier that it is still easy to agree when writers such as Dworkin, Raz, or Finnis insist that irrelevant senses of words should be filtered out in putting forward a philosophical argument. The difficulties that need further consideration occur in a middle ground, between acknowledging the significance of semantic indeterminacy and insisting on concepts being 'univocal' in the accounts of law they contribute to.

Difficulties in this area have little to do with general debates in anthropological linguistics about how far semantic distinctions reflect cultural distinctions and influence cognitive categorisation, the traditional ground of 'linguistic relativism' debates around the Sapir–Whorf hypothesis (Gumperz and Levinson 1996). The issues here are more concerned with the level in a conceptual hierarchy at which theoretical analysis of law can most successfully take place. In contrast with the critique of fixed legal concepts I have put forward, for example, a distinction is often emphasised between two levels of analysis: the level of unified concepts (abstract, ideal notions) and a level of conceptions (particular instantiations, or realisations of such concepts). To illustrate that distinction, Dworkin many years ago outlined a scenario in which he instructs his children to behave 'fairly'. In doing so, he says he anticipated two possible outcomes: first, that in applying the concept of 'fairness' his children might go beyond any particular examples of conduct he would have thought of himself; and second, that he would be prepared to modify his own view in light of alternative conceptions of fairness which underpinned their choices. The significance, for Dworkin, was that his children's actions, and his concession by way of response, do not affect the 'fairness' concept itself. That concept, he maintains, exists above the varying conceptions of it; and the true meaning of his instruction was that his family should be guided by the concept of 'fairness', while allowing for disagreement over controversial cases created by varying conceptions of that concept.

Dworkin's scenario serves in part to clarify a distinction he was making between two types of legal rule: rules amenable to further development in use but based on a large number of overlapping, agreed instances (concept-based rules) and rules where detail is specified and which are therefore less amenable to flexibility of interpretation (conception-based rules). This distinction appears valuable in accounting for the tendency of legislation to follow different conventions in different periods and legal systems (especially for modern common-law legislation to reach into more areas of life and be more voluminous and detailed than previously). As refutation of the contestability of concepts, however, the scenario seems inconclusive. How far, for example, does Dworkin's scenario depend on the contrast he draws between concept and conception, and how far is it coloured by an extra dimension – that of family hierarchy – which he introduces in passing, in that a 'law of the father' dimension complicates prospects for contestability of what an overarching concept of fairness should be. Clarification of the example also seems needed on how the children's alternative conceptions related to complexities of the particular word *fair* that Dworkin had used in giving them the instruction.

Varying Dworkin's scenario slightly in order to draw out such difficulties, by creating a hypothetical situation based on *justice*, may highlight a more substantial role for interpretation in how concepts and conceptions work. Imagine that a city mayor exhorts a gathering of her officers to 'dispense', 'do', or 'administer' *justice* (the three commonest verbs, in order of frequency, which immediately precede *justice* in the Oxford English Corpus [OEC], in contrast with *obstruct, escape*, and *delay* as the three most frequent verbs related to different kinds of actor linked to *justice*). In this modified scenario, it is first of all difficult to know whether there is one or several different instructions, because what *justice* means is inflected by each particular verb of which it is made the grammatical object. Now imagine that, following the instruction, one officer gives public property away, another takes out writs, and another inflicts punishment on people. (This is inevitably somewhat strained, reflecting simplification already present in the earlier scenario.) Each of the officers' responses derives from an alternative interpretation of *justice*, based on established senses: 'quality of being just' (construed here as some kind of *social justice* objective, justice as a balancing of all interests to be achieved including by resource redistribution); 'administration of law and judicial proceedings' (justice as a matter of proceedings in legal institutions); and 'punishment or retribution' (rendered more graphic in the now obsolete metonymic sense of the word *justice* reported in OED sense 2b, 'gallows'). To be credible, each of these responses by an officer would need to be enriched considerably. But in outline they suggest that an account framed in terms of a dynamic conceptualisation or construal of *justice*, narrowed and altered by context, might offer more insight into what justice is than an account formulated in terms of conceptions treated as varied embodiments of a static, superordinate concept. One reason for preferring a 'contextualised' account is that it fits better with the word's recognised semantic indeterminacy. Characteristics of such indeterminacy include how *justice* prompts a similar pattern of alternative interpretations through its vagueness (e.g. whether *justice* can extend to extrajudicial detention, deportation, or drone strikes) as well as through its contestability (e.g. whether 'proper' *justice* is achieved better by 'redistribution of resources' or by 'putting people in prison for longer'). Deciding which of the two analyses should be preferred seems to depend further on how the notion of 'concept' is understood (including how static or dynamic concepts are, and what internal structure they are assumed to have). It also depends on how far abstract cultural concepts should be thought of as being constituted in the course of their use in particular verbal and cultural contexts (for further discussion, see Nuyts and Pederson 1997; Croft and Cruse 2004; Geeraerts 2010: 240–49).[13]

Conduit, Competence, and Mystification

The other remaining topic to be addressed concerns the claim I made at the beginning of this chapter: that semantic indeterminacy in the general terminology of law may function as a conduit for communication between the legal sphere and wider public. In introducing that possibility, I presented semantic variation between a professional legal group and other social groups descriptively: as a matter of overlapping meanings in different domains associated with subgroups in a larger, overall language community. No relations of power, standards of correctness, or order of priority within the social hierarchy were countenanced. A contrasting view of such semantic variation would however be that it shows in the given society an endemic and potentially dangerous failure of comprehension and associated ignorance of the law. A polemical account might go on to insist on greater respect for professional legal discourse as a society's guarantor of correct meaning (e.g. as opposed to use or abuse of words with

[13] Such a contextualised view of concepts is hardly unknown in law. The jurist Glanville Williams argued over seventy years ago that context gives meaning to a word by indicating which other word it is opposed to. He gives the example of *freedom*, which he says has no single meaning: 'freedom versus imprisonment; freedom versus legal duty; freedom versus deprivation of the franchise; freedom versus imposition; freedom versus economic bondage; freedom versus determinism; freedom versus licence – all these are different meanings.' (Williams 1945: 301). Alongside *freedom*, Williams notes a similar characteristic in other 'chameleon words', as he calls them, including *democracy*, *law*, *right*, *property*, and *interest*.

inconsistent meanings or implications in various political and other kinds of rhetoric).

Surprisingly little theoretical attention has been given to such questions in linguistics, as far as I know. One way of beginning to explore them, however, is through philosophical arguments regarding a social 'division of linguistic labour' put forward in Putnam's article 'The Meaning of Meaning' (1975), taken up by other writers including Bartsch (1987) (for discussion of connections with the socioculturally situated nature of meaning more generally, see Geeraerts 2010: 244–58). Putnam's main arguments were not about normative meaning, and certainly not about law, but rather a critique of the psychological account of meaning (i.e. the view that meanings exist in the mind rather than in features of the things words refer to). His exposition of differences between specialised and general understandings of words comes halfway through a far more wide-ranging philosophical argument (Putnam 1975: 223–29).

Starting from the observation that the author himself cannot distinguish an *elm* from a *beech* tree, seeing both merely as deciduous trees, Putnam argues that for many words (in a modern society very many, and not only technical words – but his arguments are restricted to so-called natural-kind words) it is only experts in a given area who fully comprehend the essential properties of referents, which for Putnam provide the proper basis of meaning. Further, he suggests, whatever we take as full understanding is subject to change (e.g. as the result of scientific advances). Many language users (here I extend possible instances speculatively from Putnam's concrete, natural-kind words such as *elm*, *gold*, or *tiger* to abstract terms such as *hedge fund*, *efficiency*, *well-being*, or *rights*) will only understand what they mean partially, in his 'externalist' sense. Our understanding, Putnam suggests, often takes the form instead of reduced stereotypes (typically, a prototypical concept plus semantic extensions depending on how much any particular language user is motivated to know, given their social situation). On this basis Putnam postulates, at least for natural-kind terms, 'a division of linguistic labour' which he outlines through an analogy between a social community and a factory (Putnam 1975: 227). Variably according to the different social groups they belong to, language users according to Putnam engage in a kind of 'semantic deference' to whichever class of speakers in the population is taken to possess the relevant expertise to stipulate correct referents for the words a particular language user needs to use. The result (subject to variation between societies as regards the degree of prestige and trust they are willing to accord to experts) is some kind of tacit 'correct terminology' authority conferred on experts who may, in different circumstances, be scientists, chefs, boat-builders, gardeners, or others. Putnam argues that, in our use of imperfectly understood vocabulary items, we attune or orientate towards the usage of such experts (but in doing so nevertheless need to understand words at some threshold level ourselves, if we are to be competent language users). At the level of a whole society, language in Putnam's view functions like a massive, hierarchically ordered machine that works collectively, with cooperation but also subordination governing the different extents of understanding of what things around us are or mean – a fundamentally different view from the flat structure of signifying contrasts associated with traditional descriptive linguistics.

Philosophical speculations of the kind Putnam puts forward may seem a long way from practical issues of people attributing different meanings to general legal terms in different walks of life. But one notable attraction of Putnam's approach is that – exceptionally for academic linguistic thinking – it directly addresses linguistic normativity not only as a matter of constraints imposed on what people say but also in what words mean. The semantic normativity made visible in his approach is concerned with whether meanings meet some standard of correctness and, if so, what confers the relevant standard or combination of standards, given that full understanding of all aspects of a modern society is something impossible for any individual language user to achieve.

What implications follow from such arguments is not straightforward. Clearly there can be no direct transposition of Putnam's arguments onto discussion of abstract rather than concrete words; some points which may be convincing in relation to natural-kind terms will not apply to abstract legal terms because of the very different notion of 'reference' they call for. Another reason Putnam's ideas in this area have not been widely discussed is that the social ramifications of his conception of linguistic norms – that some level of competence is needed to be a functioning member of a language community but that deferring to the semantic expertise of others in particular domains is normal – is widely considered rebarbative and 'authoritarian' (for discussion, see Geeraerts 2010: 255–56). As regards legal terminology that provides essential terms in the general vocabulary of wider political and moral debate, even in a democracy, presumption of correctness on this view might be thought to rest with lawyers' expert knowledge rather than being spread across the more heterogeneous population. Non-lawyers' understandings of such key words would be assumed, in Putnam's terms, to rest merely on stereotypes, and should yield to the semantic jurisdiction of legal experts (presumably either by paying for advice or being confined to listening rather than speaking).

In contrast to this hierarchical way of ordering language in a pluralistic society, Bartsch (1987) encourages an alternative conception of linguistic norms. While acknowledging the possibility of serious norm-conflicts, especially firefights around disputed interpretations at occasional social flashpoints, Bartsch argues that more constructive forms of political engagement are possible, especially where situations can only resolve or move forward through social cooperation. That basic fact about situations, she suggests, encourages people to be more pragmatic and tolerant of semantic flexibility, including vagueness, simplification of complex material, and slippages of meaning. Semantic indeterminacy, she argues, may in some circumstances even facilitate satisfaction of a higher-order communicative norm, whether of promoting efficiency in the exchange of information or in managing social interaction (Bartsch 1987: 209–18).

In the present state of understanding, discussion of what follows practically from key words about law circulating in general vocabulary can move very quickly from what is known into fantasy politics, such as the notion that Bartsch's position might somehow make it possible to 'take back the law' into democratic control. But if we keep closer to Putnam's and Bartsch's actual positions, the implications are more limited. One view broadly aligned with Putnam's account, as has been suggested earlier, points towards semantic jurisdiction over key terms of law being maintained by a specialist professional elite. Their power over meaning would not be limited to being exercised in law itself, where (despite initiatives including alternative dispute resolution and cases argued by self-representing litigants) it would be difficult for a legal system to function otherwise; it would also diffuse through wider channels of normative influence into other social domains, including politics. Given the scale of reservations expressed in some studies of legal language (e.g. Mellinkoff's [1963] and Tiersma's [1999] accounts of the development of the legal profession as the establishment of a mediaeval oligarchy exploiting specialist linguistic knowledge for the purpose of rent-seeking), such a view would be questionable, or even unpalatable, to many. But though Bartsch's alternative vision of linguistic norms offers a vision of a more participative and negotiated society, it is in obvious tension with law's obligation ultimately to assert some kind of definitive social order after balancing the benefits of such order against personal and group freedoms.

As yet, there is little to go on in forming a better general view of how legal–lay communication can function, beyond acknowledging simultaneous separation and yet porosity between legally decided meanings and the circulation of general 'law' words. It is clearly desirable, in our twenty-first-century political culture, to understand tensions in the use of abstract vocabulary with greater clarity and calculation of social effect than how such terms were viewed in the early days of democracy in the United States by Alexis de Tocqueville (2003 [1838]). Aristocracies, Tocqueville argued in his essay 'How American Democracy Has Modified the Language', had been static, and their use of language reflected political inertia. Democracies, in contrast, encourage constant agitation of ideas as well as competition between them as old thoughts disappear, reappear, or are 'split into minute shades of meaning' (2003: 554). For Tocqueville, the implications of the political and linguistic shift from aristocracy to democracy, and the taste for change which accompanied it, were mixed. Writers, he argued – taking as an example his own use of the word *equality* – rarely dwell on a single thought but instead 'point their aim at a knot of ideas, leaving the reader to judge which of them has been hit' (2003: 555). A 'secret fascination' for imprecise ideas, he believed, displayed itself most clearly in 'constant use of generic and abstract terms and a peculiar way of using them' (2003: 557–58). Tocqueville's enthusiasm for a republic of ideas built on such terms was tempered, accordingly, by caution on account of their uncertain meaning: 'One abstract word', he warned, 'is like a box with a false bottom: you put into it the ideas you want and take them out again unobserved' (2003: 558). Such a risk, it seems, continues to exacerbate the already complicated interplay between general words used in controlled circumstances in law and their potentially more expansive use in political discourse and 'ordinary language'.

REFERENCES

Austin, J. (1979 [1956]). *Philosophical Essays*. Oxford: Clarendon Press.

Baker, P. and McEnery, T. (2015). *Corpora and Discourse Studies: Integrating Discourse and Corpora*. Basingstoke: Palgrave.

Barak, A. (2005). *Purposive Interpretation in Law*. Princeton, NJ: Princeton University Press.

Bartsch, R. (1987). *Norms of Language*. Harlow: Longman.

Bentham, J. (1970 [1780]). *Of Laws in General*. Edited by H. L. A. Hart. London: The Athlone Press.

Carston, R. (2011). 'Legal Texts and Canons of Construction: A View from Current Pragmatic Theory', in M. Freeman and F. Smith (eds.) *Law and Language: Current Legal Issues 2011*, Vol. 15. Oxford: Oxford University Press, 8–33.

Cassin, B. (ed.) (2014). *Dictionary of Untranslatables: A Philosophical Lexicon*. Translation edited by E. Apter, J. Lezra and W. Wood. Princeton, NJ: Princeton University Press.

Chomsky, N. (1965). *Aspects of the Theory of Syntax*. Cambridge, MA: MIT Press.

Coulthard, M. and Johnson, A. (2007). *An Introduction to Forensic Linguistics: Language in Evidence*. London: Routledge.

Croft, W. and Cruse, D. (2004). *Cognitive Linguistics*. Cambridge: Cambridge University Press.

Cruse, D. (1986). *Lexical Semantics*. Cambridge: Cambridge University Press.

Crystal, D. and Davy, D. (1969). *Investigating English Style*. London: Longman.

Durant, A. (2006). 'Raymond Williams's *Keywords*: Meanings "Offered, Felt for, Tested, Confirmed, Asserted, Qualified, Changed"'. *Critical Quarterly* 48(4): 1–26.

Durant, A. (2010). *Meaning in the Media: Discourse, Controversy and Debate*. Cambridge: Cambridge University Press.

Dworkin, R. (1986). *Law's Empire*. Cambridge, MA: Harvard University Press.

Empson, W. (1951). *The Structure of Complex Words*. London: Chatto and Windus.

Endicott, T. (2000). *Vagueness in Law*. Oxford: Oxford University Press.

Finnis, J. (1979). *Natural Law and Natural Rights*. Oxford: Clarendon Press.

Foucault, M. (2001). *The Order of Things: An Archaeology of the Human Sciences.* London: Routledge.
Fuller, L. (1967). *Legal Fictions.* Stanford, CA: Stanford University Press.
Gallie, W. B. (1956). 'Essentially contested concepts'. *Proceedings of the Aristotelian Society* 56, 167–198.
Geeraerts, D. (2010). *Theories of Lexical Semantics.* Oxford: Oxford University Press.
Goodrich, P. (1986). *Reading the Law: A Critical Introduction to Legal Method and Techniques.* Oxford: Blackwell.
Greenawalt, K. (2010). *Legal Interpretation: Perspectives from Other Disciplines and Private Texts.* New York: Oxford University Press.
Greenawalt, K. (2013). *Statutory Interpretation and Common Law Interpretation.* Oxford: Oxford University Press.
Gumperz, J. and Levinson, S. C. (1996). *Rethinking Linguistic Relativity*, Cambridge: Cambridge University Press.
Hart, H. L. A. (1989). 'Jurisprudence'. In Urmson, J. O. and Rée, J. (eds.) *The Concise Encyclopaedia of Western Philosophy and Philosophers* (revised edition). First published in 1960. London: Unwin Hyman, 155.
Hart, H. L. A. (1994 [1961]). *The Concept of Law* (2nd ed.). Oxford: Clarendon.
Hutton, C. (2014a). *Word Meaning and Legal Interpretation: An Introductory Guide.* Basingstoke: Palgrave.
Hutton, C. (2014b). 'Defining ordinary words for mundane objects: legal lexicography, ordinary language and the word vehicle'. In Mac Aodha, M. (ed.) *Legal Lexicography: A Comparative Perspective.* Farnham: Ashgate, 177–200.
Kay, C. and Allan, K. (2015). *English Historical Linguistics.* Edinburgh: Edinburgh University Press.
Kelly, J. (1992). *A Short History of Western Legal Theory.* Oxford: Clarendon Press.
Mac Aodha, M. (ed.) (2014). *Legal Lexicography: A Comparative Perspective.* Farnham: Ashgate.
Mattila, H. (2016). *Comparative Legal Linguistics: Language of Law, Latin and Modern Lingua Francas* (2nd ed.). London: Routledge.
Mehl, S. (2013). 'Thinking linguistically about keywords: polysemy, semantic change and divergent identities'. Keywords Project website (http://keywordsproject.pitt.edu).
Mellinkoff, D. (1963). *The Language of the Law.* Eugene, OR: Resource Publications.
Mertz, E. (2007). *The Language of Law School: Learning to "Think Like a Lawyer".* New York: Oxford University Press.
Nuyts, J. and Pederson, E. (eds.) (1997). *Language and Conceptualization.* Cambridge: Cambridge University Press.
Putnam, H. (1975). 'The Meaning of Meaning'. In *Mind, Language and Reality*, Philosophical Papers vol. 2. Cambridge: Cambridge University Press, 215–271.
Quine, W. (1960) *Word and Object.* Cambridge, MA: MIT Press.
Raz, J. (2009). *Between Authority and Interpretation: On the Theory of Law and Practical Reason.* Oxford: Oxford University Press.
Scalia, A. and Garner, B. (2012). *Reading Law: The Interpretation of Legal Texts.* Berkeley, CA: Thomson/West.
Sinclair, J. (ed.) (1987). *Looking Up: An Account of the COBUILD Project in Lexical Computing.* London: Collins.

Skinner, Q. (1998). *Liberty before Liberalism.* Cambridge: Cambridge University Press.
Soames, S. (2011). 'What Vagueness and Inconsistency Tell Us About Interpretation'. In Marmor, A. and Soames, S. (eds.) *Philosophical Foundations of Language in the Law.* Oxford: Oxford University Press, 31–57.
Solan, L. (2010). *The Language of Statutes: Laws and Their Interpretation.* Chicago: University of Chicago Press.
Sperber, D. and Wilson, D. (1995). *Relevance: Communication and Cognition* (2nd ed.). Oxford: Blackwell.
Stubbs, M. (2001). *Words and Phrases: Corpus Studies of Lexical Semantics.* London: John Wiley & Sons.
Tiersma, P. (1999). *Legal Language.* Chicago: University of Chicago Press.
Tocqueville, A. de (2003 [1838]). *Democracy in America.* Harmondsworth: Penguin.
Urmson, J. O. and Rée, J. (eds.) (1989 [1960]). *The Concise Encyclopaedia of Western Philosophy and Philosophers* (revised edition). London: Unwin Hyman.
Waldron, J. (1994). Vagueness in Law and Language: Some Philosophical Issues. *California Law Review* 82: 509.
Wierzbicka, A. (2006). *English: Meaning and Culture.* Oxford: Oxford University Press.
Wierzbicka, A. (1997). *Understanding Cultures through Their Key Words.* Oxford: Oxford University Press.
Williams, G. (1945). 'Language and the Law', 61 *Law Quarterly Review*, in 4 sections, at 71, 179, 293, 384, reprinted in Schauer, F. (ed.) (1993). *Law and Language.* Aldershot: Dartmouth Press, 71–183.
Williams, R. (1958). *Culture and Society 1780–1950.* London: Chatto & Windus.
Williams, R. (1983). *Keywords: A Vocabulary of Culture and Society* (2nd ed.). London: Fontana.
Williams, R. (1989). *Resources of Hope: Culture, Democracy, Socialism.* London: Verso.
Wood, P. (2016). *The Fall of the Priests and the Rise of the Lawyers.* Oxford: Hart.

3 Hiding in Plain Sight: The Category of Ordinary Language and the Case Law Domain of Transgender Marriage[1]

Christopher Hutton

EDITORS' NOTE TO CHAPTER 3

Judges, Christopher Hutton observes, invoke the term 'ordinary language' frequently in the course of legal interpretation to convey the idea of plain or commonsense, everyday meaning. The most basic canon of common-law statutory interpretation is based on the concept: the plain or ordinary language rule, sometimes known as the literal rule. Other standards of linguistic usage and meaning applied by courts (e.g. related to technical or trade terminology) are defined in relation to it. Yet despite the presumed transparency or self-evident nature of what is 'ordinary', the meaning of the term remains obscure. This inevitably confuses appeals to the concept in deciding cases, or, on an alternative interpretation, provides a source of judicial autonomy and latitude, potentially disguising ideological aspects of reasoning that may have played a part in reaching a judgment. One generally accepted function of the category of 'ordinary speech' is that it should bridge the insider culture of legal interpretation and the world of general, commonplace speech. But as Hutton puts it, there is nothing 'ordinary' about the kind of ordinary language that courts refer to.

In his analysis, Hutton introduces and discusses key aspects of intellectual history surrounding the debate on what ordinary language means, not only in law but in literary criticism and linguistic philosophy. In doing so, he shows how what is considered to be 'ordinary language' is a product rather than a preexistent object of such debates, and that the term has been defined in different contexts in opposition to a wide range of concepts including literary language, technical language and misuse. In the narrower legal context, Hutton also discusses the anomalous position of ordinary language in relation to a contrast drawn in law between questions of law and questions of fact, a distinction that is not only significant as regards status within the development of law based on judicial construction of meaning but also determines what evidence if any

[1] The support of Hong Kong RGC GRF award HKU 745412H is hereby gratefully acknowledged.

(e.g. from dictionaries) might be called on to demonstrate membership of the category in question. On the basis of his discussion, Hutton concludes that ordinary language is a kind of legal fiction: a construct devised for particular purposes in law as a way of treating something (in this case, the heterogeneity and complexity of actual social use of language) as if it were something different (something stable, homogeneous and transparent).

In a final, extended section of the essay Hutton turns from theoretical issues associated with ordinary language to a detailed case study, examining appeals to the ordinary language categories of 'man', 'woman' and 'sex' in case law related to transgender marriage in several jurisdictions. Combining this case study with earlier theoretical observations, Hutton's essay challenges the reassuring simplicity offered by the concept of 'ordinary language': that some notional version of language can be used to represent, or even embody, everyday reasoning and good sense. Instead, Hutton shows how variation and indeterminacy in language provide judges with interpretative space to define and redefine important and difficult social categories, including fundamental categories associated with gender and marriage.

Hiding in Plain Sight: The Category of Ordinary Language and the Case Law Domain of Transgender Marriage

The category 'ordinary language' is a key component of modern legal reasoning and a powerful weapon in the soft power arsenal of the common law judge. It is a Janus-faced category, fundamental to the insider culture of common law interpretation, yet pointing outwards beyond law to the world of everyday discourse and commonplace speech. Ordinary language, it is argued here, is a specialized legal category hiding in plain sight, one that thereby evades close analysis and theoretical investigation. This chapter seeks to exoticize its ordinariness, showing that it is the product of a complex set of intellectual trends, and that there is ultimately nothing 'ordinary' about it. The paradoxically hidden visibility of the category provides the judge with a high degree of interpretative autonomy, at the same time as it potentially obscures the deeper legal as well as ideological reasoning shaping the judgment. In order to contextualize and historicize ordinary language as a category, the discussion first sketches debates in law, literary theory and philosophy and then traces the evolution of ordinary language arguments in a particular case law domain, namely that of transgender marriage.

Legal Language and Ordinary Language

The most familiar rule of legal interpretation relies on the notion of ordinary language: 'The concept that words and phrases are to be given their "ordinary meaning" is considered to be so foundational by courts that it is applied when interpreting virtually every type of legal text' (Slocum 2012: 40). This is the default rule – it is overridden for example where a statutory definition is provided, or a definition is laid down in the case law, or where a term is deemed to belong to legal rather than ordinary language, or to a specific subgroup or trade rather than to the linguistic mainstream. The question of legal versus ordinary language raises a familiar complex of issues in relation to the (im)possibility of a truly plain, that is publicly transparent and readily comprehensible, language of the law (Morrison 1989; Tiersma 1999: 28–29; Mattila 2012: 31). For some commentators, technical legal language is essentially an extrapolation from ordinary language for a specialized purpose: 'legal language is based on ordinary language' (Mattila 2016: 1). For others, legal concepts 'cannot be reduced to ordinary language concepts, for the former have a much sharper and more restricted function than the latter' (Samek 1977: 63). On this view, legal language has its own lexicon which involves 'terms related to each other in ways different from those of the ordinary language', and therefore must be 'autonomous of the ordinary language' (Jackson 1997: 47; see Klinck 1992: 136; Cao 2007: 16–17). Hayden White takes an intermediate approach, arguing that the legal process involves a 'back and forth between the language of the law and the languages of other disciplines and communities', including 'the ordinary language of the culture that is normally spoken by the parties, the witness, and the jurors (if there are any)' (White 2008: 3–4). Lawyers translate and mediate between different ways of talking, and are not 'permanently enclosed in a single conceptual and linguistic system'; law as an institution is 'in principle open to innumerable ways of thinking and talking, new systems of knowledge and discourse' and that is 'crucial to its democratic legitimacy' (White 2008: 5). In similar fashion, Mathews (1986) argues that legal language is constrained by its embedding in ordinary language.

What these and similar discussions fail to highlight is the central role of the category 'ordinary language' (and related concepts such as 'ordinary meaning', 'ordinary and natural meaning') in legal reasoning. There is a well-known dictum to the effect that the 'meaning of an ordinary word of the English language is not a question of law'; yet ordinary meaning is not strictly a matter of 'fact' either, since 'proper construction is a question of law'.[2] The category of ordinary language is paradoxically neither a legal nor a non-legal category; it is neither unequivocally empirical, nor recognized as fictional. Strictly speaking, dictionaries, for example, are not evidence but rather 'aids to the memory and understanding of the court'.[3] This is because the status of ordinary language and of ordinary language argumentation cannot be seen to depend on a particular mode of investigation into, or presentation of, the 'facts' of ordinary language use.

[2] Lord Reid in *Brutus v Cozens* at 861. [3] *Nix v Hedden* at 306–07.

When faced with a semantic or interpretative problem, the judge must first determine whether the issue at stake is one that concerns a legal meaning, a trade-specific, subcultural or technical non-legal meaning, or an ordinary meaning. This determination may be crucial in deciding the outcome of the case, since it will indicate which of the major identifiable meanings is the relevant one for the legal issue at hand. If the judge determines that an ordinary meaning is at stake, she or he has a further range of options, including invoking linguistic intuition, appealing to common sense, consulting a dictionary, drawing on various analogies in the case law or, in rare cases, seeking expert linguistic guidance. The judge may frame the issue explicitly in terms of ordinary meaning, or talk of plain, natural, everyday or commonsense meaning, or just simply 'the meaning'.

In invoking ordinary meaning, law is responding to the democratic imperative, namely that those subject to law's control are held accountable in terms and under categories that they can theoretically understand, and giving credence to the idea that the language of law and the language of the society in which it is embedded are at least to a degree compatible or commensurable. It bridges the otherwise unbridgeable gap between law as a highly specialized and ultimately coercive social domain and law as transparent and accountable practice, open to the outsider gaze and to lay conceptual scrutiny. However the appeal to 'ordinary meaning' is always the product of a prior legal analysis set against a particular nexus of facts, actions, parties and legal principles. Ordinary language is a category of legal analysis, not an autonomous, external set of definitional criteria that constrain legal interpretation.

Literary Language and Ordinary Language

William Wordsworth, in the preface to the *Lyrical Ballads* (1802), spoke of his desire 'to choose incidents and situations from common life, and to relate or describe them, throughout, as far as was possible in a selection of language really used by men' or in what he termed 'the very language of men' (1802: vii, xviii). He evoked the state of 'humble and rustic life' and in his own terms 'purified' its language for his poetic purposes (1802: viii). This language arose 'out of repeated experience and regular feelings' and was 'a more permanent, and a far more philosophical language, than that which is frequently substituted for it by Poets' (1802: ix). 'Real language' for Wordsworth was free from the false personifications, vanities and caprices of poetic diction, and was rooted in the language of prose. Coleridge sought by contrast 'an organic yet humanly perfected language capable of voicing an idealized national life' (Dowling 1986: 26), drawing on 'his own originary wellspring of modern, vernacular poetry in Dante' (Valenza 2009: 168). Coleridge's 'vision of the *lingua communis*' did not derive 'from a language anywhere in circulation'; it was remote from 'popular language', not an expert language of poetry but rather a 'universal' one, removed 'from the common train of conversational life, even when it references or represents that life'. Coleridge's term *lingua communis* called attention 'to the removal or elevation of this special use of language from ordinary use' (Valenza 2009: 168). Impressed by Luther's Bible translation and under the influence of Herder, Coleridge wrote of High German that it was 'indeed a *lingua communis*, not actually the native language of any province, but the choice and fragrancy of all the dialects' (Coleridge [1817] 1984: 210; Dowling 1986: 22–23; Hackert 2012: 161–62). Given its ambivalent status, this aspired-to literary language could be seen itself as ordinary (i.e. not self-consciously poetic or literary), or be itself contrasted with the ordinary and everyday. In their contrasting ways, both Wordsworth and Coleridge were seeking a language which conveyed the ordinary without being grounded in it, and without suggesting the common or the popular, in effect a paradoxically ordinary yet transcendent, abstract, free-floating language which did not draw attention to itself as originating in a particular social or cultural domain, or in attention-drawing linguistic artifice. The paradox reflects the wider ambivalence of intellectual Romanticism toward language politics, standardization and the pursuit of the vernacular as a register which was both 'ordinary' yet nonetheless was to serve the functions of the displaced written classical languages and retain the prestige and dignity associated with high written forms.

In the twentieth century the status of literary versus ordinary language became a key theoretical issue. Russian formalism is associated with arguments for the autonomy and formal-linguistic distinctiveness of literary language. Jakobson saw 'literariness' as residing in formal linguistic features of literary artifacts; literature, in particular poetry, displayed 'organized violence committed on ordinary speech' (Jakobson 1923, cited in Karcz 2002: 118). It is 'this roughening up of ordinary language into tortuous "formed speech" that makes poetry poetry rather than a weather report' (Rivkin and Ryan 2004: 4). Shklovsky stressed the defamiliarization effect of the literary work; defamiliarization or estrangement was achieved by the 'deforming' of ordinary language and discourse (Eagleton 1996: 2). Since habitualization 'devours work, clothes, furniture, one's wife, and the fear of war', it works to numb the self in its relation to the world; art and literature offers the possibility that 'one may recover the sensation of life', by making the familiar unfamiliar and slowing down or thickening our perceptions (Shklovsky [1917] 2004: 16). This view of literary language as autonomous was likewise integral to New Criticism, where literary language was viewed as being 'of a different ontological order than ordinary language, in that it is both autonomous, neutral, and free from contaminating subjectivity' (Clifford 1987: 125).

The reception of structuralism in the United States and the rise of academic linguistics gave impetus to postwar attempts to capture the specific features of literary and in particular poetic language (Jakobson 1960; Carreter 1976). The disciplinary boundary between linguistics and literary studies was challenged by linguists who saw literary texts as 'accessible to analysis by existing methods of linguistics' (Halliday 1964: 302; Fowler 1966; Schwartz 1970). On this view, literary language was part of ordinary language, albeit a specialized sub-domain of it. Fabb and Durant argued that the literary lacked formal properties that distinguish it from non-literary language; further, both literary and non-literary language share register-switching, and can perform the same communicative acts (Fabb and Durant 1987: 6–7). What Fabb terms the 'development hypothesis' viewed literary language as 'governed only by rules and constraints which are available to ordinary language, and which refer only to representations which are present (at some stage in a derivation) in ordinary language' (Fabb 2010: 1220). This model however could not accommodate 'artificial literary language', such as that found in the experimental avant-garde (Fabb 2010: 1220).

The literary–ordinary distinction was challenged by theorists who rejected the notion of the literary altogether (see Eagleton 1996: 117, Alexandrov 2007: 97–98). Stanley Fish targeted the distorting effect of defining literariness against ordinary language: 'the very act of distinguishing between ordinary and literary language, because of what it assumes, leads necessarily to an inadequate account of both' (Fish 1973: 44). A neutral, referential or propositional ordinary language is in this way contrasted with value-laden literary language: 'The trivialization of ordinary language is accomplished as soon as one excludes from its precincts matters of purpose, value, intention, obligation, etc., everything in short that can be characterized as human' (Fish 1973: 44). Given that literary language is understood as a deviation from ordinary language, the result is that 'ordinary language loses its human content, and literature loses its justification for being because human content has been declared a deviation' (Fish 1973: 45). Fish's 'liberating' conclusion is that 'there is no such thing as ordinary language' (Fish 1973: 49). This conclusion however misses the point that the category of 'ordinary language' relates primarily to a mode of reasoning about literature – its existence or non-existence is in this sense beside the point.

Philosophy and Ordinary Language

In the twentieth century, a dispute arose within Anglo-American philosophy between those who saw ordinary language as 'deficient or faulty' and the idea that it was basically 'all right' (Chappell 1964: 2). For Logical Positivism, an ideal philosophical language would be the product of abstracting away from, or radically transcending, the confusions of ordinary language (see Carnap 1928a, 1928b). Ordinary language philosophy rejected this search for a conceptually pure language, arguing that 'ordinary language is the basis of all language', and 'the conceptual basis of all inquiry and indeed of all characteristically *human* activities' (Caton 1963: xi, emphasis in original). This approach involved 'the description of the use of ordinary language and a coherent reconstruction of the "common sense" of a particular group or society' (De Jong and Werner 1998: 235). G. E. Moore's technique, according to Malcolm, consisted in showing how statements such as 'There are no material things' went against common sense and ordinary language, that is violated the ordinary way that phrases such as *material things* were used (Malcolm [1942] 1964: 8–9; Chisholm 1951; Ambrose 1970: 250–53). If two people disagreed about whether a certain animal was a fox or a wolf, this would be a linguistic disagreement with a right and wrong answer. But if one of the disputants, while agreeing that the animal would normally or ordinarily be called a fox, argued that it was nonetheless a wolf, this would be an absurdity, since 'ordinary language *is* correct language' (Malcolm [1942] 1964: 15, emphasis in the original). Ordinary language philosophers frequently use banal classification to illustrate their arguments: a mule is not a horse (Baier 1951: 54), a fox is not a wolf (Malcolm [1942] 1964: 15), and a vixen is a fox (Parker-Ryan 2010: 130–32).

Ordinary language was 'the language which defines the boundaries within which people speak the same language or at least the same dialect' and which 'makes possible their daily dealings with one another'; by definition this language is known by 'everyone in the linguistic community apart from young children' and while it is not a precise category it 'must be at least in principle at least vaguely specifiable or there would be no linguistic communities' (Caton 1963: vi–vii). Yet if ordinary language was 'a collective term for the ways in which people ordinarily talk', then the analysis of 'ordinary parlance' might logically be the task of various branches of linguistics and of lexicography, or even potentially 'experimental and statistical methods' such as those found in psychology and sociology (Borgmann 2012: 120). Philosophers resisted the claims of empirical disciplines such as linguistics to inform them about use in any philosophically relevant sense (Harris 1988). Ryle's emphasis was on *ordinary usage*, the paradigm uses of a word or phrase, whether technical or non-technical (Ryle [1953] 1964: 31). In this sense the opposite of ordinary use was 'misuse', and the opposite of 'ordinary usage' was 'non-stock use' (Borgmann 2012: 121). For Ryle, types of non-stock or non-standard uses of a word include the 'metaphorical, hyperbolical, poetical, stretched and deliberately restricted uses of it' (Ryle [1953] 1964: 26). This was not a question of frequency but rather an 'appeal to what we do and do not say, or can and cannot say' (Ryle [1953] 1964: 38). Wittgenstein's famous formulation of this approach is as follows: 'For a *large* class of cases of the employment of the word 'meaning' – though not for all – this word can be explained in this way: the meaning of a word is its use in the language' (Wittgenstein [1953] 2009: para. 43). Anyone who calls a horse a *mule* does not understand the language game of these labels, and is presumptively not a fully competent member of the language community. The notion of the stock uses of a word was criticized by Ernst Gellner in his *Words and Things*, under the heading 'the argument from paradigm cases' (Gellner 1959: 30–37; Hanfling 2000: 74–93; Parker-Ryan 2012). According to Gellner, the later Wittgenstein made a 'cult' of common sense (1959: 31–32), seeing human beings as employing 'a diversity of language games, which were concrete activities in concrete contexts'. Wittgenstein argued that to go beyond these socially grounded language games was to make 'strange moves', and traditional philosophical inquiry was 'the malfunctioning of linguistic systems' and 'self-defeating thought' (Gellner 1959: 140). On this reading of Wittgenstein, the category of ordinary language ends where philosophical nonsense begins.

The argument from ordinary language philosophers has been that 'the ordinary use of the bulk of words in standard cases' is knowable directly, that is, available and accessible without specialized inquiry: 'All Englishmen, except the incapacitated, morons and very young children, do know the language. Hence we all know the ordinary use of words' (Baier 1951: 52). Cavell relies explicitly on the native speaker: 'Such speakers do not, in *general*, need evidence for what is said in the language they are the source of that evidence' (Cavell 1964: 78; Mulhall 1998: 11). The philosopher can make 'use of himself as subject in his collection of data', and while this 'may be more informal than the descriptive linguist (though not more than the theoretical linguist using examples from his native speech)' (Cavell 1964: 78). An individual speaker might 'forget or remember certain words, or what certain words mean', but he does not remember or forget the language as a whole. Claims about ordinary language, unlike statements about language history or subgroup usage, do not require empirical investigation beyond introspection or reference to native speaker norms: 'All that is needed is the truth of the proposition that a natural language is what native speakers of that language speak' (Cavell 1964: 79). Similarly, for Hacker 'to specify the correct use of a familiar word' there is no need to do social surveys, since 'a competent speaker of a natural language by definition knows how to use the common (and, if he is a specialist, the technical) words he uses' (Hacker 2013: 946). The philosopher 'does not need to consult anyone – only to reflect, and occasionally to use a good dictionary to jolt one's memory'. The task is not merely to remember 'features of usage with which any competent speaker or technical practitioner is familiar', rather the philosophical skill consists in 'selecting and marshaling those features of usage that will illuminate the problem at hand' (Hacker 2013: 946). This argument could be transposed without difficulty into a description of common law adjudication.

The aim of ordinary language philosophy was that of 'unpicking, one by one, a mass of seductive (mainly verbal) fallacies' (Austin 1962: 3–4). Many traditional philosophical problems were attributable 'to an obsession with a few particular words, the uses of which are over-simplified', whereas 'our ordinary words are much subtler in their uses, and mark many more distinctions, than philosophers have realised' (Austin 1962: 3). Philosophers had a tendency to stretch the meanings of words to become first 'obscurely metaphorical' and then 'ultimately meaningless'. Austin's notion of ordinary language was of it 'as a wonderfully intricate instrument', whose 'intricacies and distinctions are not idle, but rather marvelously and subtly fitted to serve the multiplicity of our needs and desires in communication' (Grice 1988: 57). For Grice, a 'properly regulated and directed' process of 'linguistic botanizing' (descriptive linguistic analysis) was an essential part of philosophical analysis, even if Austin's faith in the dictionary was, he felt, misplaced (Grice 1988: 57).

There is a strong link between Austin's ordinary language philosophy and the legal philosophy of H. L. A. Hart, most notably *The Concept of Law* ([1964] 1994). Austin saw ordinary language as the product of an evolutionary process of conceptual refinement (Austin 1956: 8): 'Our common stock of words embodies all the distinctions men have found worth drawing, and the connexions they have found worth marketing, in the lifetimes of many generations'. These distinctions 'have stood up to the long test of the survival of the fittest'. Whereas philosophy might profitably draw on these basic distinctions of ordinary language (using philosophical thought experiments), law's relation to ordinary language was more complex. In 'hard cases', law was obliged 'first to be careful with, but also to be brutal with, to torture, to fake and to override, ordinary language' (Austin 1956: 12). This understanding of hard cases corresponded precisely to Hart's model of law. For Hart, law 'runs out' once the application of general abstract categories such as *vehicle* to the factual matrix of the case becomes problematic. Once they pass beyond the framework of ordinary language categories, judges move from legal certainty to hard cases and the domain of judicial discretion (Hart 1994; Hutton 2014a: 53–55, 2014b). Proper law, as opposed to discretionary adjudication, is equated with the domain of ordinary language. In hard cases, law, like Jakobson's literary language, operates a kind of violence upon ordinary language.

Transgender Case Law, Marriage and Ordinary Meaning

Issues of transgender identity confront law with problems of definition and classification at a fundamental level. Terms like *man* and *woman* are quintessentially 'ordinary', and such terms are rarely explicitly defined in case law or in statutes. Where transgender persons have sought to marry in their affirmed sex (i.e. to affirm a sexual identity incompatible with that found on their birth certificate), courts have adopted a variety of reasoning strategies. For example, in *Talbot (otherwise Poyntz) v Talbot, John David (otherwise Talbot, Mabel)*, Ormrod J found the marriage void, on the simple grounds that the husband was a 'woman'. In *Corbett v Corbett* (at 83), the same judge, a qualified medical practitioner, had to rule on the status of the marriage between the Hon. Arthur Corbett and April Ashley, who had been registered as a boy at birth and undergone sex reassignment surgery in 1960. Ormrod J noted that this was 'the first occasion on which a court in England has been called upon to decide the sex of an individual and, consequently, there is no authority which is directly in point' (at 105). The decision in *Corbett* is known for the establishment of criteria, which if congruent, determined legal sex for the purposes of marriage: (1) chromosomal, (2) gonadal (i.e. presence or absence of testes or ovaries), (3) genital (including internal sex organs), and perhaps 'hormonal factors or secondary sexual characteristics' (at 100). For the purposes of marriage, subjective or psychological factors were not relevant; these were a matter of gender, not sex. The 'fundamental purpose' of law was 'the regulation of the relations between persons and between persons and the state or community', and such legal relations could be classified into 'those in which the sex of an individual is either irrelevant, relevant or an essential determinant of the relationship' (at 105). Over 'a very large area' law was 'indifferent to sex' and the authorities were entitled to accept that someone registered at birth as male 'should be treated as a woman for national insurance purposes, as in this case' (at 105). The question at issue therefore was not the meaning of the word *woman* in general but 'what is meant by the word "woman" in the context of a marriage', since for the judge the case was not about the determination of 'the "legal sex" of the respondent at large' (at 106).

The case is often read, understandably, as the imposition by law of a bio-essentialist framework on the definition of legal sex for the purpose of marriage. But the judge was quite explicit that the biomedical facts, while relevant, could not determine how the legal category was applied. Biology did not offer a purely binary distinction, so it was law's task to impose one. In an academic lecture, Ormrod stressed that law as a system was an 'artefact', a 'system of regulations which depends on precise definitions', whereas biological phenomena could not be 'reduced to exclusive categories'. Medicine often could not give categorical answers: 'living organisms refuse to fall into clearly defined groups' (Ormrod 1972: 78). This would seem to leave a gap in Ormrod's reasoning: if law does not follow the biomedical facts, where is its reference point found for the definition of *woman* in the context of marriage? One answer is that the 'sex change operation' could not affect the validity of the marriage, which was dependent on the 'true sex of the respondent' (at 89).

'True sex' is however neither a legal nor a scientific concept. It appears out of nowhere in the judgment, a rabbit pulled out of the judicial hat. To make sense of this category it needs to be understood as reflecting a partially submerged common sense or ordinary language argument. For Ormrod, the ordinary meaning of *marriage* was conclusive. For a marriage to be valid, the parties had to be 'of different sexes', since 'that is what the word means' (Ormrod 1972: 85). Further, in a letter to an Australian academic, Dr. Henry Finlay, sent in the late 1980s, Ormrod wrote (cited in Gilmore 2011: 58):

> The real issue in *Corbett* was the meaning of the word 'marriage'. It is agreed that it means the formal union of a man and a woman. The only question, therefore, was of construction! Giving the word 'woman' its natural and ordinary meaning, could April Ashley be described as a woman? The answer must be No!

Why then did the judge not simply evoke ordinary meaning or common sense in the judgment? The answer lies in the Court of Appeal decision in *S Y v S Y* (1963), where it was held that an artificially enlarged vagina was no bar to consummation and there were dicta to the effect that such a procedure should not been seen necessarily as 'producing something different in kind from a vagina artificially created from nothing' (at 59, per Wilmer LJ). If April Ashley could have been shown to be intersex, then her subjective or psychological sense of identity might have determined her legal sex for the purpose of marriage, and allowed for consummation: 'But for this [*S Y v S Y*] decision the respondent would have had no defence to the prayer for a decree of nullity on the ground of incapacity' (per Ormrod J, at 105). Given this decision of a senior court, the ordinary language argument could not stand on its own, but operating as a 'crypto-category' it nonetheless underpins the decision. In effect, the meaning of *woman* for the purpose of marriage was also the ordinary and natural meaning of the word in general. This reflected 'true sex' understood as reflecting biological criteria, in the context of the 'essential role of a woman in marriage' (at 106). Ordinary language is the medium through which the biomedical and the legal domains are brought into alignment.

Following the decision in *Corbett*, Parliament passed the Nullity of Marriage Act (1971) and then the Matrimonial Causes Act (1973), which in section 11c required that the parties to a marriage be respectively *male* and *female*, though these terms were not defined within the statute. Hong Kong also passed legislation to the same effect (described later in the chapter). In *Bellinger v Bellinger* the Court of Appeal, the argument turned on whether this lack of definition allowed the Court to supply an interpretation reflecting shifts in social attitudes and medical opinion and recognize an affirmed (postoperative transsexual) identity, or whether this was a matter for legislation. The court declined to overrule *Corbett*. In the judgments there was no discussion of the 'ordinary meaning' of *male* and *female*, though in his dissenting judgment Thorpe LJ noted that the *Oxford English Dictionary* had in a second, modern definition of *gender*: 'A euphemism for the sex of a human being, often intended to emphasise the social and cultural, as opposed to the biological, distinction between the sexes' (cited at 185) and argued that *Corbett*'s rejection of 'the developing concept of gender' no longer held good.

Following the Court of Appeal decision in *Bellinger*, Chisholm J, in the Australian case of *Re Kevin*, upheld the validity of a marriage between a 'post-operative female to male transsexual', Kevin, and a woman, Jennifer. Kevin had obtained a new birth certificate and passport, both stating his sex as male. Testimony was heard to the effect that Kevin was living a life 'that those around him perceive as a man's life'. Chisholm J also subjected the reasoning in *Corbett* to sustained criticism, pointing out that Ormrod J's contention that a person's biological constitution at birth determined their legal sex for the purpose of marriage was unsupported, and represented neither a statement of law nor fact (paras. 77 to 84). The Attorney General, in objecting to the marriage certificate, had submitted that the meaning of the word *man* was that pertaining in 1961 and also the one set out in *Corbett*. Both sides accepted that the issue concerned 'the meaning of the word "man", a word that both sides accept is an ordinary, everyday word' (at para. 126). On the question of the relevant time point, Chisholm J argued that the authorities favoured taking the 'ordinary, contemporary meaning', but in any case the question depended essentially on context (at para. 129). Even *Corbett* 'drew on the available medical evidence' rather than 'adopting the meaning of the word at some earlier date' (at para. 132). The word *man* should be given its 'ordinary contemporary meaning', and that in determining that meaning it should be read within 'the context of the legislation, the body of case law on the meaning of "man" and similar words, the purpose of the legislation, and the current legal, social and medical environment' (at para. 136).

Chisholm J surveyed the case law which included decisions to the effect that a postoperative individual would be recognized in their affirmed sex, but not a preoperative one. In *R v Harris*, the idea that a person's self-classification as male or female should be the decisive criterion was rejected, and in *Secretary, Department of Social Security v State Rail Authority*, Black CJ stated that in ordinary English usage 'words such a "male" and "female", "man" and "woman" and the word "sex" relate to anatomical and physiological differences rather than to psychological ones', and cited extensively from dictionary definitions. He concluded that 'it would be going well beyond the ordinary meaning of the words in question to conclude that a preoperative male to female transsexual, having male external genitalia, is a "woman" for the purposes of the Social Security Act and may be a "wife" as that expression is defined in the Act'. However Black CJ (at 304, cited in *Re Kevin*, at para. 152) explicitly distanced his view from *Corbett*:

> Whatever may once have been the case, the English language does not now condemn post-operative male-to-female transsexuals to being described as being of the sex they profoundly believe they do not belong to and the external genitalia of which, as a result of irreversible surgery, they no longer have.

Such a person, unlike someone who has not undergone a surgical procedure, 'may be said, according to ordinary English usage today, to have undergone a sex change' (cited at para. 153). In the same case, Lockhart J had also drawn on how terms such as *woman* 'are generally understood in Australia today' (at 312, cited in *Re Kevin* at para. 156). Chisholm J concluded therefore that 'unless the context indicates reasons for a different approach, words like "man" and "woman" in legislation will be treated as ordinary words, and will normally be taken to refer to the reassigned sex of post-operative transsexuals' (at para. 158). Chisholm J also referred to policies adopted by a number of official Australian agencies, to 'Australian values', and surveyed developments in medical research. He concluded that the word *man* should be given 'its ordinary meaning' in marriage as in other legal areas (at para. 289), and there were strong grounds for preferring consistency across different domains of law, as far as possible (at para. 306). In conclusion, in the context of marriage 'the word "man" has its ordinary current meaning according to Australian usage' (at para. 330 (10)).

One important unstated factor at work in *Re Kevin* is that Australia has no Bill of Rights or similar legislation. The argument, to be persuasive, needed to be couched in traditional common law terms of ordinary meaning, rather than in terms of fundamental rights. That meaning, as set out, in the judgment is a complex rhetorical construct, drawing on medical, legal and administrative and social factors. No explicit claim is made as to its empirical status as a reflection of actual usage among the Australian public. In upholding the decision, the Family Court of Australia (in *Attorney-General (Cth) v "Kevin and Jennifer"*) concurred that once it is determined that 'words in a statute should bear their contemporary ordinary everyday meaning, it becomes [...] a question of fact to determine what that meaning is'. They accepted Chisholm J's determination (at paras. 377–79).

At about the same time as the decision in *Corbett* the New York Supreme Court ruled that 'plaintiff and defendant are not and have not ever been "husband and wife" or parties to a valid marriage' (*Anonymous v Anonymous*, at 501). In *M.T. v T.J.*, the New Jersey Supreme Court declined to follow the reasoning in *Corbett*, arguing that 'a person's sex or sexuality embraces an individual's gender, that is, one's self- image, the deep psychological or emotional sense of sexual identity and character' (per Handler, J.A.D., at 87). However subsequent cases in the United States accepted the *Corbett* approach. In *Re Ladrach*, the Ohio court did not discuss questions of definition, but simply took the sexual characteristics of the individual at birth as determinative. In *Littleton v Prange*, the Court likewise made no reference to ordinary meaning, posing the question as 'can a physician change the gender of a person with a scalpel, drugs and counseling, or is a person's gender immutably fixed by our Creator at birth?' (at 244). In *re the Estate of Marshall G. Gardiner*, the Kansas Supreme Court rejected arguments to the effect that there was a material question of fact as to the sexual identity of J'Noel at the time of the marriage. The question was purely one of statutory construction: 'There are no disputed material facts. We disagree with the decision reached by the Court of Appeals. We view the issue in this appeal to be one of law and not fact. [...] The interpretation of a statute is a question of law, and this court has unlimited appellate review' (at 135). The court quoted both legal and general dictionaries, asserting that the words *sex*, *male* and *female* 'in everyday understanding do not encompass transsexuals' and that the 'plain, ordinary meaning of "persons of the opposite sex" contemplates a biological man and a biological woman and not persons who are experiencing gender dysphoria' (at 135). It followed that 'J'Noel does not fit the common meaning of female' (at 135). In *Kantaris v Kantaris*, the Florida Court of Appeal concluded that 'we must adhere to the common meaning of the statutory terms and invalidate any marriage that is not between persons of the opposite sex determined by their biological sex at birth' (at 161).

When the *Bellinger* case reached the House of Lords, not only had the *re Kevin* decision been made, but the European Court of Human Rights had found in favour of the transgender party in case of *Goodwin v United Kingdom* (though this was not specifically a marriage case), holding that the United Kingdom was in breach of articles 8 and 12 of the European Convention. Lord Nicholls of Birkenhead stated that to recognize Mrs Bellinger 'as female for the purposes of section 11(c) of the Matrimonial Causes Act 1973 would necessitate giving the expressions "male" and "female" in that Act a novel, extended meaning: that a person may be born with one sex but later become, or become regarded as, a person of the opposite sex' (at 6). Lord Hope of Craighead accepted that, as in *Re Kevin*, the question turned on the ordinary not any technical meaning of the words *male* and *female*, but noted that 'no evidence' in relation to contemporary usage in Britain had been placed before the Court. The definition in the *New Shorter Oxford Dictionary* (1993) included in its definition of *male* 'the sex which can beget offspring'. The ordinary meaning could not accommodate a transsexual person 'within its scope', and even in Australia contemporary usage drew a distinction between preoperative and postoperative. Such distinctions raised 'questions of fact and degree which are absent from the ordinary meaning of the word "male" in this country'. The single characteristic which distinguished male from female across the animal kingdom 'was the part which each sex plays in the act of reproduction' (at 12). While finding against Mrs Bellinger, the court issued a declaration of incompatibility with the European Convention on Human Rights.

The House of Lords decision in *Bellinger* implied there was a difference between Britain and Australia as to the ordinary meaning of *man* and *woman*. When the same issue arose in Hong Kong, the High Court followed closely the reasoning in *Bellinger*.[4] Andrew Cheung J focused primarily on word meaning, citing case law discussions and dictionary definition from the *Shorter Oxford English Dictionary* (6th edition, 2007, cited at para. 138). The issue however was 'the use of the relevant words, whether in English or Chinese, in Hong Kong' (at para. 139). The judge drew on his own intuition: 'the Court's own understanding is that post-operative transsexual people in Hong Kong are still, in ordinary, everyday usage and understanding, referred to as such', and not simply as a *man* or a *woman*. This was the case both 'in the English language or in the Chinese language' (at para. 140). Although the phrase *sex change operation* was widely used, 'as far as the Court observes', this did not represent a general 'understanding or acceptance' that someone's sex had truly been changed (at para. 140). The applicant had not established that 'the relevant words, according to their ordinary, everyday usage in Hong Kong nowadays, encompass post-operative transsexuals in their assigned sex' (at para. 141). The Court of Appeal (*W v Registrar of Marriages*, 2010, lead judgment by Fok JA) accepted that what evidence there was about local usage did not support the idea that transsexuals were generally referred to as *male* or *female* (at para. 71): 'certainly at the time Corbett was given statutory effect in Hong Kong, I consider that the ordinary dictionary meanings of "woman" and "female" were complete and accurate definitions of those words and that they were not capable, without more, of accommodating a transsexual person within their scope' (at para. 72).

The Court of Final Appeal (*W v The Registrar of Marriages*, 2013), in allowing the appeal, argued that while 'ordinary meaning' was relevant in the sense that there was no special or technical meaning at stake, the issue should not obscure 'the crucial importance of context and purpose when construing the relevant provisions', since the question was not an abstract one 'about whether a post-operative transsexual woman is "a woman" in some abstract or general sense' but whether she was a woman for the purpose of marriage. As Ormrod J had argued in *Corbett* (at para. 50), 'context and purpose' were crucial. For that reason, the judgment did not address the arguments about 'some textual ordinary meaning' but viewed the matter in the light of the legislative history since *Corbett*: 'That approach, in our view, leaves no room for a debate on "ordinary meaning" nor on whether the "always speaking" provisions deserve an updated meaning' (at para. 53). The ordinary meaning was not to be determinative, since the issue was sexual identity in relation to marriage. In essence the Court accepted that the Registrar had construed correctly the relevant statutes, but did not wish to base that judgment on a discussion of ordinary meaning. It then ruled that the *Corbett* criteria were incomplete, in that they omitted 'the sociological and social elements of a person's sexual identity' (at para. 118) and

4 W v Registrar of Marriages (HCAL 120/2009).

that, in terms of constitutionality under the Basic Law and the Bill of Rights, these provisions 'impair the very essence of the right to marry' (at para. 119).

The dissenting judgment by Mr Justice Chan PJ focused primarily on ordinary meaning, arguing that the meaning contended for by the applicant 'is different from the ordinary meaning of these words' and amounted to 'a radical change to the traditional concept of marriage' (at para. 159). As in *Bellinger*, there was no evidence 'that these words have acquired any new contemporary meanings which are different from what is commonly understood by these words'. Noting the *re Kevin* decision where 'it was held that there was evidence that the contemporary meaning of these words in Australia has changed', the judge concluded that 'the situation varies in each country, depending on its social and cultural conditions' (at para. 161). In sum, there was 'no evidence showing that for the purpose of marriage, the ordinary meanings of man and woman in Hong Kong have changed to accommodate a transsexual man and woman'; nor was there any evidence 'that the social attitudes in Hong Kong towards the traditional concept of marriage and the marriage institution have fundamentally altered' in favour of the general social acceptance of transsexualism (at para. 188).

The invocation of ordinary language and the citing of dictionary definitions of *man* or *woman* is correlated with a rejection of the transgender party's affirmed identity (Hutton 2011). In Hart's terms, none of these transgender marriage cases are hard cases. Even where ordinary language arguments are not explicitly deployed, ordinary language operates as a powerfully normative, crypto-category, in a sense at too basic or intuitive a level to submit to analysis: 'A meaning that seems to leap off the page, propelled by its own self-sufficiency, is a meaning that flows from interpretative assumptions so deeply embedded that they have become invisible' (Fish 1987: 403). Ordinary language arguments frequently reflect judicial and ideological conservatism, in particular where constitutional rights are at issue: 'Constitutionalism is about contestation, ordinary language about political closure' (Davis 1996: 508). The exception of *Re Kevin* reflects the lack of a Bill of Rights or other constitutional human rights in Australian law, so that a reform-minded judge cast a set of social, medical, moral and human rights arguments in terms of ordinary meaning. Ordinary language arguments need to be analyzed in their immediate judicial and sociopolitical context and across different case law domains.

Conclusion

In *The Elusiveness of the Ordinary* (2002) Rosen argues for the centrality of 'ordinary experience' as an orientation point in grounding philosophical debate. The ordinary, and ordinary language in particular, is a key tool of modern intellectual culture, with a complex history in literary theory, philosophy and law. By 'ordinary language' is meant a neutral, classless, non-regional, non-specialist, orderly, stable reservoir of words, their meanings, typical referents, and characteristic uses and typical patterns of combination ('collocations'). Ordinary language is an abstract construct yet, depending on the context, it is explicated with reference to notions such as community and native speaker, identified with the 'English language' or 'standard English' and illustrated by resort to reference works such as dictionaries or to linguistic intuition.

Ordinary language arguments are strictly speaking questions of law, since issues of construction are not questions of fact; yet ordinary language is also understood as a question of fact, an extra-legal, factual resource for informing legal decision-making. Within legal reasoning, ordinary language is therefore neither an empirical nor non-empirical category, or, rather, both empirical and non-empirical. It is nobody's language, or everybody's; sometimes it is implied that it is the language itself which takes a view about the nature and order of things and processes, rather than actual people, individually or collectively, as if it were the English language which was adjudicating the case. If ordinary language categories are treated as social norms, then a kind of crudely intuitive moral majoritarianism can result. In *R (Quintavalle) v Secretary of State for Health*, Lord Bingham stated (at para. 9):

> There is, I think, no inconsistency between the rule that statutory language retains the meaning it had when Parliament used it and the rule that a statute is always speaking. If Parliament, however long ago, passed an act applicable to dogs, it could not properly be interpreted to apply to cats; but it could properly be held to apply to animals which were not regarded as dogs when the Act was passed but are so regarded now.

This statement is widely quoted, but it suggests, without explicating, an unproblematic, consensus-driven ordinary language normativity.

Ordinary language is not, and cannot be, an empirical or descriptively grounded category. What seems 'ordinary' to a judge in the context of legal argument is not ordinary in any empirically ascertainable sense. The construction of the ordinary within legal discourse has nothing in common with any empirically based method of measuring, aggregating, recording or documenting actual linguistic usage. Ordinary language is in this sense a legal fiction. The notion of legal fiction is itself, of course, highly contentious (Smith 2007), and does not of itself tell us much. Classic legal fictions involve an awareness that certain states of affairs are being treated 'as if' they were true (Fuller 1967). To designate ordinary language as a legal fiction is to move the category conceptually from outside law, from its unscrutinized or taken-for-granted status, to a position fully within it. This has the benefit of greater transparency, since it affirms that the category is a representation by law to itself of what constitutes 'ordinary language', rather than a stable, externally generated or maintained social category which law simply invokes.

The fiction arises because law requires a linguistic baseline or foundational set of conceptual orientation points for its interpretative practice. It follows that actual evidence about ordinary linguistic usage is not *prima facie* relevant, since a legal fiction by definition cannot be filled out with empirical facts. It is of course open to law in general, or to an individual judge faced with a particular linguistic-factual nexus, to stipulate whether, and if so, in what way, evidence for usage in 'ordinary language' should be treated as relevant. The fictional status of ordinary language accounts for the tensions between the judges' views of meaning and interpretation and those of linguists interested in legal interpretation (see Solan 1993, 1995, 1999; Hutton 1996, 2005; Aprill 1998; Ainsworth 2006). One benefit of stating clearly that ordinary language is a fiction of law is that it enables us to make clearer precisely what is at stake in many disputes about legal interpretation within the law, and in those between lawyers and other classes of professional language experts such as linguists. A further benefit is that it enables us to define more precisely a key feature of common law jurisprudence, namely the interpretative autonomy of the judge.

REFERENCES

Ainsworth, J. (2006). Linguistics as a knowledge domain in the law. *Drake Law Review* 54: 651–669.

Alexandrov, V. (2007). Literature, literariness, and the brain. *Comparative Literature* Spring 59: 97–118.

Ambrose, A. (1970). Three aspects of Moore's philosophy. In *G.E. Moore: Essays in Retrospect*, 80–88. London: Allen & Unwin.

Aprill, E. (1998). The law of the word: dictionary shopping in the Supreme Court. *Arizona State Law Journal* 30: 275–336.

Austin, J. L. (1956). A plea for excuses. *Proceedings of the Aristotelian Society* 57: 1–30.

Austin, J. L. (1962). *Sense and Sensibilia*. G. J. Warnock (ed.). London: Oxford University Press.

Baier, K. (1951). The ordinary use of words. *Proceedings of the Aristotelian Society* 52: 47–70.

Borgmann, A. (2012). *The Philosophy of Language: Historical Foundations and Contemporary Issues*. The Hague: Nijhoff.

Cao, D. (2007). *Translating Law*. Bristol: Multilingual Matters.

Carnap, R. (1928a). *Der Logische Aufbau der Welt*. Leipzig: Meiner Verlag.

Carnap, R. (1928b). *Scheinprobleme in der Philosophie*. Berlin: Weltkreis-Verlag.

Carreter, F. (1976). The literal message. *Critical Inquiry* 3: 315–332.

Caton, C. (1963). Editor's introduction. In *Philosophy and Ordinary Language*, v–xii. Urbana-Champaign: University of Illinois.

Cavell, S. (1964). Must we mean what we say? In V.C. Chappell (ed.), *Ordinary Language: Essays in Philosophical Method*. Englewood Cliffs, NJ: Prentice-Hall, 75–112.

Chappell, V. C. (1964). Editor's introduction. In *Ordinary Language: Essays in Philosophical Method*. Englewood Cliffs, NJ: Prentice-Hall, 1–4.

Chisholm, R. (1951). Philosophers and ordinary language. *The Philosophical Review* 60: 317–328.

Clifford, J. (1987). Ideology and discourse: a historical perspective. *Journal of Advanced Composition* 7: 121–130.

Coleridge, S. (1984). *Biographia Literaria*. James Engell and Walter Bate (eds.). Princeton, NJ: Princeton University Press. First published 1817.

Davis, D. (1996). The twist of language and the two Fagans: please sir may I have some more literalism! *South African Journal on Human Rights* 12: 504–512.

De Jong, H. and Werner, W. G. (1998). Continuity and change in legal positivism. *Law and Philosophy* 17: 233–250.

Dowling, L. (1986). *Language and Decadence in the Victorian* Fin de Siècle. Princeton: Princeton University Press.

Eagleton, T. (1996). *Literary Theory: An Introduction* (2nd ed.). Oxford: Blackwell.

Fabb, N. (2010). Is literary language and development of ordinary language? *Lingua* 120: 1219–1232.

Fabb, N. and Durant, A. (1987). Editors' introduction. In *The Linguistics of Writing; Arguments between Language and Literature*. Manchester: Manchester University Press, 1–14.

Fish, S. (1973). How ordinary is ordinary language? *New Literary History* 5: 41–54.

Fish, S. (1987). Still wrong after all these years. *Law and Philosophy* 6: 401–418.

Fowler, R. (1966). Linguistics, stylistics; criticism? *Lingua* 16: 153–165.

Fuller, L. (1967). *Legal Fictions*. Stanford, CT: Stanford University Press.

Gellner, E. (1959). *Words and Things*. London: Victor Gollanz.

Gilmore, S. (2011). *Corbett v Corbett: once a man, always a man*? In S. Gilmore, J. Herring and R. Probert (eds.) *Landmark Cases in Family Law*. Oxford: Hart, 47–72.

Grice, P. (1988). Reply to Richards. In R. Grandy and R. Warner (eds.) *Philosophical Grounds of Rationality: Intentions, Categories, Ends*. Oxford: Clarendon Press, 45–108.

Hacker, P. (2013). Oxford philosophy and the linguistic turn. In M. Beaney (ed.) *The Oxford Handbook of the History of Analytic Philosophy*. Oxford: Oxford University Press, 941–946.

Hackert, S. (2012). *The Emergence of the English Native Speaker*. Boston: de Gruyter.

Halliday, M. (1964). The linguistic study of literary texts. In H. G. Lunt (ed.) *Proceedings of the Ninth International Congress of Linguistics*. The Hague: Mouton, 302–307.

Hanfling, O. (2000). *Philosophy and Ordinary Language: The Bent and Genius of Our Tongue*. New York: Psychology Press.

Harris, R. (1988). Murray, Moore and the myth. In R. Harris (ed.) *Linguistic Thought in England 1914–1945*. London: Duckworth, 1–26.

Hart, H. (1994). *The Concept of Law* (2nd ed.). Oxford: Clarendon Press. First published 1961.

Hutton, C. (1996). Law lessons for linguists? Accountability and acts of professional classification. *Language and Communication* 16: 205–214.

Hutton, C. (2005). Authority and expertise in forensic linguistics. *Language and Communication* 25: 183–188.
Hutton, C. (2011). Objectification and transgender jurisprudence: the dictionary as quasi-statute. *Hong Kong Law Journal* 41: 27–47.
Hutton, C. (2014a). *Word Meaning and Legal Interpretation.* Basingstoke: Palgrave.
Hutton, C. (2014b). Defining ordinary words for mundane objects. In M. M. Oadha (ed.) *Legal Lexicography: A Comparative Perspective.* Farnham: Ashgate, 177–200.
Jackson, B. (1997). *Semiotics and Legal Theory.* Liverpool: Deborah Charles Publications.
Jakobson, R. (1923). *On Czech Verse especially in a Comparison with Russian Verse.* Berlin: Opoyaz.
Jakobson, R. (1960). Closing statements: linguistics and poetics. In T. Sebeok (ed.) *Style in Language.* Cambridge, MA: MIT Press, 351–377.
Karcz, A. (2002). *The Polish Formalist School and Russian Formalism.* Rochester, NY: University of Rochester Press.
Klinck, D. R. (1992). *Words of the Law: Approaches to Legal Discourse.* Montreal: McGill-Queen's Press.
Malcolm, N. (1964). Moore and ordinary language. In V.C. Chappell (ed.) *Ordinary Language: Essays in Philosophical Method.* Englewood Cliffs, NJ: Prentice-Hall, 5–23. First published 1942.
Mathews, M. (1986). OK for starters: Minister of Law and Order v Hurley. *South African Journal on Human Rights* 2: 333–338.
Mattila, H. (2012). Legal vocabulary. In L. Solan and P. Tiersma (eds.) *The Oxford Handbook of Language and the Law.* New York: Oxford University Press, 27–51.
Mattila, H. (2016). *Comparative Legal Linguistics: Language of Law, Latin and Modern Lingua Francas.* Surrey: Ashgate.
Morrison, M. (1989). Excursions into the nature of legal language. *Cleveland State Law Review* 37: 271–336.
Mulhall, S. (1998). *Stanley Cavell: Philosophy's Recounting of the Ordinary.* Oxford: Clarendon Press.
Ormrod, R. (1972). The medico-legal aspects of sex determination. *The Medico-Legal Journal* 46: 18–32.
Parker-Ryan, S. (2010). Reconsidering ordinary language philosophy: Malcolm's (Moore's) ordinary language argument. *Essays in Philosophy* 11: 123–149.
Parker-Ryan, S. (2012). Ordinary language philosophy, Internet Encyclopedia of Philosophy, http://www.iep.utm.edu/ord-lang, accessed July 16, 2015.
Rivkin, J. and Ryan, M. (2004). Introduction: Formalisms. In J. Rivkin and M. Ryan (eds.) *Literary Theory: An Anthology.* Malden, MA: Blackwell, 3–6.
Rosen, S. (2002). *The Elusiveness of the Ordinary: Studies in the Possibility of Philosophy.* New Haven, CT: Yale University Press.
Ryle, G. (1964). Ordinary language. In V.C. Chappell (ed.) *Ordinary Language: Essays in Philosophical Method.* Englewood Cliffs, NJ: Prentice-Hall, 24–40. First published 1953.
Samek, R. (1977). On contracting. *Dalhousie Law Journal* 4: 62–75.
Schwartz, E. (1970). Notes on linguistics and literature. *College English* 32: 184–190.
Shklovsky, V. (2004). Art as technique. In J. Rivkin and M. Ryan (eds.) *Literary Theory: An Anthology.* Malden, MA: Blackwell, 15–21. First published 1917.

Slocum, B. (2012). Linguistics and 'ordinary meaning' determinations. *Statute Law Review* 33: 39–83.

Smith, P. J. (2007). New legal fictions. *Georgetown Law Journal* 95: 1436–1495.

Solan, L. (1993). *The Language of Judges*. Chicago: University of Chicago Press.

Solan, L. (1995). Judicial decisions and linguistic analysis: Is there a linguist in the court? *Washington University Law Quarterly* 73: 1069–1080.

Solan, L. (1999). Can the legal system use experts on meaning? *Tennessee Law Review* 66: 1167–1199.

Tiersma, P. (1999). *Legal Language*. Chicago: University of Chicago Press.

Valenza, R. (2009). *Literature, Language, and the Rise of the Intellectual Disciplines in Britain, 1680–1820*. Cambridge: Cambridge University Press.

White, J. B. (2008). Establishing relations between law and other forms of thought and language. *Erasmus Law Review* 1: 3–22.

Wittgenstein, L. (2009). *Philosophical Investigations. Philosophische Untersuchungen*. Revised 4th ed., P.M.S. Hacker and J. Schulte (eds.). West Sussex: Wiley-Blackwell. First translated edition 1953.

Wordsworth, W. (1802). *Lyrical Ballads with Pastoral and other Poems*. Vol. 1. London: Longman.

CASES CITED

Anonymous v Anonymous 67 Misc.2d 982, 325 N.Y.S.2d 499 (N.Y. Sup. Ct. 1971).

Attorney-General (Cth) v "Kevin and Jennifer" [2003] Fam CA 94.

Bellinger v Bellinger [2001] EWCA Civ 1140. 2003 WL 1610368 (2003).

Brutus v Cozens [1973] AC 854.

Corbett v Corbett [1971] 2 All ER 33.

Goodwin v United Kingdom (2002) 35 EHRR 18.

Kantaris v Kantaris 84 So. 2d 155 (2004).

Littleton v Prange 9 S.W.3d 223 (Tex. App.–San Antonio 1999).

M.T. v T.J. 40 N.J. Super. 77 (1976).

Nix v Hedden 149 U.S. 304 (1893).

R v Harris (1988) 17 NSWLR 158.

R (Quintavalle) v Secretary of State for Health [2003] 2 AC 687.

Re Kevin 165 FLR 404 (2001).

Re Ladrach 32 Ohio Misc.2d 6 (1987).

re the Estate of Marshall G. Gardiner 73 Kan. 191, 42 P.3d 120 (2002).

Secretary, Department of Social Security v State Railroad Authority (1993) 43 FCR 299.

S Y v S Y [1963] P 37, [1962] 3 WLR 526.

Talbot (otherwise Poyntz) v Talbot, John David (otherwise Talbot, Mabel) (1967) 111 S.J. 213.

W v Registrar of Marriages (CACV 266/2010).

W v The Registrar of Marriages [2013] HKCFA 39.

Part II

Imperfect Fit between Legal Categories and Social Discourse

Part II

4 Effects of Translation on the Invisible Power Wielded by Language in the Legal Sphere: The Case of Nepal

Katsuo Nawa

EDITORS' NOTE TO CHAPTER 4

In this chapter, Katsuo Nawa addresses a major challenge language poses to satisfactory cross-cultural understanding of law. Interlingual indeterminacy, he claims – that is slippage and uncertainty when concepts are transferred between languages – can introduce what amounts to a renegotiation of power relations where (usually smaller) jurisdictions transplant legal concepts from other, usually globally more influential legal systems. Such renegotiation, perhaps unforeseen and unmonitored, may operate in different directions and potentially serves different political or religious interests.

The detailed example through which Nawa explores this complex problem concerns the delineation of religious freedom in the Nepali Constitution. The resulting concept of religious freedom, he suggests – in ways likely to surprise many Western readers – has little to do with individual choice but confers instead the right to maintain the religion of one's community. Converting a person from one religion to another, by contrast, is not permitted as an expression of religious freedom. This major difference between the Nepali and Western understanding of religious freedom cannot be reduced, Nawa suggests, to political pragmatism in the context of modern Nepal but results from significant conceptual differences associated with the Nepali term *dharma* and the English term *religion*, the former term having a much stronger meaning of collectivity.

Modern Nepali law is written and is official only in the Nepali language. But the legal system has incorporated over time many Western legal concepts through borrowing and translation. In the process, it has become common for the Nepali government to engage in two-way translation: translating Western concepts from a range of sources into Nepali, then translating Nepali law into English for public information purposes. Since the effective meaning of each term needs to be established within the social realities of the country which adopts that term, it cannot simply be understood by reference to the Western source language; and subsequent English translation of the Nepali law will not fully reflect the legal meaning contained in the Nepali text either, sometimes because of significant differences in semantic scope of the words used in the two different languages.

Nawa's central example of legal translation and transplantation difficulties concerns the systematic omission in English translation of important lines of text included in the Nepali Constitution and in every Act of Nepali law. Because these sections of textual material are no longer translated, their meaning is simply unavailable to the target language reader. The lines of text in question are Sanskrit eulogies containing etymologically non-Sanskrit words, and index crucial power relations by symbolizing an authority higher than the King reigning at the time when a law is promulgated. Since the printing of the eulogies predates modern Nepali law, their continued presence in the modern era indicated a persistent source of power outside the modern Constitution. The fact that the termination of this practice in 2006 required a legislative act, Nawa argues, lends support to the interpretation that the eulogies are more than insignificant remnants of an earlier cultural practice that can be dispensed with simply by not translating them or omitting them altogether.

Effects of Translation on the Invisible Power Wielded by Language in the Legal Sphere: The Case of Nepal

This chapter deals with how power may be exercised invisibly through language in the legal sphere by showing how translated terms used in both the formulation and understanding of legal systems present major difficulties as regards precise conceptualization. In particular, it examines a series of key words and sentences used in various modern Nepali legal documents, with a particular focus on the country's Constitutional law and on the long-term effect of the choice of a word or a sentence in the periodically recurrent process of enactment of the constitutional law of a non-Western country in a non-Western language. The Nepali case is highly significant in this respect, in that Nepal is one of a relatively small number of non-Western countries which have not been formally colonized throughout their modern history, and in which no Western languages have ever had official or semi-official legal status. Even though the Nepali government has translated some acts, including its Constitutions, from Nepali into English, the English versions are the only translations which cannot be treated as official legal texts.

The basic premise of this chapter was clearly articulated by the lawyer Michael Halton Cheadle, quoted by Mara Malagodi in her thorough analysis of the 1990 Nepali Constitution, "Every single word of a legal document is important; each word casts a long shadow within which the process of interpretation takes place once the document is promulgated" (Malagodi 2013: 159). In this respect the Nepali case shares the basic characteristic of any legal documents, but as modern Nepali law has been written in Nepali, in tracing "the process of interpretation" we also have to reconstruct various hidden effects of translation erased from legal texts-artifacts. In this chapter, I deal with "long shadows" cast by several words and sentences adopted in the modern Nepali law in the long process of the transplantation and adaptation of what might be roughly conceptualized as the modern Western legal system. Simply scrutinizing and evaluating the former in terms of the latter here is to miss the dynamics of what has been going on in the Nepali legal sphere. First, "the modern Western legal system" has never been a really monolithic system, but an accumulation of various different and sometimes mutually inconsistent national and international legal systems on the one hand and various different and often mutually incompatible theories constructed by scholars on the other.[1] Moreover, its components have frequently been revised and renovated in various different directions.[2] As Nepali jurists, bureaucrats, politicians, and activists have developed their understanding of changing trends in contemporary law and jurisprudence in relation to their own peculiar situation over the decades, the history of the modern Nepali legal sphere can only be understood dialogically. Second, especially in many Asian countries, the introduction of the modern legal system was brought about in part by translation of modern legal vocabulary, in many cases using the words and roots of a non-Western classical written language traditionally used in (using English terminology uncritically for the moment) "legal", "religious", and/or "political" spheres. The long-term effects or "shadows" of this translation might have been subtle and difficult to trace, but they are nevertheless substantial. Not only do the social realities of the country collide with much of what is presupposed in the Western legal concepts, but "literal" connotations of these translated terms can also affect various legal and sociocultural processes, to the extent that laws in the non-Western language cannot be fully understood solely through Western legal vocabulary. In this sense, such laws are not transparent, not only to the outsiders but also even to the insiders.[3]

[1] A glimpse of the legal history of Japan in the Meiji era, during which there was considerable debate concerning which Western legal system, French or German for instance, should be adopted as the primary model of each code, would suffice to demonstrate the point.

[2] Amendments of various codes of a state after ratification of an International Convention would be the clearest examples.

[3] I could not include the following edited volume in the discussion that follows, as it was published after I sent my final draft to the editors: Gellner, Hausner and Letizia (eds.) (2016) *Religion, Secularism, and Ethnicity in Contemporary Nepal.*

The problem here is not the possibility or impossibility of translation, in general. Two-way translation has somehow been accomplished many times by the government of Nepal, first by fixing Nepali equivalents for various modern Western concepts in the legal sphere, and secondly by translating Constitutions and other acts written in Nepali into English. What needs to be discussed is, using the terminology of Michael Silverstein (2003), the "semanticogrammatical" uncertainty and indexical or "transductional" slippage caused by the process. In what follows I deal first with a sentence almost always printed in the Constitutions and other acts in modern Nepal as text-artifacts before 2006, but, as far as I know, never translated but simply omitted in their governmental English translation. Here, the problem is the untranslatable illocutionary force of these lines, which has been virtually hidden to all those who read Nepali laws only in English. Then, in order to trace the complicated "long shadows" of particular translations, both as semanticogrammatical intercultural gloss and as transduction, I discuss two key Nepali words which were introduced in modern legal documents as well as in other contexts as the equivalent of two modern Western concepts. The trajectory of the two Nepali terms has turned out to be contrastive: one has been used until now with the strong South Asian connotations the word has had, while the other, once used as the equivalent of a Western concept, was suddenly problematized widely due to the undesirable connotation it contains and then quickly replaced by another word. Before going into the detail, however, a brief introduction to the history of modern Nepal is necessary.

Modern Nepal and Its Legal History[4]

The modern history of the political entity now called Nepal began with the "unification" or "conquest" of its territory by the Shah dynasty from Gorkha in the late eighteenth and early nineteenth century. Nepal was defeated by the British East India Company in the Anglo-Gorkha war (1814–16) and lost more than one-third of its territory, but survived as an independent political entity. Notably, as Richard Burghart (1996: 226–60) has demonstrated brilliantly, Nepal was not a modern nation-state but a South Asian Hindu kingdom in 1816: its modern history can be described as a process of becoming a modern nation-state of a particular kind.

From 1846 to 1951, Nepal was substantially ruled by the Ranas, who virtually monopolized the country's power and wealth. In 1854, *Ain*, the first comprehensive legal code in modern Nepal, widely known as the 1854 *Muluki Ain*, was promulgated. In this code, each and every person living in Nepal, whether

[4] See Whelpton 2005 for a history of Nepal written in the twenty-first century.

or not he or she was traditionally a member of a caste society, was treated as a member of a particular group or *jāt*. Moreover, each and every *jāt* in Nepal legally occupied a particular position in the national "caste" hierarchy, while each *jāt* could keep its own sociocultural and religious tradition unless it contravened the basic Hindu norms of the state (Höfer 1979). Thus *Muluki Ain* might be conceived as a unique amalgam of some basic premises of traditional South Asian Hindu kingdoms and the Western conception of a territorial state.

After the end of the Rana regime in 1951, political negotiation among various actors, notably the King and various political parties, continued for ten years. While the Interim Government of Nepal Act was quickly promulgated by King Tribhuvan in 1951, it was only in February 1959 that King Mahendra promulgated the Constitution of the Kingdom of Nepal, on his own initiative. The first general election took place and the Nepali Congress won. King Mahendra, however, led a successful royal coup in December 1960, removing the Congress government and banning political parties. The King promulgated the new Constitution in 1962, which prescribed the party-less "Panchayat" democracy and propagated the national unity of equal Nepali citizens under the Hindu king, without any substantial consideration of sociocultural, linguistic, or religious diversity within the country.

The People's Movement of 1990 brought the Panchayat regime to an end, and the new Constitution was promulgated by King Birendra in the same year. Nepal constitutionally turned into a "multiethnic, multilingual, democratic, [...] Hindu and Constitutional Monarchical Kingdom" (article 4(1)). Under this new constitution, a general election was held on three occasions, in 1991, 1994, and 1999, although the government changed much more frequently. In 1996, the Communist Party of Nepal (Maoist) began their "People's War", which turned into a ten-year Civil War. After King Birendra and all his family were killed in June 2001, the new king, King Gyanendra, gradually seized power by disregarding political parties, to the extent that he assumed full executive powers in February 2005. The king's move, while achieving little substantial outcome in terms of his countermeasures against the "Maoist insurgency", brought the Parliamentary political parties and the Maoists closer. The second People's Movement of 2006 brought Gyanendra's direct rule to an end, and the Civil War officially ended in November 2006. After a series of long and tough negotiations among multifarious actors, including various identity-based organizations and some international agencies, the Interim Constitution of Nepal was promulgated in January 2007, in which the Nepali nation is prescribed as having "multiethnic, multilingual, multireligious and multicultural characteristics" (article 3). After further political twists and turns, notably the Madhesi movement in the Tarai or plains area, the Constitutional Assembly Election was held in April 2008. The assembly itself was dissolved in May 2012 without drafting the Constitution, and the second Constitutional Assembly Election was held in November 2013. The new Constitution of Nepal was promulgated on September 20, 2015, but the political instability still continues in February 2016.[5]

As is pointed out by Malagodi (2013: 24), there are few academic studies on the modern legal history of Nepal in European languages, though the law of modern Nepal before 1951, in general, and the Muluki Ain of 1854, in particular, are relatively well studied (Gaborieau 1977: 193–235; Sharma 1977; Höfer 1979; Fezas 1993; and Michaels 1997 among others). A book on the constitutional history of Nepal written in the early 1990s (Chaturvedi 1993) was almost solely based on the then current trope of democratization,[6] while Michael Hutt (1994) critically scrutinizes the drafting process of the 1990 Constitution. Richard Burgert's attempts of critical reconsideration of the history of modern Nepali nation, state, kingship, and religion (collected in Burghert 1996) are not legal history per se.[7]

Two studies are worth particular attention here. With his typical *Sachlichkeit* ("objectivity"), David Gellner, in his article on group rights and individual rights in Nepal, extracts three different models of the relationship between culture and collectivity in the modern history of Nepal: "the hierarchical, caste-based model of the Rana period; the citizen-based, developmental, and culturally homogenizing model of the Panchayat period; and perhaps unrealizable, multicultural, 'different but equal' model of the ethnic activists of today" (Gellner 2001: 193). True, these are convincing and illuminating as heuristic models. On the other hand, as discussed later with regard to the concept of *dharma*, Gellner's argument might be criticized as too Western and too schematic in some places. Furthermore, when he criticizes the essentialist multiculturalist view of cultural divisions largely shared in Nepal,[8] describing it as an "unrealized, and perhaps unrealizable" model, he seem to undervalue the fact that his first and second models are the failed models that are most probably unrealizable in the future, as well as the strong possibility that the individualistic model he recommends, with its strong emphasis on hybridity, would also be "unrealized, and

[5] Because I wrote this chapter before the promulgation of the new constitution, I can only mention these developments briefly, mainly in footnotes.

[6] I adopted the word *trope* here, as almost all the political leaders in Nepal since the late 1950s, including King Mahendra and King Gyanendra, have alleged themselves to be pro-democracy, propagating their own plans for democratization of Nepal. Chaturvedi's book straightforwardly praises multi-party democracy, without seriously considering the diversity of the population of Nepal.

[7] As discussed later, Chiara Letizia's multidimentional study on secularism in Nepal (2012, 2013, 2015) includes detailed scrutiny of legal texts and court cases.

[8] That is, cultural diversity within Nepal is recognized while each culture is imagined essentialistically.

perhaps unrealizable" in toto, as it is quite evidently not the panacean solution to the conundrum of individual and group rights.[9]

The other notable study is Mara Malagodi's monograph on Nepali constitutional history, which focuses on the drafting process and application of the 1990 Constitution and is certainly an epoch-making contribution to the field. The particular strength of Malagodi's work lies in her thorough analysis of Nepali legal documents, supplemented by rich information from sources, including interviews with politicians, lawyers, bureaucrats, activists, and scholars. Her basic analytic scheme, despite these impressive qualities, is less convincing. What she calls the "ancient" Nepali notion of constitutionalism, for example, is far less monolithic and static, and far more complicated and perspectival, than she presupposes. By essentializing this notion unhistorically, she sidesteps the process of how such "ancient" elements have been reinterpreted and partially adapted in different ways by various actors, thus betraying what she calls her own "historical institutionalist" approach. Moreover, Malagodi's book seems too heavily reliant on the current trope of inclusion/exclusion without seriously scrutinizing the validity of the heavily loaded concept of inclusion historically.

The problems that surface in these two previous contributions clearly derive from a series of conundra related to individual and group rights, citizenship and minority, (possibly strategic) essentialism and hybridity, which have been debated across academic disciplines in the social sciences and humanities for decades, without any clear theoretical or practical solution that every theorist, let alone activist, would be convinced by. To explicate the detail of these tangled debates is clearly beyond the scope of this chapter. Rather, what I would like to do here is to focus on one particular element that has complicated the whole issue in this globalizing world: the effect of translation as practiced in the legal sphere. The fact that I am a scholar educated in the semi-periphery of the world system of academics is not incidental to my whole argument. As a scholar who learned various Western concepts first in Japanese, second in English, and then in some other European and non-European languages, I have always been compelled to grasp these concepts not as self-evident and transparent across languages, but as problematic and only partially translatable. Certainly I am not a specialist in Nepali law: I am a sociocultural anthropologist who has taken some interest in the historical relation between various populations in Nepal and the Nepali state. I should also admit that every Nepali jurist, as well as every serious Nepal specialist, has already recognized the phenomena discussed here. I hope however that my preliminary and non-specialist

[9] Will Kymlicka's well-known argument on liberalism, nationalism, multiculturalism, and citizenship (Kymlicka 2001), for instance, reveals the complexity of the conundrum, while to what extent his dichotomous framework is applicable to Nepal is another matter.

intervention can shed light on this relatively neglected aspect of the conundra in question.

The Unprescribed and Untranslated Power of Sanskrit

As pointed out earlier, the official text of each constitution and act in modern Nepal has been written in Nepali. To be sure, the government of Nepal has also published English translations of some of them for decades. But unlike in many other South Asian countries, the English translations are not official texts, having no authority in the legal sphere in Nepal. Indeed, from 1962 the Constitutions of Nepal have specified Nepali as the official language of Nepal.

Surprisingly, however almost every modern law in Nepal, including its Constitutions, contained until 2006 several lines which are not in Nepali syntactically and morphologically. Moreover, these lines have been totally invisible to those who access the law in Nepal only through its governmental English translation, since the lines have neither been transliterated into Roman alphabet nor translated into English, but simply omitted from that translation. On the other hand, many Nepali jurists and lawyers themselves would not care at all about these lines as they consult articles of an act, since the lines have nothing to do with the main contents of the law. In order to explain how this can be the case, in this section I investigate the pragmatics of the lines in question.

Where do we encounter these lines? Leaving out the cover page and table of contents, every Nepali act as a text-artifact starts with the name of the act and the year in the Vikram Sambat, the Nepali official calendar which starts in 57 BCE. The date of authentication and publication of the act, and the list of amending acts (if any) follow, and then the number of the act, "Act Number 67 of the year 2019" in the case of the new *Muluki Ain* of 1963. Then come the lines in question, just before the main content of the act. It is easy to find the lines, as they are often printed in larger font than the main text.

The following is the transliteration of these lines from the 1990 Constitution of Nepal.

svastiśrī girirājacakracūḍāmaṇi naranārāyaṇetyādi vividha virudāvalī virājamāna mānonnata mahendramālā parama nepālapratāpabhāskara parama gauravamaya tejasvī tribhuvanaprajātantraśrīpada parama ujjvala kīrtimaya nepālaśrīpada parama projjvala nepālatārā parama pavitra õrāmapaṭṭa parama jyotirmaya suvikhyāta triśaktipaṭṭa parama suprasiddha pravala gorakhādakṣiṇavāhu paramādhipati atirathī parama senādhipati śrī śrī śrī śrī śrīmanmahārājādhirāja vīrendra vīra vikrama śāhadeva devānām sadā samaravijayinām. (śrī 5 ko sarakāra, 2047vs: 1)

Two words towards the end, "devānām" and "samaravijayinām", clearly show that this prose is morphologically not in Nepali but in Sanskrit; they are genitive plural of the words *deva* and *samara-vijayin* respectively. The five *śrīs*, often abbreviated as "śrī 5" in Nepali and normally rendered into English as "His Majesty", was the honorific for Nepali Royal family members.[10] "śrī 5 mahārājādhirāja vīrendra vīra vikrama śāhadeva", usually rendered in English as His Majesty King Birendra Bir Vikram Shah Dev, is the name of the king of Nepal who reigned from 1972 to 2001. Also note that "śrīmanmahārājādhirāja vīrendra vīra vikrama śāhadeva" is not nominative but vocative. Words like "triśaktipaṭṭa" and "gorakhādakṣiṇavāhu", on the other hand, are well-known as the names of orders of Nepal. We can thus easily conclude that the lines are a eulogy to the current king of Nepal. Indeed, this sentence, called *praśasti* in Nepali, consists of different honorific titles of the King, the core of which might be roughly translated as "Hail His Majesty King Birendra Bir Vikram Shaha, always victorious King of Kings [or God of Gods]".[11]

The same lines have appeared in various acts promulgated between the mid-1970s and 2001. In the early years of the reign of the king Mahendra, it was:

svastiśrī girirāja cakracūḍāmaṇi naranārāyaṇetyādi vividha virudāvalī virājamāna mānonnata ojasvirājanya projjvala nepālatālā ati ojasvi tribhuvana prajātantra śrīpada ōrāmapaṭṭa atula jyotirmaya triśaktipaṭṭa atipravala gorakhā dakṣiṇavāhu mahādhipati philḍa mārśal ra sarvocca kamyāṇḍara inacīpha śrī manmahārājādhirāja śrī śrī śrī mahendra vīra vikrama jaṁgabahādura śāhabahādura śamśera jaṁga devānām sadā samaravijayinām. (śrī 5 ko sarakāra 2021vs: vol. 1: 1)

Interestingly, this eulogy contains various non-Sanskrit words from Persian, like *jaṁga*, *bahādura*, and *śamśera*, as well as English-derived *kamyāṇḍara*

[10] Malagodi rendered śrī panch "five times bless blessed" (2013: 139), while Whelpton (2005: 62) rendered Shri Panch Sarkar as "Five-Times Illustrious Ruler".

[11] It would be difficult to provide an appropriate English translation here of this *praśasti*, and especially beyond the capacity of someone such as myself who is not an Indologist or historian. The main difficulty lies in the multilayered heavy-loadedness of almost every word. It is true that *triśaktipaṭṭa* and *gorakhādakṣiṇavāhu* are usually rendered as "three divine powers" and "Gurkha right arm" respectively. But such denotational glosses do not clarify much unless one considers the fact that these are also the names of orders of Nepal. In a similar vein the first three compound nouns, *girirāja* (lit. 'mountain king'), *cakracūḍāmaṇi* (lit. 'wheel-crest jewel'), and *naranārāyaṇa* (*Nara* and *Nārāyaṇa* is often used to refer to a pair of deities, and *nara* also means "man") would be very unclear unless account is also taken of the fact that they are listed as examples of the "vividha viruda" (various panegyrics) for the Hindu king of Nepal; the words would also need to be set in a context provided by detailed knowledge of South Asian civilization. In contrast, it is a version of the modern history of Nepal that is indexed by the word *tribhuvanaprajātantraśrīpada*, a version of modern history according to which King Tribhuvan in 1951 established *prajātantra* or "democracy" (on this word, see pp. 111–114) by bringing the oligarchical Rana regime to an end. Note, however, that it is still possible to discuss the pragmatics of the eulogy as a whole without getting into detailed, semanticogrammatical intercultural glosses and context for each term. Indeed, as is discussed later there had been a considerable amount of change in the words of the eulogy, even though its basic structure had remained identical for more than two centuries.

inacīpha (Commander in Chief). After the Royal coup in December 1960, however, the eulogy changed significantly:

svastiśrī girirājacakracūḍāmaṇi naranārāyaṇetyādi vividha virudāvalī virājamāna mānonnata mahendramālā ojasvirājanya ati tejasvī tribhuvana prajātantraśrīpada ati kīrtimaya nepālaśrīpada projjvala nepālatārā õ rāmapaṭṭa atulajyotirmaya triśaktipaṭṭa ati pravala gorakhādakṣiṇavāhu paramādhipati atirathī parama senādhipati śrī śrī śrī śrī śrīmanmahārājādhirāja mahendra vīra vikrama śāhadeva devānām sadā samara vijayinām. (śrī 5 ko sarakāra, 2020vs: 1)

In this version, adopted from the New *Muluki Ain* of 1963, non-Sanskrit terms were either deleted or substituted by an etymologically Sanskrit term (from English *kamyāṇḍara inacīpha* to *senādhipati*, for instance). The number of śrī was increased. We may say thus that the eulogy was 'Sanskritized' and reinforced. This coincided with the basic policy of his Majesty's Government of Nepal at the time to integrate and develop Nepal under the aegis of the Hindu King. Note however that one cannot understand the sentence purely through knowledge of classical Sanskrit: The term *tribhuvana*, for instance, refers to the name of the former King, while *prajātantra* is the modern compound to denote the Western concept of democracy made of two Sanskrit words. A similar eulogy appeared not only in the 1962 Constitution (śrī 5 ko sarakāra 2019vs: 1), but also in various acts promulgated in the 1960s and early 1970s.

Next, compare the eulogy used in early years of Mahendra's reign with the following lines.

svastiśrī girirāja cakracūḍāmaṇi naranārāyaṇetyādi. vividha virudāvalī virājamāna mānonnata śrī manmahārājādhirāja śrī śrī śrī. mahārāja surendra vikrama sāha bahādūra. samsera jaṁga devānāṁ sadā samara vijayīnām. (śrī 5 ko sarakāra, 2022 (1910)vs: 1)

These lines appear in the first comprehensive legal code of modern Nepal, *Ain* of 1854, widely known as 1854 Muluki Ain. Much shorter than the eulogies after 1950, the basic structure, as well as the use of the non-Sanskrit terms like *bahādūra* and *samsera* [sic], is the same. Interestingly, below this eulogy, two other eulogies are printed, for the then previous King Rājendra Vikrama Sāha [sic] to the left, and the crown prince Trirokya to the right. The photocopied first page of an original *Ain* included in the reprint version confirms that these eulogies certainly appeared in an original version, with each eulogy preceded by a stamp.[12]

As is widely known among historians, eulogy with a royal stamp, starting with the word "svasti" and ending with "devānāṁ sadā samara vijayīnām", has a much longer and wider history than the modern Nepali law. For instance, *Śāhakālakā abhilekha*, one of the most reliable historical source books on

[12] On different versions of the 1854 Ain, see Fezas (2047vs).

late eighteenth and early nineteenth century Nepal, contains many documents issued in the name of Pṛthvi Narayan Shah, known as the founder of modern Nepal, and his early successors. One of them goes:

svasti śrīgirirājacakracūḍāmaṇi naranārāyaṇetyādi vividhavirudāvalīvirājamāna mānonnata śrīmanmahārājādhirāja śrīśrīśrīmannṛpapṛthvīnārāyana śāhadevānāṁ sadā samaravijayīnāṁ. (Vajrācārya ra Śreṣṭha 2037vs: 45)

Despite the difference of punctuation and several words including the name of the king, the continuity is evident. Moreover, eulogies containing the same structure also appeared in documents of other dynasties, notably the Sen Dynasty of Vijaypur. For instance, a beautiful color photocopy of one such document, issued by King Mahipati Sen of Vijaypur in 1783vs (1726), with a black stamp of the king, is included in Krauskopff and Meyer (2000: 1).[13]

Tracing the genealogy of the eulogy in this way, we can now discuss the trajectory and changing pragmatics of the Sanskrit eulogy in modern Nepali law. The eulogy derived from the documentational tradition of pre-modern South Asian Hindu kingship. Pragmatically, a standardized sentence praising the King in Sanskrit and a Royal stamp guaranteed the authority of these documents. The Gorkha kings already used that scheme in their Royal documents long before the conquest of the Kathmandu valley. Indeed, these documents had been called *lālmohar* (literally "red stamp"). When *Muluki Ain* was promulgated in 1854 as the first comprehensive legal code of modern Nepal, the then authorities decided to apply this old tradition of *lālmohar*. Their decision is highly significant, as the *Muluki Ain* also shows a clear divergence from the Hindu legal tradition of Dharmashastra, in that it was not written in Sanskrit but in a vernacular, Nepali. Also note that, even though the king had no real political power in the Rana period, it should have been the King of Gorkha (or Nepal), not the Rana Prime Minister of Nepal, who had the authority to promulgate the law.

In the late Rana period and the first few years of the post-Rana period, there seems to have been a short period of time during which the eulogy was not used for legal acts. Several acts promulgated between 1990vs and 2007vs seem to lack this eulogy (e.g. śrī 5 ko sarakāra 2021vs: vol. 1: 221; vol 2: 731, 736). The 1951 Interim Government of Nepal Act also lacks the eulogy (śrī 5 ko sarakāra 2011vs). After that period, however, the eulogy reappeared, and as I have suggested it became more and more Sanskritized and elongated throughout the latter half of the twentieth century. Also note that, at least since the Panchayat period, the eulogy appeared in acts but not in regulations.

[13] This is the oldest document included in the volume. Interestingly, the editors do not translate but transliterate the eulogy part (Krauskopff and Meyer 2000: 115).

The basic pragmatic structure of the *praśasti* was preserved in post-1951 Nepali acts. The sentence, by the name of the King, guaranteed the authority of the act. A eulogy of a particular act always indexed the King reigning at the time of its promulgation. Once written down, that would never be modified, which is why the official Anthology of Nepal Acts compiled in the early Panchayat era contains various different eulogies for different kings, as well as several acts without one (śrī 5 ko sarakāra 2021vs). More importantly, the eulogy in a sense presupposes a higher order authority than the King himself. Remember that the whole sentence is not declarative but vocative, a form of direct address. Someone addresses and praises the King, and then the law is authorized and sanctioned in the name of the King. As the whole sentence is written in Sanskrit, it is most probably Brahmans who praise the King. The language is crucially important, and cannot be properly transduced, as a denotationally perfect translation of the lines into English cannot exert the illocutionary force of the original text. Moreover, the sentence was written in almost every law in Nepal including its Constitutions, even while the country was a Constitutional Hindu monarchy. The power of the eulogy, and power conferred by the eulogy, clearly came from outside the modern legal system of Nepal, as the sentence was not based on the Constitution.[14] Indeed, one can say that Nepali laws and Constitutions were sanctioned by the eulogy if one admits its illocutionary force, though it was also true that it had been less and less certain for more and more people what this eulogy really authorized, and how.[15]

Finally on this topic, let us look at the fate of the eulogy in the early twenty-first century. In acts promulgated in the reign of the king Gyanendra (2001–06), we can see the longest *praśasti* in the modern history of Nepal:

> svastiśrī girirājacakracūḍāmaṇi naranārāyaṇetyādi vividha virudāvalī virājamāna mānonnata vīrendramālā mahendramālā parama nepālapratāpabhāskara ojasvirājanya parama gauravamaya tejasvī tribhuvanaprajātantraśrīpada parama ujjvala kīrtimaya nepālaśrīpada parama projjvala nepālatārā parama pavittra õrāmapaṭṭa parama mahāgauravamaya supradīpta vīrendraprajātantrabhāskara parama jyotirmaya suvikhyāta triśaktipaṭṭa parama suprasiddha pravala gorakhādakṣiṇabāhu paramādhipati atirathī parama senādhipati śrī śrī śrī śrī śrīmanmahārājādhirāja jñānendra vīra vikrama śāhadeva devānām sadā samaravijayinām. (śrī 5 ko sarakāra 2061vs: 1)

There are relatively few acts during the King Gyanendra's reign, however, because after he dismissed the then prime minister Sher Bahadur Deuba in

14 In fact it contradicted the Constitution, which prescribed that the official language of Nepal was Nepali.

15 Alan Durant has suggested to me that, in some respects, the eulogy has affinities with the enacting formula to be found at the beginning of UK or U.S. statutes. I agree, but interestingly every Nepali law also has a preamble (prastāvanā) section which contains a sentence roughly corresponding with UK or U.S. enacting formula. It can thus be said that Nepali acts were doubly sanctioned until 2006.

October 2002, no acts (*ain*) were passed or enforced in Nepal until the 2006 People's Movement, and all legislation was introduced by ordinances (*adhyādeś*) from the King.

After the 2006 People's Movement, the Nepalese Government (not His Majesty's Government of Nepal any longer) published a new series of Nepal Ain Sangraha (Anthology of Nepali Laws; *nepālasarakāra*, 2066–7vs.). In the first volume, on the first page of every act promulgated before the second People's Movement, a small icon of scissors is printed immediately after the number of the act.[16] In the footnote the scissors icon is clarified as signifying "deleted according to the gaṇatantra sudṛḍhīkarṇa tathā kehī nepāla kanūna saṁśodhana garne ain, 2066 (Republic Reinforcement and some Nepali Acts Amendment Act, 2066vs)". Article 110 (1) of the act states 'śrī 5's praśasti' in current acts are removed. In laws promulgated after the second People's Movement in the anthology, on the other hand, there is neither the mark of scissors nor the eulogy. The long tradition of Hinduistic and monarchical sanction of law thus ended in Nepal. The fact that the lines in the acts could be deleted only through an article of a new act revealed in the end the fact that, far from being an innocent decoration with an archaic flavor, the lines had been something to be dealt with legally, in order to modify all current acts of Nepal to make them compatible with the basic principle of the New Nepal.

"Right to Religion" or "Right Concerning *Dharma*"[17]

Since 1959, Nepali Constitutions have prescribed a "right to religion", even while the country was a Hindu kingdom. However, there has been a huge gap between what has been prescribed in the Constitution and the Western concept of "freedom of religion" (Gellner 2001; Malagodi 2013). Moreover, unlike the case of the *praśasti* discussed previously, the gap clearly appeared in the governmental English translation of the Constitutions in two ways: first, the term "religion" was qualified by the clause "as handed down to him or her from ancient times"[18] before the 2015 Constitution;[19] and second, it has not been permitted "to convert another person from one religion to another" (Government of Nepal 2010: 12; 2015: 13).[20] It might look easy to conclude

[16] The icon differs from volume to volume.
[17] I discuss this issue from a different angle, comparing Japanese and Nepali translation of the concept of "religion", in another article (Nawa 2016).
[18] The Nepali word I render as "ancient times" changed from *sanātana* in the 1990 Constitution (19(1)) to *parāpūrva* in the 2006 Interim Constitution (23(1)). Considering the Hinduistic implication of the term *sanātana* (Letizia 2012: 84), it might be possible to detect traces of another phase of word politics here.
[19] The term *dharma* is defined in a clearly different way in the 2015 Constitution (26(1)).
[20] The actual number of prosecutions against proselytization declined in post-1990 Nepal (Letizia 2012: 67).

straightforwardly that there is therefore no real freedom of religion in Nepal. However, as the official text of the Constitutions of Nepal is written in Nepali, and as the universal applicability of the concept of religion has been fundamentally questioned, especially after the strong criticism by Talal Asad (1993), we should instead investigate what is written in the Nepali text before jumping to such a conclusion.

As is widely known, in Nepali as well as in Hindi and many other South Asian languages the word *dharma* has been used as the equivalent of the Western concept of "religion". Two points should be noted, however. First, the term *dharma* (unlike the term *prajātantra*, which I discuss in the next section) is not a newly coined compound noun but a word widely used throughout South Asia and beyond from ancient times. Second, the word *dharma* traditionally, and even today, denotes a quite different range of spheres from the term "religion".[21] Indeed, it can also be translated, for instance, as "law", "custom", "piety", "duty", "justice", "merit", or "faith". My basic hypothesis here is that, though legal usage of *dharma* as "religion" can easily be distinguished from other usages in most cases, the connotations of the already existent term *dharma* have affected understanding of the concept of dharma as "religion". To consider this hypothesis, let us trace the history of intersections between the Western and Nepali concepts.

In his classic monograph on Muslims in Nepal, Marc Gaborieau analyzes the use of Nepali terms regarding "religion" in 1854 and 1935 *Muluki Ain*s (Gaborieau 1977: 201–09). According to his analysis, three words, *majhap* (or *majhab*), *dharma*, and *mat*, appeared in these *Ain*s. The etymologically Arabic word *majhap* was used as the comprehensive and neutral term to denote "religion", probably as the broad equivalent of the Western concept. The term *dharma* either meant religious duty, or referred only to certain religions like Hinduism, excluding those which were categorized as *mat*. *Mat*, literally meaning "opinion", referred to foreign, irreligious (*vidharmī*) "religions" which would cause harm to the caste-based social order: Christianity, Islam, and in 1935 *Muluki Ain*, Kabīr-Pantha. Furthermore, quoting a long article from 1935 *Muluki Ain*, Gaborieau pointed out that, within the Kingdom of Gorkha, to propagate and preach irreligious and foreign beliefs like Kabiī-Pantha, Islam, Christianity, and so on, which disturb religion and distinction of castes, was prohibited (Gaborieau 1977: 205). Interestingly, the article listed Ārya-Samāj, Brahma Samāj, Rāmkṛṣṇa, Ballabha, Jhannākhannā, Jainism, Nāsika, and Rām-kabīr as exceptions, while there was no direct mention of the "religions" of those who are now called *janajāti*.

[21] See Olivelle (2009) for a collection of essays dealing with various aspects of the history of the concept from Indologist perspectives. Pravat (2013) discusses the concept of dharma in the context of law and justice in Nepal.

This conceptually divisive treatment of "religion" was replaced by a one-to-one equation between *religion* and *dharma* in the late Rana period. Indeed, the word *dhārmiksvatantratā* (roughly "religious autonomy" or "religious freedom") appeared in Article 4 (prescribing "Fundamental Rights") of the (never actually promulgated) Government of Nepal Act, 1948. In the 1951 Interim Government of Nepal Act, the word *dharma*, or *dhārmik*, certainly does not appear in Article 17(2) which prescribes rights of citizens, while Article 15 (1) clearly prohibits governmental discrimination against any citizens on grounds only on *dharma*. Then, since 1959, *dharma sambandī hak* ("right concerning *dharma*") has been prescribed in Nepali Constitutions, basically as the right to maintain the *dharma* of one's own community (śrī 5 ko sarakāra 2015vs, 2019vs, 2047vs; nepāla sarakāra 2069vs). It has been prohibited to convert someone to another *dharma*, while there was no mention of conversion by free will.

David Gellner (2001: 185) comments on the situation of religion in the Panchayat period that "religion had still not become entirely a matter of individual choice". In the same vein, Mara Malagodi (2013: 86) points out that in the 1959 Constitution, "the Right to Religion – for the first time in Nepal's constitutional history – was limited and defined religion as 'handed down from ancient times'". I would argue, however, that these comments are highly problematic and Western-centric, in that they treat the Nepali concept of *dharma* solely in terms of the Western concept of religion, as a deviation from the religious prototype. In the previous paragraph, I did not translate but transliterated the word *dharma* intentionally. Indeed, I believe that the article is far more natural and comprehensible if one reads it as prescribing something not on religion but on *dharma*, as the word *dharma* very often, though not always, has the strong connotation of collectivity. Moreover, the Nepali word *dharma*, not the English word *religion*, is the word to be interpreted and utilized in the legal sphere in Nepal in the last resort, even though it is also well-known that the word *dharma* in this context should have a distinct denotation equivalent to the English term *religion*. To what extent the gap between the two concepts has been intentionally exploited by those who drafted the Constitutions is largely yet to be known. I would argue, however, that we cannot understand the issue of "religion" in Nepal without considering the sense of naturalness that these Nepali provisions would convey.[22]

[22] Letizia (2012, 2013, 2015) already studied the other side of this topic by discussing the issue of secularism and *dharmanirapekshatā*, the highly contested translation of the English word, in the post-1990 Nepal. The following remark on the Hinduistic view of the concepts is worth noting: "One of the 'undesirable' effects of *dharma nirapeksa* is the reduction of this multi-level notion of *sanatan dharma* to the narrow western sense of 'religion' as one of the many religious paths (considered equal by a neutral state) that an individual can select and follow" (2012: 84).

As is pointed out by David Gellner (2001) among many others, many *Janajāti* (nationalities) activists who fought for a secular Nepal against the Hindu dominance shared this conception of *dharma*. Moreover, the globally circulating concept of "indigenous peoples", which is clearly connected with the issue on cultural rights of particular groups of people (not individuals), has brought further twists into the debate.[23] Again, the collectivistic connotation of the term *dharma* seems to have affected the whole debate. Indeed, while the word *dharmanirapeksha* (literally "not depending on dharma" or "no expectation to dharma":[24] Nepal turned into a *dharmanirapeksha* country as a result of the 2007 Interim Constitution partly because of *Janajāti* activism) has been used as the equivalent of the English term *secular*, many activists have strongly demanded equal recognition and positive treatment of various *dharmas* by the government.

Many anthropologists have reported a range of repercussions of this conceptual uncertainty at the local level. William Fisher's description, which follows, of a meeting of the Thakalis, now officially one of the most "advanced" indigenous nationalities in Nepal, to set up a national association in April 1983 in Pokhara, is particularly suggestive:

> A wide variety of strongly held views concerning Thakali tradition were expressed. Some parties held that the Thakali should embrace Hinduism because it was the religion of their putative high-caste Thakuri forefathers; others that their forefathers were not Thakuri but Bhote or Tibetans and they should thus readopt Tibetan Buddhist practices; and yet others that they had never systematically followed Buddhist practices and now was not the time to start. Some speakers took the less doctrinal view that they should restore pure Thakali tradition, whatever that might be (an opinion often expressed with the qualification that the speaker himself was not professing to know what, exactly, Thakali tradition was). Other speakers urged that they stop arguing about religion (*dharma*) and agree to leave the matter up to individuals. (Fisher 2001: 4)

Here, the majority of people shared the premise that Thakali as a people should have their own *dharma*, though some, probably following the Western conception of religion, argued that *dharma* should be a matter of individual choice. The understanding of the concept *dharma* in this way fluctuated between its "Western" individualistic and modern Nepali collective usages.

Susan Hangen wrote in her ethnographic study that "[r]eligious freedom was associated with democracy, and people saw the possibility of following their 'own religion' (aphno *dharma*) as an indicator of political freedom in the post-1990 multi-party era" (2010: 132). She then analyzes the process through which the Gurungs in far eastern Nepal became (according to their own perception,

[23] Note that Nepal ratified the Indigenous and Tribal Peoples Convention, 1989 (ILO-Convention 169) in 2007.

[24] Letizia (2012: 70) renders this term as "autonomous from/indifferent, impartial to *dharma*".

returned to) Ningma Buddhists. Interestingly, they never used Ningma Buddhist shrines in Sherpa villages nearby. Hangen quotes an explanation offered by an unmarried village woman, "while Gurungs and Sherpas have the same books and the same religion, they each needed their own *gumbā* and their own lamas because 'we are separate societies'" (2010: 142). This argument is intriguing, as she clearly distinguishes two boundaries of *dharma*: the boundary of a *dharma* as a religious doctrine, accompanied by a set of practices on the one hand, and the boundary of "our *dharma*" which must coincide with their ethnosocial or *janajāti* boundary, on the other.

Finally in this connection, it should be pointed out that not all Nepali people have been convinced about the constitutional provision on the "right concerning dharma". Notably many Christian activists, especially Protestants, have strongly criticized the conception of *dharma* as a collective right.[25] The crucial point here is that their criticism, as well as several of Thakalis' arguments presuming religion as an individual matter quoted earlier, has been generally comprehended by many other Nepalis, though not necessarily agreed. Those who propagate the collective "right concerning dharma" from various different positions generally also recognize the possibility that *dharma* might be a matter of individual choice. Theoretically, the adoption of the word *dharma* to gloss the English term *religion* was both an application of an already existent word to a new context and a translation of a foreign concept at the same time. In the "long shadow" of this dual endeavor lies the oscillating in-betweenness of the modern Nepali concept of *dharma*, which can be fully understood neither solely in terms of the South Asian concept of *dharma* nor in terms of the Western concept of religion.

"Democracy": "Word Trap" in Translation?

In the case of the concept of *dharma*/religion, South Asian connotations of the Nepali word have exerted a strong influence on its modern usage as the translation of the Western concept of religion. Obviously, this is not the only possible trajectory of a Nepali word used as the equivalent of a Western legal concept. Notably, a word might be problematized long after it has become established, on account of connotations deriving from its originally Sanskrit components. The word *prajātantra*, which was the official and most frequently used Nepali equivalent of the English word *democracy*, is such a case.

The term *prajātantra*, a calque or "loan translation" using two Sanskrit words, was long used as the Nepali equivalent of the English term

[25] Gellner's (2001: 190) following argument is thus clearly an overstatement: "What all Nepali political parties, pressure groups and revolutionaries seem to agree on is an essentialist view of the cultural divisions they argue over."

democracy. Nepal has been constitutionally a "democratic" country since 1951, after it turned from being a caste-based Hindu territorial state into a nation-state. The 1951 Interim Government of Nepal Act contains the word *prajātantrātmak* (democratic) (śrī 5 ko sarakāra, 2011vs: 1), while the 1959 Constitution contains *prajātantra* (śrī 5 ko sarakāra, 2016vs: 1), both in the Preamble. The 1962 Constitution did not contain the word *prajātantra* except in its *praśasti*; but by its first amendment the words *prajātantra* and *prajātāntrik* were inserted in various articles in order to redefine the basic state system as a party-less democratic Panchayat System (śrī 5 ko sarakāra, 2019vs, 2025vs). Indeed, from the 1960s to the 1980s, His Majesty's government propagated the idea that the system realized true Nepali *prajātantra* (democracy) based on their own old tradition of *panchāyat* (councils), being different in this way from Western multi-party democracy, necessarily in order to ensure the independence and harmonious development of the Kingdom of Nepal. Of course, for political party activists the Panchayat regime was not democracy at all, because it lacks a multi-party system. They fought for a "real" *prajātantra*. Both sides, however, shared use of the term *prajātantra*, which was understood straightforwardly as "democracy" in a wider meaning.

But what, it is still worth asking, does the term *prajātantra* mean in Nepali? Two points should be taken into consideration here. First, as previously mentioned, the word is a newly coined calque to translate the word *democracy*. Second, the word *prajā* has the connotation of a subject of a monarch. Interestingly, an authoritative Nepali Dictionary published in 1983 by the Royal Nepal Academy defines the word *prajātantra* as follows:

> (1) a system of governance operated by the representatives of people elected by the subject (*prajā*) or people (*janatā*); a state system whose power of governance is in the hand of the representatives of people. (2) governance operated by the people, for the people, and by the opinions of and on the advice of the people. (Nepāla Rājakīya Prajnā-Pratiṣṭhāna 2050vs: 865, my translation)

With no difficulty, this definition can be read as an explanation of the term *democracy*. The compatibility of the word with monarchy is not foregrounded, as the word *prajā* is juxtaposed with more neutral word *janatā*. Indeed, it can be said that Nepal under the Panchayat regime was *prajātantra* only in the sense of the first sentence contained in (1), not in the sense of the other definitions. All these points suggest that here the term *prajātantra* was understood as a straightforward equivalent of the Western concept of democracy. This is not the whole story, however. As Malagodi (2013: 136) has pointed out, "the term *prajā* (people) retains a sense of subject-hood: there cannot be a *prajā* unless there is a *rājā* (King)". She continues, "So, the 1990 Constitution, while establishing fundamental rights for all Nepali citizens, implicitly still makes them the King's subjects" (ibid.). Indeed, in the Preamble of the 1959 and 1962

Constitutions, the word *prajā* (subject) was used clearly in contrast with *rājā* (king). In particular, the wording of the Preamble of the 1959 Constitution, "to establish democracy [*prajātantra*] in Nepal by giving fundamental rights to the people [*prajā*]" (śrī 5 ko sarakāra, 2016vs: 1) suggests a strong possibility that the drafters of the Constitution recognized the monarchical connotation of the term.

The 1990 Constitution defined the nation as "a multiethnic, multilingual, democratic (*prajātāntrik*), [. . .] Hindu and Constitutional Monarchical Kingdom". After the restoration of the multi-party system in 1990, not only the government but also the vast majority of politicians continued to use the term *prajātantra* with few problems. At that point, multi-party democracy turned into a true *prajātantra*. On the other hand, some Leftists who wanted Nepal to be a republic already questioned the term in the 1990s. Notably, in the famous forty-point demand sent by Baburam Bhattarai, the Chairman of the United People's Front, Nepal just before the beginning of the People's War, it was not the term *prajātantra* but the terms *gaṇatantra* (republic) and also *janagaṇatantra* (people's republic) that were used, in contrast with *rājatantra* (monarchy). For the mainstream political parties, however, *prajātantra* was something to be defended even into the early 2000s, especially against the King Gyanendra's gradual control over power. In March 2004, for example, I saw activists of major political parties using the slogan "prajātantara jindābād (Hail the democracy)", as well as, "nirankush rajtantra murdabad" (death to the repressive monarchy [or kingship]) in political rallies against the then King Gyanendra in central Kathmandu. Importantly, no one in the demonstration was shouting "rajtantra murdabad" (death to the monarchy).

Things have continued to change, however. The word *prajātantra*, long used as the official translation of *democracy* in Nepal as a constitutional monarchy, was suddenly replaced by a new word, *loktantra*, towards the last period of the direct rule of the King Gyanendra.[26] On the one hand, many Nepalis in that period strongly recognized the importance of the fact that the word *prajā* has the connotation of "subject" of the king. Here, the meanings of a lexeme used as a long-established calque were found to be referentially and socially inadequate. Interestingly, parliamentary parties, unlike Maoist groups, did not use the word *gaṇatantra*, a word already established as the equivalent of *republic*, probably because the word was too straightforwardly aimed against the monarchy itself. The newly employed word *loktantra*, on the other hand, neither signifies the

[26] According to Renslee Doorenspleet and Bal Gopal Shrestha, it was after the television address by King Gyanendar on February 1, 2006, that the Seven-Parry Alliance and the protesters all stopped using the word *prajātantra* (Doorenspleet and Shrestha 2013: 248). For another explanation of the word *loktantra*, see Adhikari (2014: 189–91).

existence of the king nor denotes "republic" directly. The word was quickly and widely accepted throughout Nepal, while the term *prajātantra* became a marked term strongly conveying the idea of "democracy with a king". The term *loktantra* was also quickly adopted in the legal sphere as the equivalent of *democracy*, notably in the 2007 Interim Constitution of Nepal. Nepal became a federal democratic republican state (saṁghīya loktāntrik gaṇatantrātmak rājya) as a result of the fourth amendment to its Interim Constitution in 2008, in the first Constituent Assembly.

Whether and to what extent those who started to use *prajātantra* as the equivalent of *democracy* in Nepali legal documents considered the subtle nuances of *prajā* is largely unknown. But the word has functioned as a possibly not fully intended "word trap" – an intersection between competing and sometimes mutually exclusive social meanings – until many activists recognized its problematic meanings and implications. On the other hand, the shift from *prajātantra* to *loktantra* has not been without difficulties, as the word *prajātantra* was so firmly established as a neutral and transparent equivalent for *democracy*. Indeed, the Democratic People's Republic of Korea is still called Prajātāntrik Janavādī Gaṇatantra Koriyā in Nepali. There is almost certainly no intended irony in this wording.

Conclusion

In this chapter, I have scrutinized some of the complicated effects of translation on the invisible exercise of power through language in the legal sphere, by tracing the trajectories of a single sentence and two key words which frequently appear in modern Nepal legal texts. The eulogy in Sanskrit tacitly exercised the power, from one perspective, to authorize all modern Nepali law including its Constitutions extra-constitutionally. The inherent connotation of the word *dharma*, the term selected to translate the word *religion*, has affected the whole legal and political discourse on "religion", because of its nuances and implications. The word *prajātantra*, long established as the calque for *democracy*, was quite suddenly abandoned by many Nepalis after they problematized some of its various meanings. I have focused on a kind of latently interlingual "in-betweenness" and indeterminacy which Nepali, along with other non-Western and probably also Western, legal documents have had as a result of processes of transplantation and adaptation of already existing conceptualizations between legal systems. It is in part through such indeterminacy of meaning that what might be vaguely called the Nepali Establishment exerted its power, notably by shaping and limiting the range of public discourse. It is within this discursive in-betweenness that legal and political issues in modern Nepal have been negotiated.

REFERENCES

Adhikari, A. (2014). *The Bullet and the Ballot Box: The Story of Nepal's Maoist Revolution*. London and New York: Verso.

Asad, T. (1993). *Genealogies of Religion. Discipline and Reasons of Power in Christianity and Islam*. Baltimore: The Johns Hopkins University Press.

Burghart, R. (1996). *The Conditions of Listening: Essays on Religion, History and Politics in South Asia*. Delhi: Oxford University Press.

Chaturvedi, S. K. (1993). *Nepal: Internal Politics and Its Constitution*. New Delhi: Inter-India Publication.

Doorenspleet, R. and Shrestha, B. G. (2013). "The Ebb and Flow of Nepalese Democracy". In V. Arora and N. Jayaram (eds.) *Routing Democracy in the Himalayas: Experiments and Experience*. London: Routledge, 232–261.

Fezas, J. 2047vs. The Nepalese Juridical Tradition and Its Sources: A List of the Ain Books Kept in the National Archives. *Abhilekha* 8: 121–134.

Fezas, J. (1993). Custom and Written Law in Nepal: The Regulations Concerning Private Revenge for Adultery According to the Code of 1853. In G. Toffin (ed.) *Nepal: Past and Present: Proceedings of the France-German Conference Arc-et-Senance, June 1990*. New Delhi: Sterling Publications, 3–20.

Fisher, W. F. (2001). *Fluid Boundaries: Forming and Transforming Identity in Nepal*. New York: Columbia University Press.

Gaborieau, M. (1977). *Minorités Musulmanes dans le Royaume Hindou du Népal*. Nanterre: Laboratoire d'ethnologie.

Gellner, D. N. (2001). From Group Rights to Individual Rights and Back: Nepalese Struggles over Culture and Equality. In J. K. Cowan, M.-B. Dembour and R. Wilson (eds.) *Culture and Rights: Anthropological Perspectives*. Cambridge: Cambridge University Press, 177–200.

Gellner, D. N., Hausner, S. L. and Letizia, C. (eds.) (2016). *Religion, Secularism, and Ethnicity in Contemporary Nepal*. New Delhi: Oxford University Press.

Gellner, D. N., Pfaff-Czarnecka, J. and Whelpton, J. (eds.) (1997). *Nationalism and Ethnicity in a Hindu Kingdom: The Politics of Culture in Contemporary Nepal*. Amsterdam: Harwood Academic Publishers.

Hangen, S. I. (2010). *The Rise of Ethnic Politics in Nepal: Democracy in the Margins*. Oxford: Routledge.

Höfer, A. (1979). *The Caste Hierarchy and the State in Nepal: A Study of the Muluki Ain of 1854*. Innsbruck: Universitätsverlag Wagner.

Hutt, M. (1994). Drafting the 1990 Constitution. In M. Hutt (ed.) *Nepal in the Nineties: Versions of the Past, Visions of the Future*. Delhi: Oxford University Press, 28–47.

Krauskopff, G. and Meyer, P. D. (eds.) (2000). *The Kings of Nepal and the Tharu of the Tarai: The Panjiar collection of fifty royal documents issued from 1726 to 1971*. New York: Rusca Press, and Krtipur: Centre for Nepal and Asian Studies, Tribhuvan University.

Kymlicka, W. (2001). *Politics in the Vernacular: Nationalism, Multiculturalism, Citizenship*. Oxford: Oxford University Press.

Letizia, C. (2012). Shaping Secularism in Nepal. *European Bulletin of Himalayan Research* 39: 66–104.

Letizia, C. (2013). The Goddess Kumari at the Supreme Court: Divine Kingship and Secularism in Nepal. *FOCAAL: Journal of Global and Historical Anthropology* 67: 32–46. Doi: 10.3167/fcl.2013.670103.

Letizia, C. (2015). Shaping Secularism through the Judiciary in Nepal: Case Studies from the Kathmandu Supreme Court. In Losonczi, P. and Van Herck, W. (eds.) *Secularism, Religion, and Politics: India and Europe*. New Delhi: Routledge, 190–210.

Malagodi, M. (2013). *Constitutional Nationalism and Legal Exclusion: Equality, Identity Politics, and Democracy in Nepal*. New Delhi: Oxford University Press.

Michaels, A. (1997). The King and Cow: On a Crucial Symbol of Hinduization in Nepal. In Gellner D. N., Pfaff-Czarnecka, J. and Whelpton, J. (eds.) *Nationalism and Ethnicity in a Hindu Kingdom: The Politics of Culture in Contemporary Nepal*. Amsterdam: Harwood Academic Publishers, 79–99.

Nawa, K. (2016). Triangulating the Nation-State through Translation: Some Observations by a Japanese Anthropologist Working in Nepal. *International Quarterly on Asian Studies* 47(3–4): 11–31.

Nepāla Rājakīya Prajnā-Pratiṣṭhāna 2050vs(2040vs) *Nepalī Bṛhat Śabdakoṣa*, Kathmandu: Nepāla Rājakīya Prajnā-Pratiṣṭhāna.

nepāla sarakāra, 2066vs. *gaṇatantra sudṛḍhīkarṇa tathā kehī nepāla kanūna saṁśodhana garne aina*. http://www.lawcommission.gov.np/site/sites/default/files/Documents/ganatantra-sudhridikaran.pdf

nepāla sarakāra, 2066–7vs, *Nepāla Aina Saṅgraha* khaṇḍa 1–17. kānūn tathā nyāya mantrālaya, kānūn kitāba vyavasthā samiti.

nepāla sarakāra, 2069vs. *nepālako antarima saṁvidhāna 2063*. http://www.lawcommission.gov.np/index.php?option=com_remository&Itemid=17&func=fileinfo&id=163&lang=en

nepāla sarakāra, 2072vs. *nepālako saṁvidhāna 2072*. http://www.lawcommission.gov.np/?workflow_state=prevailing-laws-constitution

Olivelle, P. (ed.) (2009). *Dharma: Studies in its Semantic, Cultural and Religious History*. Delhi: Motilal Banarsidass.

Pravat, P. S. (2013). The Changing Discourse of Social Justice in Nepal. Arora, V. and Jayaram, N. (eds.) *Routing Democracy in the Himalayas: Experiments and Experiences*. London: Routledge, 262–291.

Sharma, P. R. (1977). Caste, Social Mobility and Sanskritization: A Study of Nepal's Old Legal Code. *Kailash* 5(4): 277–299.

Silverstein, M. (2003). Translation, Transduction, Transformation: Skating Glossando on Thin Semiotic Ice. In P. Rubel and A. Rosman (eds.) *Translating Cultures: Perspectives on Translation and Anthropology*. Oxford: Berg, 75–105.

śrī 5 ko sarakāra, 2011vs. *nepāla antarīma śāsana vidhāna*. [the publisher not mentioned]

śrī 5 ko sarakāra, 2015vs. *nepāla adhirājyako saṁvidhāna*. kāṭhamāḍaũ: kānūna tathā nyāya mantrālaya.

śrī 5 ko sarakāra, 2019vs. *nepālako saṁvidhāna 2019*. kāṭhamāḍaũ: kānūna tathā nyāya mantrālaya.

śrī 5 ko sarakāra, 2020vs. *mulukī aina*. kāṭhamāḍaũ: kānūna tathā nyāya mantrālaya.

śrī 5 ko sarakāra, 2021vs *nepāla aina saṁgraha (2020 sālasamma kāyama rahekā ainahārūko saṁgraha)* khand 1–3. kāṭhamāḍaũ: kānūna tathā nyāya mantrālaya.

śrī 5 ko sarakāra, 2022(1910)vs. *śrī 5 surendra vikrama śāhadevakā śāsanakālamā baneko mulukī aina*. kāṭhamāḍaũ: kānūna tathā nyāya mantrālaya.

śrī 5 ko sarakāra, 2025vs. *nepālako saṁvidhāna 2019 (2023 sāla māgha 14 gate prārambha bhaeko pahilo saṁśodhana sahita milāieko rūpamā)*. kāṭhamāḍaũ: kānūna tathā nyāya mantrālaya.

śrī 5 ko sarakāra, 2047vs. *nepāla adhirājyako saṁvidhāna*. kāṭhamāḍaũ: kānūna kitāba vyavasthā samiti.

śrī 5 ko sarakāra, 2061vs. *pratilipi adhikāra ain, 2059, tathā pratilipi adhikāra niyama, 2061*. kāṭhamāḍaũ: kānūna kitāba vyavasthā samiti.

Vajrācārya, Dhanavajra, ra Ṭekbahādur Śreṣṭha, 2037vs, *śāhakālakā Abhilekha* [pahilo Bhāga]. kāṭhamāḍaũ: nepāla ra eśiyālī anusandhāna Kendra, Tribhuvana viśvavidyālaya.

Whelpton, J. (2005). *A History of Nepal*. Cambridge: Cambridge University Press.

5 The Language of Film and the Representation of Legal Subjectivity in Juno Mak's *Rigor Mortis*

Marco Wan

EDITORS' NOTE TO CHAPTER 5

Marco Wan's chapter explores how people are sometimes viewed as a distraction from or interference with dominant perceptions of law as a matter of principles and proceedings. A less familiar story, because usually only told in fictional and media representations *about* law, rather than within law itself, concerns the personal impacts of law. Such impacts need not be of a kind felt by victims of crime, as valuably articulated in victim impact statements in serious criminal cases, but may be to do with how legal change affects people's lives more generally or collectively, for instance how law is interwoven with personal values or popular culture. Publications do exist which address how law is perceived, understood, and experienced by its subjects, especially ethnographic studies or case narratives which look at life histories behind particular cases. But in general the lived experience of law seems almost necessarily not to touch law itself. Even legal advocacy in adversarial settings restricts what can be said about personal experience in the courtroom, in that examination of witnesses is directed towards building a specific case and obstructing an alternative account of the same events and experiences. Personal dimensions of legal experience are not entirely unspoken, nevertheless. They surface in different kinds of expression, especially in literary and media works that employ a kind of language which is not 'legal' in being concerned with how law functions formally but still deeply concerned with how law works in other respects. In this essay, Marco Wan contends that what he describes as 'legal subjectivity' – a category alongside that of the 'legal subject' or 'person subject to the law' – can be conveyed in socially important ways by the language of film. His example is that of the horror film *Rigor Mortis*, which explores legal uncertainties facing postcolonial Hong Kong. In Wan's account, ghostly figures which appear to symbolize some kind of temporal dissonance in the film may help viewers to think themselves into the legal turbulence that has accompanied changes in political power since 1997. Chinese vampire films were popular in Hong Kong before the imminent handover of sovereignty from Britain to China, and were read at that time, Wan suggests, as reflecting anxieties about what a haunting past might bring to the present. The reappearance of such films in Hong Kong today, he argues, signifies a return of the colonial past. Unlike in the earlier films, however, the main characters in the film he discusses are not so much haunted by their past as destroyed by longing for the past. According to Wan, nostalgia and tension between present and past conveyed by the film's symbolic language are symptomatic of unease over the (in)compatibility of the common law which represents the city's colonial legacy and the new Chinese constitutional order that has become part of the city's legal structure. The legal subject is torn between two sets of values: an experience dramatized in the film's communicative structure. If *Rigor Mortis* on Wan's reading offers an account of how legal subjects can survive such a struggle, that account turns on the idea that unwillingness to let go of what is past or bygone can be dangerous.

The Language of Film and the Representation of Legal Subjectivity in Juno Mak's *Rigor Mortis*

The legal order of postcolonial Hong Kong has often been described as a hybrid system straddling English common law and Chinese civil law. Britain transferred the city's sovereignty back to China in 1997, and since then the constitutional culture of Hong Kong has been characterized by an uneasy tension between the legal vision of its new sovereign power and the conception of law derived from the time of colonial rule. Hong Kongers at times find themselves negotiating between the British and the Chinese legal *nomoi*, and between the past of British governance and the present of Chinese authority. What is the impact on legal subjectivity, or the experience of being a legal subject, in this hybrid constitutional order? And more importantly for the purpose of this volume, what language can we draw on to articulate this new, bifurcated subjectivity? The language of the law, while of course constitutive of this subjectivity, arguably fails to express the experience of living in such a new legal order.

Drawing on a growing literature on 'law and film' studies, and focusing on the example of Juno Mak's film *Rigor Mortis* (2013), this chapter argues that film constitutes an important discourse for understanding legal subjectivity in postcolonial Hong Kong. It shows that the 'language of film' – by which I mean the various grammatical elements involved in how the images on the screen are put together, including symbolism, cinematography, sound, lighting, and graphics – provides a means of expressing this legal subjectivity. As the director Martin Scorsese has recently pointed out, there exists a distinctive '*language* of cinema' which creates meaning visually as well as verbally, and 'that language has taken us in many directions' (2013: unnumbered). In a society dominated by television, video on demand, film, GIFs, and a myriad of image-based advertisements, 'we have no choice but to treat all these moving images coming at us as a language. We need to be able to understand what we're seeing, and find the tools to sort it all out'. In a more academic vein, the law-and-film scholar Richard Sherwin has argued that in an age in which the law has become inextricably intertwined with elements of popular culture, lawyers need to cultivate their 'visual literacy' in order to understand the visual jurisprudence of cinema and the image (2011: 37).[1] Part of being conversant in the 'language of cinema' described by Scorcese, and of developing the 'visual literacy' advocated by Sherwin, is the ability to explore the legal-historical significance of cultural symbols in film. One such cultural symbol is the *geong si* (or 'Chinese hopping vampire') in Hong Kong cinema; the *geong si* was a cinematic icon in the 1980s, and its reappearance at a time of intense legal conflict brought about by unresolved tensions in a complex legal subjectivity is an event which calls out for analysis. A Chinese vampire needs to be distinguished from a 'Western'-style vampire. *Geong sis* are often portrayed in mandarin robes, and the hopping derives from the folkric practice of 'corpse driving' in Ancient China, in which a *fatsi*transported the dead back to their home provinces for burial (Teo 1997: 223). The *fatsis* are said to make the corpses 'hop' with their arms outstretched by means of their incantations. As we will see later, film scholars have argued that the figure of the Chinese hopping vampire can be read as a moment of temporal disturbance in Hong Kong society. This chapter argues that in Mak's film the return of the *geong si* signals the return of the colonial past, and that its unholy resurrection points to a disturbance in the postcolonial present. More specifically, it contends that the uneasy continuation of the past in the present, and the temporal disturbance marked by the reappearance of the dead on the twenty-first-century screen, can be understood as a cinematic metaphor for the entanglements between nostalgia for British colonial rule and the recognition of the reality of Chinese sovereignty that are constitutive of legal subjectivity in post-1997 Hong Kong.

Constitutional Structure and Legal Subjectivity in Postcolonial Hong Kong

The hybridity of the legal system in post-1997 Hong Kong is encapsulated in the formulation 'One Country, Two Systems'. Hong Kong is an integral part of the Chinese state, but at the same time it is supposed to be largely autonomous, and preserves many of the economic, social, and legal structures that characterized the period of British rule. The hybrid structure is clearly stated in the General Principles of the Basic Law, the city's mini-constitution. Though Hong Kong is undeniably 'an inalienable part of the People's Republic of China',[2] it enjoys

[1] On the language of film more generally, see Bordwell (1989) and Dick (2010).

[2] The Basic Law of the Hong Kong Special Administrative Region of the People's Republic of China, Article 1.

'a high degree of autonomy'[3] and retains 'all laws previously in force' under British governance, including 'the common law, rules of equity, ordinances, subordinate legislation and customary law' except for those that contravene the Basic Law.[4] At the time of the retrocession in 1997, the city's mini-constitution, like its residents, was imagined to embody the best of British and Chinese traditions, to be a unique blend of East and West. Despite this rosy view, however, there was already a nascent sense that the two legal systems might not fit seamlessly together, and that the two legal cultures may not be easily compatible. Speaking at Oxford University a few years after the handover, the then Secretary for Justice, Elsie Leung, noted that 'the implementation of the concept of "One Country, Two Systems"' was 'unprecedented' and would be 'by no means an easy task' (2001). She acknowledged that there was 'many a problem left over from history' yet to be resolved in the new constitutional framework, though she concluded that she was confident that 'One Country, Two Systems' would successfully provide a 'model' for the resolution of such problems.

The major constitutional conflicts that have occurred since the handover can be understood as a continuing negotiation between the new, Chinese legal order and the persistence of the common law values and concepts operating in Hong Kong. In 1999, the right of abode saga sparked the first major constitutional controversy. It revolved around the question of whether children born in Mainland China of at least one parent who is a Hong Kong permanent resident would be considered permanent residents in Hong Kong. The Court of Final Appeal ruled in the children's favour. Concerned about an unmanageable influx of people into the city, the Hong Kong government sought an interpretation from the Standing Committee of the National People's Congress in China, a move which led to uproar in the local legal profession.[5] This reaction was in part caused by fundamental differences between the constitutional arrangement under the English legal system, in which the courts interpret the laws, and the arrangement under the Chinese legal system, in which the National People's Congress Standing Committee also has the power to interpret laws. Significantly, under the Basic Law it is this Standing Committee that holds the power of final interpretation. For Hong Kong lawyers trained in the common law, Beijing's interference in the ruling of the final appellate court was tantamount to putting the independence of the local courts under threat. From the Chinese perspective, however, the intervention of the Standing Committee was a proper means of dealing with the right of abode problem. The second major constitutional debate took place in 2002, when the Hong Kong government attempted to introduce national security legislation locally. The proposed law, which covered treason, sedition, theft of state secrets, and subversion, carried maximum life prison sentences for these offences. This led to an unprecedented

3 Basic Law, Article 2. 4 Basic Law, Article 8.

5 For a comprehensive discussion of the cases from the right of abode controversy, see Chen (2002).

demonstration on July 1, or Chinese National Day, in 2003. Organizers estimated that over 500,000 people participated despite the oppressive heat of the summer, compared to their original expectation of 100,000 people. The police placed the figure at 350,000 (CNN, 2003). At the crux of the demonstration was again a fundamental mistrust of the legal culture of China on the part of many Hong Kongers. Accustomed to the freedoms guaranteed by the common law, they were suspicious of the impact the new legislation would have on fundamental rights such as freedom of expression and access to information. It was unclear, for example, whether possession of writings critical of the Communist party would trigger liability, or whether there would be new restrictions on what one could say about the Chinese government. There were also concerns that freedom of association would be undermined, as links with groups banned by the mainland Chinese government could be illegal under the proposed law.[6]

Finally, the more recent debates over electoral reforms can also be seen as a clash between the continuing British legacy and the reality of the new constitutional order. The British government introduced gradual democratization in Hong Kong in the final decades of British rule, and fueled aspirations for full democracy among many Hong Kongers.[7] However, as the sovereign state China has made clear that it has the final say over selection of the city's Chief Executive, and that it would refuse to appoint anyone it regarded as 'unpatriotic'. Qiao Xiaoyang, the chairman of the Law Committee under the National People's Congress, said that only candidates who 'love the country and love Hong Kong' would be considered acceptable to the Central Government, and explicitly ruled out of the race members of the opposition party, many of whom came to political prominence before the handover (But and Lee 2013). 'As long as they insist on confronting the central government, they cannot become the chief executive', he said. Statements such as those by Qiao fueled local discontent, as they gave an impression that the establishment of full democracy in Hong Kong would not be allowed by the Chinese government. The aspiration for genuine universal suffrage can be understood as a continuation of the path to democratic development which began in the final decades of colonial rule, when Hong Kongers were led to believe that the gradual democratization which began with District Board elections was the first step towards full democracy.

The major constitutional events since the handover, then, can be understood as attempts to unravel the entanglements between a continuing commitment to British legal values and systems (whether real, remembered, or imagined) and the realities of the new legal order under Chinese sovereignty. This hybrid

[6] For an analysis of different dimensions of the national security law, see Fu, Petersen, and Young (2005).

[7] For a discussion of constitutional developments in the 1980s, see Chen (1989).

legal framework, perhaps unsurprisingly, houses within it what can be called a 'legal subjectivity', or the lived experience of being a legal subject, that is equally complex; and some Hong Kongers are still in the process of negotiating between, on the one hand, the colonial legacy which has been formative of their subjectivity for so long and a new sense of belonging which they were expected to have towards China on the other. This dual legal subjectivity can be understood as an identity that reflects the hybridity of the city's constitution: both Hong Kong identity and Hong Kong's constitution are products of Chinese and British influence. However, they differ in one crucial respect: whereas constitutional dualities can be resolved by processes of judicial interpretation, incompatibilities in subjectivity or cultural identity express themselves in different ways and are much harder to resolve. The cultural critic Howard Choy has pointed out that for Hong Kongers, 'the question of becoming Chinese again' after the handover 'cannot be discussed without reference to its Britishness', and further argued that their identity had become a 'schizophrenic' one, torn between two sets of values that are hard to reconcile (2007: 55).

The frequent appearance of the colonial flag during demonstrations in Hong Kong around the time of the screening of Juno Mak's film *Rigor Mortis* arguably reflects this conflicted subjectivity. Participants in the anti-government protests regularly displayed the Union Jack on the streets, as they somewhat paradoxically associated colonial rule with a freer, more politically stable regime. One protestor said she supported use of the flag because it represented 'the freedoms we had under the British' (Boehler 2013: unnumbered). She added that the flag 'was a way of expressing the difference in history and values between Hong Kong and the authoritarian People's Republic of China'. A journalist observed that the colonial flag became 'a symbol for those who advocate a distinct cultural and political identity' for the city. However, perhaps it was not necessary to interpret the appearance of the flag as expressive of a demand for an entirely distinct or separate political identity. As another journalist noted, 'calls for secession from the mainland, or independence, have never emerged as mainstream public opinion' (Cheung 2012). Rather, the appearance of the flag could be more simply understood as indicative of the continuing presence of the colonial past in postcolonial Hong Kong. For the generation that had lived through colonial rule, remembrance of the economic prosperity of the 1980s and 1990s, as well as the relative political stability of that period, necessarily influenced how they remember the time of British governance, and for some people these memories led to a sense of nostalgia for British presence. For a younger generation, born in the late 1990s, the time of colonial rule was a blank canvas onto which they could project visions of a less politically divisive society. The flag also recalls a time prior to the intense economic competition from across the border, and can be read as part of a local reaction to 'competition from mainlanders in nearly everything, from hospital beds and baby milk formula to property'. For some Hong Kongers, then, Britishness became a loose association of political stability, economic development, and the guarantee of reliable legal structures. Yu Zhengsheng, a member of the Communist Politburo Standing Committee in China, has noted that 'the Chinese people will not accept some Hong Kongers waving the colonial flag' (Cheung, Lee and Li 2013). The fact that an official from the nation's top advisory body found it necessary to comment on the reappearance of the colonial flag is itself indicative of the perceived intensity of colonial nostalgia in Hong Kong. The colonial past constantly returns, in the symbolic form of the flag, to haunt the new regime.

This context of a continuing British presence in debates about Hong Kong law and identity, and of the constant return of a colonial past which should have been put to rest, provides a new interpretation of the figure of the Chinese hopping vampire in Juno Mak's homage to the vampire films of the 1980s, *Rigor Mortis*. Thinking about the symbol of the *geong si*at the specific legal-historical juncture in which it reappears offers a new way of understanding the endurance of this figure in the Hong Kong film imaginary. *Rigor Mortis* is Mak's directorial debut, and is co-produced with Takashi Shimizu, who has directed a number of internationally acclaimed Japanese horror movies including the series of feature films comprising the *Ju On* franchise. At first sight, the film does not seem to have much to do with questions of Hong Kong law, subjectivity, or coloniality; but more careful reading of the language of film it uses shows a range of implied and symbolic connections. The film opens with Chin Siu Ho, who plays himself and who rose to fame starring in vampire films in the 1980s, moving into a housing estate. His career had ended a long time ago due to the demise of the genre of vampire films, and as his fortune waned his wife and son also abandoned him. Surprisingly, however, he is forced to confront a vampire once again: his neighbor, Mui, turns to dark magic in order to resurrect her beloved husband, but only succeeds in bringing him back as a hopping vampire. The vampire that has been brought back becomes an unstoppable force of evil when it combines with the ghosts of two sisters, one of whom had been raped and subsequently hung herself in Chin's apartment, while the other had been killed trying to rescue her sister from the rapist. Another strand to the narrative concerns the rapist's wife: traumatized by the death of the sisters and the horrific deed of her husband, she goes insane and spends her days wandering around aimlessly in the housing estate. The warden of the estate takes pity on her and her son, and allows them to squat in an unused backroom in the building. Central to the plot are two *fatsis*, or contrasting Daoist shamans with special powers to deal with vampires and other creatures of the undead, who also happen to live on the estate. The evil *fatsi* helps Mui to raise her husband from the dead, while the heroic *fatsi*, Yau, sides with Chin and becomes his ally against the vampire. The final scene however constitutes a narrative turning point: we learn in the final ten minutes of the film that none of the incidents were real. Chin, unable to face the reality of his failure, hangs himself in the housing estate, and the film's *denouement* is that the entire narrative was nothing more than a figment of his imagination, a last effort to revive his glorious past as the star of a hopping vampire movie. Mui's husband had died a long time ago, Yau is just a waiter in an eatery that Chin had walked past, there has been no rape, and there were no dead sisters. The film, then, is about nostalgia and reluctance to let go of one's past. In the following section, I will argue that the figure of the vampire, and the film's broader depiction of the undead, can be read as a representation of Hong Kongers' complex relation to the city's colonial history.

Ghosts and the Presence of the Past

The past is a constant presence in *Rigor Mortis*, and the co-mingling of what has been, what is now, and what is yet to come can be read as a way in which the film language expresses nostalgic sentiments for the colonial past. Ghosts are a constant presence in the film, and critics have pointed out that they can often be read as markers of temporal disturbance in the wider political and constitutional framework. Sek Kei writes that with the signing of the Sino-British Joint Declaration in 1984, through which the return of Hong Kong to China became a certainty, Hong Kongers 'suddenly realized that a spectre is haunting their city – the spectre of 1997, the year when the city's sovereignty returns to Communist China' (1989: 13). Hong Kong's Chinese affiliation, which had been relegated to the past because of the reality of colonial rule, suddenly came back to haunt it. Sek Kei continues by noting that 'the result is a general sense of bewilderment and unease, intangible but undeniably real. Little wonder that whenever we turn our eyes to the silver screen, we keep seeing ghosts'. In the 1980s, these ghosts symbolised anxieties about a Chinese identity which had been relegated to the past but which was not quite dead. In 2013, the year *Rigor Mortis* was shown, ghosts arguably continue to connote a temporal disturbance, but this time, the past which haunts post-handover Hong Kong is the colonial past. The undying nostalgia that finds expression through the waving of the British flag in the anti-government demonstrations outside the cinema is articulated as the symbolism of the ghost in the language of film: the spectral presence that refuses to be laid to rest is like the colonial flag that rises in the protests, something that should be dead and gone and yet insistently returns to haunt Hong Kong. Ghosts, then, can be interpreted as an expression of the affective ties to the past in Hong Kong's legal subjectivity.

Rigor Mortis is populated by ghosts. In the first scene at the eatery where Yau works as a chef, we are told that he is busy preparing food for the regular customers. When he mentions a dish usually ordered by a customer called Lai, another customer reminds him that Lai had passed away. Yau looks up, and says: 'Just because she has passed away doesn't mean she doesn't need to eat!' As he walks away, we catch up a glimpse of Lai's ghost. The ghost is created by superimposing the image of a woman onto the frame, and hence appears more ethereal than the living. The presence of ghosts, in the form of images which we only catch a glimpse of but which are nonetheless present, can be read as a way of embodying those intangible nostalgic sentiments about the colonial past, sentiments which are not quite graspable in the language of the law but which the language of film can express through visual means. This conflation of the past and the present, the state of liminality between the ghostly and the living, is further underscored by the use of lighting in the film: most scenes are in hues of grey and blue, such that the skin tone, the physical surroundings, and the general ambiance of the living and the dead become indistinguishable, and it becomes hard to tell whether we are seeing someone who is living, or someone who has returned another time.

An incident involving Chin early in the film further illustrates this point. When Chin first moves into the estate, he steps outside his apartment to investigate a noise in the corridor, and sees the wife of the rapist. She is dressed in white, and is kneeling on the floor eating the food which had been left on the small altar outside the apartment across the hallway. The food is intended for the hungry ghosts wandering the corridors, and when Chin first confronts her, he – like the audience – is unsure whether she is a ghost or a human being. This uncertainty as to whether someone belongs to the realm of the dead or the living, or whether she belongs to the past or the present, can be understood as the film's way of expressing the constant presence of the colonial past in contemporary Hong Kong. As Chin tries to make sense of her presence in the corridor, we hear music from the vampire film of the 1980s, and again there is a ghostly presence, a procession of the dead which goes through the corridor. This spectral procession, so vivid in the eyes of Chin and by extension the eyes of the viewer, is directly taken from a vampire film of the 1980s. In this scene, the appearance of ghosts from the glorious days of vampire film, coinciding with the days of the colonial regime, figuratively expresses the idea that some Hong Kongers cannot quite let go of their memories. They would rather be haunted by them than admit to themselves that they no longer have any material presence. Nowhere is the co-presence of the living and the dead more insistently thematized than in the figure of Chin himself: for much of the film, we assume that he is still alive, and not until the final scene do we realize that in fact he has already hung himself. However, throughout the film he has a red mark on his neck, where the loop of the rope would have been. In retrospect, we realize that the mark signifies that what we think of as a living person is already dead. But that realization only comes when we look backwards and search for answers in the past.

Finally, it is worth noting the number of the apartment Chin moves into: 2442. In Chinese culture '4' is an unlucky number, and '2442' connotes death and misfortune. More significantly, the number is the same when read either forwards or backwards. Audrey Yue has argued that the notion of (be)hindsight, coined by the American queer theorist and literary critic Lee Edelman, has particular resonance in Hong Kong cinema: 'Hong Kong's identity crisis [...]', she argues, 'was marked by its inability to distinguish the "pre-" from the "post", or the front from the back', and it is precisely this disruption of binary logic which underpins the notion of (be)hindsight within which geographical terms such as forward/backward or front/back overlap and intertwine with temporal concepts such as before/after and past/future (2000: 364). Yue's argument seems to shed light on the significance of the apartment number here. When reading '2442', it is impossible to tell the difference between moving ahead and moving back, progress and regression, between the past and the future because reading the figure in either direction yields the same number. The apartment is a place of death no matter how you read it.

Chinese Hopping Vampires and the Return of History

The most potent symbol for the return of the past in Hong Kong cinema is the Chinese hopping vampire. Critics have often made a link between the figure of the vampire and history. Mak himself noted that Chinese vampires and the folklore of corpse-driving are 'based on a historical time period', and admitted that 'it's the whole vibe that fascinated me' (Napolitano 2013). Film scholar Dale Hudson has observed that 'the specific historical settings of *geong si* films establish the convention that the *geong si* appears during times of political, social, and spiritual imbalance' (2009: 212). As such, their appearance is particularly telling when it comes to analyzing displaced colonial sentiments. He goes on to note that in the 1990s 'the emergence of the *geong si* cycle occurs with a moment of imbalance in Hong Kong following the 1982 discussions of the colony's future'. *Mr. Vampire*, the first and most popular of the vampire films, appeared in 1985, only a year after the Sino-British Joint Declaration, and was followed by a number of sequels between 1986 and 1992. Through the figure of the vampire, each of these films put on screen Hong Kongers' confrontation with their anxieties about the return of the Chinese past that suddenly became palpable because of the certainty of the retrocession.

If the vampires from the films of the 1980s can be read as reflections of anxieties about the return of the Chinese past in the years leading up to decolonization, the release of *Rigor Mortis* in 2013 marks it as a product of postcolonial Hong Kong cinema, and signals that the vampire's relationship to history in this film needs to be configured differently. The past still returns in a monstrous form, as a soulless corpse which does not belong to the contemporary world and which harms all those it comes into contact with. However, in 2013, Chinese sovereignty is the present, and it is the period of colonialism which is configured as history. As in the case of the ghosts, the past that returns is the colonial past. Furthermore, as in the case of ghosts, the vampire stands in for a continuing entanglement with the past in the construction of Hong Kong legal subjectivity. The symbolic significance of the vampire changes: the vampire no longer reflects the horror of the return of a long banished Chinese identity, but can be interpreted as a figure for an interminable longing for the time of colonialism. And the film suggests that such inability to let go of the past can be detrimental to contemporary Hong Kong.

The casting of the *geong si* in *Rigor Mortis* is significant in this respect. The character is played by Richard Ng Yiu Hon, one of the most popular actors in Hong Kong cinema of the 1980s. His filmography includes mostly action films and comedies, though he also starred in a number of horror films, including *Mr. Vampire 3* (1987). His face is instantly recognizable to a Hong Kong audience. By the time he starred in *Rigor Mortis*, he was already 74 years old. Casting Ng in the film has the effect of reminding the audience of the passage of time: the actor who was popular and well-loved in the 1980s is now an old man and, like the genre of vampire films, at the end of his career. As we watch Mui attempt to bring back her beloved husband from the dead, we are also witnessing an attempt to bring back to the screen an ageing actor who had been popular in colonial Hong Kong. The affective ties to the past behind Mui's unholy turn to dark magic can therefore be said to operate on multiple levels: literally, through Mui's love for her husband; more generally, through the audience's fond remembrance for Ng and the lively characters he used to play; and more generally still, through the audience's nostalgic feelings for the colonial past which temporally coincided with the appearance of Ng's most popular films. Furthermore, as in the case of the ghosts, it is at first impossible to tell whether Mui's husband is alive or dead: he tells her he will return in a dream, and it is only after she wakes up that the audience realizes he was already dead.

The desire to bring back the past is represented as a source of evil in the film. The scene in which Mui carries out the ritual of resurrection comes almost directly out of a local horror movie from the 1980s. In accordance with vampire folklore, in order to bring back a loved one from the dead, Mui needs to cover the corpse with earth, close the coffin, and make her wish in blood. The corpse is controlled by an enchanted mask, and Mui is given specific instructions not to remove it, an instruction she subsequently defies. The room in which the ritual takes place is dark and eerily lit by candles, and shades of red in the background connote blood and death. The *fatsi* notes that the resurrection will bring 'the life force from the dark side' into the corpse, and that it constitutes 'a movement against the heavens'. The film presents the Daoist ritual as a form of voodoo or sorcery. The danger of this kind of dark magic becomes apparent immediately after the ritual: as soon as it is over, the *fatsi* starts coughing horribly, and collapses onto the floor as his own life is compromised in order to raise the dead. The insistence on bringing back the past in this way comes at the price of posing a very real danger to one's life in the present.

The complexity of the relationship between present and past is refracted in a sequence in which Mui is in conversation with her husband. He has now been resurrected and is standing in front of her. She is altering his clothes for him, as she used to do when he was alive. This sequence constitutes an astute portrayal of the range of psychological reactions it is possible to have to a past that is yearned for but which is gone forever, a range that encompasses disavowal, recognition, fear, despair, and determination. The sequence opens with Mui speaking to her husband about their daily lives, such as how the weather had turned cold earlier in the day. Yet it quickly becomes apparent that the sequence is not so much a conversation as a monologue: even though Mui is speaking to her husband, she is in fact talking to herself because her husband's corpse shows no sign of comprehending. The moving camera, which follows her as she walks around the corpse, underscores her solitude by leaving her husband's face out of frame. The perversity of engaging in conversation with a corpse suggests that unwillingness to let go of the past is a form of insanity, like inability to differentiate between the living and the dead. To ask a corpse whether he liked the food she prepared for him at dinner is a symptom of delusion. Her unstable mental state is also a form of paranoia: she tells that corpse that she is certain she has gained weight because the people at the eatery next to the housing estate are plotting against her: 'yes, that must be it', she mutters to herself. Mui's monologue seems to suggest that we risk descending into madness if we continue to treat the past as a continuing presence in our lives.

However, Mui's denial is mingled with recognition that her husband is in fact dead; the disavowal is not entirely successful and an element of mental clarity can still be found within her delusion. In the middle of the monologue, she looks up at her husband, and her eyes widen as reality hits her: 'My dear, please don't abandon me. You promised me you'd return!' As she speaks, she starts to sob uncontrollably; she leans forward slightly for support, but realizes that none is forthcoming as the corpse is empty and cannot react to grief. Reluctance to let go of the past, in the form of the beloved husband, is marked by awareness that insisting on its return is also impossible. The same slow, mournful music which plays throughout the entirety of the sequence underscores the continuity of the two states of denial and recognition: there is no single moment at which the reality hits. Rather, the disavowal of death is all the more tragic because it is always colored by the realization that the past cannot return.

In the final part of the sequence, denial takes over once again: her expression hardens and her voice becomes deeper and more certain, as she mentally pushes away reality and becomes determined to indulge in the past. She tells herself that her husband did not eat anything not because he is dead, but simply because he did not like the food she made that night. She also admonishes him for smoking, as if he was a living person whose health could deteriorate. As the sequence ends, the camera focuses on the metallic mask on the face of the corpse, signaling that the mask will become significant later in the narrative: Mui will take it off in a further attempt to revive her husband as she sinks deeper into her delusion. The camera's focus on the mask foreshadows its removal. The cinematography is of course verbally silent, but it is full of meaning, suggesting that our fixation on the past can lead us to do things we will later regret.

The *fatsi* tells Mui that she would be able to bring her husband back to this world more completely if she offered the *geong si* the blood of a child. Mui is at first reluctant to kill, but in the end she leads her neighbor's child to her bathroom where the *geong si* is hiding, and locks him in there. However, the plan goes awry: instead of bringing the empty corpse back to life fully, the sacrifice of the child instills a kind of bloodlust in the *geong si*, and also gives it superhuman strength. The *fatsi* who colludes with Mui is killed during the vampire's rampage, and his dying words to Yau, the other *fatsi* in the estate, are that things had spun out of his control. The guard becomes collateral damage in the process: while he is patrolling the estate, he discovers that the *fatsi* and Mui have been dabbling in black magic, and Mui kills him in the *fatsi*'s apartment so he would not leak their secret. The film suggests that stubborn insistence on bringing back the past, no matter how understandable our feelings of love and nostalgia, will only lead to chaos and despair.

Confronting the Past

The ghosts and the *geong si* in *Rigor Mortis*, both of which signify the disruptive presence of the past, combine in the climax of the film. The two supernatural kinds of being complement each other: the *geong si* is an empty corpse without a spirit, the two sisters are spirits without a physical body. The power of the ghosts is transferred to the vampire, and it becomes virtually unstoppable. Chin's final confrontation with the *geong si* can be read as Hong Kong's final confrontation with the colonial past, represented on screen as a figure that is both powerful and malevolent. It indicates that standing up to the continuing influence of the past is not only difficult, but dangerous, and one may perish in the endeavour.

The confrontation scene places *Rigor Mortis* firmly in the tradition of Hong Kong vampire films, in that it is structured by an amalgamation of elements of kung fu and horror that is characteristic of the genre. Ng Ho has pointed out that 'Hong Kong's "vampire movies" are Kung Fu movies which utilize the revived spirits of the dead', and adds that this stylistic heterogeneity lies behind the success of the original *Mr. Vampire* in 1985 (1989: 29). Chin's battle with the *geong si* is highly choreographed: the summersaults, the parrying, and the outstretched palms are all directly taken from local kung fu movies. Mak reinvigorates this original stylistic innovation by updating the technology; the computer-generated imagery adds a nightmarish quality to the scene and underscores that the fight takes place in the realm of the supernatural. For example, when the vampire forces Chin to the ground, the cement floor suddenly turns into liquid, and Chin safely passes through the ground and falls into a body of water.

Chin is no match for the vampire. After all, how does one destroy the force of a past that one nonetheless wants to hold on to? However, there is a turning point in the confrontation scene: dawn approaches, and the vampire is burned alive under the glare of the red sun. The symbolic significance of the sun is worth unpacking. The camera focuses on the bright red sun for several seconds, and the sunrise changes the entire color scheme of the sequence: the grey and blue tone which had been dominant throughout the film is momentarily displaced by the sunlight. In a Chinese context, the most famous allusion to a bright red rising sun is the song *East Is Red*, which is adapted from a folksong and glorifies Mao Zedong. It was the *de facto* anthem of the Cultural Revolution, and an integral part of Mao's efforts to establish his personality cult. In fact, it was 'so totemic that it was first sound broadcast back to earth when China successfully placed a satellite into orbit in 1970' (Foster 2009). The song opens with the lines: 'The East is red, the sun rises. From China comes Mao Zedong.' The Chairman is thus portrayed as the light guiding the nation. The song also uses the sun as a metaphor for the Communist party: 'The Communist Party is like the sun. When it shines on a place, it will become bright. Where there is the communist party, there is liberation of the people'. In this context, the rising sun in the film appears evocative of the symbol of the sun in a song like the *East Is Red*, and can be read as a symbol of Chinese patriotism. The redness of the sun also evokes the official colour of the Communist Party. The vampire is burned to ashes by sunlight, and its destruction seems to indicate that the unwanted presence of the colonial past can be destroyed when Hong Kongers finally embrace the new Chinese sovereign and take pride in new allegiance to it. 'Where there is the Communist Party, there is liberation of the people': the confrontation scene in *Rigor Mortis* arguably reflects the sentiments of the *de facto* Chinese anthem in a symbolic register.

However, the film also seems to suggest that feelings of colonial nostalgia cannot be banished so easily, nor can the sun be so easily embraced. As the *geong si* burns to the ground, Mui appears on the scene and looks around her with sadness in her eyes. Her gaze falls on her former husband. She says 'My dear, why don't we go. We should go, ok?' Then, picking up a shard of broken glass on the ground, she slits her throat and collapses. Her suicide can be interpreted in a number of ways. It could be a gesture of remorse, as she kills herself to make up for the suffering she has caused other people. It could be a gesture of despair, as she becomes utterly lost from her encounter with dark magic and can no longer face life. In the present analytic frame, it could be further interpreted as an indicator of her inability to let go of the past: faced with a life in which she must accept that her beloved husband is truly gone, she would rather kill herself than continue to live. The film suggests that letting go of the past also means putting an end to who one is. One cannot live without the continuing presence of the past, even if one believed this presence is a monstrous one.

The final scene of the film returns the viewer to the reality within the film: Chin is already dead, the vampire and the ghosts never existed, and the evil *fatsi* who used black magic to resurrect the dead is in fact an employee at the morgue. What, then, of the experience of living with the complex, bifurcated legal subjectivity which the return of the *geong si* figure can be understood to represent? One answer lies in the final scene. The audience is told that someone has come to identify Chin's corpse. 'What is your relationship to the deceased?' this person is asked. The man replies: 'I'm his son'. The appearance of Chin's grown-up son gestures to the new generation in Hong Kong. Would they be able to let go of their colonial past, or would they, like Chin and Mui, be unable to live in its absence? Perhaps because of its own preoccupation with figures of the past, the film does not give us any easy answers about the future: the final scene is shot with a camera that is out of focus, and it is impossible to see the son clearly. The ending seems to suggest that any picture of how the new generation of Hong Kongers will deal with the city's colonial past remains hazy.

REFERENCES

The Basic Law of the Hong Kong Special Administrative Region of the People's Republic of China

Boehler, P. (2013). 'Disgruntled Hong Kong Embraces Union Jack as Symbol of Freedom'. *Asian Correspondent*, 25 January.

Bordwell, D. (1989). *Making Meaning: Inference and Rhetoric in the Interpretation of Cinema*. Cambridge, MA: Harvard University Press.

But, J. and Lee, C. (2013). 'Opponents of Beijing Ineligible to Be CE: Top Chinese Official'. *South China Morning Post*, 24 March.

Chen, A. H. Y. (1989). 'From Colony to Special Administrative Region: Hong Kong's Constitutional Journey'. In R. Wacks (ed.) *The Future of the Law in Hong Kong*. Hong Kong: Oxford University Press, 76–126.

Chen, A. H. Y. (2002). 'Hong Kong's Legal System in the New Constitutional Order: The Experience of 1997–2000'. In J. F. Chen, Y. W. Li and J. M. Otto (eds.) *Implementation of Law in the People's Republic of China*, 213–245.

Cheung, G. (2012). 'Beijing finds Hongkongers' Nostalgia for Colonial Era Hard to Fathom'. *South China Morning Post*, 1 October.

Cheung, G., Lee, C. and Li, J. (2013). 'Displays of Hong Kong's Colonial Flag Offend Beijing'. *South China Morning Post*, 7 May.

Choy, H. Y.F. (2007). 'Schizophrenic Hong Kong: Postcolonial Identity Crisis in the *Infernal Affairs* Trilogy'. *Transtext(s)s Transcultures: Journal of Global Cultural Studies* 3: 52–66.

Dick, B. F. (2010). *Anatomy of Film*. Boston: Bedford/St. Martin's.

Foster, P. (2009). 'East Is Red is the Siren Song of China's New Generation'. *Telegraph*, 10 May.

Fu, H. L., Petersen, C. and Young, S. N. M. (eds.) (2005). *National Security and Fundamental Freedoms: Hong Kong's Article 23 Under Scrutiny*. Hong Kong: Hong Kong University Press.

Hudson, D. (2009). 'Modernity as Crisis: Geong Si and Vampires in Hong Kong Cinema'. In Brown, J. E., and Picart, C. J. (eds.) *Draculas, Vampires and Other Undead Forms: Essays on Gender, Race and Culture*. Baltimore: Scarecrow Press, 203–235.

'Huge Protests Fills Hong Kong Streets' (2003). *CNN.com*, 2 July. Accessed June 13, 2015. http://edition.cnn.com/2003/WORLD/asiapcf/east/07/01/hk.protest/

Leung, E. (2001). 'The Continuity of Hong Kong's Legal System', Speech at the Asia-Pacific Society, Oxford University, 4 March.

Napolitano, D. (2013). 'Fresh Life for Hong Kong's Vampire Genre'. *Wall Street Journal*, 24 October.

Ng, H. (1989). 'Abracadaver: Cross-Cultural Influences in Hong Kong Vampire Movies'. In C. T. Li (ed.) *Phantoms of Hong Kong Cinema*. Hong Kong: HKIFF/Urban Council, 29–35.

Scorsese, M. (2013). 'The Persisting Vision: Reading the language of Cinema'. *New York Review of Books*, August.

Sek, K. (1989). 'The Wandering Spook'. In C. T. Li (ed.) *Phantoms of Hong Kong Cinema*. Hong Kong: HKIFF/Urban Council, 13–16.

Sherwin, R. K. (2011). *Visualizing Law in the Age of the Digital Baroque: Arabesques and Entanglements*. Abingdon: Routledge.

Teo, S. (1997). *Hong Kong Cinema: The Extra Dimensions*. London: BFI.

Yue, A. (2000). 'Preposterous Hong Kong Horror'. In K. Gelder (ed.) *The Horror Reader*. London: Routledge, 364–374.

Part III

Written in Silence: Hidden Social Meanings in Legal Discourse

6 Let the Fingers Do the Talking: Language, Gesture and Power in Closing Argument

Gregory Matoesian and Kristin Enola Gilbert

EDITORS' NOTE TO CHAPTER 6

In terms of the language used, advocacy is generally acknowledged as more multimodal than legal drafting or interpretation. Tempo, tone of voice, intonation and other prosodic and paralinguistic features have been discussed both by lawyers offering training and by linguists offering analysis (e.g. Conley, O'Barr and Lind 1979; Findley and Sales 2012). Less attention is typically given to gesture and movement within available space, however, partly because these aspects of communication are less precisely understood. Yet photographic records show public speakers ranging from actors and local politicians all the way through to Adolf Hitler rehearsing speech in front of a mirror, making meticulous decisions about facial expression and accompanying gestures. Powerful, even coercive speakers persuade not only through their voice but by means of gaze, facial expression, hand gestures and overall body movement. One result, for later audiences and scholars, is that there is inevitably a loss in reading print collections of famous speeches (and less of a loss, but still some, in listening to audio recordings).

Even though courtroom discourse is so clearly multimodal, it is still the case that most research has focused more narrowly on written text. In the following essay, by contrast, Greg Matoesian and Kristin Enola Gilbert present an account of how courtroom lawyers synchronize speech, gesture and gaze in putting forward their cases. The authors focus in particular on closing argument, when lawyers have a final opportunity to accentuate their previous submissions. By analyzing video recordings of the Kennedy Smith rape trial (*State v. Smith*, No. 91- 5482 CF-A-02 (Fla. Cir. Ct. 1990)), Matoesian and Gilbert show how gestures can be deployed by an attorney to provide visual cues which assist in imagining scenarios and concepts. While this extra dimension in expression is easily noticeable, the mechanisms through which gestures achieve their effect are not well understood.

Matoesian and Gilbert work in detail through illustrative sequences in order to introduce a set of tools that may allow researchers in future to analyze the inevitably complex ways that non-verbal and verbal communication work together in producing meaning. Such analysis raises further, related questions about the distribution of rhetorical resources in the hierarchical organization of courtrooms, notably questions regarding which participants are given opportunities during proceedings to reinforce their point-of-view by means of more expansive rhetorical gestures.

REFERENCES

Conley, J. M., O'Barr, W. M. and Lind, E. A. (1979). The Power of Language: Presentational Styles in the Courtroom. *Duke Law Journal* 1978(6): 1375–1399.

Findley, J. D. and Sales, B. D. (2012). *The Science of Attorney Advocacy: How Courtroom Behaviour Affects Jury Decision Making*. Washington, DC: American Psychological Association.

Let the Fingers Do the Talking: Language, Gesture and Power in Closing Argument

According to both forensic linguists and legal scholars, closing argument constitutes the most dramatic moment of an adversary trial. Rosulek (2010: 218) refers to closing as the "master narrative of the crime, investigation and trial." Stygall (2012: 380) characterizes it as a "powerful moment" in the proceedings. Heffer (2010: 212) states that it is "often considered by trial lawyers as their main performance event." Similarly, legal scholars emphasize the importance of closing argument for evaluating testimony. Mauet (2010: 387) mentions how closing represents the "culmination of the trial": an epistemological crescendo where jurors "are looking to see which lawyer *really believes* his side should win" (Mauet 2010: 398); and Tanford (1983: 133) describes how closing allows attorneys "to organize and emphasize favorable evidence, rebut your opponent's allegations, suggest ways the jury can resolve conflicting testimony, explain the law and show how the testimony leads to a verdict in your favor." Perhaps the main function of closing is to weave disparate strands of testimony from examination into a persuasive and coherent narrative.

Although closing represents the legal crescendo of a case, researchers like Rosulek (2008: 549) find that it remains "understudied" by comparison with other discursive events in the trial. Just as ironic, the few studies that focus on closing argument limit their analysis to speech, despite Mauet's (2010: 394–400) recommendation that attorneys should use "forceful" and "persuasive" gestures "to highlight major points of argument." In this chapter we examine this "understudied" – indeed totally neglected – aspect of closing argument: how gestures modulate the affective intensity and epistemic certainty of speech. We analyze how gestures synchronize with speech not only to orchestrate the rhythm of utterances but also to persuade jurors of the truth of one side and falsity of the other. We demonstrate how closing functions as a multimodal narrative in which gesture, gaze and speech transform legal evidence into institutionally organized forms of persuasive oratory: how attorneys foster the impression that they really believe their side should win by organizing and emphasizing favorable points of evidence, including explicitly by counting off and counting up inconsistencies in the prosecution's case. In our analysis, we also illustrate the wider relevance of multimodal conduct for the study of legal language and power.

The Relevance of Gesture and Multimodal Conduct for Legal Interaction

In Tiersma's (1999: 1) classic text, he states that "Our law is a law of words," and the burgeoning literature in language and law showcases how language anchors the interactional infrastructure through which evidence, statutes and precedent are forged into legal relevance. Even so, recent developments across a range of interdisciplinary scholarship show that language involves more than just words. McNeill (1992, 2005, 2012) and Kendon (2004) have demonstrated how ad hoc hand movements or speech-synchronized gestures represent mutually supportive partners in the production of meaning and utterance construction.[1] That is, co-verbal gestures form the visual and imagistic dimension of language, a co-expressive – not redundant – modality in the semiotic division of labor. Working as a semiotic gestalt, the two modalities execute a more coherent course of communicative action – conveying different aspects of meaning – than either could convey alone.[2]

If language indeed includes this visual dimension of semiotic practice, then how do gestures and other forms of multimodal conduct contribute to an understanding of language and law? A mere glimpse of trial interaction reveals that attorneys and witnesses often beat out the rhythm of their words to

[1] That is, the meaning of gesture is context-sensitive and emerges at the moment of speaking. The integration of speech-gesture emerges in the temporal synchronization of the two modalities, in which the stroke or meaning-bearing phase of the gesture co-occurs with its speech counterpart. Unlike the segmental, sequential and conventional features of speech, gesture is global (the meaning of the part emerges from the whole), non-combinatoric and, for the most part, imagistic. According to McNeill (1992) this definition excludes gestures with language-like properties, such as sign language, emblems (V for victory etc.) and so on, which impart meaning independently of speech.

[2] In this regard, gesture provides a manual modality for expression and imparts visual imagery not necessarily conveyed through speech. According to Goldin-Meadow (2003: 9) "gesture and speech never convey exactly the same information," something we will show in striking detail.

dramatize evidential points of significance, bestow an affective or emotive stance to their words and, as we will see, cumulate and quantify key strands of testimony. Legal actors may use gestures in concert with both gaze and speech to point out focal objects of attention. In fact, it is rare to find a moment when courtroom participants fail to gesture and/or deploy other forms of multimodal conduct in concert with speech.[3]

Beat Gestures

Given its crucial role in the organization of communicative practice, how does gesture function in concert with speech? McNeill's typology of "iconic, metaphoric, deictic, beat quartet" provides an analytic point of departure (McNeill 1992, 2005). Iconic gestures resemble their referents; metaphorics depict abstract content; deictics locate referents through pointing; and beats orchestrate the visual rhythms of speech and foreground important information. This last gestural form is our focus in relation to closing argument.

McNeill (2012: 15) defines beat gestures as "yellow highlighters that beat out musical time" and in the process stress significant syllables and words. Like an orchestra conductor's baton, they parse speech into prominent, visual segments (Streeck 2008). Experimental research confirms that beats not only signal emphasis but also influence the production and interpretation of prosodic prominence in their speech counterparts. According to Krahmer and Swerts (2007: 396), the "visual beat leads to a change in how prominence is realized in speech . . . and how it is perceived by observers." As they note, speech-synchronized beats increase the persuasiveness of a message compared to words, phrases or clauses without them. Maricchiolo et al. (2009: 244) found similar results: "Experimental design with control groups shows that beat gestures have an important effect on receivers' perceptions of communicative effectiveness, and persuasiveness of the message."

In this study, we show how a novel type of speech-synchronized beat not only orchestrates the rhythmic pulse of closing argument and foregrounds key strands of evidence but also, more substantively, cumulates and expands inconsistencies against the prosecution's case. That is, such beats engineer emergent forms of propositional imagery in addition to and simultaneously with their more orthodox rhythmic function, producing a multifunctional dimension of meaning that cannot be conveyed as richly through speech alone.[4]

[3] Of course in the U.S. witnesses must raise their right hand to take the oath before they can testify.

[4] According to McNeill (2005: 40) beats exhibit little structural variation in form and consist of simple up-down "flicks of the hand(s)." Though they mark points of speaker emphasis they do not represent or depict semantic content. In other words, they are non-imagistic (Kendon 2004: 99–100). As we (Matoesian and Gilbert 2015) have shown previously, however, and as we argue here, beats are much more complex than McNeill and others such as Goldin-Meadow

Along a different yet simultaneous multimodal dimension, the attorney superimposes gaze-shifting movements of participation onto rhythmic beats to foster the impression that he *really believes his side should win.* Following an ethnographic overview of the trial, the first section of the chapter demonstrates how precise coordination of speech with gesture projects multiple inconsistencies in the opposing side's case: how co-speech beats contribute to the epistemic calibration of certainty and hyper-persuasive affect through the poetic delivery of the unfolding text. The next section elaborates on the use of this rhythmically infused gesture and shows how it functions ideologically as well as persuasively in oratorical practice. As the defense attorney lets his fingers do the talking he not only magnifies the prosecution's inconsistencies but also shapes and quantifies them in poetically organized and embodied forms of discursive power.

Background of the Case

The Kennedy Smith rape trial was one of the most widely publicized and watched criminal trials of the twentieth century, and pitted charismatic defense attorney, Roy Black, against prosecuting attorney Moira Lasch. After an evening at a popular nightclub, Patricia Bowman claimed that on March 30, 1991, at 3 A.M. William Kennedy Smith raped her at the Kennedy estate in West Palm Beach, Florida. The trial took place in November–December 1991, and Smith was acquitted of second-degree sexual assault. In closing argument Black raised two themes that we address in this chapter. First, the prosecuting attorney claimed that Smith had deliberately evaded police requests for submission of evidence. Second, although the rather large and athletic Smith tackled the petite Bowman on the lawn of the estate, there was neither damage to her clothing nor marks on her body from the collision. As we will see next, Black uses these twin themes to develop inconsistencies in the prosecution's case through a novel form of staccato-like gesture that hammers home a significant piece of evidence: what we refer to as *interdigital beats* or the right index finger moving up and down the digits of the left hand.

Interdigital Beats and Obstructing Justice

We begin with example 1, in which Black argues that, in contrast to the prosecuting attorney's closing argument, the defendant never obstructed the police investigation, even surrendering voluntarily when charges were brought.

(2003: 8) have indicated. Rather than functioning as off-propositional flicks of the hand, beats may, at specific moments, exhibit considerable structural variation in form and invoke semantic imagery along with their orthodox rhythmic function and may do so simultaneously. In our view, beats are, at specific moments of discourse, multifunctional.

001 And what happens when he finds out about the allegations?

[((two open palms in front of body))

002 He calls (0.5) and *talks* to people at the home

[((left arm lateral open palm beat and hold))

003 (.)

004 He gets a *lawyer* (.) who immediately gets in *touch* with them

[((left arm lateral open palm beat)) [((lateral open palm beat))

005 (.)

006 He voluntarily

[((hits left little finger with right index finger and holds))

[((gaze at little finger for 0.5 seconds over the volitional adverb))

007 turns over all the

[((gaze returns to jury from the gaze at the finger))

008 *samples* that they want

[((IB = interdigital beat; pushes down little finger with right index finger))

009 *photographs*

[((IB on ring finger))

010 (0.6)

011 uh::: (0.4) *everything*.

[((IB on middle finger and hold))

[((highest elevation on upstroke over delay marker+vowel stretch))

Example 1 (22 seconds)

In line 1, Black poses a rhetorical question synchronized with a two-handed open palm gesture (an open palm supine, Kendon 2004). According to Muller (2004: 244), such a gesture possesses an emphatic function, offered here as a puzzle that the defense attorney proceeds to answer with a poetic listing of items (see example 1 line 1). In lines 2, 4 and 7 Black crafts a poetic metricalization of third-person pronouns and action verbs that generates a rhythmic listing of items ('he calls', 'he gets', 'he turns over'), highlighting the significance of each individual piece of evidence in the series. Expansion of the listing tokens (or particulars related to the general interrogative 'what happens' in line 1) projects onto the extralinguistic world of evidence to produce a cumulative effect against the prosecution's claims about obstructing justice: that the defendant never hindered the police investigation but cooperated voluntarily. Moreover, the attorney employs the phrasal verb in line 7 ('turns over') as the interactional platform to launch an embedded series of noun phrases in lines 8, 9 and 11 ('the samples', 'photographs', 'everything'), with noticeably marked stress on each for emphasis.

Example 1 line 001

In lines 2 and 4 he inserts an even more intricate lamination, or embedding of poetic detail, consisting of multimodal layers of inclusion. The defense attorney repeats a lateral open palm beat with the left arm fully extended and synchronized with the respective lexical affiliates: 'calls', 'gets' and 'gets' (see example 1 line 2). The upstroke of each beat occurs on the pronoun in lines 2 and 4 and the *wh*-relative in line 4 while the stroke or meaning-bearing phase of the gesture occurs on the action verb.

Moreover, the phrasal motion verb in line 7 ('turns over') not only serves as the staging point for launching the laminated pattern of NPs but also acts as a rhythmic anchor delivering an ascending progression of gestural beats that unfurls incrementally from the loosely furled hand, a process that unfolds as follows.

Example 1 line 002

In line 6, Black activates space-shifting movements from the extended left arm to a repetitive series of *interdigital beats*, in which the tip of the extended right index finger lands on and ascends up the unfurling fingers of the left hand. To contextualize the shift, he coordinates beat on the little finger with marked gaze over the volitional adverb (relating to the willingness of the agent) and little finger (see example 1 line 6). As Muller (2008: 236) mentions: "Directing the gaze at something . . . indicates speaker's focal attention" and "turns the gesture into an interactively significant object." In this instance, gazing at the little finger while simultaneously hitting it functions as a pointing gesture to signal that the gesture possesses significant evidential import and that the jury should also look at it (see Streeck 1993: 286). Moreover, he maintains gestural position with the right hand index finger latched onto the little finger of the left hand as he shifts gaze from the finger to the jury on the phrasal verb in line 7.

Example 1 line 006

However, the significant object of attention is not merely the index finger hitting the little finger of the opposite hand. More importantly, the attorney's gaze draws attention to the forthcoming interdigital list superimposed over the NPs ('samples', 'photographs', 'everything'), which the beat on line 6 activates with the hit gesture.

In line 8 Black delivers an ascending progression of interdigital increments, which begins (as noted earlier) with the tip of the right index finger pushing down the tip of the little finger on the left hand. As we have seen, the beat lands on the volitional adverb, well ahead of the NP token ('samples'). As a demonstration of the temporal synchrony between speech and gesture Black "holds" the gesture – with the right index finger merely touching the little finger of the left hand – to manage the online pace of the gesture-speech ensemble, adjusting and readjusting timing in order to synchronize precise coordination with utterance construction. When the noun finally "arrives," the gestural hold on the little finger gets pushed down from the "landing" or touching position to coordinate arrival with its lexical affiliate. In so doing, he evokes a type of visual imagery that, when one object hits another, there will be a conspicuous reaction (a point we return to later).

The next beat ascends up the ladder of the unfurling hand on 'photographs,' so that the right index finger hits and pushes down the ring finger of the left hand (see example 1 line 9). In line 11, the set-marking tag 'everything' co-occurs with the beat on the middle finger and fosters an impression that other as yet unmentioned inconsistencies might be included under its auspices (see example 1 line 11). It is also synchronized improvisationally with its gestural counterpart, as Black makes online adjustments and readjustments in the speech-gesture ensemble to manage the interactional contingencies that arise (Kendon, 2004). Similar to the beat on 'samples,' the right index finger begins upstroke on the delay marker and lands on the middle finger during the 0.4-second pause. However, the tag has not arrived; so the index finger holds position on the middle finger till it does. Notice in particular how the delay marker and pause work as interactional resources to manage coordination between speech and gesture, making online adjustments to execute temporal spacing between the two modalities. That is, the right index finger maintains beat position to wait for the set marking tag to catch up, as if maintaining a holding pattern for one another, then hits and pushes down the middle finger. This demonstrates in vivid detail how speech and gesture are executed conjointly as a speech-gesture ensemble.

In this rhythmic interplay of fingers, Black provides evidence that the defendant, in contrast with stereotypic beliefs about rapists, cooperated voluntarily with the police investigation. In the visual infrastructure where such sociocultural identities emerge, he orchestrates a polyrhythmic and multimodal expansion of inconsistent evidence against the prosecution's case on the issue of obstructing justice. By 'polyrhythmic,' here, we mean the repetition of action

Example 1 line 009

Example 1 line 011

verbs, NPs, beat gestures and marked stress on significant points of evidence, creating a state of involvement with the jury and sense of cohesion in the closing narrative. By 'multimodal' we mean an improvisational integration among gesture, gaze and speech that modulates the affective intensity and epistemic certainty of the attorney's persuasive performance. Together, these features yield an intricately balanced metricalization of oratorical power that not only magnifies the inconsistencies but counts them as well. Indeed, Black's unfolding segmentation of individual items allows jurors to focus attention on the discrete accumulation of favorable evidence contained in the list. Rhythmic repetition in the speech-gesture ensemble produces a pragmatic emphasis in which each individual item of evidential significance stands out, like each individual digit in the unfurling hand, allowing the jury to visualize the adding-up effect in a dynamic spatio-temporal movement that cannot be captured as richly through speech alone.[5]

Interdigital Beats and the Embodied Resistance Ideology

In her classic study of rape trial discourse, Ehrlich (2001) analyzed how defense attorneys organized their side of the case around what she referred to as the "utmost resistance" ideology: a powerful sociocultural practice designed to generate inconsistencies in the victim's narrative. 'Utmost resistance' – a

[5] As Jakobson (1960: 356) notes, this is the poetic function of language or a "focus on the message for its own sake." Tannen (1989: 50) also finds that repetition is "evaluative and emphasizes a point.... Repetition of phrases establishes a list-like rhythm, giving the impression that... it constitutes a long list, longer even than the one given.... The evaluative effect of the list is to communicate that the speaker finds the length of the list impressive – and so should the listener." Here we can see that the poetic function applies to multimodal conduct as well.

once-codified legal hurdle for the allegation of sexual assault – required the victim to fight off the attack physically until all resistance was overcome by overwhelming male force. By way of broad analogy, this section examines how the defense attorney mobilizes powerful inconsistencies through interdigital beats in the production of what we call an *embodied resistance ideology*, a requirement that evidence of resistance must be visible on the victim's clothing.

As mentioned earlier, Bowman claimed that the large and athletic Smith (six foot three and two hundred pounds) tackled her on the lawn of the estate after chasing her at "full tilt"; yet there was neither damage to her clothing nor marks on her body after (what Black referred to as) this "tremendous impact." In the following examples he raises the condition of Bowman's clothing after the impact.

In examples 2–4, the defense attorney uses a type (or general) category to start each narrative segment, then unpacks that type through tokens (or particular details). In example 2, he organizes the type around a forensic expert's 'minute' examination of Bowman's dress, while in example 3 he announces that the state forensic examiners even used a 'microscope.' At a finer level of granularity (example 3 line 1), Black leans his upper torso into the stressed type component 'microscope' to deliver a litany of referential detail that explicates the type. The experts not only looked at 'everything' but looked at everything 'with a microscope,' finding 'no grass stains,' 'abrasions,' 'cuts,' 'rip,' 'mud,' 'dirt,' 'soil' (lines 2–8). For still further emphasis, he produces a 1.2-second prolonged hold on the instrumental role (line 1, example 3), contextualized by an accelerated downward gesture and noticeably marked recoil off the bottom of the downstroke.[6] More formally, the hold gets built off the top of the recoil in the form of an open hand supine (or right hand palm up) gesture, as if to say: "what more could be done to find any damage to the clothing?" In this instance, Black's gestural intensifier transforms the speech event (one of listing or describing) to an evaluation of the event being described (i.e. instructing the jury how to interpret subsequent speech). As Kendon (2004: 270) suggests, such a gesture "makes a comment on something that was just said" or in this case what will be said, producing an interpretative frame for the subsequent listing. Example 2 constitutes a similar pattern. Here Black executes a 'minute' discursive analysis (lines 3–8) of the dress superimposed over the 'minute examination by Barbara Carabello' (the forensic expert in line 1 who found 'no grass stains,' 'no dirt,' etc.). Both cases demonstrate in vivid detail how referential text (or what we are saying about something) gets mapped onto interactional text (or what we are doing now) to deliver a persuasive evaluation with all multimodal cylinders firing (Silverstein 1998).[7]

6 Occasionally, the gesture stroke (or meaning-bearing phase of the gesture) will be followed by a post-stroke hold, which keeps the stroke phase in play, often for emphasis.

7 Put another way, both instances display a parallelism between narrated and narrating events.

B^ = Intradigital Beat or up down push on the same digit with right index fingerlatched onto left little finger and closed into a fist shape

IB = interdigital beat

001 The examination of the dress was done minutely (.) by

[((gaze at finger)) [((B^ [((B^ [((B^ [((B^ [((B^

[((gaze returns to jury

002 Barbara Carabello ((lowered volume))

(0.6)

003 There's no *grass* strains (0.4)

[((IB little finger))

004 There's no *dirt* (0.4)

[((IB ring finger))

005 There's no *particles* (.) of grass (0.3)

[((IB middle finger))

006 There's no *mud* (0.4)

[((IB index finger))

007 There's no *chips* of concrete (0.4)

[((IB thumb))

008 no little *stones* (0.3)

[((B2 = vertical parallel two-hand gesture))

009 *no* ***nothing*** (1.0) on this dress at all (0.5)

[((criss-crossing lateral gesture in front of body with both hands/palms down

[((eyes close/gaze downward on the double-negative))

010 N'yet this dress (.) ha::d (.) a *tremendous impact*

[((B2)) [((B2)) [((B2)) [((B2)) [((B2))

B2 = two hand parallel vertical (up/down) beats

Example 2 (23 seconds)

B1 = One hand vertical/up-down beats/chops

001 They looked at everything with a ***microscope*** (1.2) n found absolutely nothing

[((B1 + hold)) [((B1))

(2.1)

002 Not a single *grass stain* (.)

[((gaze at finger)) [((IB starting with little finger))

003 no *abrasion* (.)

[((IB

004 no *cuts* (.)

[((IB

005 no *rip* (.)

[((IB

006 no *mud* (.)

[((IB on thumb))

007 no *dirt* (.)

[((IB on index finger on down slope))

008 no *soil*

[((IB on middle finger on down slope with 1.4 second post stroke hold))

[((1.4 second post stroke hold) on *soil*)

009 *Nothing.*

[((B2 = two hands open palms vertical parallel gesture))

Example 3 (11 seconds)

B2 = Two handed open palms vertical/up-down beats

001 In the weave of the pantyhose (.) there's ***ab*** *solutely*

[((B2 [((B2 [((B2 [((B2 [((B2

002 *no* evidence.

[((B2 [((B2

(0.5)

003 There's no *sand.*

[((gaze at little finger)) [((IB-little finger

(.)

004 There's no *dirt.*

[((IB-ring finger

(.)

005 There's no *grass particles.*

[((IB-middle finger

(0.5)

006 There's no *soil.*

[((IB-index finger

(.)

007 There's no *mud.*

[((IB-thumb

(.)

008 *There's none whatsoever.*

[((B2 = two hand vertical palms parallel))

Example 4 (11 seconds)

Example 4, however, departs from the agentive role exemplified in examples 2 and 3. Instead it moves directly to material evidence: the victim's pantyhose. Even so, a striking similarity may be noted in type organization of examples 3 and 4. The defense attorney organizes evidential findings around the epistemic stance adverb 'absolutely' (the experts 'found absolutely nothing' and 'there's absolutely no evidence'), signaling degree of commitment to and level of certainty about the proposition. But there is more to 'absolutely' in both uses that bears scrutiny here, more than lexical/grammatical encoding of epistemic stance through the degree adverb. While 'absolutely' signals epistemicity at the level of grammar, it also co-occurs, first, with two-handed parallel (palms facing each other) beats in example 4 and, second, with one-handed vertical chops in example 3, which further intensify Black's alignment to his words (see example 3 line 1; example 4 line 1 downstroke; and 4 line 1 upstroke). In example 4 (line 1), he produces three vertical (up-down) two-handed beats (palms facing each other with low elevation on the beat upstroke) on 'weave,' 'of' and 'pantyhose.' After the contracted existential copula he repeats the same beat, though with an elevated upstroke – and increased acceleration on the downstroke – that lands on the first stressed syllable of the intensifier. Black repeats this marked gesture on the second syllable of 'absolutely,' the *no*-determiner and noun in a dense flurry of two-handed vertical beats that convey emotional conviction. In example 3 (line 1) he uses (one-handed) right-hand chopping gestures to accompany 'with a microscope' and the sensory verb plus object ('found absolutely nothing'). Just as important, the highly symmetrical stress on the sentence-final nouns and indefinite in example 3 (lines 02–09), and on the sentence final nouns in example 4 (lines 03–07), adds a further layering of poetic detail to the developing inconsistencies.

Example 3 line 001

Example 4 line 001 downstroke

Example 4 line 001 upstroke

After the type-indefinite introduction ('everything'), Black begins his listing process with marked gaze on the turn-initial first token (see example 3 line 2). As illustrated previously, the attorney directs gaze at the unfurling finger to start a polyrhythmic and multimodal pattern of evidential listing, gazing at the initial beat to coordinate a focus of joint attention with the jury. The deictic gaze that points to and locates attention in examples 3 and 4 aligns here with the same rhythmic pattern – on the existential plus contracted copula in example 4 (line 3) and negative particle in example 3 (line 2) – turning the gesture(s) into an "interactively significant object" (Muller 2008: 236). However, the gaze in example 2 begins on the turn-initial determiner of the type (line 1). Why does his gaze in 3 and 4 land on the token listing of items or the particulars of 'everything,' while it co-occurs on the type-category in example 2? Why does example 2 depart in this way from the rhythmic pattern?

Example 3 line 002

Or does it? The attorney's gestures in example 2 (line 1) involve not just any kind of gesture. They consist of the right index finger latched onto the little finger of the left hand (in a closed fist), and he beats out rhythm (over the words indicated) in this position (see example 2 line 1). That is, the type category interacts with a less marked, subtler, series of fist-like beats, which is why the attorney directs gaze to the determiner (example 2 line 1). Instead of ascending to the ring finger the attorney maintains position with the right index finger latched onto the little finger of the left hand in an embedded lamination of delicate gestures – *intradigital beats* – that reflect and visually demonstrate the detailed and precise examination of the dress, highlighting 'examination,' 'of the dress' and 'done minutely' by landing on an explicit point of emphasis.[8] By using this gestural variation, he regulates the tempo of the interdigital beats for the forthcoming listing tokens (or particulars) to elaborate the type (or general category). Rather than deviating from the gaze distribution seen in the other examples, Black adheres to the pattern by gazing at the initial latching touch on the little finger: a rhythmic modulation of, rather than departure from, the gaze distribution.[9]

Example 2 line 001

[8] To be more precise, intradigital beats occur with the index finger of the right hand latched onto the little finger of the left hand, beating out rhythmic significance over an entire idea unit with this latching motion in a closed fist position. That is, intradigital beats use a single digit or form for a single idea unit; they don't elaborate or unpack details. Detail-oriented interdigital beats, on the other hand, occur with the index finger of the right hand ascending up the ladder of the left hand (starting with the little finger) as each individual digit unfurls to emphasize the listing tokens. They use multiple digits for multiple idea units and unpack details visually.

[9] Furthermore, the linking of the little finger of the left hand by the index finger of the right hand prior to the onset of the token links the prosecution's examination to the findings – depicting Black as someone who merely relays information, effectively concealing his partisan role. We can see here how gaze and gesture combine to delineate participation roles in oratorical performance.

Thus, in each of the preceding examples, the attorney simultaneously gazes at and hits the little finger of the left hand with the index finger of his right hand to contextualize the significance of the rhythmic pattern. He then shifts gaze to the jury and launches a polyrhythmic fusillade of tokens that elaborate or unpack the type by (1) repeating the negative + NP and (2) segmenting the digits into discrete units. Verbally, Black repeats the existential + contracted copula, negative and NP (examples 2 and 4 lines 3–7 *There's no dirt* etc.) and the negative +NP (in example 3, lines 3–8 *no cuts* etc.). Visually, he extends the fingers of the left hand (furled together in a fist-clenched position in the starting off position), such that each individual digit unfurls incrementally from the bottom little finger to the thumb (which is extended by default). Once unfurled, each digit is then hit by the extended index finger of the right hand, pushing it down in a pronounced movement of hitting impact (once again, a crucial point we discuss later). Integrating both verbal and visual, his beat upstroke (in examples 2 and 4) co-occurs on the contracted existential copula while the stroke lands on the NP (see example 2 line 6; example 2 line 7; example 4 line 5 upstroke; and example 4 line 6 downstroke). In example 3, the upstroke co-occurs on the negative while the stroke once again lands on the NP. Just as important, each interdigital beat co-occurs with stress in either its NP affiliate or the first modifier in the NP and ends with a short pause before moving on to the next item in the series, so that the tokens appear measured out in discretely layered intervals. Finally, as the index finger of the right hand beats up and down, each unfurling digit of the left hand extends outward from its coiled/furled position and stays extended after receiving its beat in a chopping position (looking like a karate chop that transforms the starting fist position).

Such interdigital beats function to individuate, expand and cumulate individual pieces of evidential significance through finger movements along the hand. In that process, counting may be viewed not as a static or given outcome of some mathematical operation but as a micro-technique of oratorical power: counting as a situated and multimodal accomplishment. In all three examples, the manual modality adds another dimension to meaning that is not as vividly captured through the oral modality alone, merging epistemic with affective stance.

Type–Token Reflexivity

We have seen, then, that Black mobilizes multiplex laminations while integrating speech and gesture. He builds tension in his narrative through amassed repetitions: a repetitive groove that starts with a type category as a way of launching the token items. There is also a form of embedding that merits further discussion. In examples 2–4, Black produces not only type beginnings for each segment but type for ending categories too, embedding tokens between the types. In this pattern, the type elaborates each unfolding token as each token

Example 2 line 006

Example 2 line 007

Example 4 line 005 upstroke

Example 4 line 006 downstroke

elaborates the type, and provides an interpretive space for the next token in the itemized series. The segment-ending type resurrects and reaffirms the discretely anchored motifs in the type–token relationship.

In example 2, however, Black alternates the type–token pattern in line 8, from the turn-initial existential+negative (lines 3–7) to the turn-initial negative: a rhythmic reduction in lines 8–9 that maintains the sustaining texture while alternating rhythmic structure ('There's no chips, no little stones, no **nothing**'). Moreover, he departs not only from the prior repetitive frame but also from the repeating interdigital gestures (line 8) and employs a two-handed vertical gesture with the palms facing one another that co-occurs with the adjective phrase, a shifting arrangement that injects a sense of novelty into an otherwise predictable pattern (see example 2 line 8). But what is most novel about his oratorical performance is something further. Black layers polyrhythmic modulations to produce the double negative with increased stress and volume in line 9 ('no **nothing**') that repeats the turn-initial negative from line 8, intensifying epistemic and affective stance about the forensic expert's analysis of Bowman's dress (from line 1).[10] In addition, he synchronizes the double negative with two multimodal components. First, he layers it with a two-handed crisscrossing lateral gesture with the palms down (see example 2 line 9). According to Kendon (2004: 225), this type of gesture serves a performative function: "Gestures with the open hand held so palm faces downward . . . and is moved laterally in a decisive manner is an act of rejection or denial." Second, he gazes down with his eyes closed to produce a multimodal display of affect (line 9), fostering an emotionally charged impression of truth, sincerity and spontaneity. In this multi-laminated maneuver, we see speech, gaze and gesture converge and merge to execute a powerful epistemic and affective stance.[11]

Example 2 line 008

Example 2 line 009

The double negative and crisscrossing gesture recalibrate epistemic and affective value; they also figure prominently in a tightly woven contrast in line 10. In a further layering of metric modulation, Black mobilizes the double negative as the first component in a juxtaposition of contradictory elements, whose second part employs the utterance-initial contrastive adverbial ('N'yet this dress had a tremendous impact') as culmination of the argument: a rhythmic resolution synchronized with a dense flurry of vertical beats (two-handed

[10] According to Biber et al. (1999: 178), "Because of the repetition of the negative form this type of negative appears to have a strengthening effect. Here *no nothing* equals *not anything.*" But of course it is just *not anything. Not anything* is a big something for the defense.

[11] Just as interesting, Black uses the proximal demonstrative *this* in line 9 to bring the dress into a state of deictic immediacy for the jury.

parallel palms facing each other in an up-down movement) to foreground the main points of the contrast, that is, that given the 'tremendous impact' one would expect evidential residue on Bowman's clothing (see example 2 line 10).

Example 2 line 010

In examples 3 and 4 Black continues to elaborate the type–token relationship with a repetitive type-closing. In example 3, he produces a partial repeat ('nothing' in line 9, from the indefinite in line 1, 'absolutely nothing') which co-occurs with the two-handed open palm gesture, providing an "intensifier effect" on the stance-marked negative (Muller 2004: 244). In example 4, he tweaks the type-beginning (from line 1) for his type-closing (in line 8), while maintaining continuity with the initial motif ('there's absolutely no evidence and There's none whatsoever'). Here the intensifier 'whatsoever,' emphasizing the negative aspect of the statement, integrates with the two-handed vertical gesture to modify the quantifier 'none,' adding a strong emphatic stance to the token items that serves to remove any ambiguity about the proposition.

In essence, it may be suggested that the type–token relationship seeks to establish its own sphere of truth and facticity. The type frames the tokens which are included, while the tokens provide evidence for the type. Together, the two levels yield a gestalt-like configuration which reflexively draws attention to the narrative through a densely laminated and polyrhythmic integration of speech, stance and gesture. Black's deft, virtuosic twists and turns produce a dynamic that foregrounds affect by varying gestural form relative to the type–token relationship. That is, for type gestures he uses two-handed gestures; for the tokens he mobilizes interdigital beats to count off the inconsistencies or unpack the type.[12]

[12] We have noted what are potentially exceptions to this in the intradigital beats in line 1 and the gesture in line 8 in example 2. But perhaps we should temper such an observation. The

Multimodal Modulations

As we have seen, Black orchestrates several multimodal modulations of the preceding pattern. First, in example 2 he recycles the intradigital beat into an interdigital beat to recalibrate and segment the listing process. After the hold on the address term in line 2 ('Barbara Carabello'), the right index finger lifts off the latching position and then moves down to hit the unfurling little finger on the left hand, a strategic maneuver that individuates the little finger from the former intradigital grouping.

Second, he rotates gaze from left to right in an incremental (horizontal/lateral) progression as if to engage each juror by coinciding eye movement with each beat stroke in lines 3–7 (on the thumb beat he recalibrates gaze direction one increment to the right).

Third, Black not only moves his gaze direction (by moving his head) in lateral increments, he simultaneously incorporates head and upper torso vertically to build contrapuntal rhythms for heightened affect (beating with the head and torso up and down along with the first three interdigital beats in lines 3, 4 and 5): a multidimensional, multimodal and polyrhythmic layering of sound, imagery and movement.[13]

Example 3 reveals another variation, this time on the interdigital pattern. After the degree adverb and negative pronominal ('absolutely nothing'), the attorney launches an ellipted series of tokens that unpack what 'nothing' consists of. Once again, he starts with noticeably marked gaze on the initial items in the adjective phrase ('not a single'), then redirects his gaze to the jury. In this symmetrical series he proceeds once again to unfurl his fingers in an ascending progression from the little finger up to the thumb on 'mud' but then runs out of fingers as he scales the ladder of the hand! More prosaically, Black runs out of fingers on the upslope because there are so many inconsistencies. In a strikingly nimble improvisational movement, he recycles the index finger and middle finger on the downslope to create an ascending and descending progression of interdigital increments.

Also germane to the previous point, the 1.2-second prolonged post-stroke hold on the middle finger accentuates the significance of the number of inconsistencies. For McNeill (2006: 62) the "hold ensures that the meaningful part

intradigital beats also express a single idea unit like the types ('The examination of the dress was done minutely by Barbara Carabello'). The two-handed beat on *little stones* appears designed to intensify the poetic repetition occurring on the double negative in line 9. One other consideration deserves mention here. The intradigital beats contain no stress over their lexical affiliates. On the other hand, the NP items that co-occur with the interdigital beats contain stress.

13 We draw attention here to grammatical parallelism (along with stress and pausing), the right finger moving up and down, the digits of the left finger extended outward one at a time, lateral head movement and vertical or up-down motions of the head and upper torso that generate an intricately synchronized tapestry of sound, imagery and motion.

of the gesture – the stroke – remains semantically active." Perhaps the hold here, however, does more than keep the meaningful part of the gesture in play. It emphasizes the number of inconsistencies in such a way that, although Black could continue, he pauses for all practical purposes as if to say: "This is getting ridiculous and even though we could continue we'll stop here because you get the message." Speakers can in this way encode and convey motion and direction – even stance, in this context – more vividly through gesture than by means of speech alone.

Residual Semanticity

There is a further aspect of gesture not easily, or even possibly, encoded in speech. We have seen how interdigital beats recruit the index finger of the right hand to hit and push down the digits of the left hand in the action–reaction imagery. We also mentioned at the beginning of the chapter that beats may, at certain moments in the discourse, not only foreground key strands of evidential significance but also evoke aspects of propositional imagery, that is semantic content. It is time now to develop and conceptualize this multifunctionality of beats in more detail. According to the ideology of embodied resistance outlined earlier, expert scientists should have found forensic residue on Bowman's clothing because of the "tremendous impact" between her and the defendant. The fact that no evidential residue showed up under microscopic scrutiny exposes, according to the defense, a serious inconsistency in the prosecution's case. During the interdigital beats, the friction of two fingers colliding signifies the impact between one force hitting another and projects how there should be some visible consequence as a result. More explicitly, just as the interdigital beats represent a symbolic residue of touching (contact) so too should the collision between Smith and Bowman be revealed by evidential residue of the collision on her clothing. Put another way, Black shows how one force impacts another in the pushdown part of the stroke or stroke intensifier and how, by analogy, there should be residual effect on Bowman's clothing. In this action, the referential aspect of the text maps onto the here-and-now, interactional-multimodal text in a dynamic process involving what we refer to as *residual semanticity*: the way that what we are saying becomes what we are doing through an integration of text metricality and rhythmic beats (Silverstein 1998, 2004). Beats, in this instance, not only serve a pragmatic function but also convey residual semanticity or aspects of content as well.[14]

[14] Along similar lines, the ascending and descending movements on the hand (which show the increase in and direction of inconsistency) are not something easily conveyed in speech as in gesture.

Power and Multimodal Conduct in the Law

In the adversary system, the weight of evidence refers to the weight or significance of facts necessary to tilt the burden of proof to one side or the other, and such proof rests on the persuasiveness of the evidence. Which attorney really believes his side should win? Who counts off the most facts and thereby creates the most favorable impression on the jury? And, most importantly, how does one attorney mobilize power to make their account *count*?

Consider counting in more literal terms. In examples 2–4, the token items Black counts off with the interdigital beats could suffice semantically at the type level (such as "There's nothing on her clothing" etc.). Or he could convey the general meaning with some other gesture, such as a precision ring (in which the tip of the thumb touches the tip of the index finger on the same hand) or even a point (a vectorial indication in space). This demonstrates how the rhetorical force of the chosen gestures combined with other levels of language organization crystallizes and adds particularity to the evidential points – binding different discourse levels together. When scrutinized in detail, the interdigital beats accompany synonyms or noun phrases similar if not identical in meaning at the conversational level: 'grass stains' equals 'dirt' equals 'mud' equals 'soil,' and so on. What interactional work does such redundancy accomplish in the law?

The interdigital beats make each individual piece of evidence stand out, just like each individual digit stands out from the others. The beats carve up or dissect a unity into discretely layered and distinct items of significance: a microscopic division of referential detail that counts off and expands inconsistencies in the prosecution's case. That is, as the defense attorney lets his fingers do the talking he not only magnifies the prosecution's inconsistencies but also shapes and quantifies them in a poetically organized and embodied form of discursive power. In the spatio-temporal conversation among the fingers, he allows the jury to visualize that counting and cumulative process in motion.[15] This conversation demonstrates that counting is not merely a mathematical operation but a sociocultural resource in the construction of legal context.

More theoretically, we are claiming that counting, cumulating and differentiating are more richly conveyed through gesture than speech. According to Goldin-Meadow (2015: 73): "Because the representational formats underlying gesture are mimetic and analog rather than discrete gesture permits speakers to represent ideas that lend themselves to these formats (e.g., shapes, sizes, spatial relationships) – ideas that... may not be easily encoded in speech." Just as important, touching the individual digits of one hand with the finger of the other hand encodes and individuates objects more effectively than other types of gesture. As Alabini and DiRusso (1999: 52) find: "Touch is closer to the tagged

[15] Moreover, individuating the whole displays a level of precision that confers authority on his words and shows the jury that Black considers all these tokens important enough to mention individually, important enough to count off in gestural form.

object than a point; it is more clear which specific object is being indicated by a touch than a point." By touching each digit to branch off from the whole, Black signals that it warrants unique consideration as an individual item of evidence. He integrates repetition of the unfolding text with gestural rhythms to produce a semantic foregrounding affect (as mentioned earlier conveying substantive information and performing a pragmatic function simultaneously), a persuasive oratory that may tilt the balance of proof and put the defense case in the most favorable light.

And that balance of proof poses important questions and problems in relation to the resistance ideology described earlier. Embodied resistance foregrounds inconsistencies in the victim's account in and through a polyrhythmic infrastructure of interdigital beats in concert with repetitive features of speech, making 'ideology of inconsistency' invisible as a taken-for-granted process of power. In the law, inconsistency is taken as a natural incongruity or juxtaposition among contradictory facts of evidence. However, as Black unfolds the digits to individuate items of evidence from the whole (and thus increase their size/weight), he conceals their "factual" status as a unity of similar if not identical items, a multimodal ideology of language that naturalizes inconsistency in the mutual interplay of the fingers.[16] Black's beats impart a natural "feel" to his verbal rhythms and inject them – and the inconsistencies – with a powerful sense of oratorical precision. Just as crucial, inconsistency is framed from the defense attorney's perspective, while alternative possibilities remain unexplored or erased (e.g. that the victim was traumatized, that the defendant picked her up and put her on the ground or that perhaps, fearing for her safety, she didn't resist etc.). Rather than view inconsistency as a natural or objective incongruity between contradictory facts of evidence we envision it as a contextually situated and multimodally emergent naturalizing process, emerging in part from the rhythmic integration of gesture and speech. If one definition of power is the ability to make one's account count (Giddens 1979, 1984) then interdigital beats in particular and multimodal conduct in general may offer a visual way to make it count.[17]

[16] Needless to say, this notion of multimodal ideology of language derives from and builds on Silverstein's classic work on language ideology (Silverstein 1976). Matoesian (2001: 38) developed the notion of a linguistic ideology of inconsistency or that inconsistency is not merely a natural logic of contradictory pieces of evidence but a thoroughly infused logic of power and domination (at least on key occasions in the rape trial). Here we expand that idea to encompass other semiotic resources beyond speech alone.

[17] In this chapter we are not making claims about form and thus function of gesture as a one-to-one mapping of meaning. Neither are we claiming that these function in a certain way in a specific context of use. Our aim is to analyze the gesture/speech produced in the here-and-now. As a result, we make no claims that a gesture/speech ensemble typically works in a certain way, nor do we seek to extend the analysis beyond their use here. As Adam Kendon and David McNeill have indicated there is no stable, conventional meaning of gesture and speech; their meaning is spontaneously produced at that moment.

REFERENCES

Alibali, M. and DiRusso, A. (1999). The function of gesture in learning to count: More than keeping track. *Cognitive Development* 14: 37–56.

Biber, D., Johansson, S., Leech, G., Conrad, S. and Finegan, E. (1999). *Grammar of Spoken and Written English*. New York: Longman.

Ehrlich, S. (2001). *Representing Rape: Language and Sexual Consent*. London: Routledge.

Giddens, A. (1979). *Central Problems in Social Theory*. Berkeley: University of California Press.

Giddens, A. (1984). *The Constitution of Society*. Berkeley: University of California Press.

Goldin-Meadow, S. (2003). *Hearing Gesture*. Cambridge, MA: Harvard University Press.

Goldin-Meadow, S. (in press). Nonverbal communication: The hand's role in talking and thinking. In R. Lerner (ed.) *Handbook of Child Psychology and Developmental Science*. Vol. 2. New York: Wiley.

Heffer, C. (2010). Narrative in the trial: Constructing crime stories in court. In M. Coulthard and A. Johnson (eds.) *Routledge Handbook of Forensic Linguistics*. New York: Routledge, 199–217.

Jakobson, R. (1960). Closing statement: Linguistics and poetics. In T. Sebeok (ed.) *Style in Language*. Cambridge, MA: MIT Press, 350–377.

Kendon, A. (2004). *Gesture*. Cambridge, United Kingdom: Cambridge University Press.

Krahmer, E. and Swerts, M. (2007). The effects of visual beats on prosodic prominence: Acoustic analyses, auditory perception and visual perception. *Journal of Memory and Language* 57: 396–414.

Maricchiolo, F., Gnisci, A., Bonaiuto, M. and Ficca, G. (2009). Effects of different types of hand gestures in persuasive speech on receivers' evaluations. *Language and Cognitive Processes* 24: 239–266.

Matoesian, G. M. (2001). *Law and the Language of Identity*. New York: Oxford University Press.

Matoesian, G. M. (2010). Multimodal aspects of victim narration in direct examination. In M. Coulthard and A. Johnson (eds.) *Routledge Handbook of Forensic Linguistics*. New York: Routledge, 541–557.

Matoesian, G. and Gilbert, K. (forthcoming). Multifunctionality of beat gestures and material conduct in closing argument. *Gesture* 15 (1).

Mauet, T. (2010). *Trial Techniques*(8th ed.). New York: Wolters Kluwer.

McNeill, D. (1992). *Hand and Mind: What Gestures Reveal About Thought*. Chicago: University of Chicago Press.

McNeill, D. (2005). *Gesture and Thought*. Chicago: University of Chicago Press.

McNeill, D. (2006). Gesture and communication. In K. Brown (ed.) *Encyclopedia of Language and Communication* (2nd ed. Vol. 5). New York: Elsevier, 58–66.

McNeill, D. (2012). *How Language Began: Gesture and Speech in Human Evolution*. New York: Cambridge University Press.

Muller, C. (2004). Forms and uses of the palm up open hand: A case study of a gesture family. In C. Muller and R. Posner (eds) *The Semantics and Pragmatics of Everyday Gestures*. Weidler: Buchverlag, 233–256.

Muller, C. (2008). What gestures reveal about the nature of metaphor. In A. Cienki and C. Muller (eds.) *Metaphor and gesture*. Philadelphia: John Benjamins, 219–245.

Rosulek, L. F. (2008). Manipulative silence and social representation in the closing arguments of a child sexual abuse case. *Text & Talk* 28: 529–550.

Rosulek, L. F. (2010). Prosecution and defense closing speeches: The creation of contrastive closing arguments. In M. Coulthard and A. Johnson (eds.) *The Routledge Handbook of Forensic Linguistics*. New York: Routledge, 218–230.

Silverstein, M. (1976). Language structure and linguistic ideology. In P. Clyne et al. (eds.) *The Elements: A Parasession on Linguistic Units and Levels*. Chicago: University of Chicago Press, 193–247.

Silverstein, M. (1998). The improvisational performance of culture in realtime discursive practice. In R. K. Sawyer (ed.) *Creativity in performance*. Greenwich, CT: Ablex, 265–312.

Silverstein, M. (2004). Cultural concepts and the language-culture nexus. *Current Anthropology* 45(5): 621–652.

Streeck, J. (1993). Gesture as communication I: Its coordination with gaze and speech. *Communication Monographs* 60: 275–299.

Streeck, J. (2008). Gesture in political communication: A case study of the democratic presidential candidates during the 2004 primary campaign. *Research on Language and Social Interaction* 41: 154–186.

Stygall, G. (2012). Discourse in the U.S. courtroom. In L. Solan and P. Tiersma (eds.) *Oxford Handbook of Language and Law*. New York: Oxford University Press, 369–380.

Tanford, J. A. (1983). *The trial process*. Charlottesville, VA: Michie.

Tannen, D. (1989). *Talking voices*. New York: Cambridge University Press.

Tiersma, P. (1999). *Legal language*. Chicago: University of Chicago Press.

7 Questions about Questioning: Courtroom Practice in China and the United States

Meizhen Liao

EDITORS' NOTE TO CHAPTER 7

In 2015, the conviction rate in trials in China is thought to have been 99.9 percent. In the United States, the conviction rate has hovered somewhere around 90 percent since the turn of the millennium. In themselves, such statistics cannot say much about a legal system, unless they are contextualized (e.g. how often, and on what basis, prosecutors press charges; or what procedures are in place to safeguard due process). Another route into understanding legal processes in two countries, with different strengths and challenges, is by observing what goes on in their respective courtrooms. Cross-jurisdictional studies make it possible to see commonalities in seemingly disparate legal systems, as well as distinctiveness or peculiarities in how justice is delivered in one given jurisdiction – features we might otherwise not notice.

In the chapter which follows, Meizhen Liao presents such a cross-jurisdictional analysis, comparing how questions are put to defendants and witnesses (where present) in the courtroom. Courtroom questioning as a general topic has received attention by researchers in language and law from early in the field's development (Danet and Kermish 1978; Dunstan 1980). Studies have looked especially at the degree of coerciveness associated with different question forms and how questions are used as a way of controlling courtroom testimony. Liao's essay differs from such studies by offering a highly specific, comparative analysis of American and Chinese criminal courtrooms, contrasting when questions are asked, to whom, and why as well as the types of questions asked. For example, Liao's data reveal that, in contrast to the New York courtroom he studied (where most questions were directed toward witnesses), almost all questions asked in a Chinese courtroom are directed to the defendant. More strikingly for readers in common law systems, Chinese judges, unlike their American counterparts, participate very actively in questioning. Shifting from role to quantity, Liao observes that American trials last a lot longer than Chinese ones, with a far greater number of questions being asked overall. More particularly, he reports that Chinese prosecutors ask far more questions than defense lawyers do, whereas frequency of questioning is more balanced between the two sides in U.S. courtrooms. Viewed in a larger context, Liao's findings probe deep questions about background assumptions a jurisdiction makes as regards practical truth-finding, presumption of guilt, evidentiary requirements, participant roles, and the overall purpose served by a trial. Methodologically, his study also shows the potential value of analyzing legal processes through details in their linguistic expression, both quantitatively and comparatively.

REFERENCES

Danet, B. and Kermish, N. (1978). Courtroom Questioning: A Sociolinguistic Perspective. In L. Massery II (ed.), *Psychology and Persuasion in Advocacy*. The Association of Trial Lawyers of America. 413–441.

Dunstan, R. (1980). Contexts for coercion: Analysing properties of courtroom 'questions'. *British Journal of Law and Society* 7: 61–77.

Questions about Questioning: Courtroom Practice in China and the United States

Recent decades have witnessed a rapidly growing scholarly interest in the language of law, both in linguistics and in the field of law itself. The emergence of such scholarship has resulted in a rich and diverse academic literature (for an overview, see Carter 2014). However, nearly all the research produced so far has been directed towards the language of one specific legal system; rarely is work encountered that is devoted to comparative study of language use in *different* legal systems. Specifically, at present there is little or no work comparing language use in the Chinese and American legal systems. China and the United States, politically perhaps the two most important and powerful nations on the planet, have very different legal systems embodying respectively an inquisitorial and an adversarial approach. Whereas in China there is a distinct field of comparative law concerned with comparison between Chinese law and American law (and common law more generally), there is nevertheless no corresponding comparative study of Chinese and American legal *discourse*. One branch of linguistics, Contrastive Analysis (CA), does of course exist to illuminate differences between languages, and has produced major achievements in contrastive analysis of Chinese and English (for an overview, see Zhang 2006); but so far little effort has been made to compare or contrast Chinese and American courtroom discourse in particular, despite the fact that discourse study of other professional fields is flourishing both in China and in the United States (as it is elsewhere in the world).

Despite the rapid growth of forensic linguistics in general, then, there appears to be hardly any literature devoted to comparative or contrastive forensic linguistics. This chapter addresses the present paucity of research by offering an initial linguistic description of similarities and differences in courtroom questioning techniques used in Chinese and American criminal trials. Findings from the study may contribute to the development of forensic linguistics by clarifying the scope and potential of comparative or contrastive analysis. More particularly, the study aims to contribute to mutual understanding in international legal affairs by promoting better understanding of the legal systems and practices of the respective countries. Such understanding is to be especially valued at present, given that judicial reforms in China show a tendency towards learning from Anglo-American judicial practices; it is hoped the present study will help promote such legal reform.

The Research Focus

In forensic linguistics, a considerable amount of research has been undertaken on courtroom questioning. This is desirable, because questioning is essential to trials both in inquisitorial and adversarial legal systems. Such research offers a ready-made point of departure for comparative study. This chapter offers a comparative analysis, in this instance of similarities and differences in questioning techniques used in Chinese and American criminal courtrooms. Discussion is based on transcripts of two criminal trials that took place respectively in China and in the United States.

Crucial to understanding questioning in criminal courtroom trials from a comparative perspective are the following key questions: (1) What are the similarities between different styles of questioning? (This question calls for description of how questions are structured, both formally and as speech acts or events, in different languages and settings); (2) What are the significant differences between the respective kinds of questioning? (3) What are the possible *causes* for those differences? (This question is likely to involve both linguistic and legal considerations); and (4) What implications follow from the differences that exist? (This is the most open-ended and challenging area of investigation). In the account presented here, reflecting this order of priority among the research problems, emphasis moves from what kinds of questions are asked and when to who asks the questions, to whom, and why.

The findings presented this chapter are empirical rather than speculative. Research was conducted using transcripts of two criminal courtroom trials that took place in Shanghai, China, and in Brooklyn, New York, respectively. The two cases were selected from a larger corpus of Chinese and American courtroom discourse gathered by the author as part of a larger study.[1] Both qualitative

[1] This chapter forms part of the author's Fulbright research at Brooklyn Law School (2006–07), on the topic 'A Comparative Study of Chinese and American Criminal Courtroom Discourse'. Selection of the two cases was based on their relative representativeness across a range of factors, in spite of the fact that the trials took place respectively in 2006 in the United States and 2008 in China.

and quantitative approaches have been brought to bear on the data. In general, a quantitative approach seemed more suited to addressing the first two questions just described (while allowing for the general tendency of American courtroom trials to last much longer than Chinese hearings); a qualitative approach was deemed more appropriate in addressing the more explanatory questions: that is analyzing underlying factors which might be responsible for similarities and differences.

The Chinese case selected for exemplification in this chapter involved the kidnapping of a Uighur boy from Xinjiang Autonomous Region on March 28, 2008, by three farmers from Anhui Province in the middle of China, respectively named Zhang XX, Jiao XX and Liu XX. Having allegedly robbed the boy of his mobile phone, worth about 225 yuan, the three defendants, unsuccessful in their attempt to extort a ransom of 5,000 yuan from the boy's father, were alleged to have forced the child to steal from place to place in the neighboring areas until he was caught red-handed. The trial took place in the first tribunal of Minhang People's Court, Shanghai, on September 5, 2008, before a panel of three judges. The three defendants, together with their four defense lawyers, were present at trial.

The American case, *United States of America v. James Sessoms & Kenwayne Jones* (04-CR-706, DGT), was tried in the Brooklyn courthouse, in New York, on 26 September 2006. The case concerned drug trafficking and robberies during the period 8–10 July 2002, allegedly committed by a gang of drug dealers and thugs belonging to an organization based in Bedford Stuyvesant, Brooklyn, a gang known to the police for more than ten years. The two defendants, James Sessoms and Kenwayne Jones, were alleged to have become members of the gang and sold crack cocaine and committed other offenses. Jones was said to have orchestrated the robbery at gunpoint of a man in June 2002 which ended with the man being shot. In July 2002, Sessoms and Jones were alleged to have forced a drug dealer into a van at gunpoint, taken money from his pockets, bound him, blindfolded him, and along with other members of a gang they were working with, taken him from Queens to Brooklyn and kept him overnight in a building at gunpoint in an attempt to rob him of his supply of narcotics.

The Legal Context: Criminal Procedures in the Two Legal Systems

As necessary background to examining the questioning techniques in the two cases, it is necessary to describe briefly some relevant differences in criminal procedure between the two jurisdictions.

Chinese criminal procedure (as formulated in the Criminal Procedure Law of the People's Republic of China) forms part of a unique legal system that blends

(1) Roman law, particularly as transmitted via Germany to Japan; (2) traditional law, notably the legal system as developed in China over several millennia; (3) the communist legal tradition (including influences absorbed from the former Soviet Union); and (4) common law, especially most recently in the area of contract law. Proceedings are open, and take the form of a bench (i.e. non-jury) trial. The principle of presuming the innocence of the defendant was not adopted until 1996, but was in place by the time of the case under discussion. The main stages of a trial taking place according to these procedures are (1) pre-trial questioning by the judge; (2) opening statement (typically by the prosecuting party reading the indictment); (3) examination of evidence; (4) identification of evidence (which can alternatively form part of the examination); (5) argument or closing statement; (6) final statement by the defendant; (7) sentencing (either immediately after the self-defense or final statement by the defendant, or after a period of time); and, where available, (8) appeal. Chinese criminal procedure is basically the same as Chinese civil proceedings except that in the latter the dispute is between two parties typically represented by their respective lawyers, rather than between the State represented by the prosecutor and the defendant typically represented by a lawyer or lawyers either employed by the defendant himself or herself or appointed by the State. A very important feature of Chinese criminal Proceedings is that the defendant has a right to self-defense before sentencing, as prescribed by the Criminal Procedure Law, even though he or she is represented by a lawyer.

U.S. criminal procedure is importantly different in two major respects. First, it forms part of a common law system, notable for the authority given to a body of non-statutory law derived from precedents established during centuries of judicial decision-making (sometimes referred to in shorthand as 'judge-made law'). Second, the system of trial by jury (as formulated in the Federal Rules of Criminal Procedure) mandates a presumption of the innocence of the defendant, a presumption which has wide-ranging effects on presentation and testing of evidence. Major stages of a trial include (1) a pre-trial hearing without a jury; (2) pre-trial motions; (3) jury selection; (4) trial with a jury, including the stages of opening statements, examination, closing statements, jury instruction and jury verdict; (5) sentencing; and, where available, (6) appeal.

Questioning: Forms and Functions in Chinese and English

For the purposes of this chapter, it is not only the structure of trials that differs in significant ways between China and the United States. It is also important to compare how questions are performed in the two languages being used, Chinese and English, both in terms of their formal type and as regards their function. As

Table 7.1 *Types of questions in Chinese and English*

Languages	Chinese	English
Types of questions	WH-questions (特指问) (*为什么, 如何, 谁, 哪里等*) 你**为什么**去那里?	WH-questions (*why, who, where, when*, etc.) ***Why*** did you go there?
	Y/N (是非问) 你是中国人**吗**?	Y/N (Yes/No questions) Are you Chinese?
	A/N (A-NOT-A) (正反问) 你**是不是**中国人?	–
	ALT (选择问) 你**是**中国人**还是**日本人?	ALT (Alternative questions) Are you Chinese or Japanese?
	TAG (附加问) **你是中国人, 是吗**?	TAG (Tag questions) You are Chinese, aren't you?
	DEC (陈述问) 你是中国人?	DEC (Declarative questions) You are Chinese?
	RQ* (修辞问话) 这种简单得近乎愚蠢的问题也要回答吗?	RQ∗ (Rhetorical questions) Shall we answer such a stupidly simple question?

regards type, most established question types familiar from grammar books are the same in the two languages, except that in Chinese there is an additional type of question called "A-NOT-A" (affirmative plus negative) which does not exist in English. For example, a question may take the form "是不是", "对不对", "能不能", literally translated into English as 'yes not yes', 'right not right' and 'can not can', which is a variety of alternative or yes/no questions, as indicated in Table 7.1.[2]

In terms of the functions performed by these various types of question, there also seems to be a near correspondence between the two languages. A basic framework for analysis can accordingly be drawn from international studies investigating the functioning of questions in terms of the fact-value or information conveyed by answers to them, and in relation to the degree of control that questions exercise over the addressee as assessed on the basis of the availability of alternative responses to them (Goody 1978; Harris 1984; Woodbury 1984;

[2] It should be pointed out that the classification of Chinese questions here is simplified for the purpose of comparative analysis. Not every Chinese grammar book or linguist classifies Chinese questions in the same way. Most grammarians, in fact, refer to just three types of questions: WH-, Y/N and ALT. In the quantitative treatment of questions presented later, A/N questions are presented together with Y/N questions for clarity in the analysis.

Table 7.2 *Types of questions in terms of relative fact-value*

Languages		Chinese	English
	Very low	RQ (修辞问话)	RQ (Rhetorical question)
		TAG (附加问)	TAG (Tag question)
		DEC (陈述问)	DEC (Declarative question)
	Average	A/N (A-NOT-A) (正反问)	–
		Y/N (是非问)	Y/N (Yes/No question)
		ALT (选择问)	ALT (Alternative question)
	Very high	Narrow WH-questions (特指问) (谁, 哪里等)	Narrow WH-questions (*Who, where, when*, etc.)
↓		Broad WH-questions (如何, 怎样, 为什么等)	Broad WH-questions (*How, why*, etc.)

Shuy 1987; Walker 1987; Berk-Seligson 1999; Illie 1999). Among the findings to emerge from such studies is the principle that questions can be classified into two classes (a standard and a non-standard variety) according to whether they elicit an answer from the addressee. Those which *do* elicit answers are considered to be standard (or canonical) questions, while those which *do not* seek an answer (e.g. rhetorical questions) are considered non-standard. For this reason, rhetorical questions found in the data in both languages are excluded from the present study as being irrelevant; only standard questions, which function to elicit an answer, are taken into account.

Within standard questions, however, there are major differences. Such questions vary in terms of the fact-value or information that will be provided by the answer they elicit. The fact-value of an answer to a WH-question such as 'how' or 'where' is greater, for instance, than to a non-WH question such as a 'yes/no question' or 'tag question' (Woodbury 1984; Liao 2004). Even among different kinds of WH-question, the fact-value of answers to broad WH-questions, such as 'why' or 'how', is greater than answers to narrow WH-question types such as those using the interrogatives 'when', 'where' and 'who'. Table 7.2 shows question types that indicate relative fact-value or information provided by an answer elicited by the particular form of question, in order from low to high.

As suggested earlier, questions also vary in the degree of control they exercise over an addressee in terms of likely response.

Normally, the higher the fact-value of the answer a question invites, or the more information that will be provided by the invited answer to it, the less control the question exerts over the addressee. Table 7.3 shows question types listed in terms of the degree of control over the addressee exerted by the question, again in order from low to high.

Table 7.3 *Types of questions in terms of degree of control*

Languages		Chinese	English
	Very low	Broad WH-questions (宽式特指问) (为什么, 如何, 等)	Broad WH-questions (*How, why*, etc.)
		Narrow WH-questions (谁, 哪里, 何时等)	Narrow WH-questions (*Who, where, when*, etc.)
	Average	Y/N (是非问)	Y/N (Yes/No question)
		A/N (A-NOT-A) (正反问)	–
		ALT (选择问)	ALT (Alternative question)
↓	Very high	DEC (陈述问)	DEC (Declarative question)
		TAG (附加问)	TAG (Tag question)

Questioning in the Courtroom Data

With these two areas of essential context in place, it is now possible to offer a quantitative comparison of questions in the two trials. Findings are presented first regarding 'what questions are asked and when', then regarding 'who asks the questions', 'to whom' and 'why'. However, it should be made clear before we embark on the analysis proper that assignment of questions found in the data to different categories was undertaken independently first by two of my MA students and then by the author following established standards for classifying questions, with any discrepancies subsequently resolved.

The first stage of the analysis, shown in Table 7.4, shows the distribution of questions found in the data in terms of what types of questions are asked, beginning with the Chinese data. The top row presents types of questions, with WH questions divided into narrow and broad varieties. Although the second and third rows seem to present essentially the same thing, they in fact highlight or reflect different perspectives on WH-questions, Y/N and A/N questions, with the second row showing the sub-totals of narrow WH-questions and broad ones because they serve different functions and the third row treating Y/N and A/N questions as belonging to the same type. The bottom row presents the percentage of respective question types.

Table 7.4 *Types of questions in the Chinese data*

Types of questions	WH		Y/N	A/N	ALT	TAG	DEC	Total
	Narrow	Broad						
Sub-total	95	100	78	125	4	18	75	495
Total	195		203		4	18	75	495
Percentage (%)	39.39		15.75	25.25	0.8	3.6	15.15	100
			41					

Table 7.5 *Types of questions in the U.S. data*

Types of questions	WH		Y/N	ALT	TAG	DEC	Total
	Broad	Narrow					
Sub-total	2,052	2,028	5,704	217	980	2,520	13,501
Total	4,080		5,704	217	980	2,520	13,501
Percentage (%)	30.21		42.24	1.6	7.3	18.66	100

Here is the equivalent table for the U.S. data (Table 7.5).

These basic findings can be developed by adding further information. As can be seen from Table 7.6, in the Chinese trial data the WH-question comes first in terms of frequency, followed in descending order of frequency by A/N, Y/N, DEC, TAG and ALT questions. In the U.S. trial data, by contrast, the question type most asked is the Y/N question, followed in descending order by WH, DEC, TAG and ALT questions.

Although the amount of data being looked at here is very small – allowing, for instance, the possibility of personalized questioning style in the respective trials – the suggestiveness of a comparative approach is evident; and that suggestiveness is strengthened if a distribution of questions in terms of 'when questions are asked' is combined with the preceding information. In Table 7.7, a distribution of question types is presented in terms of the particular stages of the trial at which questions occurred. This is of course not a straightforward comparison, since (as explained earlier) procedures in the two legal systems do not correspond. In order to avoid a potentially misleading comparison, therefore, illustration here is confined to comparison between the most important procedures, such as examination. Table 7.7 shows the patterning in the Chinese data.

Beginning with the second row, the distribution of types of questions is presented in order of trial stages: court opening or pre-trial, examination, argument, final statement and sentencing. In the same way as in Tables 7.4 and 7.5, WH-questions and Y/N and A/N questions are first treated separately and then put together. Table 7.8 shows the equivalent U.S. data.

Table 7.6 *Frequency of types of questions compared*

Type of questions / Types of trial	WH	A/N	Y/N	DEC	TAG	ALT	Total
Chinese	195	125	78	75	18	4	495
		203					
U.S.	4,080	0	5,704	2,520	980	217	13,501

Table 7.7 *Distribution of questions in terms of trial stages*

Stages \ Types of questions	WH		Y/N	A/N	ALT	TAG	DEC	Total
	Broad	Narrow						
Court opening or pre-trial	0	32	7	17	3	4	0	63
	32		24					
Exams	95	68	71	99	1	13	75	422
	163		170					
Argument	0	0	0	7	0	1	0	8
	0		7					
Final statement	0	0	0	2	0	0	0	2
	0		2					
Sentencing	0	0	0	0	0	0	0	0
	0							
Total	95	100	78	125	4	18	75	495
	195		203					

Table 7.8 *Distribution of questions in terms of trial stages*

Stages	Types of questions						Total
	WH		Y/N	ALT	TAG	DEC	
	Broad	Narrow					
Pre-trial	5	51	60	2	16	30	164
	56						
Opening remarks	15	3	9	3	0	4	34
	18						
Exams	1,983	1,945	5,580	169	948	2,402	13,027
	3,928						
Charge conference	39	21	23	0	11	68	162
	60						
Summation	10	0	13	0	0	8	31
	10						
Closing remarks	0	0	0	0	0	0	0
	0						
Jury instruction & verdict	0	8	19	43	5	8	83
	8						
Total	2,052	2,028	5,704	217	980	2,520	13,501
	4,080						

Table 7.9 *Distribution of questions among trial participants*

Questioners \ Types of questions	WH		Y/N	A/N	ALT	TAG	DEC	Total
	Narrow	Broad						
Judge	42	21	27	62	3	9	13	177
	63		89					
Prosecutor	46	61	42	30	1	6	55	241
	107		72					
Defense lawyer	12	13	9	33	0	3	7	77
	25		42					

As can be seen, when distinguished by trial stage, most questions (as might be expected) are asked during the examination phase of proceedings, although there are also questions in the U.S. case in the charge conference and in the jury instruction and verdict; such questions are absent from their Chinese counterpart.

The next comparison asks "who asks the questions?" Again, the first table (Table 7.9) shows the Chinese data.

The first row in Table 7.9 presents the question types with WH-questions divided into narrow and broad whereas the other three rows present question types among the three main trial participants, namely, the judge, the prosecutor and the lawyer. Table 7.10 presents the equivalent U.S. data.

A more dramatic comparison is presented in Table 7.11. Relevant factors in the two cases are brought together in order to show the question types used by different participants, listed in order from most frequent to least frequent.

Complementing this interest in who addresses questions needs to be an equivalent interest in to whom questions are addressed, which is also likely to

Table 7.10 *Distribution of questions among trial participants*

Questioners \ Types of questions	WH		Y/N	DEC	ALT	TAG	Total
	Narrow	Broad					
Judge	68	141	176	110	19	0	514
	209						
Prosecutor	1,352	1,426	2,995	1,268	75	366	7,482
	2,778						
Defense lawyer	596	472	2,497	1,121	121	612	5,409
	1,068						
Clerk	2	0	3	0	0	1	6
	2						
Witness	10	13	33	21	0	1	78
	23						

Table 7.11 *Patterning of questions among trial participants*

Participants		Order from highest to lowest					
Judge	China	WH	A/N	Y/N	TAG	DEC	ALT
	U.S.	WH	Y/N	DEC	ALT	0	0
Prosecutor	China	WH	DEC	Y/N	A/N	TAG	ALT
	U.S.	Y/N	WH	DEC	TAG	ALT	0
Defense lawyer	China	A/N	WH	Y/N	DEC	TAG	0
	U.S.	Y/N	DEC	WH	TAG	ALT	0
Clerk	China	WH	0	0	0	0	0
	U.S.	Y/N	WH	TAG	0	0	0

be significant. Table 7.12 shows the Chinese data, in which nearly all questions were exclusively addressed to the defendants.

Table 7.12 *Questions to addressees*

Questioners \ Types of questions	WH		Y/N	A/N	ALT	TAG	DEC	Total	Addressee
	N	B							
Judge	42	21	27	62	3	9	13	177	Defendants
	63		89						
Prosecutor	46	61	42	30	1	6	55	241	Defendants
	107		72						
Defense lawyer	12	13	9	33	0	3	7	77	Defendants
	25		42						

In striking contrast, in the American data almost all questions were asked of witnesses (except those asked by the judge in performing his procedural duties) (Table 7.13).

Table 7.13 *Questions to addressees*

Questioners \ Types of questions	WH		Y/N	DEC	ALT	TAG	Total	Addressee
	N	B						
Judge	68	141	176	110	19	0	514	Prosecutor
	209							Defense
Prosecutor	1,352	1,426	2,995	1,268	75	366	7,482	Witnesses
	2,778							
Defense lawyer	596	472	2,497	1,121	121	612	5,409	Witnesses
	1068							
Clerk	2	0	3	0	0	1	6	Miscellaneous
	2							
Witness	10	13	33	21	0	1	78	Miscellaneous
	23							

These various dimensions of interrogative speech events fit together into an overall pattern, and allow the question to be asked: "*Why* are questions asked in these ways rather than other ways?" This issue is of course different in kind from the preceding research questions, in that it has more to do with the functions served by questions in their particular contexts, especially how far they are information-soliciting or control-managing. Table 7.14 presents Chinese data gathered across all the questions asked, now showing the fact-value or information of the answers each question type solicits, and the control exercised over the addressee.

Table 7.14 *Distribution of questions in terms of function*

	Information or the fact value			Control		
Function	High	Average	Low	High	Average	Low
Number	195	207	93	93	207	195
Percentage	39	41.8	19.78	19.78	41.8	39

The equivalent U.S. data is shown in Table 7.15.

Table 7.15 *Distribution of questions in terms of function*

	Information or the fact value			Control		
Function	High	Average	Low	High	Average	Low
Number	4080	5921	3500	3500	5921	4080
Percentage	30	43.85	25.92	25.92	43.85	30

Within the examination stage of the trials specifically, the picture is clearer. The Chinese data, beginning with direct examination, is shown in Table 7.16.

Table 7.16 *Distribution of questions in direct-examination*

Participant	Direct examination							
	WH		DEC	Y/N	A/N	TAG	ALT	Total
	B	N						
Defense lawyers	12	15	7	12	40	3	0	89
	27							

Table 7.17 shows the equivalent data for cross-examination.

Table 7.17 *Distribution of questions in cross-examination*

Participant	Cross-examination							
	WH		DEC	Y/N	A/N	TAG	ALT	Total
	B	N						
Judge	22	9	14	17	8(S)	5	0	75
	31							
Prosecutor	64	46	55	48	11(P)	8	3	235
	110							

In Table 7.17 both the judge and the prosecutor participate in cross-examination (and the judge asked almost as many questions as the defense lawyer). Table 7.18 shows the U.S. trial data, tabulating all questions used in direct examination (none from the judge).

Table 7.18 *Distribution of questions in direct-examination*

Participant	Direct exam						
	WH		DEC	Y/N	TAG	ALT	Total
	B	N					
Prosecutor	1,382	1,251	1,079	2,453	332	44	6,520
	2,633						
Defense	9	8	14	46	0	2	79
	17						

See Table 7.19 for related U.S. data for cross-examination.

Table 7.19 *Distribution of questions in cross-examination*

Participant	Cross exam						
	WH		DEC	Y/N	TAG	ALT	Total
	B	N					
Prosecutor	38	71	169	525	27	10	840
	109						
Defense	450	561	1,082	2,403	580	102	5,178
	1,011						

The two sets of tables have in common that both the defense and the prosecutor participate in examination, with the prosecutor asking more questions in direct examination and the defense counsel asking most of the questions. Differing fundamentally from the Chinese data is the fact that the judge was not involved at all in either the direct or cross-examination in the U.S. data.

Similarities and Differences between Chinese and U.S. Trials

The data presented earlier are concerned primarily with frequency of use of particular question types, and the distribution of alternative question types as assessed against a number of significant variables: the asker of the question; who the question is addressed to; the stage of the trial at which a question is asked; and the fact-value, or informational worth, of the type of question being asked. Whereas these data are taken from a single case used to typify a legal system, and so cannot claim representative significance, they do show how quantitative underpinning might be used to test intuitions regarding stylistic differences in courtroom discourse in different legal systems. With caution because of the small scale of the study, it is possible to extrapolate from the findings outlined toward general similarities and differences between use of questioning in Chinese and U.S. trials, and to highlight what appear to be some major differences between the two.

Consider similarities first. Undoubtedly what is shared by the two trials is that questioning constitutes a crucial dimension of courtroom trial process; perhaps unsurprisingly, the data confirm that questioning is a pervasive feature of courtroom trials irrespective of whether the legal system is inquisitorial or adversarial. It is not surprising either that most questions were asked during the examination stage of the respective trials. This reflects the fact that the examination phase of trial procedure, whether direct or cross, is the central stage of a court's inquiry into the facts of the case; it is in the basic structure of courtroom interaction that questions should be used for this purpose. It may nevertheless be interesting that relatively few 'alternative question' forms are found in either kind of trial discourse, Chinese or American; it seems likely that the 'alternative question' form, which is similar in function to Y/N questions and A/N questions in Chinese, may be found less efficient in legal inquiry.

Differences between the two kinds of trial in the two jurisdictions are more significant. First of all, it is important to note an overall difference in terms of the number of questions asked: 13,501 in total in the U.S. data, as compared with a meager 495 in the Chinese data. As mentioned earlier, U.S. criminal trials typically last significantly longer than equivalent Chinese cases because more witnesses are called and a more rigorous and detailed examination of witnesses takes place (in relation to the data reviewed in this chapter, it might also be noted that the facts of the particular U.S. case analyzed are more complicated). However, even the mere fact of a massively larger number of questions being asked during a first instance criminal trial in the United States seems to suggest that questioning is more central to the U.S. trial process, especially where a jury is involved, than for Chinese judges deciding whether the defendants are guilty or not guilty.

There are, however, more specific findings to note in relation to the patterning among alternative question types. These are best reviewed in the following order: what questions are asked and when; to whom questions are addressed; and why. As regards what questions are asked, in the Chinese data WH questions are most frequent, accounting for about 40 percent (39.39 percent) of all questions asked, followed in descending order by A/N (25.25 percent), Y/N (15.75 percent), DEC (15.15 percent), TAG (3.6 percent) and ALT (0.8 percent) questions. In the U.S. data, by contrast, Y/N questions are the mostly frequently asked, accounting for 42.24 percent, followed in descending order by WH questions (30.21 percent), DEC (18.66 percent), TAG (7.3 percent) and

ALT (1.6 percent). In the Chinese data, A/N questions, which as stated earlier have no direct parallel in English, account for a significant percentage; most such questions, however, were asked by the judge when performing his or her procedural duties and may distract attention from the main procedures involved in establishing facts and ascertaining innocence or guilt. Despite this important qualification, A/N questions clearly constitute a distinctive feature of Chinese courtroom questioning, and merit further study.

In terms of when particular types of question are asked, what is interesting is that most questions were asked during the examination stage. That in itself is unsurprising. But there is nevertheless a significant difference: that during this stage of the trial the Chinese judge participated in the examination by asking a significant proportion of the questions asked, while the U.S. judge, supervising procedure rather than conducting the enquiry, remained necessarily separate from this stage of questioning.

In terms of who asks the questions, there are three main types of participant: the judge, the prosecutor, and the defense lawyer. This is true both of Chinese and American trials. However, the questions asked by each of the three differ in number, question type, and stage of the trial at which they are asked. In particular, as regards the number of questions asked by the prosecution and the defense, in the U.S. data the difference in number between the two sides is insignificant: the prosecution accounts for 58.04 percent (7,482) and the defense for 41.95 percent (5,409). These data seem to reflect the requirement that the burden of proof beyond any reasonable doubt lies with the prosecution but is tested against a presumption of innocence and a full opportunity by the defense to rebut prosecution claims. In the Chinese data, by contrast, the prosecution asked most of the questions, by far, with a very sharp contrast between the number of questions asked by the two sides: 241 by the prosecution and 77 by the defense, accounting respectively for approximately 48.6 percent and 16 percent of the total number of questions. There is also a major difference in the *types* of question asked by the two sides. In the Chinese case, the prosecutor asked mostly WH questions and the defense asked mostly A/N questions, while in the U.S. case both prosecution and defense mostly asked Y/N questions. In the Chinese case, the judge also asked mostly WH (63) and A/N questions (62), while in the U.S. case the judge asked most WH questions (209) followed by Y/N questions (176). Perhaps most significantly, however, in the Chinese case the judge's questions were involved in substantial investigation of facts, while in the U.S. case, in a jury trial, the judge did not ask any factual questions at all. This reflects a fundamental difference between inquisitorial and adversarial legal systems.

In terms of who the questions were addressed to, there is a further important difference between the two legal systems. In the Chinese trial, questions were exclusively addressed to the defendants; there were no witnesses to appear and testify. Moreover, the defendant's oral confession counted as crucial evidence for the court. In the U.S. case, by contrast, questions were addressed primarily to witnesses. If a U.S. defendant chose not to testify, there would be no opportunity to put questions to the defendant in court. Such differences as regards the targets of questioning suggest that oral confession by a defendant is relied on as important, possibly even decisive evidence in the Chinese criminal procedure, while in U.S. criminal procedure witnesses' testimony in court was relied on more as evidence.

As regards *why* questions are asked, it is necessary to return to a number of points made earlier concerning the functions served by questions. It was suggested that questions serve two main functions: eliciting information or a particular kind of response and exercising control. In these respects, questions differ between the two jurisdictions in a significant way. The quantitative analysis of question functions in the Chinese trial data suggests that questions in Chinese proceedings may be more oriented to information-soliciting or the fact-value of the answers that the questions invite: questions aimed at high information, or fact-value, account for nearly 40 percent (39 percent), while questions appearing to be aimed at high or greater control account for only 20 percent (19.78 percent). In the U.S. trial, by contrast, questions similarly categorized as oriented to high information or fact-value account for only 30 percent, while those appearing to aim at control amount to 26 percent (25.92 percent). This difference in the type of questions, if borne out in a larger data sample, would suggest that questioning in U.S. trials functions more strategically as part of courtroom interaction, whereas questioning in China appears more oriented to fact-finding. Put another way, the Chinese court appears to attach greater importance to, or is more concerned about, substantial facts than about adversarial courtroom rhetoric – a typical feature of an inquisitorial system. In Chinese criminal procedure, leading questions or declarative questions (which usually take a yes/no or tag form) are not allowed either in cross or direct examination, while in the U.S. counterpart leading is not allowed in direct examination but is even encouraged in cross examination.

Finally, as regards the difference between the types of question used in the examination stages of a trial, there is a marked contrast between cross and direct examination in the U.S. data. In direct examination, WH-questions stood out, whereas in cross-examination Y/N questions were prevalent, suggesting again that questions in the U.S. context function more strategically. It was previously suggested that WH-questions (especially broad questions) are typically information-soliciting, while Y/N, declarative and tag questions function mainly to establish or maintain control. However, there is no real cross- or direct-examination data in the Chinese case; so in those data, there is no difference between direct- and cross-examination, with WH-questions at the top of both lists.

Conclusion

While acknowledging once more the illustrative nature of the comparison discussed earlier, based as it is on one case from each jurisdiction, two tentative conclusions may be drawn from the findings presented. First, comparison of questioning in courtroom discourse may be useful in revealing important differences between legal systems; accordingly, when the method is applied to two particularly important jurisdictions such as the People's Republic of China and the United States, discussion based on such data may be helpful in understanding the two legal systems in ways that would otherwise not be possible. Second, comparative work along these lines may help sustain and even extend a global shift in international affairs toward integration and inclusion. Current legal reforms in China appear to be toward learning from common law traditions, interpreted as being needed to supplement China's traditional legal values. In this context, the findings outlined earlier may help promote a specific change, by lending support to a stipulation in the newly revised Criminal Procedure Law that witnesses should appear in court to testify: a distinct feature of Anglo-American law not previously adopted in China (where absence of witnesses during trial has been a long-standing problem in criminal cases) and one likely to increase trial transparency and reduce the risk of incorrect verdicts. In the words of influential Chinese legal scholar Ping Yu, of Vanderbilt University Law School,

> Because lawyers have insufficient access to prosecution evidence and lack the means to collect their own evidence, lawyers must have an opportunity to examine the evidence presented during trial. Lawyers, however, have great difficulty in calling witnesses to testify on the stand. Prior to the enactment of the new Criminal Procedure Law, witnesses were rarely called to the stand, and defendants had few chances to confront witnesses in cross exam. . . . Complaints that witnesses, especially those who provide authorities with written testimonies, are seldom present for cross exam were widespread among lawyers. Most witnesses are exempted from presence at trial by a decision of the court, even when lawyers have applied for their presence. In cases in which witnesses are called by the court, many witnesses ignore the court order and choose to stay away. (Yu 2002)

If witnesses appear in court and testify, exclusive reliance on defendants' oral confessions in court would be greatly diminished; and the presiding judge would be able to focus more on his or her procedural duties in court rather than becoming directly involved in the court's fact-finding by asking substantive questions.

BIBLIOGRAPHY

Adelsward, V., Aronsson, K., Jonssen, L. and Lineli, P. (1987). The unequal distribution of interactional space: Dominance and control in courtroom interaction. *Text* 7(4).

Adler, M. and Longhurst, B. (1994). *Discourse, Power and Justice.* London and New York: Routledge.

Atkinson, J. M. and Drew, P. (1979). *Order in Court: The Organization of Verbal Interaction in Judicial Setting.* London: Macmillan.

Bennett, W. L. and Feldoman, M. S. (1981). *Reconstructing Reality in the Courtroom.* New Brunswick, NJ: Rutgers University Press.

Berger, C. (1994). Power, dominance, and social interaction. In M. L. Knapp and G. R. Miller (eds.) *Handbook of Interpersonal Communication.* Thousand Oaks, CA: Sage, 450–507.

Berk-Seligson, S. (1999). The impact of court interpreting on the coerciveness of leading questions. *International Journal of Speech, Language and the Law* 6 (1).

Bogoch, B. and Danet, B. (1984). Challenge and control in lawyer-client interaction: A case study in an Israeli legal aid office. In B. Danet (ed.) *Studies of Legal Discourse*, special issue of *Text* 4(1–3): 247–273.

Bourdieu, P. (1991). *Language and Symbolic Power.* Cambridge: Cambridge University Press.

Cao, D. (2004). *Chinese Law: A Language Perspective.* Aldershot: Ashgate.

Conley, J. M. and O'Barr, W. M. (1998). *Just Words.* Chicago: University of Chicago Press.

Conley, J. M., O'Barr, W. M. and Lind, E. A. (1978). The power of language: Presentational style in the Courtroom. *Duke Law Journal* 1978: 1375.

Coulthard, M. (2002). Whose voice is it? Invented and concealed dialogue in written records of verbal evidence produced by the police. In J. Cotteril (ed.) *Language in the Legal Process.* London: Palgrave Macmillian, 19–34.

Danet, B. (1980a). Language in the legal process. *Law and Society* 14: 445–564.

Danet, B. (1980b). Language in the Courtroom. In H. Giles, P. Smith and P. Robinson (eds.) *Language: Social and Psychological Perspectives.* Oxford: Pergamon, 367–376.

Danet, B. (1993). Book Review of Roger Shuy, Language Crimes: The Use and Abuse of Language Evidence in the Courtroom, Oxford: Blackwell. *Journal of Language and Social Psychology* 13 (1): 73–77.

Danet, B. and Bogoch, B. (1980). Fixed fight or free-for-all? An empirical study of combativeness in the adversary system of justice. *British Journal of Law and Society* 7: 36–60.

Danet, B. and Kermish, N. C. (1978). Courtroom Questioning: A Sociolinguistic Perspective. In L. N. Massery (ed.) *Psychology and Persuasion in Advocacy.* Washington, DC: Association of Trial Lawyers of America, 412–444.

Deirdre B. and Zimmerman, D. H. (1991). *Talk and Social Structure: Studies in Ethnomethodology and Conversation Analysis.* Cambridge: Polity Press.

D'hondt, S. (2010). The cultural defense as courtroom drama: the enactment of identity, sameness and difference in criminal trial discourse. *Law and Social Inquiry* 35(1): 67–98.

Diamond, J. (1996). *Status and Power in Verbal Interaction.* Amsterdam/Philadelphia: John Benjamins.

Drew, P. (1985). Analyzing the use of language in courtroom interaction. In T. A. Van Dijk (ed.) *Handbook of Discourse Analysis*, Vol. 3. Amsterdam: North-Holland, 133–148.

Drew, P. (1990). Strategies in the contest between lawyer and witness, cross-examination. In J. Levi and A. Walker (eds.) *Language in the Judicial Process*. New York and London: Plenum.

Drew, P. and Heritage, J. C. (1992). *Talk at Work: Interaction in Institutional Settings*. Cambridge: Cambridge University Press.

Drew, P. and Sorjonen, M.-L. (1997). Institutional dialogue. In T. A. Van Dijk (ed.), *Discourse as Social Interaction. Discourse Studies: A Multidisciplinary Introduction*, Vol. 2. London: Sage, 92–118.

Duncan, S., Jr. (1972). Some signals and rules for taking speaking turns in conversation. *Journal of Personality and Social Psychology* 23: 383–392.

Eades, D. (2000). I don't think it's an answer to the question: Silencing Aboriginal witnesses in court. *Language in Society* 29: 161–195.

Ehrlich, S. (2001). *Representing Rape*. London: Routledge.

Fowler, R. (2001). *Power*. In T. A. van Dijk (ed.) *Handbook of Discourse Analysis*. London: Academic Press, 61–82.

Fowler, R., Hodge, R., Kress, G. and Trew, T. (1979). *Language and Control*. London: Routledge & Kegan Paul.

Gee, J. P. (1999). *An Introduction to Discourse Analysis: Theory and Method*. London: Routledge.

Gibbons, J. (1994). *Language and the Law*. Harlow: Longman.

Gibbons, J. (2003). *Forensic Linguistics: An Introduction to Language in the Judicial System*. Oxford: Blackwell.

Goody, E. N. (1978). *Questions and Politeness: Strategies in Social Interaction*. Cambridge: Cambridge University Press.

Harris, S. (1984). Questions as a Mode of Control in Magistrate's Courts. *International Journal of Sociology of Language* 1984 (49): 5–28.

Harris, S. (1995). Pragmatics and power. *Journal of Pragmatics* 27: 117–135.

Heritage, J. and Clayman, S. (2010). *Talk in Action: Interactions, Identities, and Institutions*. Oxford: Wiley-Blackwell.

Hobbs, J. (1990). Topic Drift. In B. Dorval (ed.) *Conversational Organization and Its Development*. Norwood,NJ: Ablex Publishing Corporation, 3–22.

Ilie, C. (1999). Question-response argumentation in talk shows. *Journal of Pragmatics* 31: 975–999.

Itakura, H. (2001). *Conversational Dominance and Gender*. Amsterdam/Philadelphia: John Benjamins.

Levi, J. N. (1990). *Language in the Judicial Process*. New York: Plenum Press.

Liao, M. Z. (2004). *A Study of Courtroom Questions, Responses and Their Interaction*. Beijing: Law Press.

Liao, M. Z. (2005a). *Trial Communication Strategies*. Beijing: Law Press.

Liao, M. Z. (2005b). The goal-driven principle and goal analysis: A new way of doing pragmatics. *Rhetorical Learning* 3: 1–10 and 4: 5–11.

Liao, M. Z. (2009a). The goal-driven principle and communication. *Foreign Language Research* 4: 62–64 and 6: 101–109.

Liao, M. Z. (2009b). A study of interruption in Chinese criminal courtroom discourse. *Text & Talk* 29(2): 175–199.

Liao, M. Z. (2010). A comparative study of Chinese and American criminal sentencing discourse. *ESP Across Cultures* 7: 105–128.

Liao, M. Z. (2012). Courtroom discourse in China. In L. Solan and P. Tiersma (eds.) *Handbook on Language and Law*. Oxford: Oxford University Press, 395–407.
Liao, M. Z. (2013). Power in interruption in Chinese criminal courtroom discourse. In C. Williams and G. Tessuto (eds.) *Language in the Negotiation of Justice: Contexts, Issues and Applications*. Surrey: Ashgate, 33–48.
Liao, M. Z. (2015). Speech or silence: Within and beyond language and law. In L. W., Solan, J. Ainsworth and R. Shuy (eds.) *Speaking of Language and Law*. Oxford: Oxford University Press, 127–130.
Loftus, E. (1975). Leading questions and eyewitness report. *Cognitive Psychology* 7: 560–572.
Mackenzie, I. (1999). Power. In F. Ashe (ed.) *Contemporary Social and Political Theory*. Philadelphia: Open University Press, 69–87.
Matoesian, G. M. (1995). Language, law, and society: Policy implications of the Kennedy Smith rape trial. *Law & Society* 29: 669–701.
Mayr, A. (2008). *Language and Power: An Introduction to Institutional Discourse*. London: Continuum.
O'Barr, W. M. (1982). *Linguistic Evidence: Language, Power and Strategy in the Courtroom*. New York: Academic Press.
Philips, S. U. (1998). *Ideology in the Language of Judges: How Judges Practice Law Politics, and Courtroom Control*. New York/Oxford: Oxford University Press.
Shuy, R. (1987). Conversational power in FBI covert tape recordings. In L. Kedar (ed.) *Language and Power*. Norwood, NJ: Ablex, 43–56.
Shuy, R. W. (1993). *Language Crimes*. Oxford: Blackwell.
Shuy, R. W. (1998). *The Language of Confession, Interrogation and Deception*. London: Sage.
Shuy, R. W. (2001). Discourse analysis in the legal context. In D. Schiffrin, D. Tannen and H. Hamilton. (eds.) *The Handbook of Discourse Analysis*. Malden, MA: Blackwell, 437–451.
Shuy, R. (2005). *Creating Language Crimes*. Oxford: Oxford University Press.
Sidnell, J. and Stivers, T. (eds.) (2012). *The Handbook of Conversation Analysis*, London: Wiley-Blackwell.
Solan, L. M., Ainsworth, J. and Shuy, R. (eds.) (2015). *Speaking of Language and Law*. Oxford: Oxford University Press.
Stenstrom, A.-B. (1984). *Questions and Responses in English Conversation*. Malmo: Liber Foerlag.
Stygall, G. (1994). *Trial Language*. Amsterdam/Philadelphia: John Benjamins.
Tiersma, P. M. and Solan, L. M. (2012). *Handbook of Language and Law*. Oxford: Oxford University Press.
Walker, A. G. (1987). Linguistic manipulation, power and the legal setting. In L. Kedar (ed.) *Power Through Discourse*. Norwood, NJ: Ablex Publishing, 57–83.
Walsh, M. (1994). Interactional Styles in the Courtroom: An Example from Northern Australia. In J. Gibbons (ed.) *Language and the Law*. London: Longman Group, 217–233.
Weigand, E. and Dascal, M. (2001). *Negotiation and Power in Dialogic Interaction*. John Benjamins Publishing Company: Amsterdam/Philadelphia.
Wodak, R. (1980). Discourse analysis and courtroom interaction. *Discourse Processes* 3: 269–390.

Wodak, R. (1985). The interaction between judge and defendant. In T.A. van Dijk, *Handbook of Discourse Analysis*, Vol. 4: Discourse Analysis in Society. London: Academic Press, 181–191.

Woodbury, H. (1984). The strategic use of questions in court. *Semiotica* 48(3/4): 197–228.

Yu, P. (2002). Glittery promises vs. dismal reality: The role of a criminal lawyer in the People's Republic of China after the 1996 revision of the Criminal Procedure Law. *Vanderbilt Journal Transnational Law* 35: 827.

Zhang, W. Y. (2006). An overview of contrastive studies of the Chinese English and Languages. *Journal of Central China Normal University (Humanities Edition)* 45(01): 133–137.

8 Law, Language and Community Sentiment: Behind Hate Speech Doctrine in India

Siddharth Narrain

EDITORS' NOTE TO CHAPTER 8

As has been said elsewhere in this volume, language plays important roles in law on several different levels. It is the material used in legal proceedings and legal reasoning; it provides the written and printed substance of sources of law (in common law systems, legislation and law reports); and it is sometimes contested content, adjudicated in cases concerned with disputes in such varied areas as defamation, intrusions into privacy, sexual harassment, bribes or threats and hate speech. While the chapter by Siddharth Narrain which follows appears concerned with a topic in the last of these categories – hate speech as restricted expression – it is in fact concerned with all three, and the relationship between them.

Hate speech, as Narrain describes it at the beginning of the chapter, is a deeply contested terrain. If considered globally, entrenched and sharply opposed positions can be seen to be taken up both for regulating it and for permitting it, even among people who in general advocate free speech and civil liberties. Within this difficult terrain, Narrain shows how the means adopted to regulate hate speech – in India, a layering of the Universal Declaration of Human Rights (1948), protection conferred by Article 19 of the Indian Constitution (1950), and related legislation (especially sections 153A and 295A of the Indian Penal Code), all superimposed on nineteenth-century colonial English law – take the form of linguistic formulations which are not universal but highly specific, historically and culturally. The Indian experience, Narrain suggests, though particular to the sociocultural context, has important lessons for continuing global debates around the criminalization of hate speech and hurt religious sentiment.

The chapter presents its more general analysis through a close, critical reading of the history of Indian hate speech regulation. It traces the development of this area back to historical circumstances under colonial rule which led to enactment of laws seeking to protect 'wounded community sentiment', especially in the area of religion, by controlling communications 'promoting enmity between groups'. Narrain then charts the history forwards from such origins, highlighting developments associated with the adoption of the Indian Constitution (1950), challenges during the post-Partition period and then the 1960s and 1970s, leading into contemporary tensions triggered, Narrain contends, by politicized use – even hijacking – of relevant legislation when mobilized by interest groups of various political or religious persuasions as a vehicle for suppressing minority voices.

Amid current global challenges facing freedom of expression, Narrain's chapter draws attention to how far the 'language' at stake in hate speech regulation is simultaneously a matter of verbal content and its effects, on the one hand (e.g. how far manner of expression can affect whether an utterance is interpreted as opinion, and so valuable expression, or construed as for example a threat to public order) and also a matter of the wording in legislation intended to protect most kinds of language use (including especially political use in a democratic society) while restricting other kinds of language use as exceptions (e.g. in India, uses which challenge the sovereignty or integrity of the country in ways that could lend support to groups seeking political secession). Any full account of hate speech regulation, the chapter shows, needs also to engage with all the levels of language in law indicated previously. Narrain shows this in his analysis of courtroom arguments in cases concerned with what amount to efforts by dominant social groups and powerful majorities in India to mobilize current legislation as a way of restricting internal criticism, promoting communalization, and reinforcing hate – all in ways that chill speech and appear completely at odds with the aims of laws in place specifically to prevent those things happening.

Law, Language and Community Sentiment: Behind Hate Speech Doctrine in India

Hate speech is a deeply contested terrain, with entrenched and sharply opposed positions both for regulating it and for permitting it, even amongst those who in general advocate free speech and civil liberties (Matsuda et al. 1993; Schauer 2005; Barendt 2007; Dhavan 2007; Waldron 2012). Law is crucial in both creating and maintaining this category of speech, and the nature and extent of the law involved varies in different jurisdictions (Rosenfeld 2003; Hare and Weinstein 2009). Indian law regulating such speech can be traced back to colonial rule, and to a set of specific historical circumstances that led to the enactment of laws which were intended to deal with attacks on religious icons and wounded religious feelings (Donogh 1911).

Current debates around Indian hate speech law provide fertile ground in understanding the complexities of the gap that can exist between why a law is ostensibly enacted and the manner in which it is deployed. The Indian example in this respect shows how those claiming to represent specific religious or community interests can mobilize existing hate speech law, through claims of 'hurt sentiment'. In a multifaith society with a history of communal riots, such claims of hurt sentiment, it is argued, along with an implied threat of disruption of public order, act to create a major chilling effect on free speech.

Laws in India regulate various forms of what is broadly understood as hate speech. But it is rare for the term 'hate speech' to be used in judgments of the court, in statutes, or in official government documents. The language that was codified during colonial rule, and retained after independence, deals with what can be broadly categorized as 'promoting enmity between groups' and protecting 'wounded community sentiment'.

One of the rare instances where the term 'hate speech' has been used by Indian courts is in a 2014 Supreme Court judgment which resulted from a Public Interest Litigation (PIL) filed by an organization dealing with rights of migrant labour (Pravasi Bhalia Sangathan) that asked for the court to regulate hate speech generally, but mentioned the specific case of hate speech targeting migrant labourers in particular.[1] Provisions in the Indian Penal Code (IPC) (the law that lays down substantive criminal law definitions) criminalize 'promoting enmity between different groups', 'words uttered with deliberate and malicious intention of outraging religious feelings', 'statements conducing to public mischief', 'insults to religion or religious beliefs' and 'assertions prejudicial to national integration'.[2]

Besides the criminal law, there are also other pieces of legislation by means of which speech is restricted, dealing with media, elections and the protection of disadvantaged minorities.[3] There is no single hate speech law, but rather a variety of sections found across laws that criminalize different forms of what might in other jurisdictions be brought together under the category of hate speech.

Amongst these laws, the two provisions most commonly invoked by the police, often together, are sections 153A and 295A of the Indian Penal Code. The sections have an interesting history. Section 153A was an offshoot of the law of seditious libel (Donogh 1911). Earlier, sedition law had governed both

[1] Pravasi Bhalai Sangathan v. Union of India A.I.R. 2014 S.C. 1591. In March 2017, the Law Commission of India, in its 267th report on Hate Speech recommended that the Indian Parliament amend the Indian Penal Code to incorporate two new sections – section 153C (prohibiting incitement to hatred) and section 505A (causing fear, alarm, or provocation of violence in certain cases) to specifically address the question of hate speech in India.

[2] Section 153A(1): Promoting enmity between different groups on ground of religion, race, place of birth, residence, language etc. and doing acts prejudicial to maintenance of harmony; section 153B: Imputations, assertions prejudicial to national integration; section 295A: Deliberate and malicious acts intended to outrage religious feelings of any class by insulting its religion or religious beliefs; section 298: Uttering words etc., with the deliberate intent to wound the religious feelings of any person; section 505(2): Statements conducing to public mischief.

[3] These include laws that govern media such as sections 5, 6, 11, 12, 15, 16, 19 and 20 of the Cable Television Networks Act 1995, election-related law such as sections 8, 8A, 123(3)A and 125 of the Representation of Peoples Act 1951, and laws intended to address historic discrimination such as section 3(x) of the Scheduled Castes/Scheduled Tribes (SC/ST) Prevention of Atrocities Act 1989.

public order disruptions that emerged from the relationship between citizens and the government and also the relationship between communities. After the British Parliament passed an amendment in 1898,[4] section 153A governed only the relationship between communities. Section 124A, the law that governed 'disaffection against the government', continued to govern sedition (Donogh 1911: 61–68). Section 153A was the subject of further discussion during the Constitutional Assembly debates and during debates around the First Amendment to the Indian Constitution in 1951, discussed in more detail later in the chapter.

Thomas Macaulay, who drafted the Indian Penal Code, was influenced fundamentally by Benthamite ideas, but language used in sections such as 153A went against Bentham's attempt to create a scientific jurisprudence, in which language had to be stable for the law to be certain and communicable (Ahmed 2009: 179). The reason Bentham made an exception for these sections, it has been argued, was his understanding of a peculiar Indian vulnerability to mental anguish he felt arises from insults related to caste, religion or women (Ahmed 2009: 179).

Section 295A was enacted soon after the colonial government had found itself in the midst of a controversy over the circulation of a pamphlet titled *Rangeela Rasool* (*The Colourful Prophet*) in Lahore, then part of the undivided province of Punjab. The publication of this pamphlet in 1924 had led to widespread mobilization by the Muslim community, which intensified when the Lahore High Court acquitted the accused (the printer), saying that the existing law only criminalized acts of promoting enmity between religions and not insult to religious figures: the argument was that insulting the Muslim community was illegal but that insulting the prophet was not. This distinction was made in direct response to growing protests against the pamphlet from the Muslim community, and led to a charged and polarized environment especially in the province of Punjab. The three High Court judgments made at that time reached different views on the issue, thus casting doubt on the legal position.[5] Resulting uncertainty led to a legislative amendment and the introduction of section 295A, which criminalized "deliberate and malicious acts intended to outrage religious feelings of any class by insulting its religion or religious beliefs" (Nair 2013). Thus the law moved from protecting attacks against religious communities to attacks against the sentiment of persons belonging to a religious community, specifically attacks that took the form of insulting religion or religious beliefs.

Procedurally, under section 196(1)(a) of the Code of Criminal Procedure (CrPC), prosecutions under sections 153A and 295A of the IPC require prior sanction from the central or state government. Although this has worked as a

[4] See section on 'Changes in the 1960s and 1970s' in this chapter.

[5] Raj Paul v The Emperor, A.I.R. 1927 Lah 590; Devi Sharan Sharma & Anr v King Emperor A.I.R. 1927 Lah 594; Kali Charan Sharma v Emperor, A.I.R. 1927 All 649.

safeguard against malicious prosecutions by private parties in some cases, it has also resulted in very few prosecutions against members of powerful political parties, even when they are clearly in violation of the law.

Hate Speech in the Framing of the Indian Constitution

The proceedings of the Fundamental Rights Subcommittee of the Constitutional Assembly, which were conducted in April 1946, offer significant insights into the strong opinions for and against hate speech provisions in the criminal law. The debates centred on whether restriction of the fundamental right to freedom of expression should extend to cover speech that is 'likely to promote class hatred'. Such discussion formed part of a larger debate on the wording 'public order or morality' in the measure proposed by C. Rajagopalachari, a member of the subcommittee. The debates show that members of the subcommittee were acutely aware of the draconian nature of section 153A and its potential to curb speech.

Alladi Krishnaswami Iyer, a member of the subcommittee, began the discussion by suggesting that 'class hatred' should be added to the exception to the right to the freedom of speech and expression. At that point in the discussion, the only alternative proposal was to include the terms 'defamation' and 'sedition' in the exception, and he felt that these terms would not adequately cover the problem of class hatred; indeed they might have the unintended result of giving people carte blanche to promote it (Rao 2010: 231). Iyer argued that the amendment was needed to prevent speeches and other utterances likely to foster communal hatred (Rao 2010: 232). K. M. Panikkar suggested that the term 'class or religious hatred' should be added (Rao 2010: 232).

The proposals to include class or religious hatred as a restriction to the freedom of speech and expression were met by stiff resistance from some members of the committee. Syama Prasad Mookerjee, an erstwhile member of the Hindu right-wing party the Hindu Mahasabha, argued that it would be dangerous to include the terms 'class or communal hatred', since to do so would allow for a skewed use of the law, by means of which the majority party would be able to get away with the same speech that their opponents could be convicted for (Rao 2010: 232).

K. M. Munshi added to this the further observation:

> The right of free expression is now recognised all over the world, and it has been felt that speeches or writings tending towards communal or class hatred, if they do not go to the extent of causing violence or crime, should be permitted. This is the case in all civilized countries. The reason why 'class or communal hatred' was omitted was that it was felt that it might permit the units (i.e. provinces) to make all kinds of drastic laws; and all constitutional experts are of the view that up to the point where it leads to a breach of

peace or public order, any amount of public expression should be permitted. (Rao 2010: 231)

The discussion between Iyer, Mookerjee and Munshi was followed by discussion on whether section 153A of the IPC would be nullified if the exception they were discussing were to be adopted in the Constitution. K. M. Panikkar pointed out that the issue at hand was different from 'class hatred', as the whole of socialist philosophy was based on a theory of class war (Rao 2010: 232). Bakshi Tek Chand then intervened with a passionate plea not to include this term in the proposed clause.

I think the clause as it stands should not be amended. My experience shows that there is no section in the whole Indian Penal Code which has been more abused by the government of the time than section 153(a). As you know, no action under section 153(a) can be taken unless sanction is obtained from the executive. Now, when the bureaucratic government was there, sanction was given to prosecute a certain newspaper simply because it write [sic] articles against the police. It was argued and held that the police force was a class by itself and that the newspaper was creating hatred against the police. The man concerned was sentenced to two year's imprisonment. This is about the class part of it. Again, when members of the majority committee write against the minorities whether they are Hindu or Muslim, no sanction is given. When the minorities write against the majority, sanction is given. So, I say that, as Dr. Ambedkar said, this should be limited only to occasions when there is grave danger to public order. I think the clause as drafted should stand. (Rao 2010: 232)

H. C. Mookherjee, founder member of the Hindu nationalist party the Bharatiya Janata Sangh, added a further point based on his own professional experience:

We started a certain periodical in Bengal. As soon as the first issue came out, unofficial warning was given to us that unless we stopped, action would be taken under section 153. We had to stop it. So, I am afraid that, so far as we are concerned, we do not feel quite safe, if we had a provision of that sort. (Rao 2010: 232)

Given such strong reservations about the proposal, a decision on the matter was postponed and eventually no mention of inciting 'class hatred or communal hatred' was included as an exception to the right to freedom of expression. As a result, laws in India that deal with hate speech (wounding religious sentiment/promoting enmity between groups) are justified under a broader 'public order' exception to the right to freedom of speech and expression guaranteed under Article 19(1)(a) of the Indian Constitution.[6]

[6] Article 19(1)(a) reads: All citizens shall have the right to freedom of speech and expression. The exception to Article 19(1)(a) is outlined in Article 19(2) 'Nothing in sub-clause (a) of clause (1) shall affect the operation of any existing law, in so far as such law imposes reasonable restrictions on the exercise of the right conferred by the said sub-clause in the interests of the sovereignty and integrity of India, the security of the State, friendly relations with foreign States, public order, decency or morality or in relation to contempt of court, defamation or incitement to an offence'.

Development of Hate Speech Law during and after Partition[7]

In India, the next major set of developments related to hate speech law occurred during the post-Partition period (the late 1940s and early 1950s). The government of the first Prime Minister of independent India, Jawaharlal Nehru, introduced changes to Article 19(1)(a) in the First Amendment to the Indian Constitution in 1951.[8] The immediate reason for such changes was a series of High Court judgments, most notably a Madras High Court decision striking down provisions of the Madras Maintenance of Public Order Act, 1949 (*Romesh Thapar*), and of the East Punjab Public Safety Act, 1949 (*Brij Bhushan*). These pieces of legislation gave the government a high degree of control over the press through the power of pre-censorship (by means of section 7(i)c East Punjab Public Safety Act, 1949) as well as blocks on circulation (section 9(1-A) of the Madras Maintenance of Public Order Act, 1949). Since the High Courts had said that these laws could not be held to satisfy the 'security of state' exception to Article 19(1)(a), Nehru's government decided to amend the Constitution in order to introduce an exception based on 'public order', 'incitement to an offence' and 'friendly relations with foreign states'. These measures would allow for greater restrictions on speech.

The wording of these changes was deliberated in a Select Committee, a number of whose members warned that the changes would bring in unreasonable restrictions to the freedom of speech and expression. Nehru, responding to these charges in a speech in Parliament, argued that

> We live in a haunted age. I do not know how many Hon'ble members have that sense and that feeling – we in this country or in the world – of ghosts and apparitions surrounding us, ideas, passions, hatred, violence, preparations for war, many things which you cannot grip, nevertheless which are more dangerous than other things.[9]

Nehru went on to specifically invoke the memory of Partition:

> How many of you remember, or have you forgotten, three and a half years ago, in this city of Delhi in the month of September 1947 in Punjab, in that entire body of western Pakistan, what happened? This constitution was not there, but I am not thinking of the constitution. Where was freedom anywhere – not constitutional freedom but the freedom of normal human impulses – where were those freedoms? Do you think any

[7] The Partition of British colonial India into India and Pakistan, which took place in August 1947, was preceded by months of horrific violence and mass migration of Muslims into Pakistan and Hindus and Sikhs into India.

[8] For a detailed account of the debates during the lead-up to the First Amendment, see Arudra Burra, 'Arguments from Colonial Continuity: The Constitution (First Amendment Act)', 1951, (December 7, 2008), available at SSRN: http://ssrn.com/abstract=2052659.

[9] *The Parliamentary Debates, Official Report*, Part II, 9626 (May 29, 1951).

constitution will prevent me from dealing with such a situation? No. Otherwise the whole constitution goes and the country goes.[10]

Nehru identified the horrors of Partition, and the need for section 153A in particular, as specific reasons for amending Article 19(1)(a). Through emphasis on such justifications for the changes, Nehru ensured that a host of criminal provisions, including sections 153A, 124A, 295A of the IPC and 99A of the Code of Criminal Procedure (CrPC), survived constitutional challenges.

Changes in the 1960s and 1970s

The next significant changes in hate speech law were made between 1961 and 1972. This period saw the defeat of the Indian army in the 1962 India–China war. It also saw the onset of the post-Nehru era and gradual splintering of complete Congress dominance, as well as the demand for secessionism made through Dravidian agitation in Tamil Nadu.

The Criminal Law Amendment Act of 1961 introduced changes both to section 153A and to section 295A. Significantly, an explanation previously incorporated into section 153A was dropped. That explanation had originally been introduced at the insistence of Sir Griffith Evans, after concerns were raised regarding the possibility of abuse of the law during final deliberations of a British Parliamentary Select Committee on 18 February 1898, related to making section 153A a separate offence. At the time, the prohibition against promoting class hatred was part of the English law of sedition; but the proposed offence was not included in Indian law. The explanation read,

> It does not amount to an offence within the meaning of this section to point out, without malicious intention, and in honest view to their removal, matters which are producing, or have the tendency to produce, feelings of enmity or hatred between different classes of Her Majesty's subjects. (Donogh 1911: 165)

The 43rd Report of the Law Commission of India on 'The Offences Against the National Security (1971)', while remarking on the changes made through the Criminal Law Amendment Act 1961, observed that the main purpose of the law was to punish persons who questioned the territorial integrity of India in a manner that undermined the safety and security of the country.[11] As per the report, Article 19(2) of the Constitution was amended to include an exception 'in the interests of sovereignty and integrity' of the country in order to ensure that freedom of speech and expression could not be misused by those

[10] Ibid.

[11] Law Commission of India, *43rd Law Commission Report on Offences Against the National Security*, August 31, 1971, Para 1.10, p. 5.

supporting secession from India. The report links this amendment to changes the government introduced to the Criminal Law Amendments Act 1961 which brought amendments to sections 153A and 295A.[12]

These political developments were reflected in the Law Minister A. K. Sen's justification for the Constitutional (Sixteenth) Amendment of 1963. Sen defended the amendment by arguing that

> some of the decisions of the Supreme Court have made it quite clear that the words "security of state" is a limited expression and it does not comprehend any power to ban organizations or political activities.... [The] purpose of this Constitution (Amendment) Bill is mainly that we want to appropriate powers for the Government to impose restrictions against those individuals or organizations who want to make secession from India or disintegration of India as political issues for the purpose of fighting elections.[13]

The minister justified the amendment in the interest of outlawing secessionism, in the absence of which the situation in India, the minister said, would be the same as in 1940 when the Muslim League first put forward the idea of the Partition of India. Parliament overlooked the point made by some members that the Dravida Munnetra Kazhagam (DMK), a Dravidian party with a strong following in the southern state of Tamil Nadu that had openly demanded secession from the Indian Union, had already dropped secessionism from its charter.[14]

After all these changes, the restrictions on the freedom of speech and expression in Article 19(2), which prescribed the limitation in Article 19(1)(a), read as follows:

> (2) Nothing in sub clause (a) of clause (1) shall affect the operation of any existing law, or prevent the State from making any law, in so far as such law imposes reasonable restrictions on the exercise of the right conferred by the said sub clause in the interests of the sovereignty and integrity of India, the security of the State, friendly relations with foreign States, public order, decency or morality or in relation to contempt of court, defamation or incitement to an offence.

The changes outlined here led to the explanation to section 153A, a crucial safeguard under the penal law, being dropped, as well as a further narrowing of the constitutional guarantee of freedom of speech and expression. While the exception to 19(1) based on sovereignty and integrity is not invoked as much as the public order exception, it has allowed for the introduction of section 153(B) through the Criminal Law Amendment Act 1972, which criminalizes 'imputations and assertions prejudicial to national integration', a broadly framed provision that has been invoked over the years, sometimes along with section 153A.

[12] Lok Sabha Debates, 22 January 1963, pp. 5759–5841; and Lok Sabha Debates, 2 May 1963, pp. 13409–13506 cited in Coordination of Democratic Rights Organisations, *The Terror of Law: UAPA and the Myth of National Security*, New Delhi, April 2012.

[13] Ibid. [14] Ibid.

The Significance of Language in Judicial Doctrine

These detailed historical changes have a continuing, contemporary significance. The Indian Supreme Court and High Courts of various states have over a period of time upheld the constitutionality of sections 153A and 295A, mostly on the ground that these laws fall within the scope of the 'public order' exception in Article 19(2) of the Constitution.[15] Within Indian legal doctrine, there are now two divergent strands of thought on 153A and 295A.[16] The first involves the principle of ordered security, in which emphasis is placed on creating an atmosphere of safety and peace without which creativity and freedom are meaningless. In accordance with this principle, courts have to give deference to protecting public order rather than allowing for freedom of speech, in the interests of security. Justice Krishna Iyer enunciated this principle powerfully in the *Lalai Singh Yadav*[17] case, in which the Supreme Court struck down an Uttar Pradesh government order banning a translation of the Ramayana in Hindi by the radical Tamil social reformer Periyar. The government claimed that, by treating the main characters with disdain, the author had offended the sentiments of the majority Hindu population. While in fact the court struck down the ban on procedural grounds, the observations of the Justice Krishna Iyer outlined the limits of the court's approach.

The second strand of judicial thought is enunciated powerfully in a dissenting High Court judgment,[18] in which Justice Bhimasankaran says that curbs on freedom of speech are a greater evil than any consequences which may follow as a result of such freedom, and that one must not be afraid of error as long as there is also freedom to speak the truth. In this case the Andhra Pradesh High Court upheld the validity of a government ban on a book, which presented itself as a scientific take on the Bible, on the ground that the book would outrage the religious feelings of Christians.

The courts have responded to numerous claims of hurt sentiment, many of which are related to extracts or parts of larger narratives taken out of context, by holding that the overall narrative of the publication or film in question must be taken into account. A significant factor that courts also take into account in section 153A and section 295A cases is the manner of language used by the speaker in question. Courts have allowed criticism of religion as long as the language used is restrained, and appears to be in the form of rational argument.

[15] Ramji Lal Modi v State of Uttar Pradesh, A.I.R. 1957 S.C. 620 (section 295A upheld); Gopal Vinayak Godse v State of Maharashtra, A.I.R. 1971 Bom. 56 (section 153A upheld).

[16] For a more detailed account of these two strands of judicial thought see Narrain, S., Hate Speech, Hurt Sentiment and the (Im)Possibility of Free Speech, *Economic and Political Weekly*, Vol. LI, No. 17, 23 April 2016, pp. 119–126.

[17] State of Uttar Pradesh v Lalai Singh Yadav (1976) 4 S.C.C. 213.

[18] N. Veerabrahmam v State of Andhra Pradesh, A.I.R. 1959 A.P. 572.

Pratap Bhanu Mehta has linked this judicial approach to the 'Hobbesian dread that religion releases passions in which the agency of citizens is impaired' (Mehta 2015). According to Mehta, legal reasoning that emphasizes restrained language allows the state to step in to restore order, but in doing so also to escape from its responsibility to protect speech. This line of legal reasoning inevitably assumes that all art and political discourse must either be conducted in civil language, and if it is not conducted in civil language there must be a specific and discernable reason for its use. It does not take into account the numerous forms of satire, popular humour, political dissent, literary work and other use of language where the whole point is to use uncivil, shocking and coarse language.

Mehta's concerns bring to mind the argument made by the legal scholar Eric Barendt, who has argued against distinguishing between hate speech and acceptable speech based on the nature of language (coarse versus sophisticated), since the law should not for instance discriminate against the freedom of speech of those who are in some way less articulate (Barendt 2013).

The approach taken by the Indian judiciary has in some cases led not only to inconsistent rulings, but to an effective 'Heckler's veto',[19] as it has been called, which hangs over the head of Indian artists, students, political dissenters and anyone who wishes to exercise their right to free speech. Perhaps the most obvious example of this problem brought about by this strand of judicial reasoning is to be found in rulings by the Karnataka High Court and Supreme Court in *Baragur Ramachandrappa*,[20] where the judges asked the author of a controversial book to remove a chapter that had hurt the sentiments of the dominant and politically powerful Veerashaiva community (because he had dared to portray in his narrative one of the saints revered by the community as having being born out of wedlock). The judges appear to have been influenced by organized demonstrations of outrage against the book, which they refer to directly in their judgments. This is just one example of a series of incidents in India where communities have mobilized around claims of hurt sentiment, and leveraged existing law to prevent speech that challenges the dominant narrative about a given community. This apparent misuse of the law has created a situation in which powerful interests within a community, or powerful

[19] The term 'Heckler's Veto' has been coined by Harry Kalven in the context of African Americans protesting for their civil rights in the Southern states of the United States in the 1950s, to refer to a situation when a speakers right is curtailed for fear of a negative reaction from someone opposed to the speech. Harry Kalven, The Negro and the First Amendment 140 (1965) cited in Ruth McGaffey, 'The Heckler's Veto: A Reexamination', 57 Marq. L. Rev. 39, 40 (1973) available at http://scholarship.law.marquette.edu/mulr/vol57/iss1/3.

[20] Baragur Ramachandrappa & Ors. v State of Karnataka & Anr., (2007) 5 S.C.C. 11; Baragur Ramchandrappa & Ors. v State of Karnataka And Anr., 1998 Cri.L.J. 3639.

communities that are able to leverage hate speech law to their advantage, can sideline alternative traditions, critical voices, and anyone who dares to contest established traditions.

This approach taken by the courts needs to be read in the light of its broader approach to the link between speech and the threat to public disorder. When it comes to balancing free speech rights against the threat to public order, there are two available strands of case law: the more 'speech protective' one (exemplified by *Ram Manohar Lohia*[21]) which has recognized that there are two kinds of speech: those that distinguish between speech acts which directly impact public order and speech acts that only indirectly bring about such a result, and a less 'speech protective' strand of case law that conflates all speech acts as directly impacting public order (as exemplified by *Ramji Lal Modi*[22]) (Bhatia 2015: 45–82).

Compare this situation to doctrine around public order and free speech in other jurisdictions. In the United States, the Brandenburg test[23] is followed as providing that advocacy of violence alone, or in itself, is not per se illegal. The Brandenburg test distinguishes between advocacy and incitement, criminalizing only speech that goes beyond advocacy and amounts to incitement to breaches of public order (Bhatia 2015: 68). Under English law, the Privy Council, in striking down a provision of Antigua's Public Order Act, which criminalized false statements likely to disturb public peace, held that the law did not satisfy the proximity requirement between the speech act and the public disorder it was supposed to be responsible for (Bhatia 2015: 70–71). The South African Constitutional Court in *Islamic Unity Convention v The Independent Broadcasting Authority*[24] struck down a section of the Code of Conduct for broadcasting services that proscribed 'advocacy of hatred ... that was likely to prejudice relations between sections of the population' (Bhatia 2015: 71–72). The Court held that not all advocacy of hatred was likely to prejudice relations

[21] In The Superintendent Central Prison, Fatehgarh v Dr. Ram Manohar Lohia, 1960 2 S.C.R. 821, Lohia, the General Secretary of the Socialist Party, was arrested for instigating people against paying agricultural tax. The Supreme Court held that for a restriction on speech to be valid, there needs to be a proximate nexus to public order, and it could not be too remote in the chain leading to public disorder.

[22] Ramji Lal Modi v State of Uttar Pradesh [1957] 1 S.C.R. 860. This case related to the prosecution of an editor of a magazine that promoted the protection of the cow. The Muslim community opposed the magazine as hurting its religious sentiments, and said its content could lead to public disorder. The Court in this case considered whether section 295A IPC would apply and rejected an argument that there was a subset of content that could outrage religious feelings yet not lead to public disorder.

[23] Brandenburg v Ohio, in which the Supreme Court struck down criminal syndicalism laws in the state of Ohio.

[24] Islamic Unity Convention v The Independent Broadcasting Authority, 2002 (5) B.C.L.R. 433 (CC).

between sections of the population. In European law, the European Court of Human Rights has distinguished between speech that is hostile to government and speech that incites violence[25] (Bhatia 2015: 72).

When judged in the light of these comparisons, Indian doctrine around hate speech and public order shows that there has generally been a movement towards conflation of language, expressed in a contested speech act, and resulting public disorder, and that such conflation has led to strategic use of the law by dominant community interests.

Hate Speech Laws, Language and Anti-Minority Sentiment

Legal academics and others who have followed the application of these laws in India have shown repeatedly that these laws are mobilized by powerful interests within communities, sometimes for publicity and at other times in order to stifle expression that is at odds with the dominant narratives of communities, as well as sometimes by the dominant majority in order to further their agenda of communalization of society (Dhavan 2007).

In a large number of the resulting cases, the claims being made are what Mazzarella and Kaur term ‘profitable provocation’: a strategy used to gain media attention and free publicity (Mazzarella and Kaur 2009: 172–205). When exploited to make possible such provocation, the law arguably becomes a vehicle or platform for mobilization, especially since once a trial court admits the claims in question, the verdict in the case does not matter much. To this extent, the legal process may be turned into an instrument of harassment, rather than a way of controlling it: a phenomenon that legal academics (Dhavan 2008) and Indian appellate courts themselves have remarked on.[26]

[25] Seher Karatas v Turkey, No. 33179/96, judgment of 9 July 2002; Karkin v Turkey, Application no. 43928/98, judgment of 23 September 2003; Kizilyaprak v Turkey, Application no. 27528/95, judgment of 2 October 2003; Abdullah Aydin v Turkey, Application no. 42435/98, judgment of 9 March 2004.

[26] See Bilal Ahmed Kaloo v State of Andhra Pradesh, A.I.R. 1997 SC 3483. The Court upheld charges against Kaloo based on a violation of the Arms Act but overturned charges under section 124A, section 153A and section 505(2) of the Indian Penal Code. The Court at the end of its decision said: ‘Before parting with this judgment, we wish to observe that the manner in which convictions have been recorded for offences under Section 153A, 124A and 505(2), has exhibited a very casual approach of the trial court. Let alone the absence of any evidence which may attract the provisions of the sections, as already observed, even the charges framed against the appellant for these offences did not contain the essential ingredients of the offences under the three sections. The appellant strictly speaking should not have been put to trial for those offences. Mechanical order convicting a citizen for offences of such serious nature like sedition and to promote enmity and hatred etc. does harm to the cause. It is expected that graver the offence, greater should be the care taken so that the liberty of a citizen is not lightly interfered with.’

The roots of this difficulty are deeply embedded. The history of contestation over hate speech laws in India began during colonial rule, for example, and continued during the Constituent Assembly Debates, emerging again during the debates around the First and Sixteenth Amendments to the Constitution. Voices opposing the penalizing of speech have persistently warned of misuse, a clamping down of political dissent and the appropriating by the majority of a law which purportedly protects minorities. Such misgivings have not been misplaced. The law, becoming more than a space of contestation, is a now a means by which discourse around hate and hurt can be constituted to further the strategic aims of political and religious groups.

Mobilization of sections 153A and 295A of the IPC by interest groups of various political persuasions suggests that there is something inherent in the framing of these laws that is being taken advantage of. What is unique about Indian law in this area is its combination of the framing of the law (as explicitly impacting community interests, both in terms of promoting enmity against the 'other community' as well as wounding community sentiment framed as the feeling of a class of citizens), and the historical background of the law which is related to violence between religious groups and the threat of secession. These unique factors have over time helped entrench the law in this area, making it unlikely for any legal challenge based on Article 19(1)(a) to succeed.

Justifications for hate speech law include the need to protect minorities and vulnerable groups from speech that in itself amounts to a verbal act of discrimination against a target group, undermines the security of vulnerable groups of society, and silences the voices of these groups, thus discouraging them from participating in public discourse (Barendt 2013). Sections 153A and 295A, the two Indian laws discussed here, do not satisfy these criteria, as they are based on identity-based claims, in which a conflation takes place between attacks on the beliefs of persons or icons that persons hold sacred and attacks on the persons and collective groups who hold those beliefs (Barendt 2013).[27]

There is little evidence to set against the problem identified here with the way hate speech laws are framed in India to prove that hate speech laws have served as an effective deterrent against anti-minority sentiment. For instance, in the state of Maharashtra, leaders of the powerful Hindu right wing party, the Shiv Sena,[28] have regularly expressed anti-minority sentiments which have been reported widely by the media and even published editorials in their Marathi language mouthpiece *Saamna* attacking communities based on their religion

[27] Barendt specifies this as one form of speech restriction that should not be imposed, as he disagrees with such conflation.

[28] For an academic account of the factors behind the rise of the Shiv Sena, see Hansen (2001).

and ethnicity during the communal riots in 1992–93 in which over 900 persons died (Mehta 2008). Bal Thackeray, leader of the Shiv Sena at the time of the riots, was named by a state government-instituted Commission of Inquiry, the Justice B.N. Srikrishna Commission, as responsible for directing violence against Muslims during one phase of the riots (Punwani 2014).

Prosecutions of Shiv Sena leaders under existing hate speech laws have been rare, as they require government sanction; and many cases were dropped when the Shiv Sena came to power in an alliance with the BJP, the Hindu nationalist party that has an all-India presence (Punwani 2014). Bal Thackeray, who faced hate speech cases for his editorial in the Shiv Sena mouthpiece *Saamna*, successfully challenged the allegations in the Bombay High Court. The case dealt with editorials that Thackeray had written after the 1993 communal riots in Muslim-dominated areas of Mumbai after the demolition of the Babri Masjid (a mosque in Ayodhya at a spot that Hindu fundamentalists claim was built on the birthplace of Lord Ram).[29] Thackeray, in the editorials in *Saamna*, had described the Muslim community living in specific areas of the city as traitors, and called the areas in which they lived 'mini-Pakistan'.[30] The editorials in Saamna also accused Muslims of being loyal to their religion rather than the nation,[31] and pointed a finger at the government suggesting that the state administration was going soft on Muslims.[32]

The Bombay High Court, when faced with the question of whether such writing amounted to hate speech, held that the writing did not express ill will, spite or hatred against the Muslim community as a whole, and only targeted a section of the Muslim community.[33] The High Court held that, though it was true that in some of these articles 'due to the emotional outburst high-flown and caustic language is used', this in itself did not fall within the mischief of section 153A.[34] Perversely, the High Court ruled that, since communal harmony had been restored in Mumbai, it was not desirable to reopen these issues.[35] Such refusal by the High Court to consider the *Saamna* editorials as hate speech, and the dismal record of prosecutions of Shiv Sena leaders under sections 153A and 295A in Maharashtra, stands as an example of what Bakshi Tej Chand and Syama Prasad Mookerjee warned against during the Constitutional Assembly debates: the prospect that the majority or ruling party would be able to get away with hate speech, while hate speech law could be used to prosecute and harass those in the opposition and those who are not powerful enough to leverage the law to their advantage.

[29] For an English translation of the content of editorials published in the *Saamna* at this time, see 'What Saamna Said', *Frontline*, Vol. 17, Issue 16, 5–18 August 2000, http://www.frontline.in/static/html/fl1716/17160160.htm.

[30] Joseph Bain & Ors. v The State of Maharashtra & Ors., 1995 *Cri.L.J.* 1316 at Para 18.

[31] Ibid. at Para 24. [32] Ibid. at Para 19.

[33] Ibid. at Para 27. [34] Ibid. [35] Ibid. at Para 30.

Conclusion: Lessons from Indian Hate Speech Law

The particular way in which hate speech laws have been mobilized in India can be encapsulated in an interesting and topical example. In a case decided by the Supreme Court in 1988, the petitioner claimed that the Koran should be proscribed under sections 153A and 295A, since its content amounted to hate speech.[36] The Court not only dismissed the claim, holding that the Koran could not be the subject of such legal proceedings, but observed that examining the legal claims of the petitioner would result in consequences that these very laws were trying to prevent.[37]

Considered together, nevertheless, the factors outlined in this chapter – the specific history of hate speech provisions, justification of retaining these laws under the public order exception to freedom of expression, and the Indian courts' collapsing of hurt sentiment and incitement into public order – form a potent cocktail that has allowed for a dangerous mobilization of claims of hurt sentiment.

Hate speech laws in themselves are context specific, and globally there have been multiple ways in which the challenge of curbing hate speech has been approached. The Indian experience, though specific to its particular sociocultural context, has important lessons for global debates around the criminalization of hate speech and hurt religious sentiment. Much of the problem with the way in which hate speech law is mobilized relates to a strong underlying current that the Indian public continues to be susceptible to being incited to public disorder, based on identity and community-based provocation. This is in turn connected with a judicial doctrine of privileging security over free speech, following a doctrine that is unable to recognize that not all hate speech is likely to cause violence.

In these ways, the Indian experience provides a cautionary tale for those advocating increased regulation of hate speech in order to protect the rights of vulnerable minorities, or those asking for regulation of hurt sentiment in the wake of controversies such as that over the Danish cartoons or widespread circulation online of the film *Innocence of Muslims.* As debates around hate speech become global, it is crucial to remember that the language of hate speech laws reflects specific histories, and has to be read in relation to a complex set of historical and cultural factors that determine how such laws are used. Mobilization by community groups, as we see in the Indian case, can be used by dominant groups and powerful majorities to restrict internal criticism, and at other times to reinforce hate in ways that are completely at odds with the purported aims of the laws in question.

[36] Chandmal Chopra v State of West Bengal, 1988 *Cri.L.J.* 739. [37] Ibid.

REFERENCES

Ahmed, A. A. (2009). Specters of Macaulay: Blasphemy, The Indian Penal Code and Pakistan's Predicament. In W. Mazzarella and R. Kaur (eds.) *Censorship in South Asia: Cultural Regulation from Sedition to Seduction*. Bloomington, IN: Indiana University Press, 172–205.

Barendt, E. (2007). *Freedom of Speech* (2nd ed.). Oxford: Oxford University Press.

Barendt, E. (2013). "Hate Speech", Lecture given at Hull University, 21 November, www2.hull.ac.uk/fass/pdf/Eric%20Barendt-HATE%20SPEECH.pdf

Bhatia, G. (2015). *Offend, Shock, or Disturb: Free Speech under the Indian Constitution*. New Delhi: Oxford University Press.

Burra, A. (2008). *Arguments from Colonial Continuity: The Constitution (First Amendment Act)*, 7 December 1951, available at SSRN, http://ssrn.com/abstract=2052659

Coordination of Democratic Rights Organisations (2012). *The Terror of Law: UAPA and the Myth of National Security*, New Delhi, April.

Dhavan, R. (2007). *Harassing Husain: Uses and Abuses of the Law of Hate Speech*. New Delhi: Sahmat.

Dhavan, R. (2008). *Publish and Be Damned: Censorship and Intolerance in India*. New Delhi: Tulika Books.

Donogh, W. R. (1911). *A Treatise on the Law of Sedition and Cognate Offences in British India*. Calcutta: Thakker, Spink and Co.

Hansen, T. B. (2001). *Wages of Violence: Naming and Identity in Postcolonial Bombay*. Princeton: Princeton University Press.

Hare, I. and Weinstein, J. (eds.) (2009). *Extreme Speech and Democracy*. Oxford: Oxford University Press.

Kalven, H. (1965). The Negro and the First Amendment 140. Cited in R. McGaffey (1973) The Heckler's Veto: A Reexamination. *Marquette Law Review* 57 (1): 39–64, available at http://scholarship.law.marquette.edu/mulr/vol57/iss1/3

Law Commission of India, 43rd Law Commission Report on Offences Against the National Security, August 1971.

Matsuda, M. J., Lawrence, C. R., Delgado, R. and Crenshaw, K. W. (1993). *Words That Wound: Critical Race Theory, Assaultive Speech and the First Amendment*. Boulder, CO: Westview Press.

Mazzarella, W. and Kaur, R. (eds.) (2009). *Censorship in South Asia: Cultural Regulation from Sedition to Seduction*. Bloomington, IN: Indiana University Press.

McGaffey, R. (1973). The Heckler's Veto: A Reexamination. *Marquette Law Review* 57(1): 39–64, available at http://scholarship.law.marquette.edu/mulr/vol57/iss1/3

Mehta, D. (2008). Words That Wound, Archiving Hate in the Making of Hindu and Muslim Publics in Bombay. In N. Khan (ed.) *Beyond Crisis: Re-evaluating Pakistan*. New Delhi: Routledge India.

Mehta, P. B. (2015). The Crooked Lives of Free Speech: Liberals Lose Plot from Paris to Delhi. *Open Magazine* 7(5), 4–10 February.

Nair, N. (2013). Beyond the 'Communal' 1920s: The Problem of Intention, Legislative Pragmatism, and the Making of Section 295A of the Indian Penal Code. *Indian Economic Social History Review* 50: 317–340.

Narrain, S. (2016). Hate Speech, Hurt Sentiment and the (Im)Possibility of Free Speech, *Economic and Political Weekly* LI (17), 23 April: 119–126.

The Parliamentary Debates, Official Report, Part II, May 29, 1951.

Punwani, J. (2014). *Why There's No Noise about the Mumbai Riots*, 14 February, http://www.rediff.com/news/column/jyoti-punwani-why-theres-no-noise-about-the-mumbai-riots/20140204.htm

Rao, S. (ed.) (2010). *The Framing of India's Constitution: Select Documents* Vol. 2. Delhi: Universal Law Publishing.

Rosenfeld, M. (2003). Hate Speech in Constitutional Jurisprudence: A Comparative Analysis. *Cardozo Law Review* 24 (4): 1523–1568.

Schauer, F. (2005). The Exceptional First Amendment, KSG Working Paper No. RWP05–021, http://ssrn.com/abstract=668543, February.

Waldron, J. (2012). *The Harm in Hate Speech*. Cambridge, MA: Harvard University Press.

'What Saamna Said', (2000) *Frontline*, Vol. 17, Issue 16, 5–18 August, http://www.frontline.in/static/html/fl1716/17160160.htm.

Part IV

Conflict between Linguistic and Legal Ideologies

9 When Voices Fail to Carry: Voice Projection and the Case of the 'Dumb' Jury[1]

Chris Heffer

EDITORS' NOTE TO CHAPTER 9

Sometimes 'voice' is lost in courtroom communication. That is what Chris Heffer sets out to show in this chapter. *Voice* is a word subject to polysemy and considerable vagueness, of course, so one part of Heffer's task is to establish the scope he will give the term, or the range of meanings he will draw on simultaneously (from *voice* as 'audible articulation' through to voice as 'assertion of point-of-view'). In the course of the chapter, Heffer sets out a model of (mis)communication he has devised called the Voice Projection Framework, and he applies that model to a case of fundamental misunderstanding between judge and jury.

'Losing' voice relates to features of the institutional context of courtroom communication, including an in-built power imbalance between speakers, procedural constraints governing the right to speak, and the problem of multiple legal audiences (which Heffer examined in detail in his book *The Language of Jury Trial: Corpus Aid Analysis of Legal Lay Discourse* (2005)). By contrast, 'projecting' a voice involves not only how a message is 'voiced' and 'heard' but also the extent to which both the speaker and hearer commit to authority and/or accommodation between their respective positions.

In a widely discussed English case involving the defendant Vasiliki Pryce – famous due to the identity of its protagonist rather than on account of its legal significance – the jurors sent ten questions to the judge during their deliberation. Both by the judge and in the national press, the questions, which were widely reported, were construed as reflecting the jurors' inability to comprehend the basic purpose of their presence at the trial, or even as simply a sign of their collective stupidity. Heffer presents an alternative account. He sets out to explain *why* the judge's and jurors' voices failed to project successfully to each other.

[1] This chapter is a much shorter and very considerably revised version of a Working Paper published in the Cardiff Working Papers in Language and Literature: 'Projecting Voice: Towards an Agentive Understanding of a Critical Capacity'. I am very grateful to Alison Wray, John Conley, Martin Kayman, Michael Toolan and an anonymous reviewer for providing acute and incisive feedback on various drafts of the paper.

By applying his Voice Projection Framework, Heffer describes how the jurors' questions, in his view, actually demonstrated legal-linguistic competence and perceptiveness about indeterminacies in the judge's directions.

The factors that Heffer takes into account in explaining miscommunication between jurors and judges are typically concerned with the institutional design of courtroom interaction. For example, he highlights how the voices of individual jurors are suppressed in jury communication to the judge, with the result that the apparently collective voice represented by the forewoman camouflages potentially major internal tensions. Jurors, he also notes, are prevented from explaining themselves to the public because of their justifiable fear of being found in contempt of court. Judicial communication is further complicated, Heffer argues, by the fact that judges address multiple audiences at the same time: the jurors, the parties of the trial, judges in higher courts who may review the case on appeal, and possibly also the media and wider public. In doing so, they can easily align their speech more to one audience than another, with a potentially damaging effect on communication with any one group.

When Voices Fail to Carry: Voice Projection and the Case of the 'Dumb' Jury

In this chapter, I apply a model of (mis)communication I have been developing to a case of fundamental misunderstanding between judge and jury. In the Voice Projection Framework, a speaker's perspective (voice) will be conveyed, or 'projected', to an interlocutor in such a way that it may or may not lead to what Bakhtin described as 'actively responsive understanding' (Bakhtin 1981). Projection involves the way a message is 'voiced' and 'heard' but also the extent to which both speakers and hearers commit to authority and/or accommodation. In the high-profile English case of Vasiliki Pryce (2013), when the jury failed to reach a verdict, the judge dismissed them as showing 'absolutely fundamental deficits in understanding'. The media almost unanimously construed this event as being emblematic of a failing jury system: of pig-ignorant jurors (the tabloids) or a woefully inadequate system of justice (the broadsheets). Rather than being indicative of a 'dumb' jury, though, the miscommunication in this case can be explained in terms of a failure of the judge's and jurors' voices to project successfully to each other due to fundamental problems regarding voicing, hearing, authority and accommodation.

After an introduction to the case, I briefly outline the key elements of the Voice Projection Framework. Then I apply the framework to the Vasiliki (Vicky) Pryce jury questions first by analyzing the judge's voicing in his summing-up to which they respond and then by exploring aspects of projection in relation to both the jury's questions and the judge's answers.

Introduction: A Case of a 'Dumb' Jury?

In the jurisdiction of England and Wales, serious indictable offences (e.g. murder and manslaughter, rape and robbery) are tried in Crown Courts before a judge and a jury of twelve randomly selected and anonymous citizens (potentially including legal professionals). A large but ever-dwindling number of cases that could alternatively be tried 'summarily' in Magistrates' Courts (so called either-way cases such as theft, burglary and dangerous driving) are also tried by jury in Crown Courts. In trial by judge and jury, the judge is responsible for legal matters, including conveying the law relevant to the case to the jury in his final 'summing up', whereas the jury is responsible for applying the law (as conveyed to them by the judge) to the evidence they have heard in court. The jury determine during their secluded post-evidential deliberation whether or not the defendant is guilty, whereas the judge will sentence the defendant if found guilty. Despite continual cutbacks by successive governments and attacks on its unprofessional nature by the media and some academics, the 'costly' and 'amateur' jury system still enjoys widespread support from both the public and legal professionals in the United Kingdom and has been empirically established as a 'fair' system of justice in both the United States and the United Kingdom (e.g. Thomas 2010).

Despite the central role of the jury in determining the outcome of a case, jurors are rendered institutionally dumb (speechless) by trial procedure. They do not speak in court,[2] they deliberate behind closed doors and they deliver their verdict via the 'foreman' in one or two words: 'guilty' or 'not guilty'. This public silence can in turn lead to a pervading fear in some sectors of society that some of those unheard jurors may also be too 'dumb' (stupid) to hear a case fairly and thus ensure that justice is done. The media, institutionally oriented to preferring the exceptional to the typical, will therefore tend to seize on any case in which any breaking of the jury's silence might be construed as evidence for a 'dumb' jury.

One notorious case of a putative 'dumb' jury occurred at the end of the first trial of the well-known UK economist Vasiliki (Vicky) Pryce. In February 2013, Pryce went on trial in London for subverting the course of justice after it emerged that (ten years earlier) she had taken driving penalty points for her ex-husband and Cabinet Minister Chris Huhne. Huhne had pleaded guilty to the offence and resigned from government but Pryce decided to claim the very rare and controversial defence of marital coercion (Coughlin 1994): namely, that she was coerced to take the points by her husband and so was

[2] It is now quite common for English jurors to send written questions to the judge to ask the witness but they do not speak out loud.

morally innocent.[3] The high profile case went before a jury and senior judge at Southwark Crown Court. The jury heard the evidence and the judge's summing-up, including directions on the law and a review of the evidence (Sweeney 2013a). Then, during what must have been difficult deliberations, the jurors sent Judge Sweeney ten questions relating to his legal directions and the constraints on their deliberation (see Appendix). The questions appeared to shock the legal professionals in court. The prosecution submitted to the judge that the jury's questions 'aimed at attempting to understand the fundamental purpose of their presence' and Judge Sweeney remarked that they showed 'absolutely fundamental deficits in understanding'. When the jury failed to reach a verdict, the judge's remarks in turn led to front-page headlines about the stupidity of some jurors, the need for qualifying IQ tests and the inadequacy of the jury system as a whole.[4] Very few commentators questioned whether the judge's harsh evaluation of the jury was justified in the context. The leading British researcher on the jury (Thomas 2014) subsequently and rightly noted that one should not arrive at conclusions about the jury based on one such 'exceptional case'. But the overwhelming perception, including that of Thomas, was that the questions *did* demonstrate alarming deficits in understanding.

Furthermore, this is not one of those cases where the judge's instructions were, as a whole, legally and/or linguistically impenetrable, as was the case, for example, with the OJ Simpson criminal trial in the United States (see Tiersma 2001). From both legal and linguistic perspectives, the judge's summing-up to the jury is in many ways exemplary. As a whole, it is well constructed, well written, logical and coherent, and it follows many of the recommendations made by linguistic and legal researchers intent on improving the comprehensibility of jury instructions: it provides a clear 'road map' through the instructions (Dumas 2000); it integrates the trial evidence with the legal directions (Auld 2001); it offers narrative illustrations of some of the legal points (Heffer 2006); and it sets out a clear 'Route to Verdict' (JSB 2010: 3) indicating, in order, the set of questions the jury needs to answer and the evidence that needs to be considered in relation to each of those questions. The judge not only read out his instructions but also provided a written copy of them for the jury to refer to during deliberation. From his own perspective, then, one can understand the judge's

[3] The defence had already been abolished in most other common law jurisdictions. It was subsequently abolished in England and Wales in 2014 by Section 177 of the Anti-social Behaviour, Crime and Policing Act 2014.

[4] A few examples: 'Are some people just too stupid to serve on a jury' (James Delingpole, *Daily Express* Feb. 22); 'Do we need IQ TESTS for juries? Vicky Pryce trial has exposed a breathtaking level of ignorance and stupidity' (Melanie Phillips, *Daily Mail* Feb. 20); 'Eight women, four men . . . and not much of a clue' (*Daily Mail* Feb. 20); 'Juries? It's time they went the way of the ducking stool.' (Simon Jenkins, *Guardian* Feb. 21); 'The Pryce of a jury's failure' (Joshua Rozenberg, *Guardian* Feb. 21).

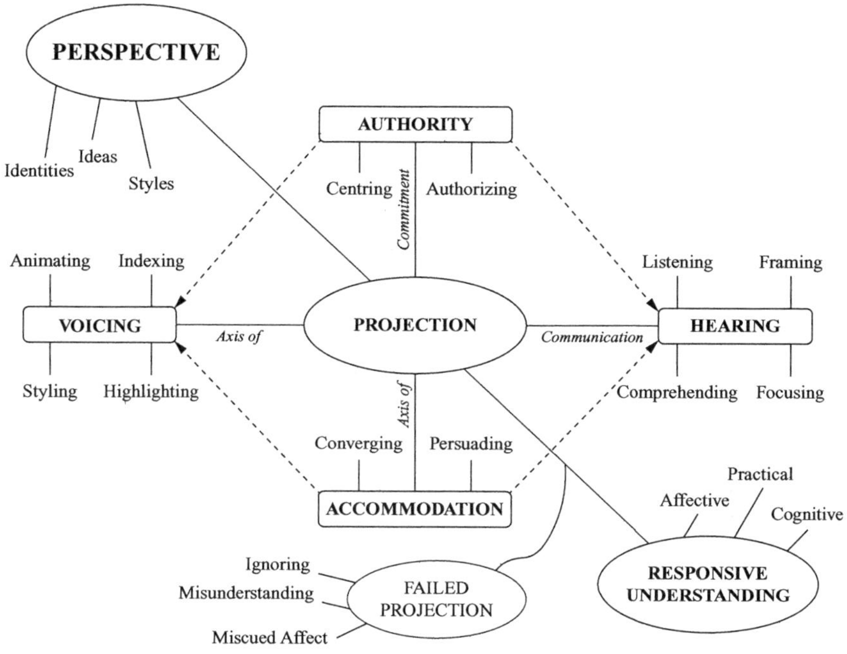

Figure 9.1 The Voice Projection Framework

exasperated comment in the trial that 'it is actually all there and has been there the whole time'.

Nevertheless, the cognitive deficit argument (the 'dumb' jury) does not stand up well to cross-examination. Several of the jury's questions, as we shall see, show legal-linguistic competence, are legally perspicacious and identify actual gaps and ambiguities in the judge's directions. Others raise fundamental questions about the nature of legal evidence. The one clearly surprising question has, I shall suggest, been worded in such a way as to invite assistance from the judge in dealing with a 'difficult' juror. In this chapter, then, I shall argue that the communication breakdown derives not from deficits in understanding but from a failure of both the professional (judge) and lay participants (jurors) to project their voices effectively.

The Voice Projection Framework

In the Voice Projection Framework, voice consists in three key elements – perspective, projection and responsive understanding – as indicated in Figure 9.1. **Perspective** in this model broadly covers the ways of being (Identities), ways of thinking (Ideas) and ways of speaking (Styles) that the speaker or group of speakers projects to a listener or audience when they are 'given voice'. **Responsive understanding** is the minimal level of response we seek from an audience when we convey our perspective: it is when they understand what we are 'getting at' to the point where they are able to actively respond – positively or negatively – to what we have said. It is not necessarily agreement or compliance but it will leave us feeling that we have 'been heard'. **Projection** is the way voice carries to an audience, or, in terms of Figure 9.1, it is the way voice travels from perspective to responsive understanding. Projection can be both active and passive: one can expend a great deal of effort in trying to make oneself understood, but one's perspective may still not carry to the audience for a multitude of reasons. Though successful projection will lead to responsive understanding, crucially, voices can fail to project, resulting in such phenomena of miscommunication as **ignoring**, for example, when a witness's evidence is discounted because the court couldn't understand his accent; **miscued affect**, as when an audience laughs at something that was meant to be serious; and plain **misunderstanding**, as when the hearer understands something quite different from that intended.

At the heart of the Voice Projection Framework is an articulation of projection. The key elements of projection outlined in the following paragraphs combine communicational aspects (voicing and hearing) with power aspects (authority and accommodation). The elements are mostly drawn from wide-ranging work in discourse analysis (e.g. Gumperz 1992, Blommaert 2005), linguistic anthropology (e.g. Bauman and Briggs 1990, Goodwin 1994, Hymes 1996) and related fields. The interaction of these elements can be very complex and there is no easy way of assessing the chances of successful projection. However, the object of the framework is to encourage holistic consideration of a variety of factors rather than just, for example, the comprehensibility of texts or accommodation to the audience.

Voicing, or giving semiotic expression to one's perspective, involves projecting both physically (**animating**) and discursively (**styling**). **Animating** is physically conveying voice through sound, sign and other forms of semiosis. When the *performative* aspects of animation are mediated through indirect discourse or writing, as very frequently happens in institutional contexts, it can mean not only loss of physical voice but also loss of meaning: the loss of 'all the emotive-affective features of speech' in indirect discourse (Voloshinov 1973: 128) or the loss of structure, emphases and implications in transcription (Tedlock 1983). **Styling**, or the selecting and arranging of words, sentences, paragraphs and so on, involves a number of key strategic choices such as that between *conforming* (following standards) and *creating* (showing individuality). It also involves *opening up* to different perspectives or 'voices' (*dialogic discourse*, Bakhtin 1981) or *silencing* other voices in favour of a single perspective (*monologic* *discourse*). The effect of styling strategies on voice projection is very much dependent on context. For example, conforming can help when the audience is well versed in the standards, but is detrimental when the audience does not know those standards (think legal writing for lawyers or non-lawyers).[5]

Voicing also involves guiding audience interpretation by pointing to particular ways of reading what is said (**indexing**) and stressing the salience of certain elements (**highlighting**). Through **indexing**, the speaker can actively *point to* (index) a particular aspect of the language or context that provides a preferred frame of interpretation. Words and other signs can index something about their form or use (metapragmatic), about how they should be interpreted, how they relate to context or how they should be valued (Gumperz 1982, 1992). For example, winking to a third party might index that what you are saying to the addressee is a lie and that you are complicit in keeping the truth from her. The speaker can also actively **highlight**, or try to show what is most salient, in a piece of discourse through selection, performance and styling. Professional practices in particular tend to highlight institutionally relevant details and let the personal stories that lay people bring recede into the background.

Although speakers can anticipate and guide hearing, hearers can also actively or unreflectively impose their own interpretations and interests on what they hear, and this might result in weakened projection. **Hearing** involves both physical **listening** (or reading) and mental **comprehending**: voice will fail to project if the audience is not paying attention or has impaired hearing or difficulty reading, or if the discourse is too complex or the hearer/reader not sufficiently intelligent to understand. Hearing also involves important interpretative practices, notably schematic **framing** and selective **focusing**, which, as indicated earlier, are guided though not at all determined by the speaker's indexing and highlighting. Frames help to interpret the unsaid within an activity in a given 'community of practice' (Lave and Wenger 1991). However, since frames are often community-specific, or even idiosyncratic, the same type of speech event can be framed in very different ways by different individuals and communities, and with different values. Closely connected with framing is **focusing**, which makes salient certain aspects of the voicing and backgrounds others. Goodwin (1994) notes how the archaeologist and the farmer will see quite different things in a patch of dirt: the archaeologist will frame it as a dig and focus on stains and artefacts; the farmer will frame it as arable land and focus on soil quality. If aspects of what we hear are not salient to us, they recede into the background and will either not be noticed or will be noticed and then *forgotten*.

Working in conjunction (or disjunction) with a communicative axis of voicing and hearing is an axis of commitment to authority and/or

[5] As illustrated in this paragraph, higher-level categories of Projection (as indicated in Figure 9.1) are in **bold**. Subcategories not indicated in Figure 9.1 and emphases are in *italics*.

accommodation. **Authority**, the source of institutional power, constrains the possibilities for both voicing and hearing (and thus projection) by imposing discursive and other norms through the practices of **centring** (working centripetally towards increasing normativity) and **authorizing** (conferring authority and legitimacy on speakers and discourse). **Centring** is the process by which 'centring institutions' (Silverstein 1998; Blommaert 2005) such as family, peer group, profession and State competitively impose their own normative standards in a *polycentric* world. Given that the centres to which we orient are not equal but stratified (some are valued much more highly than others), orienting to local community discursive norms in styling (whether in using a non-standard dialect, a restricted code, a 'foreign' language or a specialized professional language) will inevitably lead to loss of voice in the wider community if the norms diverge (Silverstein 1998). **Authorizing**, or the conferring of authority and legitimacy on speakers and discourse, both helps to project voices across space and time and can hinder projection in a given context. An *authorized voice* such as a Supreme Court judge is empowered to effect change in the law by issuing judgments that deviate from the prior authoritative discourse of earlier judgments (Heffer 2013). They then project their voice through others by acting as the source of the words, as 'principal' in Goffman's terms (1981: 144). The ensuing *authoritative discourse* (Bakhtin 1981: 342), originating in the agency of an authorized voice, is then perceived by speakers in germane discursive contexts (e.g. a trial judge delivering legal instructions) as a structural constraint on voicing: it leaves us little option in terms of how we style our message. *Authoritative discourse* will thus travel relatively intact *in form* across time but precisely because it is impervious to context, it can soon fail to project to audiences beyond a specialist community (words that made sense to ordinary people a hundred years ago might not make sense now). What is required in such cases is contextual **accommodation** to the audience.

Accommodation, or the extent to which speakers adapt their speech to the audience, involves practices of **converging**, or adapting to the communicative norms of the speaker, and **persuading**, or being rhetorically efficacious. **Converging** can facilitate both comprehension and solidarity, and thus help to project voice. In institutional contexts, converging can involve lay participants moving towards professional discourse norms or professionals moving towards everyday discourse norms. Speakers need both the capacity and motivation to converge. They need the *communicative competence* (Hymes 1972) to 'pass' to a greater or lesser extent as members of a given discourse community. Converging with specialized discourse communities is more difficult than converging with general ones: a speaker might be able to narrate effectively in conversation but not in court. Converging also requires motivation: ritualistic institutional discourse is often not primarily aimed at communication at all (Heffer 2013), while professionals often use the excuse of authority to avoid having to converge (Heffer 2006). Though converging with the local community's discursive norms is likely to facilitate comprehension, successful voice projection generally requires an orientation to **persuading** rather than simply informing the audience. Where speakers are motivated to respond to a rhetorical situation, as with trial lawyers determined to win their cases in adversarial courts, audience-oriented rhetoric will naturally ensue. Where extrinsic motivation is lacking, though, institutional speakers may hide behind authority and 'impermeable' authoritative discourse. Where voicing is not oriented towards being heard, towards actively responsive understanding, it is *recitation*, or voicing to be voiced. Re-citing what has been said before, particularly in ritual, can occur irrespective of audience understanding. Authoritative discourse, then, is always in danger of not projecting when it is recited rather than communicated rhetorically.

Many Voices, Many Hearers: The Pryce Jurors and the Judge's Audiences

The preceding outline of the Voice Projection Framework assumes, for explanatory simplicity, that we are dealing with a single speaker/writer or homogenous group communicating with a given type of audience. The reality of many institutional contexts is more complex than this and this needs to be borne in mind when applying the framework. Indeed, one of the key reasons for the communication breakdown between judge and jury in the Pryce case is arguably because certain voices and certain audiences were suppressed.

Jurors are thrust together 'from all walks of life' (as judges are wont to say) to form a forced and fleeting virtual community. There is a hidden heterogeneity, then, in the singular 'jury' that defies attempts to conceive it as a 'common' community with shared conditions or interests. Jurors are certainly drawn from '*the* community', where community is understood purely as 'locality', but otherwise they may have little in common in a globalized world. Southwark, the London locality in which the Vicky Pryce trial took place, is particularly heterogeneous, with, for example, 34 per cent of its population born outside the United Kingdom, and 32 per cent belonging to ethnic minorities.[6] However, the twelve individual voices of the jury, which may be heard in all their diversity in the jury room, are hidden from public (and even researcher) hearing.

In the media reaction to Judge Sweeney's comments, the jurors' own voices were again silenced by the Contempt of Court Act 1981, which, unlike in the

[6] *The Guardian* Data Blog 26 May 2011 at www.theguardian.com/news/datablog/2011/may/26/foreign-born-uk-population# and 18 May 2011 at www.theguardian.com/news/datablog/2011/may/18/ethnic-population-england-wales. Some of the right-wing tabloids made an implicit or explicit link between the visible ethnic minority status of most of the jurors and their 'deficits' in understanding (e.g. Littlejohn 2013).

United States, prohibits any interviewing of jurors in any form about their deliberations. The circumstantial evidence available from the textual records points to a situation of discursive conflict: the deliberation was very long (fourteen hours) for a legally simple case; it passed to a majority verdict phase; Question 5, as discussed later, was **styled** in a way that suggested distance between the author of the questions and the juror that originated the question; the jury ultimately failed to reach agreement; and the forewoman **highlighted** tensions when, in her final note to the judge about the possibility of reaching a verdict, she underlined 'highly unlikely' twice. The *polyvocality* of the deliberation, though, is for the most part lost as the questions travel back to court and beyond. First, most of the questions are lifted from their interactional situation of conflict and entextualized in a *univocal* and ordered written list. The requirement to present the questions in written form means that the distinctive voices (physical, discursive and rhetorical) of the individual jurors are lost. We cannot know for sure whether the person who wrote out the questions is merely **animating** the questions of other jurors or authoring them, nor how many principals are involved (theoretically, each question might represent a different juror's voice or a combination of different voices), nor how much conflict and negotiation went into the **styling** of the questions. We can speculate that the first eight questions, sent out at the same time and showing stylistic similarities, are authored by the forewoman and I shall both make this assumption and focus on those questions.

If that is the case, though, some of the jurors will have already lost voice in the process of converting oral sentiment into rational text from a given authorial perspective. Question 5 in particular seems to be **styled** by the forewoman to convey a metapragmatic comment on the juror who is the source of the question:[7]

Q5. Can *a juror come to a verdict* based on a reason that was *not presented in court* and has *no facts or evidence to support it?*

Firstly, by using the indefinite article ('can **a** juror') in place of the collective 'we' or 'the jury', the forewoman appears to be deliberately singling out the discordant voice of an indefinite individual juror. Secondly, this discordant voice is projected as not merely wanting to 'consider' or 'take into account' the proffered reason as one of many elements that might support a given verdict but quite simply to 'come to a verdict' based on this reason. Finally, that 'reason' is presented in an entirely negative fashion: '*not* presented in court'; '*no* facts or evidence to support it'. The **styling** of the question, then, seems to **index** it

[7] It is quite possible (though this is speculative) that we can hear the original voice of the juror in the individually submitted Question 10: 'Would religious conviction be a good enough reason for a wife feeling she had no choice i.e. she promised to obey her husband in her wedding vows, he ordered her to do something and she felt she had to obey?'

to the hearer as 'stupid', though this is not how it appears to have been **framed** by the judge. Consider how the question might have been **styled** if the author had aligned with the principal (and the forewoman demonstrates through her other questions that she is perfectly capable of styling in this manner):

Q5B. *Can we consider a possible form of coercion* that was not presented in court *but might be inferred from the evidence as a whole?*

This is a far more reasonable question. The answer would still be 'no', but would be due to the specific law of evidence (fact finders should consider only reasons presented in court) rather than universal laws of reasoning (basing our decisions on facts and evidence rather than pure conjecture). It is quite possible, then, that the forewoman has distorted one or more dissenting voices in the jury, thus preventing that voice from projecting effectively to the judge. And those voices may not actually be 'dumb' but might be challenging the very nature of the controversial law on marital coercion.

Once the questions are written, they are further decontextualized as they are removed from the jury room. They are subsequently recontextualized by the judge who will have read them out in court (**animated** but probably not *performed*) with new accents and intonations and without knowledge of the discursive history of deliberation that led to their entextualization. They are now perceived as a univocal *monologic* text that conforms to the legal institutional view of the jury as a single counterbalancing side of the judicial scales: the judge determines the law; the jury determine the facts. In its institutional role, the jury, like the judge, is singular and speaks with one voice through the 'foreman'. The judge tells the jury that, in deciding the facts 'you bring, and are entitled to use, your joint experience of life and your common sense'. However, the *polyvocality* of deliberation remains locked in the jury room. The judge's metapragmatic comment on the questions as demonstrating 'absolutely fundamental deficits in understanding' then steers their recontextualization in the media through the metapragmatic **frames** of 'stupid jury' or 'defunct system'. The voice of the individual jurors has by this stage long been lost.

We can also not assume that the judge is always focused on conveying his perspective to the jury. Judges are mindful of at least three different audiences: the jury, the legal parties at trial and the higher tribunals that might review the case. In high-profile cases like this one, they will also be aware of the media. Importantly, Judge Sweeney, during the course of the trial, had written a twenty-eight-page Ruling on Marital Coercion that shifted the persuasive burden of this defence from Defence to Prosecution (Sweeney 2013b). Whereas previously the Defence was required to prove marital coercion on the balance of probabilities, now the Defence only needed to adduce some evidence that the marital coercion defence applied and the burden was now on the Prosecution to prove beyond reasonable doubt that the wife was not coerced by her husband. The jury was not made aware of this, as they are sent out of court whenever legal matters are discussed. Nevertheless, it is well recognized that the primary function of the judge's summing-up to the jury must be to communicate the law effectively to the jury so that they are in a position to apply that law to the case in hand. If the jury do not 'get it' then, irrespective of their actions in deliberation and irrespective of the reactions of other potential audiences, the judge's voice will not have projected successfully to the jury. Similarly, assuming the institutionally homogeneous status of the jury, if the judge fails to understand what the jury are 'getting at' then their univocal voice will have failed to project (as indeed it failed to project to the media).

The Voice of the Judge

We cannot hope to understand the jury's questions (see Appendix) without some understanding of at least the immediate communication to which they respond: the judge's summing-up on the law (his 'legal directions', 'instructions' or 'jury charge').

Authority and the Styling of the Judge's Instructions

Authority is clearly central in judges' instructions to juries and very significantly determines both the **styling** and the degree to which judges can **accommodate** to jurors. In many U.S. jurisdictions the judge can merely **animate** 'pattern' legal instructions authored by legal committees (Dumas 2000) but in England and Wales, judges have considerably more discretion to **style** their own instructions and the recent move has been *away* from pattern instructions rather than towards them (JSB 1999, 2010). Judges are, though, still constrained by *authoritative discourse* and there is still the risk that the wording they choose will be criticized by the higher courts, the legal **centring** institutions according to the Voice Projection Framework. There is accordingly a discursive tension in British judges between merely **animating** authoritative legal discourse and using their *authorized voice* to **style** the instructional texts. Individual **styling** is essential for projection in this case since it permits the judge to **accommodate** to the lay audience (a point taken up in the following section).

The *authoritative discourse* at the heart of the judge's directions in this trial is that relating to marital coercion. Marital coercion was originally a legal presumption that a man's wife was under his control and so would naturally be coerced into conspiracy and consequently be morally if not legally innocent. There had long been dissenting voices against this presumption, not least Mr Bumble in *Oliver Twist* who railed that 'If the law supposes that, . . . the law is a ass – a idiot' (Dickens 1837–39/1970: 489). Several controversial cases eventually led to the presumption being abolished by statute in 1925, but that statute at the same time introduced the possible *defence* of marital coercion:

[O]n a charge against a wife for any offence other than treason or murder it shall be a good defence to prove that the offence was committed in the presence of, and under the coercion of, the husband. (Criminal Justice Act 1925, Section 47)

The defendant, then, in claiming this defence rather than relying on the previous presumption, now had to prove as more likely than not that she was under the coercion of her husband.

Judge Sweeney, in his directions to the jury in *Pryce*, points out that 'the defence of marital coercion' is 'the critical issue in this case'. He then directs them as follows:

(1)[8] The law recognises, via the defence of marital coercion, that a wife is morally blameless if she committed an offence **only** because her husband was present and coerced her – that is put pressure on her to commit the offence in such a way that, as a result, her will was overborne (in the sense that she was impelled to commit the offence because she truly believed that she had no real choice but to do so).

(2) A wife's will would not have been overborne (in the sense that I have just described) if, for example, she was persuaded by force of argument to choose (albeit reluctantly) to commit the offence rather than to take another course, or if she was persuaded (albeit reluctantly) to commit the offence out of love for, or loyalty to, her husband or family, or to avoid inconvenience (whether to herself or others). Her will must have been overborne in the sense that she was impelled to commit the offence because she truly believed that she had no real choice but to do so.

(3) It is not, however, for the defendant to prove that Mr Huhne coerced her – rather it is for the prosecution to prove that he did not do so. The Prosecution may do that (as they seek to in this case) either by making you feel sure that Mr Huhne was not present when Ms Pryce committed the offence, or by making you feel sure that her will was not overborne (i.e. that she was not impelled to commit the offence because she truly believed that she had no real choice but to do so).

(Summing-up, *R v Pryce*. Emphasis in original.)

The three paragraphs in turn: (1) define 'marital coercion', (2) indicate what it does not cover, (3) indicate that the burden of proof is on the prosecution. Paragraph 3 is clearly in contrast with the 1925 statute, a point to which I shall return.

One might expect at least the definitional paragraph to be dominated by the *authoritative legal discourse* of statutes and judicial judgments. However, as the following annotated paragraph shows, only a few words in the direction come

[8] I have numbered the paragraphs for ease of reference. There is no numbering in the document available online, which I assume is the written version of the directions made available to the jury.

from the 1925 Act – 'wife' (not husband or partner), 'husband . . . present' (not elsewhere), 'defence' (not presumption), 'coercion' (not duress) – and the lack of definition of 'coercion' in the Act leads to the inclusion of three key terms from judicial judgment: 'pressure', 'will was overborne' and 'impelled'.

> The law recognises, via the **defence** of marital **coercion**, that a **wife** is morally blameless if she committed an offence only because her **husband** was **present** and **coerced** her – that is *put pressure on her* to commit the offence in such a way that, as a result, *her will was overborne* (in the sense that she was *impelled* to commit the offence because she truly believed that she had no real choice but to do so).
>
> (**Bold** = statutory discourse; *italics* = judicial opinion; underline = legal terms; dotted underline = formulaic phrases found in legal register)

The remaining words, then, are not merely **animating** *authoritative legal discourse* but are also **stylistically** *conforming* to legal *register*. There are specific legal terms such as 'the defence of marital coercion' and more general ones such as 'commit an offence'. A term such as 'morally blameless' is not found in legal dictionaries but is either explicitly or implicitly opposed to 'legal blame', particularly in the expression 'legally culpable but morally blameless', and goes to the heart of the distinction between legal and moral accountability (Arenella 1991) that is central to the issue of marital coercion. We also find formulaic phrases that are not exclusive to legal *register* but are typically found in legal discourse across common law countries and in particular textual environments: 'The law recognizes', 'only because', 'in such a way that as a result', 'because [s/he] truly believed that [s/he]', 'had no real choice but to do so'. Finally, the paragraph conforms to the typical definitional syntax of legislation (Bhatia 1994): it is one long sentence with multiple complex embedding that, as psycholinguists have shown, can cause problems in comprehension.

We might predict that such a paragraph, heavily permeated as it is with *authoritative legal discourse* and legal *register*, will not project well to a jury unversed in such language. The communicative burden, then, would seem to be on the judge. However, the judge is also engaged in communication with the legal community. He is fully aware of his *authorized voice* as he *creates* a new, judicially authored direction. He is also likely to be aware, given the rarity of the marital coercion defence, that he is *creating authoritative discourse* in the process.

Accommodation: Reciting Rules versus Persuading People

We have established in the last section that even in the paragraph of the judge's directions that is most highly constrained by **authority**, there is room for **styling** and thus for **accommodation**. However, **styling** does not presuppose **accommodation** since the author might orient towards *reciting* rather than

persuading. As is often the case in legal definition, we hear different strata of **voicing** lying on top of each other like an ancient building that has been extended piecemeal over the centuries as owners have responded to changing circumstances. Thus the 'coercion' of the statute is first defined by a trial judge as the 'will' being 'overborne' (*R v Richman*)[9] and then this is *authorized* by a High Court judge (*R v Shortland*).[10] Next, 'overborne' is defined in terms of being 'impelled' (*D.P.P. For Northern Ireland v Lynch*),[11] which in turn is recognized as needing glossing. In his full direction on marital coercion (cited earlier), the judge tries to **focus** jury hearing by **highlighting** his definition of 'coercion' through slightly reformulated repetition reflecting the slightly different contextualizations of the three paragraphs:

her will [was/must have been/was not] overborne ([in the sense/i.e.] that she [was/was not] impelled to commit the offence because she truly believed that she had no real choice but to do so).

This is reminiscent of the famous Rule of Three enunciated by the Bellman in the *Hunting of the Snark*: 'What I tell you three times is true' (Carroll 1898/2006: 15).[12] He repeats this formula again in his Route to Verdict at the end of the summing-up. However, the legal-linguistic belief that **highlighting** a phrase through repetition, both within a summing-up and across time, will make it cognitively salient and thus comprehensible to the jury confuses salience with comprehension (Heffer 2013). The syntax here is complex. There is also a reversal of everyday definitional and rhetorical practice: *rarer* words are used to explain a more common word. While, in the Oxford English Dictionary's (OED's) frequency information, 'coercion' is a band 5 word (1 to 10 occurrences per million words), a band described as 'literate vocabulary associated with educated discourse' (OED 2017), 'overborne' is a band 2 word (less than 0.01 occurrences per million words), a band described as consisting in 'terms which are not part of normal discourse and would be unknown to most people'. Indeed, 'overborne' occurs only thirteen times in the British National Corpus of English (BNC) and nine of these citations relate to legal reports on cases involving coercion or consent. 'Overborne' is then explained with the still 'literate' band 5 term 'impelled'. While such less-than-comprehensible legal language might be attributed to the *authoritative discourse* of statute and precedent, it is notable that, in his response to the jury's question on marital coercion

[9] 'she had to prove that her will was overborne by the wishes of her husband' (*R v Gary Richman and Ann Richman*).

[10] *R v Shortland* ([1996] 1 Cr. App. R.116).

[11] Lord Simon: 'Coercion' in its popular sense denotes an external force which cannot be resisted and which impels its subject to act otherwise than he would wish.' (*D.P.P. for Northern Ireland v. Lynch* [1975] A.C. 653).

[12] My thanks to Alison Wray for this link.

(discussed later), the judge simply removes the discursive layer of 'overborne' altogether:

A1: The law requires that a husband was present and coercion was to such an extent that she was impelled to commit an offence because she truly believed she had no real choice but to do so.

It is simply not the case, then, that the judge is prevented by *authoritative discourse* from converging further with the jury. Successive guidelines to English judges (JSB 1999, 2010) have insisted that judges should not be 'slaves to wording' and that communication with the jury is paramount, while empirical investigation has indicated an extraordinary range of stylistic convergence and divergence amongst English Crown Court judges delivering legal directions to juries (Heffer 2005: 157–75). Defining a difficult term with a more difficult one can only be classified as 'divergence' whereas ritualistic repetition could not possibly be conceived as 'convergence' (Heffer 2013).

Further evidence of divergence within the marital coercion direction can be drawn from the fact that the judge's written Ruling on marital coercion includes almost identical paragraphs to those he would deliver in the summing-up,[13] *except that* in the Ruling, designed to be read by fellow legal professionals, the judge glosses the two uncommon terms 'overborne' and 'impelled' with the two 'everyday language' band 6 words (10 to 100 occurrences per million) 'overcome' and 'forced':[14]

> Her will must have been overborne *(i.e. overcome)* in the sense that she was impelled *(i.e. forced)* to commit the offence because she truly believed that she had no real choice but to do so. (my emphasis)

The judge thus appears to recognize the need to provide assistance with the language for his fellow legal professionals in the Ruling but not for the lay jury in his summing-up. A likely explanation for this is that in the summing-up, or at least in the part where he sets out his legal directions, he is oriented to **authority**, to the legal **centring** institutions and thus to *reciting* rules, whereas in the Ruling he is oriented to *rhetoric* – to **persuading** his audience of fellow legal professionals.

In summary, then, at least with regard to the crucial legal direction on marital coercion, the judge, probably both mindful of the dangers of appeal and following his legal-linguistic habitus (Heffer 2013), was pulled discursively towards **authority** and away from **accommodation** and this will have hindered

[13] The ruling was made orally (but with the jury sent out) before his summing-up on 19 February 2013 but was written up and published on 7 March 2013. It is not clear, then, whether the direction in the summing-up is a recontextualization of the paragraph in the ruling or vice versa.

[14] The *Collins English Dictionary Online* puts both 'overcome' and 'forced' in their band of most frequent or 'very common' words (top 4,000) (Collins 2013).

his attempt to project his legal perspective to the jury. There are few if any signs in this direction of **converging** with everyday communicational norms and his Ruling for fellow professionals is more persuasive than his summing-up to the lay jury.

The Voice(s) of the Jury and Judicial Hearing

The jury's questions come in response to the judge's oral and written summing-up and were construed by the judge as evidence of serious mishearing. I argue in this section that, though the questions constitute a limited amount of data, several of them suggest actively **responsive understanding** of the judge's directions while the judge's own responses are likely not to have projected well.

Jury Converging with Legal Discourse, Judge Diverging from Lay Discourse

A lay jury might be excused for struggling with legal language. Yet the jury's questions demonstrate a considerable degree of *legal communicative competence* and thus clear signs of an attempt to **converge** with legal discourse. This is evident from the first question in the jury's list:

Q1. You have defined the defence of marital coercion on page 5 of the jury bundle and also explained what does not fall within the definition by way of examples. Please expand on the definition, provide examples of what may fall within the defence, specifically 'will was overborne' and does the defence require violence or physical threat?

Legal terms such as 'jury bundle',[15] 'defence of marital coercion' and 'will was overborne' might merely be echoing expressions used by the judge in his summing-up. More significantly, though, the question uses formulaic phrases belonging to a legal *register* that are *not* used in the summing-up and that are unlikely to have been used elsewhere in the proceedings. For example, 'fall within the definition' and 'fall within the defence' are almost exclusively used in legal contexts: all fourteen citations of 'fall within the definition' in the BNC are in legal contexts whereas 'fall within the defence' does not occur. Use of such terms as 'at the material time' and 'notice of intent to prosecute' in other questions confirms that there is at least some *legal communicative competence*.

The question also demonstrates an orientation to legal-institutional **framing** of the trial events. The judge's summing-up could be seen as his legal 'diagnosis' (Agar 1985: 149) of the more fully voiced personal testimony of witnesses

[15] The 'jury bundle' is the collection of documents relating to the case provided to each of the jurors.

that has been presented to the jury. The jury question shows an ability to orient to the judge's institutional **framing** by identifying a substantial oversight in the judge's directions. *Authoritative* legal opinion has established that judges should define not only what the defence of marital coercion does *not* include (as the judge does in the second paragraph of his direction) but also what it *does* include (e.g. psychological bullying) (*R v Shortland*). It has also established that judges should make quite clear that the defence does *not* require violence or physical threat (*R v Cairns*). So the jury is quite perspicaciously identifying gaps in the judge's directions. In placing this question first and **styling** it in a legal fashion, the forewoman is arguably **indexing** that she has at least some awareness of legal discourse.

Yet the judge does not appear to pick up on the indexing of this competence, perhaps because it is part of his own background legal *competence* and thus not perceptually salient, or worthy of **focus**.[16] Most significantly, the judge, in dealing with the questions, re-orders them so that the one demonstrating greatest legal-linguistic competence (Question 1 in the jury's list) is demoted to eighth place while the one that is arguably deliberately styled by the forewoman to indicate a juror's incompetence (Question 5, discussed earlier) is placed first (Guardian 2013a, 2013b). The psychological effects of primacy are well-known: people pay more attention to the first item in a list and impressions of a person change according to whether the first items in a list are positive or negative (Asch 1946). It is difficult to imagine, then, how Question 5 could not have created a negative impression of the jury on the judge's audiences when he promoted it to first position. I am not suggesting that the judge *deliberately* misrepresented the jury's perspective when he re-ordered the questions; I am more inclined to believe that he was simply dealing with the 'easy' questions first before tackling the more substantial ones. However, the net effect of this re-ordering on the legal and media audiences may well have been **miscued affect**: ridicule rather than rational consideration.

Another *institutionally* **framed** directive question showing **convergence** with legal discourse is the one on the criminal standard of proof:

Q4. Can you define what is reasonable doubt?

The Judicial College (formerly Judicial Studies Board), the body that trains and advises English and Welsh judges, has long recommended not using the very poorly understood legal expression *beyond reasonable doubt* at all and replacing it with the everyday paraphrase *sure*:

> The prosecution proves its case if the jury, having considered all the evidence relevant to the charge they are considering, are sure that the defendant is guilty. Further explanation is unwise. (JSB 2010: 16)

[16] Alternatively, he might be defending himself from a potential loss of face.

It has always been considered 'unwise' to attempt to explain 'reasonable doubt' and most judges are happy to keep with the *sure* paraphrase (Heffer 2005: 170). Unfortunately, Judge Sweeney told the jury in summing-up that 'must make you feel sure of guilt' is 'the same as, but no more than, the proof of guilt beyond reasonable doubt'. Once again he is moving from the common expression to the rare one: 'beyond reasonable doubt' is set as the standard against which to measure the 'novel' expression 'make you feel sure', rather than vice versa. If the judge, in responding to the question, had been oriented to **persuading**, he might have told the jury simply to consider whether the prosecution had made them feel sure of guilt and not to worry about the meaning of 'reasonable doubt'. Instead, he seeks the apparent safety of legal **authority**:

A4: The prosecution must make you feel sure beyond reasonable doubt. A reasonable doubt is a doubt that is reasonable. These are ordinary English words that the law does not allow me to help you with, beyond the written directions.

First, against explicit legal recommendation (e.g. JSB 2010), he qualifies plain English 'sure' with the legal term 'beyond reasonable doubt' (which the jurors have already indicated they do not **comprehend**). Second, he utters the common judicial tautology 'A reasonable doubt is a doubt that is reasonable', which in fact is only true if 'reasonable' is understood as 'rational' rather than its more common contemporary meanings of 'moderate' or 'fair' (Heffer 2007). Third, he utters the common judicial myth 'These are ordinary English words' (that can therefore be understood by jurors), which has been shown to be empirically false (Heffer 2013). Finally, he points out that 'the law does not allow me to help you with' the term. Unlike the jury, then, with respect to legal discourse, he shows few signs of **convergence** with everyday communicational norms.[17]

Styling Obligation

A second pair of questions (2 and 7) is styled in terms of legal obligations in assessing the evidence:

Q2. In the scenario that... what *should* the verdict be?

Q7. Does the defendant have an *obligation* to present a defence?

These **index** an orientation to legal-institutional **framing** but request clarification on legal points that are not self-evident, or betray some ambiguity for the non-expert. Question 7, on the defendant's obligations, illustrates this well.

[17] My object here is not to criticize the judge, who has clearly made an effort to accommodate to the jury in much of his summing-up, but to suggest that, in providing such an evidently unhelpful response, he must have been focused on authoritative recitation rather than rhetorical projection.

The judge's Ruling on marital coercion is a twenty-eight-page document arguing the case for reversing the persuasive burden of proof from the defence to the prosecution (Sweeney 2013b). This constitutes a significant change in the law and is an example of a judge using his *authorized voice* to 'make law'. The carefully argued Ruling, like judicial judgments or opinions, is a piece of *rhetorical* discourse that engages with other voices. As Mertz points out with regard to U.S. judicial opinions, 'The reference within the texts of many opinions . . . indexes an exchange in which multiple points of view have been acknowledged' and 'the hegemonic voice' of the judge is forced 'to explicitly recognize and respond to these alternative views' (Mertz 1996: 139). We thus hear the arguments put forth by defence and prosecution and the various competing voices on the issue through time. This is a classic dialogic text, a fine exercise in rhetoric. In the summing-up, though, this is recontextualized for the jury as *authoritative monologic discourse*:

> It is not, however, for the defendant to prove that Mr Huhne coerced her – rather it is for the prosecution to prove that he did not do so.

In response to the jury's question on the issue, the judge is categorical:

A7: There is no burden on the defendant to prove her innocence and there is no burden on her to prove anything at all. The defendant does not have an obligation to present a defence.

Thus the many conflicting voices that contributed to the judge's eventual decision on this matter, and that are engaged with openly in the Ruling, are silenced and the persuasive burden (which has only just been reversed by the judge) is presented as a timeless truth. This is the *authorized voice* of the judge that is speaking rather than the *authoritative discourse* of legal history and it would be particularly confusing for the forewoman if she did in fact have some experience with the law.

Focusing the Evidence and Forgetting Equity

A third set of the jury's questions (3, 6 and 8) is **styled** in terms of what is legally permissible in assessing the evidence:

Q3. . . . *can* inferences be drawn to arrive at a verdict?

Q6. *Can we* infer anything from the fact that . . .

Q8. *Can we* speculate about the events . . .

These do orient to *institutional* **framing** but also engage *narrative* **framing**, which considers all aspects relevant to an overall narrative understanding of events. The questions address an area where the law of evidence lacks certainty: the difficult line between inference and speculation.

Question 3 is a case in point:

Q3. If there is debatable evidence supporting the prosecution case can inferences be drawn to arrive at a verdict? If so can inferences/speculation be drawn on the full evidence or only where you have directed us to do so?

The forewoman **highlights** *inferences* being drawn but then, in referring back to her main question, she makes the institutional 'mistake' of mentioning 'speculation' alongside 'inferences'. In doing so she is recognizing that it is not at all easy to draw the line between the two. Indeed this difficulty is well recognized in the legal community: 'The difference between an inference and mere speculation is a fine line to distinguish.... At some point, the link between the facts and the conclusion becomes so tenuous that we call it "speculation." When that point is reached is, frankly, a matter of judgment' (Watt 2011: 104–105). In academic discourse, to 'speculate' often means to apply a lower evidential standard but not one that is wholly uncalled for (I have explicitly speculated several times in this chapter). In legal discourse, on the other hand, others are seen to speculate while 'we' draw valid inferences.

The judge, though, responds to the question with a firm binary categorization:

A3: The drawing of an inference is a permissible process. Speculation is not.

Against a murky background of real life evidence with all its epistemological nuances and uncertainties, the judge **highlights** through parallelism the 'permissible process' of inferencing: Inferencing, the logical drawing of conclusions from the evidence, is the permissible legal *figure* against a background of impermissible speculation, just as admitted 'material' evidence is the *figure* against a background of 'immaterial' evidence. However, the judge is not the only voice on this. The lawyers in the trial encourage jurors to think in narrative as well as logical ways. Prosecuting counsel told the jury in his closing speech that ultimately 'you have to look hard at her and decide what kind of person she is and that exercise will probably tell you the answer'. He is relying on the folk narrative script that 'when two powerful, clever, affluent people decide on a course of action you probably conclude that they do that with their eyes open'. Defence counsel replied in his own closing argument that 'Bullies, domineers, don't just use their fists. They don't have to. Clever people like Mr Huhne have other ways of controlling and domineering'. In deciding such narrative scenarios (Pennington and Hastie 1991), it is very difficult indeed to draw the line between inference and speculation.

One reason for believing the Pryce jury to be 'dumb' is that legal professionals considered the case a 'simple' and clearly delineated one. Yet that is only the case if you orient to the law as your normative **centre**. Some jurors orient instead to morality or their common sense of justice (Finkel 2001). The defence of marital coercion in particular appeals to natural law and justice and the distinction between legal culpability and moral blamelessness: one can be wrong in law but excused in life. Some of the jurors, then, might have been applying 'equity', or 'the recourse to principles of justice to correct or supplement the law as applied to particular circumstances' (Garner 2009). Interestingly, the application of equity follows *successful* not *failed* projection: you have to 'get' the law before you can reject it. However, whereas judges are said to draw on equity to 'supplement' existing law to bring about a just result, juries (at least in the United States) are said to 'nullify' the law, to make it void or invalid. In other words, judicial equity is projected as resulting in a gain to society while jury equity is considered to be an inevitable loss. Yet the history of jury equity (as much as this can be known – [Finkel 2001]) suggests that the jury's silent but empowered voice in such cases has frequently been a gain. Juries have made their voice heard in eighteenth-century England when they refused to convict for petty capital crimes and again in the twenty-first century when they have refused to convict in euthanasia cases. In the Vicky Pryce case they may have objected to the requirement that the husband needed to be physically present to apply overbearing psychological pressure, as this fails to take account of what we know about controlling and domineering spouses (Follingstad and DeHart 2000). Or they may have simply disagreed with the judge's view of Pryce, as suggested subtly in his summing-up and stated explicitly in his sentencing remarks after the retrial, that she was 'controlling, manipulative and devious' (Sweeney 2013c). It is perhaps significant in this respect that eight of the twelve jurors were women and ten appeared to belong to ethnic minorities.[18] Rather than the jury *forgetting* the judge's instructions then, the judge may have been *forgetting* jury equity.

Failed Projection

It is this last point about forgetting jury equity that is the key to interpreting the judge and jury's failure to project successfully to each other. Figure 9.2 summarizes the key elements of voice projection in this case, with plain type indicating points relating to the judge's projection and italics indicating points relating to the jury's projection.

The central issue is one of **authority**. Whereas the judge orients to the law alone as his normative **centre**, the jury orients not only to the law but also to the community's (or communities') sense of morality and natural justice.

[18] The ethnic composition, as well as the gender composition, can only be anecdotal since it is not possible to obtain any information on jurors in England and Wales.

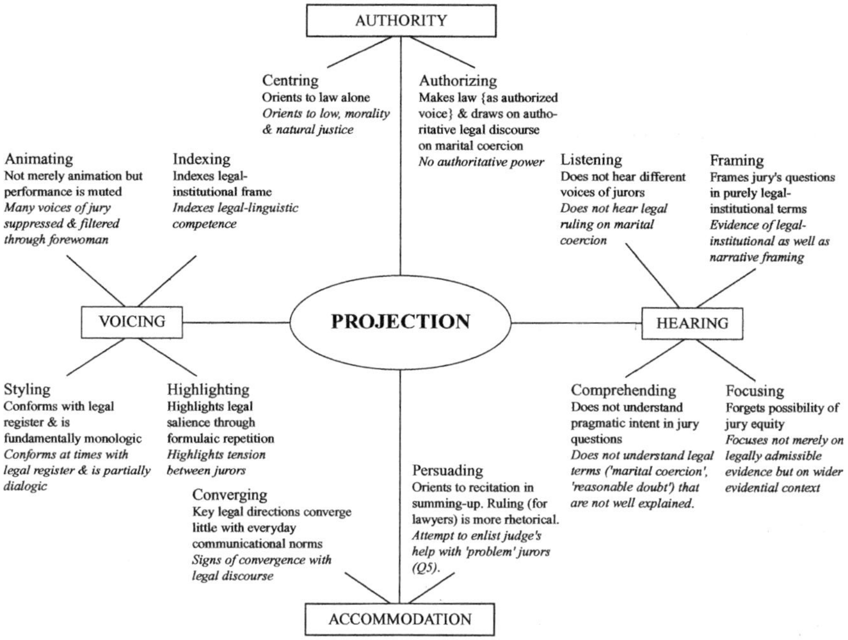

Figure 9.2 Key Elements Affecting the Judge and *Jury*'s Voice Projection

However, in the trial context, the judge has the full weight of **authority** behind his orientation, both as an *authorized voice* 'making' the law on marital coercion and as a reciter of *authoritative legal discourse.* The jury, on the other hand, only has **authority** to deliver a verdict. This power imbalance has consequences for both **hearing** and **accommodation**. In terms of **hearing**, the judge fits the evidence he has heard in the trial into a *legal-institutional* **frame**, backgrounding any elements that do not fall tightly within that frame. The jury **index** an understanding of that *legal-institutional* **frame** but (like lawyers in closing arguments) also frame that evidence in narrative terms that go beyond legal-institutional strictures; this may lead to **focusing** on elements in the wider evidential context that are not 'heard' by the judge. In terms of **accommodation**, the judge has no immediate need to risk going beyond *authoritative legal discourse.* Taken as a whole, his summing-up is a model of instructional clarity but his key legal directions (those for the most part queried by the jury) **converge** little with everyday communicational norms despite the jury's own attempt to **converge** with legal discourse. He thus *recites* rather than **persuades**, **highlighting** legal salience through repetition of formulas not understood by the jurors. His **styling** consequently *conforms* with legal *register*, which the forewoman succeeds in emulating, but which is not necessarily **comprehended** by the other jurors. Finally, though the forewoman seems to fail to convey her perspective to the judge (who, apparently focused on the legal semantics, misunderstands the pragmatics of Question 5), we must not forget that the other jurors' voices are filtered through (and perhaps suppressed by) the forewoman herself.

Conclusion

In their seminal study of the American jury, Kalven and Zeisel (1971: 219) noted that 'in many ways the jury is the law's most interesting critic' and that jurors are often critical of 'the nicety of the law's boundaries'. What we see in the Pryce jury's questions is a group of individuals struggling with the niceties of these boundaries. Considering the way the judge projects his own voice, with a preference in the key directions for recitation of rules over persuasion of people, and the way he appears to fail to hear (and thus respond to) the jury's narrative framing of events, the jury, rather than forgetting the judge's directions, appear to be actively responding to them as best they can. The questions they ask show an awareness of the law but also challenge its subtle distinctions and even its very foundations. This is arguably precisely what is required of the jury as a democratic institution. Nevertheless their perspective clearly failed to project to the judge and they also clearly failed to persuade each other.

The Voice Projection Framework outlined and applied here can help produce a richer and more holistic analysis of such institutional contexts. One could certainly discuss the linguistic complexity of the marital coercion direction or the nicety of the law's legal and linguistic boundaries without recourse to such a model. The claim, though, is that the framework can help 'give voice' even to those who, like a jury in court, mostly remain silent. The advantage of the framework is that it encourages the analyst to consider multiple aspects of the discursive context, not only at the time of the speech event but through its discursive history (to the extent this can be established). For example, a legal instruction conveyed to the jury needs to be considered not only in relation to its authoritative discursive history, which might significantly constrain styling, but also in relation to communication policy arising from centring institutions such as the Judicial College, which in this case promotes more active accommodation to the jury. And it can never be assumed that audiences will hear what is intended by the speaker or even that the speaker is the source of the message. The framework thus opens up avenues of investigation that go well beyond a single text in its immediate (institutional) context and is particularly useful in cases where opportunities to voice are restricted and/or the possibility of alternative interpretations is considered limited.

Ultimately, the aim of this framework is to raise awareness of contexts where people's voices are not projecting successfully and to help promote change that will ensure actively responsive understanding. However, I have indicated here that this does not just concern minority 'powerless' voices but also powerful voices. Powerful speakers have far more resources at their disposal to ensure that their voices do project successfully to less powerful audiences, but in many cases they need to be made more aware of this. The Voice Projection Framework can help articulate why even powerful speakers can find themselves losing voice while using it, often with serious institutional consequences.

APPENDIX: THE PRYCE JURY QUESTIONS

Q1. You have defined the defence of marital coercion on page 5 of the jury bundle and also explained what does not fall within the definition by way of examples. Please expand on the definition, provide examples of what may fall within the defence, specifically 'will was overborne' and does the defence require violence or physical threat?

A: The pressure applied by the husband need not involve violence or physical threats. The law requires that a husband was present and coercion was to such an extent that she was impelled to commit an offence because she truly believed she had no real choice but to do so.

Q2. In the scenario that the defendant may be guilty but there may not be enough evidence provided by the prosecution at the material time when she signed the notice of intent to prosecute to feel sure beyond reasonable doubt, what should the verdict be, not guilty or unable or not safe to bring a verdict?

A: Turning to page three of my written directions, the direction is combining the burden and standard of proof with the need for a majority verdict. If, having carefully considered all of the evidence, at least 10 of you feel sure of the guilt of the defendant then it would be your duty to return a verdict of guilty. On the other hand, if after careful consideration at least 10 of you were feeling less than sure of guilt, then it would be your duty to return a verdict of not guilty. And so it follows that if at least 10 of you are not sure, the appropriate verdict is one of not guilty.

Q3. If there is debatable evidence supporting the prosecution case can inferences be drawn to arrive at a verdict? If so can inferences/speculation be drawn on the full evidence or only where you have directed us to do so?

A: The drawing of an inference is a permissible process. Speculation is not. In this case the evidence on which the prosecution relies is largely undisputed, and where you are willing to draw inferences from that is entirely a matter for you.

Q4. Can you define what is reasonable doubt?

A: The prosecution must make you feel sure beyond reasonable doubt. A reasonable doubt is a doubt that is reasonable. These are ordinary English words that the law does not allow me to help you with, beyond the written directions.

Q5. Can a juror come to a verdict based on a reason that was not presented in court and has no facts or evidence to support it?

A: The answer to that question is a firm no. That is because it would be completely contrary to the directions I have given you.

Q6. Can we infer anything from the fact that the defence didn't bring witnesses from the time of the offence, such as the au pair or neighbours?

A: You must not, as I have now emphasised many times, speculate on what witnesses who have not been called might have said or draw inferences from their absence. Her evidence is that no one else, other than Mr Huhne, was present when she signed the form.

Q7. Does the defendant have an obligation to present a defence?

A: There is no burden on the defendant to prove her innocence and there is no burden on her to prove anything at all. The defendant does not have an obligation to present a defence. In this case the defendant has given evidence and it is for you to judge the evidence from her in the same way you would any other witness.

Q8. Can we speculate about the events at the time Miss Pryce sent the form or what was in her mind when she sent the form?

A: The answer to that is an equally firm no. The position in a criminal trial is that no one must speculate. There is a difference between speculation, which is not permitted, and inference, which is the drawing of common-sense conclusions from the facts of which you are also sure. Speculation is guesswork. That is not the same as inference at all.

Q9. The jury is considering the facts provided but is continuing to ask the questions raised by the police. Given that the case has come to court without answers to these questions please advise on which facts in the bundle the jury should count on to determine a not guilty or guilty verdict.

A: You must decide the case on the evidence [put before the court]. It is for you to decide which you consider to be important, truthful and reliable then decide what common-sense conclusions you can safely draw. It is not for me to tell you which piece or pieces of evidence are important and which are not. That is a matter for you to decide.

Q10. Would religious conviction be a good enough reason for a wife feeling she had no choice i.e. she promised to obey her husband in her wedding vows, he ordered her to do something and she felt she had to obey?

A: This is not, with respect, a question about this case at all. Vicky Pryce does not say that any such reason formed any part of her decision to do what she did. Answering this question will not help you in any way whatsoever to reach a true verdict in this case. I must direct you firmly to focus on the real issues in this case.

(Rayner 2013)

REFERENCES

Agar, M. (1985). Institutional discourse. *Text* 5(3): 147–168.

Arenella, P. (1991). Convicting the morally blameless: Reassessing the relationship between legal and moral accountability. *UCLA Law Review* 39: 1511–1622.

Asch, S. (1946). Forming impressions of personality. *Journal of Abnormal and Social Psychology* 41. 258–290.

Auld, R. E. (2001). *Review of the Criminal Courts of England and Wales: Report*. London: Stationery Office. Available online at http://www.criminal-courts-review.org.uk. Accessed 20 June 2005.

Bakhtin, M. (1981). *The Dialogic Imagination*. Austin: University of Texas Press.

Bauman, R. and Briggs, C. L. (1990). Poetics and performance as critical perspectives on language and social life. *Annual Review of Anthropology* 19: 59–88.

Bhatia, V. K. (1994). Cognitive structuring in legislative provisions. In J. Gibbons (ed.) *Language and the Law*. London: Longman, 136–155.

Blommaert, J. (2005). *Discourse*. Cambridge: Cambridge University Press.

Carroll, L. (1898/2006). *The Annotated Hunting of the Snark*. New York: W.W. Norton and Co.

Collins (2013). *Collins English Dictionary Online*. Glasgow: Collins.

Coughlin, Z. (1994). Excusing women. *California Law Review* 82(1): 1–93.

Dickens, C. (1837–39/1970). *Oliver Twist*. Geneva: Edito-Service.

Dumas, B. (2000). US pattern jury instructions: Problems and proposals. *Forensic Linguistics* 7(1): 49–71.

Finkel, N. J. (2001). *Commonsense Justice: Jurors' Notions of the Law*. Cambridge, MA, and London: Harvard University Press.

Follingstad, D. R. and DeHart, D. D. (2000). Defining psychological abuse of husbands toward wives: Contexts, behaviors, and typologies. *Journal of Interpersonal Violence* 15(9): 891–920.

Garner, B. (ed.) (2009). *Black's Law Dictionary*. St. Paul, MN: West Publishing Co.

Goffman, E. (1981). *Forms of Talk*. Philadelphia: University of Pennsylvania Press.

Goodwin, C. (1994). Professional Vision. *American Anthropologist* 96(3): 606–633.

Guardian (2013a). Vicky Pryce trial: 10 questions jury asked the judge. *The Guardian*. 20 February. http://www.theguardian.com/law/2013/feb/20/vicky-pryce-trial-10-questions.

Guardian (2013b). Vicky Pryce jury can reach majority verdict, says judge. *The Guardian*. http://www.theguardian.com/uk/2013/feb/20/vicky-pryce-jury-can-reach-majority-verdict.

Gumperz, J. J. (1982). *Discourse Strategies*. Cambridge: Cambridge University Press.

Gumperz, J. J. (1992). Contextualization revisited. In P. Auer and A. Di Luzio (eds.) *The contextualization of language*. Amsterdam: John Benjamins, 39–53.

Heffer, C. (2005). *The Language of Jury Trial*. Basingstoke: Palgrave.

Heffer, C. (2006). Beyond 'reasonable doubt': The criminal standard of proof instruction as communicative act. *The International Journal of Speech, Language and the Law* 13(2): 159–188.

Heffer, C. (2007). The language of conviction and the convictions of certainty: Is 'sure' an impossible standard of proof? *International Commentary on Evidence* 5(1): Art. 5.

Heffer, C. (2013). Communication and magic: Authorized voice, legal-linguistic habitus and the recontextualization of 'beyond reasonable doubt'. In C. Heffer, F. Rock and J. M. Conley (eds.) *Legal-Lay Communication: Textual Travels in the Law*. New York: Oxford University Press, 206–225.

Hymes, D. (1972). On communicative competence. In J. B. Pride and J. Holmes (eds.) *Sociolinguistics: Selected Readings*. Harmondsworth: Penguin, 269–293.

Hymes, D. (1996). *Ethnography, Linguistics, Narrative Inequality: Toward an Understanding of Voice*. London: Taylor and Francis.

JSB (1999). *Crown Court Benchbook: Specimen Directions*. London: Judicial Studies Board.

JSB (2010). *Crown Court Benchbook: Directing the Jury*. London: Judicial Studies Board.

Kalven, H. and Zeisel, H. (1971). *The American Jury*. Chicago: University of Chicago Press.

Lave, J. and Wenger, E. (1991). *Situated Learning: Legitimate Peripheral Participation*. Cambridge: Cambridge University Press.

Littlejohn, R. (2013). After this farce, Huhne must wish that he'd pleaded not guilty too! *Daily Mail Online*. 21 February. http://www.dailymail.co.uk/debate/article-2282525/After-farce-Huhne-wish-hed-pleaded-guilty-too.html – ixzz2jZ0guhuX

Mertz, E. (1996). Consensus and dissent in U.S. legal opinion: Narrative structure and social voices. In C. Briggs (ed.) *Disorderly Discourse: Narrative, Conflict and Inequality*. New York: Oxford University Press, 135–157.

OED (2017). *OED Online*. Oxford University Press, http://www.oed.com/. Retrieved 7 July 2017.

Pennington, N. and Hastie, R. (1991). A cognitive theory of juror decision making: The story model. *Cardozo Law Review* 13: 519–557.

Rayner, G. (2013). Vicky Pryce jurors given further directions by judge in speeding points case. *The Daily Telegraph*. 20 February. http://www.telegraph.co.uk/news/uknews/crime/9882943/Vicky-Pryce-jurors-given-further-directions-by-judge-in-speeding-points-case.html.

Silverstein, M. (1998). Contemporary transformations of local linguistic communities. *Annual Review of Anthropology* 27: 401–426.

Sweeney, J. (2013a). 'R -v- Vasiliki Pryce and Christopher Huhne: Sentencing remarks of Mr Justice Sweeney.' Available at http://www.judiciary.gov.uk/media/judgments/2013/r-v-pryce-huhne-sentencing-remarks. Retrieved 7 March 2013.

Sweeney, J. (2013b). 'R v Vasiliki Pryce – Reasons: Marital Coercion.' Available at http://www.crimeline.info. Retrieved 7 March 2013.

Sweeney, J. (2013c). 'Summing-up in R v Vasiliki Pryce.' Available at http://www.crimeline.info/news/pryce-jury-summing-up. Retrieved 7 March 2013.

Tedlock, D. (1983). *Spoken Word and the Work of Interpretation*. Philadelphia: University of Pennsylvania Press.

Thomas, C. (2010). *Are Juries Fair?* Ministry of Justice Research Series 1/10, Available at http://www.justice.gov.uk/publications/research.htm.

Thomas, C. (2014). Exposing the myth of jury research. *Criminal Law & Justice Weekly*. 9 December. http://www.criminallawandjustice.co.uk/features/Exposing-Myth-Jury-Research.

Tiersma, P. (2001). The rocky road to legal reform: Improving the language of jury instructions. *Brooklyn Law Review* 66. 1081–1099.

Voloshinov, V. N. (1973). *Marxism and the Philosophy of Language*. Cambridge, MA: Harvard University Press.

Watt, D. (2011). *Watt's Manual of Criminal Evidence 2011*. Toronto: Carswell.

10 Ideology and Political Meaning in Legal Translation

Janny HC Leung

EDITORS' NOTE TO CHAPTER 10

For interpreters, who perform in front of an audience, it is against the professional code of ethics to conduct themselves in a way that could give rise to an appearance of bias. Even so, there is no shortage of research publications which document how personal bias seeps into the practice of interpreting. In literary translation, typically a more reclusive activity, there is an equivalent body of research that shows how ethnocentricity and ideology impact on lexical and other choices made in the course of translating. But with legal translation it is less clear how ideology plays a role. By analogy with what happens in interpreting, however, it is reasonable to suppose it may. Although processes of legal translation are not generally subject to public scrutiny, it is still possible, Janny Leung argues in this chapter, to gauge how particular approaches to legal translation may reflect power relations and to assess the nature of the role they play in maintaining or potentially transforming aspects of social structure.

When lawyers interpret a legal text, one of the first questions they ask is what authority that text has. If legal status is in this way crucial to legal interpretation of a text, then it is logical that the equivalent issue should arise as regards how legal texts are produced. Leung also argues, however, that legal status is not the only indicator of power which influences the working and meanings of legal translation. Status, she claims, is complex, and not only legally but also socially determined. An illustration she presents in support of this view is that of jurisdictions in decolonizing territories, where a 'source-oriented' translation strategy is commonly adopted in circumstances where law is translated from the language of a departed colonial power into a vernacular. In contrast, she notes, a move is often made toward a 'target-oriented' approach where raising consciousness about language equality and giving more attention to notice, in the sense of delivering accessible public information, is recognized as a requirement of due process.

Given the saturation of law with politics – despite whatever efforts are made to claim law as an abstract formal system – Leung critiques a continuing lack of attention paid to power relations in existing theories of legal translation.

As essential further components of the field, she urges systematic analysis of forces outside a legal system which influence its processes of legal translation, and the development of more detailed and rigorous ways of understanding legal translation as social and political commentary.

Ideology and Political Meaning in Legal Translation

Prologue

Contemporary concerns with gender equality and changing social dynamics have led to revisions in Bible translation. One recently published version displays particular sensitivity to gender inclusiveness in its approach to translation: words that apply to both genders in ancient Greek and Hebrew, which have been traditionally translated into their masculine equivalent in English, are translated in gender neutral ways. For example, 'achim' in Hebrew is rendered as 'brothers and sisters' instead of 'brothers' in English, and 'anthropos' in Greek becomes 'person' instead of 'man' in English (*The Washington Post*, 17 March 2011).

The publisher justifies such a change using a target-oriented approach to translation, stating that their goal is 'to articulate God's unchanging Word in the way the original authors might have said it if they had been speaking in English to the global English-speaking audience today' (ibid.). This statement appeals to a perception that politically correct use of the English language has become a social norm today. The trend of using politically correct gender-related terms started in the 1970s, following feminist critiques of patriarchy as inscribed in English. The counter-argument made by critics of the new Bible translation is based, in contrast, on a source-oriented approach to translation. The translators argue that such updates alter 'the theological direction and meaning of the text' (ibid.), marking a departure of the translation from its source.

For the purpose of this essay it is not necessary to get into the complicated debate concerning authorship or precise meaning of the source text in this example. The insight I wish to develop is based on a more straightforward observation: that a text may be translated differently because of changing power relationships and social structures which form part of the context in which a target text is produced and will be interpreted.

This chapter shows that translation also displays such sensitivity in the legal context, challenging a fixation with linguistic meaning, textual functions, and legal effect in existing theories of legal translation. It is thus possible to read translation as social and political commentary, written within the power structures of law. I argue that, although translation approach does not neatly map onto power relations, power relations are always in the equation when translation approaches are adopted. If it is true that translation approaches are a function of power relations, it will then be logical to ask whether the question of morality arises in approaches to legal translation. Before I engage with these issues, let me begin by offering an overview of how existing theories of legal translation currently stand.

Existing Conception of the Relationship between Legal Translation and Power

In language and law studies, ideology and power are inevitably recurrent themes, both separately and in relation to each other. In a courtroom context, for example, scholars have studied how unequal power relations among trial participants are expressed in courtroom interaction (Wagner and Cheng 2011), how speech styles associated with different demographics have practical legal consequences (Conley et al. 1978; O'Barr 1982), and how court interpreters have the power to affect the outcome of a case (Berk-Seligson 1990/2002). Most studies in this area, however, focus on the practice of *interpreting*, the oral equivalent of translation, in a given legal procedure or for a series of proceedings. When it comes to legal translation, the *written* practice, the relevance of ideology and power is rarely highlighted, especially as regards translation of the language of the law itself (whether constitution, statute, or statutory instrument). This relative neglect may reflect a number of considerations: the fact that legal translators tend to be invisible in the law-making process, for example; or that there may be a team of translators involved in working on a given legal instrument, especially when it comes to legislative texts; that processes of legal translation are less available for observation and scrutiny; or that there are vetting procedures before any particular translation of a source text of law acquires legal force (so presumably any individual values that have gained a footing in the text will be filtered out at later stages of the editing process).

It is scarcely a new insight in the field of translation studies that translation can be used to achieve social or political ends. Studies of translation and power over many years have acknowledged that power relationships are a significant context of, as well as determinant of, the cross-cultural transfer of texts. Bassnett and Lefevere (1990), for instance, have suggested that analysis of the exercise of power provides one important means of explaining changes in approaches to translation. A number of studies that explore ideological forces behind translation, notably research associated with the Manipulation School (Hermans 1985) and with the 'cultural turn' (Bassnett and Lefevere 1990), dissect such forces with respect to literary translation.

There are curiously few studies, on the other hand, that consider whether, and if so how far, power relationships, sociopolitical contexts, and ideological forces are meaningful contexts for *legal* translation. By and large, current scholarship on legal translation is largely preoccupied with tension between legal and linguistic considerations at work in shaping a translation. This preoccupation, however, obscures the fact that law is not a closed system, and that through their work, whether consciously or not, legal translators are participating in the consolidation, and at times transformation, of a power structure.

Traditional conceptions of legal translation saw translation as transcoding and the reproduction of the form and meaning of the source text in the target language. In recent years more attention has been paid to pragmatics and discourse functions. Vermeer's 'skopos theory'[1] introduces a functional approach to translation (Vermeer 1996; Reiß and Vermeer 2014). In Vermeer's account, the commissioner of a translation and the translator agree upon the purpose of a translation, or the skopos of the text, which determines the appropriate strategy of translation.[2] The more divergent the function of the translation is from that of the source text, the more freedom the translator enjoys in the method of translation. This account is intuitively appealing, as one might well expect the end to justify the means (Reiß and Vermeer 2014: 90). The most comprehensive theory of legal translation to date is offered by Šarčević (1997). Admitting that achieving equal meaning in parallel legal texts is an unrealistic goal, Šarčević proposes that translator of plurilingual legal instruments should aim at producing texts that lead to the same reception – the generation of equal legal effect. In contrast to the situations that Vermeer imagines, where the function of translation and the source text may diverge, Šarčević (1997) argues that authenticated legislative texts 'always' have identical communicative function (109) and thus the production of parallel legislative texts constitutes one communicative act with the same receiver-orientation. Similar to Šarčević (1997), Cao (2007) draws attention to the legal status and communicative purpose of both the source and target language texts in her approach to legal translation.

A Critique

These accounts are essentially prescriptive and normative in nature; they serve a goal-setting function and aim to offer guidance to the legal translator. Their proposition that translation approaches cannot be assessed independently of the

1 *Skopos* is the Greek word for purpose. The skopos theory is a theory of general rather than legal translation.

2 In presenting his skopos theory in Vermeer (1996), Vermeer defines *skopos* as the purpose of translation as posited by the commissioner of the translation and as understood by the translator. Function is defined as the purpose of the translation as understood by the recipient. However, the terms 'skopos' and 'function' are often used interchangeably in the literature, including by Vermeer himself (in Reiß and Vermeer 2014).

(potentially differentiated) function of the source and the target texts and institutional purpose and constraints seems well justified. As far as their descriptive aspects are concerned, these accounts are laudable in their attempt to bring in some situational context (in terms of textual function and institutional goals respectively) into an understanding of legal translation.

However, it is also not difficult to see that existing theories of legal translation project a doctrinal and positivist understanding of law: they take an internal perspective and assume that the communicative function of a legal text is determined by its legal status (Šarčević 1997: 19). They readily accept that a legal text performs a function that it is said to perform, or that the status that a legal text enjoys is equivalent to the legal status assigned to it. This makes sense considering that many legal translators work for or within a legal institution, through employment or contract. Šarčević (1997), for example, understands legal translation as 'an act of communication within the mechanism of the law' (55). But legal status does not come about out of thin air, and what is outside of law influences the operation of law; the way law is written not only has significance for the legal system but it also says something about social organization and power struggles. If there are any socially realistic elements in these theories, they are largely confined to the linguistic aspect of translation: for example, that language is inherently indeterminate and meaning is context-dependent. Such characteristics are understood as challenges to legal translation.

If we take an external perspective to legal translation, or aim to offer a descriptively accurate, sociological account of the practice of legal translation, we see an elephant in the room in these existing theories that the concepts of 'function', 'legal effect,' and 'legal status' dance around. Textual function, the determination of legal effect, and legal status are a function of *power relations* between the source and target text. But legal status is not the sole indicator of power relations: texts that enjoy equal legal status may nevertheless have different perceived status and social status (legal status may be conferred to serve symbolic function; see Leung, forthcoming). It is only through such realization that divergent approaches applied to translating from a source text that is supposed to have the same legal status and function as the target text may be understood. In each of the accounts of legal translation mentioned earlier, reference to power has been avoided, probably because power is in apparent conflict with the ideology that the translator is an expert in language whose professionalism requires him or her to be politically neutral. Without taking power relations into consideration, however, the accounts described cannot tell a comprehensive and realistic story of wider contextual factors that may systematically affect how the translator makes his or her judgment. They also fail to address the issue of potential divergence between the institutional function of a target text and its perceived, wider social function. By contrast, this chapter seeks to present a more multidimensional account of how legal translation approaches interact with the sociopolitical context in which a legal translator works.

Although most of the examples I draw from are legislative texts, it is my contention that the argument made in this essay is equally applicable to the translation of other legal texts such as judicial opinions, legal commentaries, and private legal documents.

The Classic Dichotomy in Translation Approaches

To examine how translation approaches may be related to wider sociopolitical context, it is helpful to review existing approaches in legal translation and their perceived benefits and shortcomings. One important underlying assumption must be that perfect translation is an impossible enterprise. By treating full equivalence as an unattainable ideal which may nevertheless usefully guide the practice of translation, this premise does not deny the value of translation (including interpreting) that is practised on a day-to-day basis. Indeed, divergent approaches to translation exist only because there are different ways of approximating to an ideal translation, depending on which ideal one aims for. If full equivalence is a reachable goal, then disagreement as to the path to get there would be far less prevalent. There is room for a choice of approach precisely because no single translation approach can be used to convey the same message to the target language reader as the source text does to the source language reader.

The classic dichotomy in translation is between a source-oriented and a target-oriented approach. A source-oriented approach emphasizes fidelity to the source text, and may entail the use of techniques such as borrowing, transliteration, neologisms, or literal translation. A target-oriented approach, on the other hand, focuses on the comprehensibility of the translated text, and is associated with free[3] or idiomatic[4] translation – for example, substitution of a foreign concept with a native equivalent (e.g. from *baguette* to *naan*), a process that may be understood as domestication (Venuti 1994). Between the two extremes there has also been recognition of a third space where cultural hybridity and transformation may take place (Wagner, Sin and Cheng 2014).

As far as legal translation is concerned, there are advocates of both orientations. The strongest argument for a source-oriented approach is that departure

[3] 'Free' translation is not completely unconstrained. The 'free' translator pays attention to what the source text says, but less to *how* it is said.

[4] Idiomatic translation focuses on the target language and its readers, seeking to achieve alignment with relevant language habits. It conceals the apparent foreignness of the source text.

from the source text is 'unfaithful'. The Treaty of Waitangi, signed in 1840, is a radical example of how it may seem morally wrong to depart from the source text. That treaty played a crucial role in British colonization of the Maori in New Zealand. Despite general acceptance of the translation of the treaty, in more recent times it has been suggested (e.g. Fenton and Moon 2002) that fraudulent manipulation of the translation misled Maori chiefs into accepting the agreement, especially as regards the question of sovereignty. The translation departed so much from the original, some scholars contend, that there are actually two separate treaties[5]. The source-oriented approach has also been justified on other grounds. Literal translation has been praised for its ability to preserve the structure and even the lexis of the source language; as a strategy, this may be appealing in the legal context because it is reversible (and also in a sense, componential – individual words and phrases can be matched, allowing step-by-step comparison). Glanert (2014) argues that retaining the foreignness of a text is also a sign of respect – a reminder to the reader that a translated text has a foreign origin; by contrast, an idiomatic translation compromises the authenticity of the source language text and may be seen as ethnocentric. Similarly, Baaij (2014: 118) dismisses a target-oriented approach as not being useful for comparative legal studies, since such a translation has been 'contaminated' by the legal translator's comparative analysis. In the context of the European Union, which currently has twenty-four official languages, Baaij (forthcoming) argues that all European law should be drafted in English and source-oriented translation should be adopted in order to ensure legal integration.

On the other hand, there are frequent complaints that source-oriented translations may be incomprehensible to the reader, for the approach prioritizes the integrity of the source text over the accessibility of the target text. In a legal context, a literal translation of legislation may fail to inform citizens of their rights and obligations adequately. Writing from a sociological perspective, Ng (2014) argues that a source-oriented approach to translation reduces the interpretive autonomy of a text: a characteristic defined as the ability of a translated text to stand on its own, as contrasted with having to acquire its meaning through the source text at the time of interpretation. This argument carries particular strength in postcolonial jurisdictions, where indexical translation[6] may be used as an institutional means of allowing two or more languages to coexist and relate to each other in a legal system, while at the same time controlling that relation.

[5] See www.nzhistory.net.nz/politics/treaty/read-the-Treaty/differences-between-the-texts, by the History Group of the New Zealand Ministry for Culture and Heritage.

[6] The meaning of an indexically translated text needs to be understood in relation to the source text; literal translation is an example of such translation.

Translation Approaches and Context

As normative theories of legal translation suggest, considerations such as the legal status of a text, communication function, and the intended legal effect, should and do affect translation approaches.

For example, if the purpose of the translation exercise is comparative legal research, which is what Glanert (2014) and Baaij (2014) are concerned with, a source-oriented approach makes perfect sense. The comparative lawyer seeks to understand the foreign text in order to identify similarities and differences across legal systems; in this case it is clear that a translation approach which actively minimizes differences is unlikely to be helpful. For the purpose of comparative legal research, the target text and the source text serve radically different functions. The translated text is not law; and its interpretation does not directly affect people's lives. Instead, the text serves to inform the researcher, by facilitating his or her understanding of a foreign legal system. The stakes of misinterpretation are relatively low.

Sometimes legal texts (e.g. treaties, legislation, contracts) are also translated as reference materials for people who do not speak the dominant language to learn about law that may affect their interests. Such people may include foreigners, migrants, or members of minority communities who occupy a less powerful position in a society. Such translation may be found at immigration controls, printed on custom forms, or posted in public places frequented by tourists. In these cases, the translation will tend not to be idiomatic in the target language; in fact, sometimes translations may be rendered in a lingua franca that may not be the mother tongue of the potential reader (e.g. in English for foreign visitors coming from different countries). Sometimes the translation is a simplified summary of the original. Such translations are also common in colonial and postcolonial settings, where the former colonial language has ultimate authority and the law is translated into vernaculars to facilitate compliance.

In some cases, the same status is enjoyed by two or more language texts. Through becoming authenticated, a legal translation becomes a legal instrument that has authority to stand on its own. In bilingual and multilingual jurisdictions, an authenticated translation of a statute becomes a source of law along with its original. In other words, the law consists of a mega-text made up of two or more language versions (Leung, forthcoming). This is also what happens in treaties. As an object of legal interpretation, an authenticated translation may even come into conflict with the source text, raising questions as to what the intended legal meaning is. In this situation it is not immediately obvious which approach to translation should be adopted, given the need to balance legal certainty with accessibility to law. People who prioritize notice as a requirement of due process may urge for a more target-oriented translation; those who prioritize uniformity of legal effect may prefer a source-oriented approach to translation (e.g. Baaij, forthcoming); yet others have found middle ground through alternative methods of text production (such as bilingual drafting in Canada).

The Political Meaning of Translation Approaches

Note that where multiple legal texts have the same function and legal status, the choice between a target-oriented translation approach or a source-oriented translation approach necessarily disturbs the presumed balance of power and is not an apolitical decision, even if the justification is perfectly reasonable (e.g. due process or uniformity of legal effect). In other words, the translation approach may not only reflect power relations but also be used as a tool in maintaining or subverting the balance of power.

Authentic legal texts that have the same legal status and institutional function may nevertheless be divergent in their perceived status and social function. Even where both a source language text and a target language text are authentic sources of law, they are likely to be associated with different language communities; and the languages may well correspond with different social status. Despite the equal status conferred on languages in some bilingual and multilingual jurisdictions, such as English and French in Canada, Chinese and English in Hong Kong, the eleven official languages in South Africa, or the twenty-four official languages of the European Union, there is an implicit understanding that some languages are more dominant or relevant than others. In legal translation, more likely than not, the source language will be a more powerful language than the target language. An interesting example is judgments of the European Court of Justice[7] (ECJ), which are drafted in French but authentic in the language of procedure (McAuliffe 2012). In other words, although the language of the case enjoys higher legal status, it is a translation from French, which is the single internal working language of the court (and thus more powerful institutionally).

Although Šarčević (1997) has not incorporated power relations and social changes in her normative theory of legal translation, in her seminal book she traces the evolution of strategies used in legal translation from an early preference for literal translation to the rise of idiomatic translation, leading all the way to the bilingual co-drafting method (as employed in Canada). The analysis seems to suggest that the move away from source-oriented translation is associated with social changes such as equality of language rights and growth in national language consciousness. Let us explore this association further.

[7] More formally known as the Court of Justice of the European Union (CJEU).

Literalism and Power Imbalance

When placed in the sociolegal context of a particular locality, tension between the two translation approaches is often less an ideological conflict about textual loyalty than a power struggle. Textual fidelity in a source-oriented approach to translation may practically translate into maintaining an alignment with institutional power. This approach weakens the authority of an authenticated translation, since its meaning may need to be established by reference to the source text.

Colonization and at least early stages of decolonization are in evident ways contexts that involve power imbalance and struggles aimed at countering such imbalance. Between the fifteenth and the eighteenth century, for example, the British and other European powers colonized many territories in Asia, Africa, and the Americas. After World War II, in a fairly short period many former colonies became independent. Most often, the law of a decolonizing nation nevertheless still operates in the colonial language but with an increasing need to be translated into the local tongue. Translation in such circumstances is often literal, since in the colonial context an inferiority complex is often persistently associated with the local language being translated into, and there is often an expectation that this language should be adapted, even twisted, in order to accommodate the original. This political dimension of the translator's practice in turn permeates language and translation ideology. It becomes a common feature of rhetoric in colonies and postcolonial nations, for example, that the local languages are not sophisticated enough to express the shades or complexities of meaning contained in the imported foreign law, with the result that loanwords are frequently used in the translation of such law (see Leung 2016).

Examples of such a linguistic and social nexus are easy to find. Literal translation is used extensively in the legal sphere in Malaysia, for instance, which is a former British colony that obtained independence in 1957. Although the Malay language (Bahasa Malaysia) is now the official language of the country, legal terminology continues to borrow heavily from English; instances of such borrowing include *lokap* (lock-up), *apil* (appeal), and *saman* (summons) (Powell 2004). The principal strategy for developing legal terminology in the Malay language has been assimilation, largely on the basis that Malay had hardly been used for legal matters previously. English phonemes, morphemes, phrases, or sentence structures were simply inserted into Malay. A desire to align the resulting legal language with English and international styles of discourse is reflected in the choice of translated words such as *psikologi* for 'psychology', as opposed to the more phonetic implant *saikologi*. A regularly updated official publication *Istilah Undang-undang* ('Legal Terminology') lists thousands of Malay–English pairs, somewhere under a quarter of which are English loanwords (Powell 2004); the purely Malay words on the list are in many cases hardly accessible, either, as some of them are new coinages. The consequence is that legal translation can read like a foreign text, even though it is written in Malay. Scholars such as Faiza (1994, cited in Powell 2004) understandably therefore call for a prioritizing of Malay over English and argue that Malay terms, where available, should be used to replace English derivations. On the other hand, many established bilingual legal practitioners prefer to use English over Malay, and most law journals and law reports continue to be published in English. Such readiness to identify with the colonial language reflects not only a language habit developed during the colonial days, but also the fact that, with the retreat of the colonizer, the power of the colonial language can still linger through people (especially elites) and systems that remain in place. This continuing, active influence, according to some, contributes to a form of linguistic recolonization. Such influence intersects with the market value of globalized English acquired in recent decades as the main international language of commerce and of legal relations which underpin commerce in developing economies, which adds a counterforce to an otherwise predicted decline of the colonial language (Sonntag 2003).

A further example of the same underlying pattern of forces is that of Hong Kong, where literal translation was also prevalent at the beginning of the decolonization process which started with the signing of the Sino-British Joint Declaration in 1984. Translation of legislation – drafted and enacted in English – into Chinese began in 1989 and was completed just before the British handed Hong Kong back to China in 1997. In the early stages of such legislative translation, a 'word-for-word' approach was used to create a 'mirror-image' of the English texts in Chinese (Lai and Li 2012: 12). Previously, during colonial days, English had been acknowledged as the language of power and access. This reputation has not diminished since the handover, despite the growing importance of Mandarin. The reasons for this are complex. English is particularly vital for the legal system of Hong Kong, which has remained a common law jurisdiction frequently operating as a conduit for international trade. In fact many legal practitioners also feel that Cantonese does not have the qualities required of a legal language, and prefer using English in their legal practice (Ng 2009). A 1986 government paper clearly states that, since the common law underlies the Chinese text of the law in Hong Kong, 'the meaning of the Chinese text in the courts of Hong Kong may not be what a reader unfamiliar with our legal background (e.g. a reader in China) may think it to be' (Attorney General's Chambers: 4). This significant complication is compounded by other features of legal discourse. Neologism was used, for example, to represent foreign legal ideas such as the common law concept of 'possession' (translated as '*管有*' gun2jau5); and literal translation, paraphrasing and borrowing were also common strategies (Poon 2005). In examples cited by Poon, the Bilingual Law Advisory Committee attempted to find Chinese terms that have the same semantic scope as terms used in the English original, and this aspect of the terms chosen trumped consideration of whether those terms were in common usage. Some scholars (e.g. Zhao 2001) have expressed concern that Chinese translations of laws originally drafted in English appear to have been written in Anglicized Chinese or in some cases are simply not comprehensible. As such concerns grew, and as importance of the Chinese language continued to rise in Hong Kong's integration with China, the word-for-word translation approach was gradually abandoned[8] and legal translation in Hong Kong has increasingly paid attention to the comprehensibility of Chinese legal provisions and to policy intent.[9] Notwithstanding the need for such a significant shift of approach, parallel drafting has not been fully adopted and translation is still common practice in the preparation of bilingual law.

A final example from a very different context is the German and Dutch translations of the American constitution used in advocacy for its ratification in the founding era of the United States. Although there was no doubt that, if the constitution were ratified, only the English text would be authoritative, the text had not yet acquired legal status at that point. The translations, commissioned and translated separately in Pennsylvania and New York respectively for different audiences, both closely adhered to the original phrasing and sentence structure of the English text, and even adopted some English terms (Mulligan et al. 2014). Literal translation was the obvious choice, not because of the actual legal status of English but because of its perceived power.

Idiomacy, Emanicipation, and Beyond

Fidelity to the source text remains the fundamental principle of legal translation (Wolff 2011). Given that legal systems themselves tend to be inherently conservative, it is especially interesting therefore to consider what kinds of jurisdictions attempt to depart from that norm.

In translating the Swiss Civil Code, which was drafted in Switzerland's majority language of German, Rossel 'defended his idiomatic translation by arguing that the French-speaking population of Switzerland had a right to insist that their *Code civil suisse* be written neither in germanized French nor in gallicized German but rather in the spirit of the French language, thus upholding the principle of language equality' (Šarčević 1997: 39). Similarly, when Belgium gained independence in 1830 the majority of political leaders were French

[8] Acknowledged by the Panel on Administration of Justice and Legal Services of the Hong Kong Legislative Council in a meeting in 2001; LC Paper No. CB(2)1516/00–01.

[9] This practice coincides with a parallel trend in many civil and common law jurisdictions away from literal statutory construction in the direction of interpretation based on policy intent.

speaking. The Dutch version of the Belgian Constitution was a literal translation of the French original until language consciousness gradually promoted a more idiomatic legal Dutch in recent decades. And in Canada, the campaign for idiomatic translation was linked to broader struggles for language equality: legal French underwent a process of 'refrancization' in Quebec, and the English translation of the Civil Code was cleaned up in the manner exemplified here by Meredith (1979, cited in Šarčević 1997: 44–45):

French original (paragraph 1 of former Article 501 of Civil Code): Les fonds inférieurs sont assujettis envers ceuz qui sont plus élevés à recevoir les eaux qui en découlent naturellement sans que la main de l'homme y ait contribué.

English translation (original): Lands on a low level are subject towards those on a higher level to receive such waters as flow from the latter naturally and without the agency of man.

English translation (revised): Water must be allowed to flow naturally from higher land to lower land.

A connection between translation strategy and wider political campaigns can be so deep, in fact, that for instance the Canadian Department of Justice has gone as far as acknowledging that literal translation violates the principle of equal language rights (Šarčević 1997: 46).

In general, it would seem that the countries which attempt to move beyond literalism of legal translation are ones which overtly attach importance to equality among linguistic communities. Harmonization of potential textual differences,[10] rather than settling such differences by appeals to relative authority, may be seen for instance as an act of power balancing, to take place when – or sometimes even before – translation is undertaken. Such harmonization, which typically involves collaboration by two or more translators/draftsmen who speak a different first language, shifts the goal of translation from fidelity to the source text in the direction of equivalence of legal effect (Šarčević 1997).

However, I must caution against the inference that there is a one-to-one mapping between translation approaches and power relations. Idiomatic translation does not always imply empowerment and respect; sometimes idiomatic translation may be deployed for pragmatic reasons (e.g. exerting effective control).

Alternative Methods of Textual Production as a Politically Neutral Move

Some bilingual and multilingual jurisdictions have shown that unified legal effect does not have to be compromised in order to break away from literalism. The practice of bilingual drafting may be seen as an attempt to bring equality

[10] A process of removing potential discrepancies by comparing texts.

into the heart of the textual production process. Translation need not, on this approach, be a subsequent and subordinate action to the drafting of an original text.

For example, a text may accommodate to the target text prior to becoming a source text. A new system of multilingual drafting to underpin such equal status was introduced in the United Nations in the 1980s, in which drafts need to be amended based on recommendations from each language group before they can be finalized (Shelton 1996). In the European Union, since multilingualism is at the core of the functioning[11] of the Union, an effort is made to adjust the input texts so that they are more readily translatable into other official languages. The drafting language, which is most of the time English, goes through a process of 'deculturalization' so as to reduce the level of embedding of cultural specifics and to simplify semantics and syntax (Biel 2007). In other words, when the source text is drafted, constraints acknowledged in relation to various target languages are already being taken into account. This kind of accommodation, in advance, facilitates terminological standardization and makes what amounts to a new level of literalism in translation more feasible. Accommodation of this kind has now advanced so far that languages in the Union are affected by their use by non-native speakers, suggesting that notions of ownership of language have also shifted (van Els 2001). Linguistic equality is also a prioritized agenda in integrating newly acceded nations into the Union. Under an equal authenticity principle, the whole idea of an 'original' is destabilized; translations are not called 'translations' but referred to as 'language versions'. Correspondingly, literalism in translation loses its role as a foundation stone of what a translation should be faithful to, and fidelity to a source text becomes fidelity to the single legal instrument (with related effects on later interpretation of that legal instrument in different language versions).

Alternatively, some methods of bilingual textual production have removed the role of translation altogether. In bilingual drafting, practiced in jurisdictions such as Canada, one Anglophone common lawyer and one Francophone civilian lawyer collaborate in the drafting task related to any new statute (L'Heureux–Dubé 2002). An initial step in introducing a practice of bilingual drafting into a legal system is necessarily to elevate the status of the legal translator. Then, as part of any specific act of drafting, consultation takes place in both directions between draftsman and translator (Beaupré 1986). Thus, translators participate directly in the production of source texts rather than only in derivatives from them, having an opportunity to revise the source text though translation (Šarčević 1997). Importantly, therefore, the original *intent* of a piece of legislation may be queried and clarified at an early stage. Such a practice of

[11] The principle of direct effect and the doctrine of the supremacy of Community Law are argued only to operate effectively within a fully multilingual legal regime in Athanassiou 2006.

co-drafting revolutionizes both the traditional mode of working (which consisted of drafting followed by translation) and the alternative model of a bilingual single draftsman working largely independently. Jurilinguists equipped with both legal knowledge and language skills conceive the process of creating law in language, through bilingual drafting, in a new way, partly by being able to keep different types of audience in mind. In the case of Canada mentioned earlier, for example, four distinct audiences are engaged with: Anglophone and Francophone common law lawyers, and Anglophone and Francophone civilian lawyers. Bilingual drafting may be seen as an ambitious way of rebalancing power relations.[12]

In order to ensure uniform legal effect, sometimes translation may be neither source-oriented nor target-oriented. In multilingual drafting, supranational bodies (such as the EU) separate themselves to some extent from local languages by developing a unified terminology in order to distance themselves from specific national terms and to avoid trespassing into the territory of particular frameworks of national law. As a consequence of this distancing strategy, a resulting translation may not be particularly idiomatic for *any* of the local languages. The resulting effect of a kind of 'textual alienation' may contribute to promoting equality across member states, but arguably might make comprehension by individual citizens more challenging.

Toward a Descriptive Theory of Legal Translation

Referring to general translation, Jin and Nida (2006: 14) argue that historically translation strategies appear to follow something of a pendulum action:

> The history of translating in a particular language or cultural contexts is highly instructive. In general, however, the history consists of an alternation between literalism and unrestricted freedom. Shifts from one pole of translating to another often change over a period of time, but usually opposite tendencies exist throughout long periods of time, with people having very diverse views as to what translation should be like.

Though it is true that preferences in translation strategies have swung between literalism and freedom, subject to the underlying continuity also observed by Jin and Nida, this chapter argues that where such motion occurs it is not random, at least as regards legal translation. What may appear to be chaos or randomness close-up takes on a different and more specific shape if one steps back and adopts a macroscopic perspective that embraces history and context.

[12] The fact that Canada is not only bilingual but also bijural (i.e. English for its common law tradition and French for its civil law tradition) makes harmonization of legal texts more complicated, since both linguistic differences and differences between two legal systems need to be unified.

This chapter has not sought to find flaws in existing normative theories of legal translation. Rather, it critiques a lack of a descriptive theory of legal translation, and a lack of effort in understanding the meaning of legal translation outside the legal system. In other words, I am less concerned with what legal translators ought to do than with what is practically influencing the way they work, and how the way they work takes on a social and political meaning. A successful account of legal translation should recognize that in some cases, notwithstanding the overtly stated function of the target text, its symbolic function supersedes its practical legal function. The symbolic value of legal status explains why many postcolonial bilingual and multilingual jurisdictions that have granted official status to vernaculars have not even started translating their law into them (see examples and further discussion in Leung, forthcoming). A more nuanced understanding of function takes into account the specific ways in which translations establish, reinforce, or revise the relationship between different language communities. Such a more nuanced understanding needs to take power relations as a basic parameter of legal translation.

Although there seems to be a tendency for more equal societies to move away from a source-oriented approach to legal translation, I wish to reiterate the warning against inferring a one-to-one mapping. For one thing, sources of power struggles are multiple, involving not only sovereign power but also pressure from community and market value of languages. What should be recognized is that, although power relations cannot always be gauged through translation approaches, power always forms part of the context of legal translation. The actual and perceived status of a translation or its target language can become a factor in its meaning potential, beyond linguistic and legal meaning (which are the usually considered factors in legal translation). However, such an effect of translation status on meaning does not occur in a simple relation of single cause and effect. Strategies adopted may show not only personal attitude or bias of individual translators in any given instance, but also may amount to a fully institutionalized practice, which reflects the systematic development of an institutional translation culture and structural preferences through guidelines given to translators. Moreover, the effect of translation status on meaning impacts not only the legal status of the translation, or its reference value for legal professionals and laypersons, but also a wider perception of the target and source language community. In other words, extra-linguistic and extra-legal factors have an effect, in multiple and complex ways, on translation strategy, which in turn has social and political meaning beyond its value in the legal system.

From choice of word to the way the target text positions itself in relation to the source text, translation can be read as commentary (Mulligan et al. 2014). This powerfully stated proposition from Venuti (1998: 158) illustrates the point:

Translation is uniquely revealing of the asymmetries that have structured international affairs for centuries. In many 'developing' countries . . . it has been compulsory, imposed first by the introduction of colonial languages among regional vernaculars and later, after decolonisation, by the need to traffic in the hegemonic lingua francas to preserve political autonomy and promote economic growth. Here translation is a cultural practice that is deeply implicated in relations of domination and dependence, equally capable of maintaining or disrupting them.

Ethics in Legal Translation

Consider, finally, the moral weight implicit in the vocabulary of translation studies: 'fidelity' (and 'infidelity'), 'faithfulness' (and 'unfaithfulness'), 'loyalty', 'betrayal', and 'violence', just to name a few. Since textual fidelity is usually applied in relation to the source text, the expressions imply that source-oriented translation is somehow more ethical.

On the other hand, some have seen more moral relevance in the underlying motivation behind translation than in translation approach. In analyzing the language conflict between England and France in Shakespeare's *Henry V*, Nouss (2014: 29) discusses the ethical dimension of translation:

[T]he dual function of translation: to get to the other in order to exercise mastery over him or to get to the other so as to understand him. In other words, it is about looking for sameness or for difference. . . . Domination entails ignoring the difference; understanding means respecting it.

This analysis taps into implicit motivations which underpin translation and attempts to use translation to affect power relationships, beyond whatever explicit function a translation is said to serve. It is tempting to infer from the preceding analysis that domination is immoral and respect is moral, with the result that looking for sameness is immoral and looking for difference is moral. Although both source-oriented and target-oriented approaches to translation involve looking for sameness and difference across source and target languages and cultures, it is generally the case that a target-oriented approach demonstrates more respect to differences.

Can ethics in legal translation be linked systematically or consistently with translation approach? My position is that there is no inherent moral value in a translation approach. This view is consistent with Gentzler and Tymoczko (2002: xx), who write that "No single translation strategy can be associated with the exercise of oppression or the struggle for resistance; no single strategy is *the* strategy of power" (emphasis in original). But it is nevertheless a mistake to think that *translation* is value free, or that 'politics may play no part' in the choice between literal and free translation, simply because, for example, literalism has been advocated by both conservatives and radicals[13] (Wolff 2011: 229). The analysis developed in this chapter suggests that politics can play a major part in choices between literal and free translation, but that the exact interaction between politics and translation approaches is highly dependent on a cluster of contextual factors, including the implicit and explicit purpose of the translation and the actual and perceived status of the languages involved.

Legal certainty, accessibility, and transparency are some common motivations behind a translation approach. It is simplistic, however, to suggest that one motivation is nobler than another. Prioritizing one value over another does not automatically entail moral deficiency. On the other hand, the means to achieve these ends tends not to be ideologically neutral. If source-oriented translation is adopted in a bilingual or multilingual jurisdiction in order to ensure legal certainty, for example, one may ask why one language is chosen as the source but not another.

The broader lesson to be learnt by reflecting on the complex interrelation between different translation approaches is that, since such approaches are sensitive to power relationships, any adequate descriptive theory of legal translation needs to take this into account. Sensitivity to power relations is not automatically a critique of the ability or work of the translator. The observation calls for scrutiny, not alarm; after all, not all power is corrupt or illegitimate. Further, power imbalance may be transitional; in some cases, it is the cost of political stability during a particular period or political moment. Power relationships are, simply put, part of the context that constitutes the source and target culture that the legal translator needs to work with. Translation not only marks linguistic, cultural, or status differences across texts, but is also an instrument that creates, reinforces, and may attenuate such differences.

REFERENCES

Athanassiou, P. (2006). The Application of Multilingualism in the European Union Context. *Legal Working Paper Series* No. 2, European Central Bank (ECB).

Attorney General's Chambers Hong Kong (1986). *Discussion Paper on the Laws in Chinese.*

Baaij, C. J. W. (2014). Translation and the 'Contamination' of Comparative Legal Research. In S. Glanert (ed.) *Comparative Law – Engaging Translation.* Oxon and New York: Routledge, 104–122.

Baaij, C. J. W. (forthcoming). *Legal Integration and Language Diversity: The Case for Source-Oriented EU Translation.*

Bassnett, S. and Lefevere, A. (1990). Proust's Grandmother and the Thousand and One Nights: The 'Cultural Turn' in Translation Studies. In S. Bassnett and A. Lefevere (eds.) *Translation, History and Culture.* London: Pinter, 1–13.

[13] According to the author, the conservatives take legal texts to be sacred and the radicals think it is unethical to disguise the otherness of foreign language texts.

Beaupré, M. R. (1986). *Interpreting Bilingual Legislation* (2nd ed.). Toronto: Carswell.
Berk-Seligson, S. ([1990] 2002). *The Bilingual Courtroom: Court Interpreters in the Judicial Process*. Chicago: University of Chicago Press.
Biel, L. (2007). Translation of Multilingual EU Law as a Sub-genre of Legal Translation. In D. Kierzkowska (ed.) *Court Interpreting and Legal Translation in the Enlarged Europe*. Warszawa: Translegis.
Cao, D. (2007). *Translating Law*. Clevedon, Buffalo, and Toronto: Multilingual Matters Ltd.
Conley, J. M., O'Barr, W. M. and Lind, E. A. (1978). The Power of Language: Presentational Style in the Courtroom, *Duke Law Journal* 6: 1375–1399.
Fenton, S. and Moon, P. (2002). The Translation of the Treaty of Waitangi: A Case of Disempowerment. In E. Gentzler and M. Tymoczko (eds.) *Translation and Power*. Amherst and Boston: University of Massachusetts Press, 25–44.
Gentzler, E. and Tymoczko, M. (2002). Introduction. In E. Gentzler and M. Tymoczko (eds.) *Translation and Power*. Amherst and Boston: University of Massachusetts Press, xi–xxviii.
Glanert, S. (2014). Translation Matters. In S. Glanert (ed.) *Comparative Law – Engaging Translation*. Oxon and New York: Routledge, 1–19.
Hermans, T. (ed.) (1985). *The Manipulation of Literature: Studies in Literary Translation*. London: Croom Helm.
Jin, D. and Nida, E. (2006). *On Translation: An Expanded Edition*. Hong Kong: City University of Hong Kong Press.
Lai, A. K. P. and Li, A. S. L. (2012). Through the Looking Glass: What a Reader of Hong Kong Legislation Found There. *The Loophole – Journal of the Commonwealth Association of Legislative Counsel*, issue 1. Available at http://www.opc.gov.au/calc/docs/Loophole/Loophole_Jan12.pdf; last accessed on 18 March 2016.
Leung, H. C. J. (2016). Negotiating Language Status in Multilingual Jurisdictions: Rhetoric and Reality. *Semiotica* 209: 371–396.
Leung, H. C. J. (forthcoming). *Shallow Equality and Symbolic Jurisprudence in Multilingual Legal Orders*. New York: Oxford University Press.
L'Heureux–Dubé, C. (2002). Bijuralism: A Supreme Court of Canada Justice's Perspective. *Louisiana Law Review* 62(2): 449–466.
McAuliffe, K. (2012). Language and Law in the European Union: The Multilingual Jurisprudence of the ECJ. In P. M. Tiersma and L. M. Solan (eds.) *The Oxford Handbook of Language and Law*. New York: Oxford University Press, 200–216.
Mulligan, C., Douma, M., Lind, H. and Quinn, B. P. (2014). *Founding-Era Translations of the Constitution*. Constitutional Commentary (forthcoming); Brooklyn Law School, Legal Studies Paper No. 402. Available at SSRN: http://ssrn.com/abstract=2486301 or http://dx.doi.org/10.2139/ssrn.2486301
Ng, K. H. (2009). *The Common Law in Two Voices: Language, Law and the Post-Colonial Predicament in Hong Kong*. Stanford, CA: Stanford University Press.
Ng, K. H. (2014). Legal Translation and the Problem of Hereoglossia. In S. Glanert (ed.) *Comparative Law – Engaging Translation*. Oxon and New York: Routledge, 49–66.
Nouss, A. (2014). Translation as Ethics. In S. Glanert (ed.) *Comparative Law – Engaging Translation*. Oxon and New York: Routledge.

O'Barr, W. M. (1982). *Linguistic Evidence: Language, Power, and Strategy in the Courtroom*. New York: Academic Press.

Poon, W. Y. E. (2005). The Cultural Transfer in Legal Translation. *International Journal for the Semiotics of Law* 18: 307–323.

Powell, R. (2004). Terminological Creation and Language Shift in Malaysia's Legal System. *Current Issues in Language Planning* 5(2): 109–130.

Reiß, K. and Vermeer, H. J. (2014). *Towards a General Theory of Translational Action*. London and New York: Routledge.

Šarčević, S. (1997). *New Approach to Legal Translation*. The Hague: Kluwer Law International.

Shelton, D. (1996). Reconcilable Differences? The Interpretation of Multilingual Treaties. *Hastings International and Comparative Law Review*, 20: 611–638.

Sonntag, S. (2003). *The Local Politics of Global English*. Lanham: Lexington.

The Washington Post, 17 March 2011, New Bible draws critics of gender-neutral language. Available at http://www.washingtonpost.com/wp-dyn/content/article/2011/03/17/AR2011031703434.html

van Els, T. J. M. (2001). The European Union, Its Institutions and Its Languages: Some Language Political Observations. *Current Issues in Language Planning* 2(4): 311–360.

Venuti, L. (1994). Translation and the Formation of Cultural Identities. *Current Issues in Language and Society* 1(3): 201–217.

Venuti, L. (1998). *The Scandals of Translation. Towards an Ethics of Difference*. London and New York: Routledge.

Vermeer, H. J. (1996). *A Skopos Theory of Translation*. Heidelberg: TEXTconTEXT-Verlag.

Wagner, A. and Cheng, L. (eds.) (2011). *Exploring Courtroom Discourse: The Language of Power and Control*. Surrey, England, and Burlington, VT: Ashgate.

Wagner, A., Sin, K. K. and Cheng, L. (2014). Legal Translatability Process as the "Third Space" – Insights into Theory and Practice. In L. Cheng, K. K. Sin and A. Wagner (eds.) *The Ashgate Handbook of Legal Translation*. Surrey, England, and Burlington, VT: Ashgate, 1–11.

Wolff, L. (2011). *Legal Translation*. In K. Malmkjer and K. Windle (eds.) *The Oxford Handbook of Translation Studies*. Oxford: Oxford University Press, 228–242.

Zhao, Y. H. (2001). 'Drafting Policy On Bilingual Legislation – Comments on the Hong Kong *Securities and Futures Bill*'. LC Paper No. CB(2) 1136/00–01 (01). Available at www.legco.gov.hk/yr00–01/english/panels/ajls/papers/b1136e01.pdf; last accessed 18 March 2016.

Part V

Demands of Law and Limits of Language

11 Law and the Grammar of Judgment

Janet Ainsworth

EDITORS' NOTE TO CHAPTER 11

In this chapter, Janet Ainsworth asks a fundamental question about legal processes in an increasingly multilingual legal environment: if law is a kind of 'grammar' of judgment, then how far are its reasoning systems affected by variation in the structures, or grammars, of different natural languages in which that reasoning takes place? This question, Ainsworth argues, is particularly worth raising because legal reasoning tends to be viewed as an authoritative system for creating meaning that simply happens to take place in natural language but is somehow separate from it and superior to it.

To explore the question, Ainsworth revisits the idea of "linguistic relativity," or structural variation between languages that gives a distinctive shape to concept formation by speakers of different languages. Although a strong version of the Sapir-Whorf hypothesis regarding linguistic determinism – the claim that our thought and understanding of the world are fundamentally determined by the language we speak – has been subjected to sustained criticism, there is little doubt that some degree of linguistic relativity exists (Gumperz and Levinson 1996). For example, there are obvious blind spots of meaning not readily accessible to readers of a translation, typically aspects of meaning encoded in the source language but not translatable due to a lack of equivalents: for example, the social distinction between *tu* and *vous* in French reduced simply to "you" in English; or implied meaning or ambiguity in the source language (e.g. created by subjectless sentences in Chinese); and social meanings not manifested linguistically at all but affecting how an expression in the source language will be understood (e.g. that tea is drunk in the morning in certain cultures).

Tracing the significance of such nuances in legal contexts, Ainsworth argues that acknowledging the impact of linguistic relativity in law might have important consequences as regards courtroom interpreting. In general, she suggests, legal proceedings committed to understanding the full meaning of witness testimony should allow or even encourage interpreters to explain relevant details of their translations as context for the imperfect linguistic and cultural mapping between the languages in question. More particularly, she emphasizes the different extent to which, and ways in which, "evidentiality" (i.e. the basis on which some legally relevant fact is known or opinion offered) is encoded in two particular languages. In translated testimony, she argues, such variation and its rendering into the target language may affect the perceived credibility of a witness or some other legally important aspect of a trial.

In a multilingual and multicultural world, Ainsworth concludes – including in or even especially in bilingual courtrooms – linguistic relativism should be acknowledged as an important challenge. As regards law in particular, she urges that legal thinking should take far more seriously the question of how legal proceedings can engage with the differing grammars, and associated variation of cognition, of languages used in communication that forms the essential material of legal reasoning, rather than simply an input to it.

REFERENCE

Gumperz, J. and Levinson, S. C. (1996). *Rethinking Linguistic Relativity*. Cambridge: Cambridge University Press.

Law and the Grammar of Judgment

David Mellinkoff (1963: vii) famously wrote, "The law is a profession of words." This may explain why so much has been written about the *vocabulary* of law – its specialized lexicon and how that gets deployed. But the language of law includes more than merely its particularized professional vocabulary; the law also is marked by a kind of grammar in how that lexicon is used in legal processes and practices. The grammar of law – its internal rule structure – is expressly a grammar of judgment: guilty or not guilty, liable or not liable, lawful or unlawful. As James Boyd White (1985: 65) put it, the language of legal rules "seems to be a language of description, which works by a simple process of comparison, but in cases of any difficulty it is actually a language of judgment." Law is thus both an expression of and a vehicle for normative judgment. How normative judgment in the law is realized has long been and continues to be a fundamental project in jurisprudence (see, e.g. Schlag 1991; Spaak 2003; Postema 2012).

The aims of this chapter are more modest. This chapter poses the following question: given that the structure of law is marked by a grammar of judgment, how might that internal rule structure of law be affected by the rule structures of the natural languages in which law finds its individualized expressions? In short, does the grammar of natural language affect how judgments in the law occur? The answer to that question is significant, because the grammatical systems of natural languages differ from one another – often in profoundly basic ways. Do those kinds of linguistic variations then affect the way in which legal judgments get made? Law – in particular the processes of legal reasoning and judgment – is frequently conceptualized as a hegemonic system of meaning that merely incidentally find its expression in natural language, which is assumed to be transparently referential (see Ainsworth 2008: 14–15). If, however, the syntax of natural languages has relevance for how legal judgments are made, then law's insistence on ignoring or masking the linguistic differences among languages can be critiqued as an ideologically based assertion of power.

In examining this question, we will need to seriously consider the possibility not only that linguistic relativity exists, but also that it *matters* for purposes of communication and understanding. Before considering this, it is necessary to briefly examine the short and unhappy academic history of the idea of linguistic determinism. In its strong version, linguistic determinism is predicated on the concept that languages encode the ways in which human beings see, experience, and understand the world, and then it goes one step further to posit that different languages encode experience in different ways. That is, speakers of different languages don't just *talk* about the world differently; they actually *see and experience* the world differently as a result of the language they speak. Languages, in this theory, are thought of as inherently incommensurate and incommensurable. This strong version of linguistic determinism – often referred to as the Sapir-Whorf hypothesis after two of its primary proponents, Edward Sapir and Benjamin Lee Whorf – was extremely influential in early twentieth-century anthropology. And no wonder. Early twentieth-century anthropologists, especially the intellectual disciples of Franz Boas (see Hitchens 1994), were anxious to establish that other cultures were as worthy of respect as our own; that non-Western cultural orders were not just pallid, underdeveloped, or primitive versions of presumably superior Western culture. If every unique culture was of equal value and validity, then likewise each unique language and its encoded worldview was of equal value and validity as well. Thus, the concept of linguistic determinism – that the language one speaks channels one's thoughts and perceptions – can be seen as one facet of a progressive ideology aiming to understand the social and cultural varieties of humanity and dedicated to countering the racist presuppositions of European superiority that permeated earlier Western studies of non-Western peoples.

Yet, by the 1970s, scholarly adherents of the Sapir-Whorf hypothesis of linguistic determinism were decidedly thin on the ground. The linguist David Alford could write in 1978 (486), "It is as much in vogue today to be anti-Whorf as it was to be pro-Whorf in the early 1950's." More recently, the neuropsychologist James Anderson (1995: vii, ix) mocked the Sapir-Whorf hypothesis as the intellectual darling of "excitable undergraduates and literary critics" and pronounced that the evidence shows this "provocative hypothesis is not true."

So what went wrong? How did this progressive and humanistic concept become tarred with the brush of academic heresy? One answer to that question is found in the nature of the empirical work done by Whorf and his followers in attempting to verify this theory, work which tended to be fairly question-begging assessments done on Amerind languages such as Hopi or Navaho, for which the typical scholarly reader had little way of judging the conclusions made by the researcher. When the linguist Ekkehart Malotki (1983) published a devastatingly detailed critique of Whorf's analysis of Hopi linguistic encoding of temporality, Whorf's work came to seem amateurish and misguided to linguistic anthropologists. Moreover, many of the conclusions made by Whorf about the concepts encoded in the more familiar Western languages with which the Amerind languages were being contrasted simply fail to stand up to scrutiny. For example, Whorf himself argued that Hopi concepts of time differ from English language encoded concepts of time because the Hopi speaker must say something like "on the tenth day" whereas the English speaker uses the plural form "ten days," signifying the idea that time to an English speaker is seen as discrete, pluralizable lumps of something. But, as this example itself shows, English speakers can choose either the pluralizable count noun "days" or the conceptual unity point-in-the-stream-of-time "on the tenth day" parallel to the Hopi expression. So, is it really plausible that sometimes English speakers see the world in a Hopi way and sometimes they do not?

The strong version of linguistic determinism – that differing languages reflected fundamentally incommensurable worldviews – also failed to jibe with the experiences of many multilingual speakers. If languages were really incommensurable encodings, then those who speak more than one language would sometimes encode the world according to the cognitive patterns of one language and other times in an entirely different way. Yet while multilinguals may agree that certain expressions seem to them more or less salient depending on the language they are using at the time (Fishman 1967), they do not report that they experience the world in completely incommensurate ways as they switch from language to language.

The work of cognitive researchers like Eleanor Rosch (1979) and Brent Berlin and Paul Kay (1969) on cross-cultural basic-order categorization also served to undermine strong linguistic determinism. How people cut up the color spectrum into nameable colors, for example, was shown to be anything but random and arbitrary, as one might expect if different languages categorize and name the attributes of the external world in an autonomously based fashion. Instead, this research found that whereas the number of color categories varied between languages, what counted as a "focal" example of a color was consistent across linguistic and cultural boundaries. In short, through a converging accumulation of studies and observations, linguistic determinism of the stronger sort was in effect disconfirmed.

If those disquieting observations helped expose critical weaknesses in the empirical underpinning of strong linguistic determinism, the intellectual juggernaut that was Chomskyan linguistics, with its emphasis on the discovery and mapping of universal characteristics and rules governing all languages, made the focus on incommensurate linguistic differences seem distinctly unsystematic and unscientific. Thomas Olschewsky (1969) drove home the point, arguing that if Chomsky's view of universal grammar was correct, it spelled the death knell of linguistic determinism. Thus, the idea that differing languages encode invariably incommensurate worldviews was relegated to the closet of discarded and unproductive academic pursuits, like butterfly collecting and sentence diagraming (Alford 1978; Fishman 1980).

So, why revisit linguistic determinism? Well, for one thing, the Chomskyan paradigm of a universal grammar – having been revised, readjusted, and reconceptualized repeatedly over the decades by Chomsky himself (cf. Chomsky 1965, 1981, 1995), to say nothing of his adherents – is no longer the unquestioned orthodoxy among linguists (see, e.g. critiques by Kornai and Pullum 1990; Johnson and Lappin 1997; Evans and Levinson 2009). As the strong version of universalism in language has receded in its dominance, intellectual space now exists for a reconsideration of linguistic variability. Indeed, strong linguistic determinism – that language constrains thought – always existed alongside a more moderate concept of linguistic relativism. Linguistic relativism suggests that while human thought may not be straitjacketed in a hermetically sealed unique prison-house of one's own specific language, different languages may instead predispose their users to particularized cognitive encodings of their perceptions and memories. That is, differing languages may *incline* their users toward differing possible encodings – encodings that are simply more available, more salient, closer to hand. Since the mid-1990s, a re-evaluation of linguistic relativity has flourished in the cognitive social sciences (see, e.g. Gumperz and Levinson 1996; Leavitt 2001).

Linguistic relativism of this more moderate form better accords with the experience of multilingual language users, who are more apt to say that it's hard to say something in a particular language than that it's impossible to think of something available in one language while they are operating in another. The translator's cliché "lost in translation" suggests that the commensurability problem in translating something from one language into another is more a matter of mis-mapping of concepts interlinguistically, rather than that a concept is unthinkable interlinguistically. The last two decades have seen an explosion of empirical research exploring the relationship between the language spoken and human cognition (Boroditsky 2001; Boroditsky, Schmidt and Phillips 2003), memory (Pavenko 2003; Boroditsky, Fausey and Long 2009; Fausey and Boroditsky 2011), emotion (Perlovsky 2009), and judgment (Filipovic 2007; Fausey and Boroditsky 2010). Even the supposed universality of color categories – the area of inquiry perhaps most devastating to strong linguistic determinism – has come into question, with recent empirical research (Andrews

1994; Levinson 2000; Roberson, Davies and Davidoff 2000; Athanasopoulos 2009) showing evidence of linguistic relativity there as well; research that has led Paul Kay (Regier and Kay 2009) to reassess his earlier dismissal of linguistic relativity in that context in a co-authored article wrily entitled, "Language, Thought, and Color: Whorf Was Half Right." As it turns out, the idea that individual languages might nudge thought, perception, and memory in distinctive ways might not be so crazy after all. So, let me suggest three examples in which linguistic relativity may have relevance for the grammar of judgment in the law.

The Presence and Absence of Linguistic Politeness Tokens

Assessments about credibility – which witnesses can be believed and who should not be – are at the very heart of judgment in the law. So how do fact-finders decide who to believe? In part, credibility assessments occur on the basis of the nature of the language that the witnesses and litigants use (Conley et al. 1978). One way in which credibility judgments and culpability assessments can be impacted by language is through the use or non-use of linguistic markers of politeness. English is relatively impoverished in its lexical and syntactic markers of hierarchy and politeness in comparison to many other languages. Nevertheless, there have been mock jury studies (Parkinson 1981) showing that even in monolingual English language mock trials, jurors are more likely to believe witnesses and more likely to acquit defendants who use polite forms of language in their courtroom testimony. In addition, the use or non-use of linguistic politeness markers in reported speech are one of the interpretive discursive resources that can help fact-finders separate villains from victims, and aggressors from responders (Mason and Stewart 2001). This suggests that interpreters who fail to completely translate politeness markers in witness testimony are depriving judges and jurors of critical information needed for making appropriate judgments.

In languages with more elaborated and robust systems of politeness markers, their use provides a key index of politeness and respect, and their non-use when otherwise expected is similarly an index of impoliteness and disrespect. In short, politeness markers serve as a discursive resource for indexing of social practices in maintaining or resisting hierarchy, positionality, and attitude. In Romance languages such as Spanish, for instance, there are two, second person singular pronouns – a familiar form (*tú* in Spanish) and a polite form (*usted*). There are social conventions about when to use one versus the other, and a choice to flout that convention always has meaning. In fact, there is a verb in Spanish, *tutear*, that means to use the familiar second person pronoun, so that Spanish speakers can and do overtly make meta-comment on appropriate and inappropriate use of the second person pronoun. Sandra Hale and John Gibbons

(1997) and Susan Berk-Seligson (1988) have examined interpreting conventions in English language courtrooms in which Spanish-speaking witnesses are testifying, and both studies found that English language renderings of Spanish language reported speech did not attend to the presence or absence of the *tú-usted* politeness and deference markers. Thus, important semantic information in such cases is literally lost in translation, and the judge and jury deprived of the fuller meaning of the testimony.

Languages such as Japanese and Korean feature far more pervasive and elaborate linguistic systems of encoding politeness, social position, and deference in social interaction than Romance languages do. The systems of honorifics include differing verbs to be used, different verb endings to be applied, and prefixes to be added to nouns as indicators of the politeness, formality, and social relationships existing between the speaker, the addressee, and the subject matter of the utterance. For example, Japanese distinguishes between three classes of honorific language: *sonkeigo*, or respectful language; *kenjogo*, or humble language; and *teineigo*, or polite language. So, as an example, the verb *suru* meaning "do" would be used between intimates or familiars, it would become *shimasu* used to be polite to an addressee, *nasaimasu* to be particularly respectful to an addressee, *itasu* to express humility by the speaker, and *itashimasu* to express both speaker humbleness and politeness to the addressee. Korean, too, has a set of similar grammatical and lexical codes for politeness, hierarchy, distance, and stance toward the topic of the utterance. Korean sociolinguist Ho-Min Sohn (2006) has identified fourteen distinct linguistics levels expressing varying combinations of politeness, formality, and hierarchy.

Adherence to the appropriate linguistic standards for the interactional context sends a pragmatic signal, and flouting them quite another. These complex linguistic systems express equally complex sets of social attitudes and stances on the part of the speakers, and any culturally competent hearer understands this in her pragmatic understanding of the discourse. The meanings encoded in these honorific systems go beyond the designated references described earlier, however. Deployment, over-deployment, and under-deployment of these systems is itself a rich discursive resource for delicately tuned shades of meaning. Violating these conventions can express contempt, sarcasm, cringing deference, pretentiousness, rudeness, emotional distance, or assertions of power. If the pragmatic information so encoded were to be eliminated from the interactional record, much meaning would disappear with it.

In the English language, there really is no equivalent linguistic resource that corresponds to the lexical and syntactic systems of honorifics in Japanese or Korean. Therefore, speech in such languages, when translated into English, is inevitably shorn of considerable meaning. The meaning of reported speech is distorted when its insulting, presumptious, or deferential nature is deleted from the translated version. More generally, the judge and jury cannot accurately assess the credibility of witness testimony when so much of its pragmatic content has been bleached out of it. The many studies (e.g. Conley et al. 1978) that have demonstrated that the manner and register of witness testimony affects its reception by juries speak to the serious impact that this loss of meaning has for appropriate judgments of credibility and culpability.

How Do You Know What You Claim Is So?

As noted earlier, legal fact-finders – whether judges or juries – have to assess witness testimony for credibility. In part, fact-finders may attempt to judge the character of a witness for truthfulness, but as often as not, credibility assessment is a process of determining how the witness knows what he or she is testifying to, and how believable that source of knowledge might be. Consider the different implications for believability of the following:

John came to the apartment.
I know that John came to the apartment.
I learned that John came to the apartment.
I realized that John came to the apartment.
I think that John came to the apartment.
I assume that John came to the apartment.
John must have come to the apartment.
I guess John came to the apartment.
I heard that John came to the apartment.
Reportedly, John came to the apartment.
Supposedly, John came to the apartment.

All of these statements entail that John came to the apartment; they differ in terms of evidentiality. Evidentiality (see generally Wierzbicka 1994; Aikhenvald 2011) is the element of an utterance that tells the hearer how the speaker knows the fact being asserted. Indirect knowledge is generally considered less reliable than direct knowledge. Hence, the common law's severe restrictions on the admissibility of hearsay evidence – that is, statements made by someone out of court and reported on later by a witness in court to prove the truth of what the out of court speaker said at that time. Hearsay evidence is indirect evidence, and the common law rules of evidence consider it categorically less reliable than the direct testimony of a witness.

Some of these examples given earlier include a verb to indicate *both* that the information is from the speaker's own knowledge *and* that the speaker is vouching for the truth of the information. So these sentences don't make sense semantically:

*I know that John came to the apartment, but maybe he didn't.
*I learned that John came to the apartment, but maybe he didn't.
*I realized that John came to the apartment, but maybe he didn't.

All these would be strange and inconsistent with normal modes of expression. Rather, the speaker with reason to doubt the fact of John's coming to the apartment would hedge like this:

> I think that John came to the apartment.
> I assume that John came to the apartment.

Those examples express the speaker's sincere belief that John likely came to the apartment, based on a surmise or deduction from other facts known to the speaker, but do not vouch for it as an observed, established fact, so that "I think John came to the apartment, but maybe he didn't" is semantically fine, as is "I assume that John came to the apartment, but maybe he didn't."

In contrast, the following examples report the fact that John came to the apartment but without any first-hand knowledge of the fact and without taking a position on whether the fact is true or not:

> I heard that John came to the apartment.
> Reportedly, John came to the apartment.

They would be entirely coherent if amended as "I heard that John came to the apartment, but maybe he didn't" or "Reportedly, John came to the apartment, but maybe he didn't." The last of our examples – "Supposedly John came to the apartment" – disclaims any personal knowledge or even a surmise about the underlying fact, and the adverb "supposedly" expresses skepticism that the fact is true at all.

The examples given here all encode for the *evidentiality* of the embedded statement "John came to the apartment" – they tell the hearer something about how the speaker knows the fact being stated. Evidentiality is obviously very useful if you are a judge or juror trying to decide whether the speaker's testimony can be relied upon. But consider that first sentence:

> John came to the apartment.

It doesn't tell you anything about how the speaker knows the fact or how confident the speaker is about the veracity of the fact. Yet that sentence is a well-formed, perfectly acceptable English language sentence, and would be entirely unobjectionable from the witness stand. That is because the English language does not require evidentiality in its past tense sentences. Evidentiality is entirely optional. When present, it can be indicated through modal verbs like "must be," "ought to be," or "might be"; through additional verbs of knowledge such as "know," "learn," or "realize"; or by using verbs of deduction like "assume" or "deduce"; or verbs of mental commitment like "believe" or "think"; or verbs indicating the means of acquisition of the fact such as "heard that," "read that"; or through the use of adverbs like "reportedly" or "supposedly" or "allegedly" highlighting the lack of the speaker's personal knowledge of the fact. In short, the rules of English grammar *permit* but do not *require* speakers to use evidential markers when they make assertions or ask questions about the past, and for the most part, they don't.

Not all languages are as free and easy as English is when it comes to evidentials, however. Many language families native to North and South America require that a speaker narrating a past event provide a grammatical evidential to indicate the source of the speaker's knowledge (Faller 2004; Barnes 1984; Schlichter 1986). To fail to do so is ungrammatical in the same way that an English speaker discussing an event must tell the hearer whether the event is in the past, present, or future, and failing to use a tense marker on the verb would likewise be an ungrammatical sentence in English. (Of course, many languages find tense as optional as English users find evidentiality. Chinese and Malay, to take two examples, do not mark verbs for tense, relying on other words in the sentence or on context to make the time of the action clear when timing matters.)

Languages of the Caucasus and Turkic languages, like many Amerind languages, also require evidentiality to be marked via verb endings or infixes (Johanson and Utas 2000). Therefore, a Turkish speaker cannot simply say "John came . . . " as an English speaker can. Instead, the Turkish speaker must choose either:

John geldi
    John came (and I know this directly) or
John gelmiş
    John came (reportedly, or assumedly)

The endings *di* or *miş* to the verb stem *gel* are required parts of the verb in narrating a past event or situation. Likewise, "*Yağmur yağmış*" has to mean "I've heard that it rained" or "I surmise it has rained" or "It must have rained" but it cannot mean "It rained, and I saw or heard it rain myself." The *miş* and *di* verb endings are grammatical evidentials, necessary in Turkish, that tell the hearer how the speaker knows what she is stating as a fact, and thereby gives the hearer additional information in deciding whether the fact at issue is likely to be true or not.

Such evidentiality as occurs in Turkish is information that in English may well not be present in an utterance at all. Of course, it is perfectly possible to use evidential expressions in English, and one could imagine that, in a court of law, lawyers would be careful to always clarify how the witnesses know what they are claiming to know. A glance at any trial or deposition transcript, however, will show that even though evidential language is *available* to English speakers, they frequently fail to use it even in circumstances like giving evidence under oath where one might expect the greatest need for evidential precision. Pity the poor interpreter having to interpret for a Turkish speaking litigant – when the

English speaker fails to include evidential language in the course of testifying, the interpreter cannot simply leave it out, as the English speaker has done. The interpreter must instead interpolate some form of evidential into the translated testimony – in the process, adding or subtracting from the meaning intended by the English speaking party. Likewise, the translated testimony of a Turkish witness is likely to have the evidentials necessary for proper weighting of the witness's credibility shorn from the verb by the interpreter who is used to the English absence of evidential markers, in the process robbing the fact-finder of a key linguistic resource for assessing the testimony.

Attribution and Agency Patterns in Language and Assessments of Causation and Blame

Beyond assessing credibility, fact-finders in the law must also make decisions about what caused something to happen, who was responsible, and how blameworthy those causal agents might be. Culpability in the law is a delicate blend of causal responsibility and moral responsibility for harm, and therefore the attribution of causality and blame in legal cases is an area in which linguistic variation in how agency and causation are habitually expressed might have significance for legal decision-making.

Several cognitive science researchers are exploring just those issues through the lens of linguistic relativism. Caitlin Fausey and Lera Boroditsky (2006; 2008) have conducted a series of psychology experiments on native English speakers, native Spanish speakers, and bilingual English-and-Spanish speakers to see whether differences in how English and Spanish encode agency affect the perceptions, recall, and judgments of speakers of those languages.

Spanish and English syntax diverge in how matters of agency are expressed. English is a language which highlights agency syntactically. Subjects generally occur at the beginning of sentences and are seldom omitted, even when the identity of the subject is clear from context. Active voice, in which the doer of an action is in the subject position – "I broke a glass" – is strongly preferred in English, whereas passive voice, in which the doer is syntactically left behind in a prepositional phrase – "A glass was broken by me" – is less common. The linguist John Gibbons (2003) notes a continuum of high to low agency phrasing possible in English – from the high agency "I broke a glass" to the less agentive "A glass got broken" to the agentless "A glass broke." A similar spectrum is available to Spanish speakers, ranging from "*Rompí el vaso*" (I broke the glass on purpose) to "*Se me rompió el vaso*" (It happened that I broke the glass) to the completely agentless "*Se rompió el vaso*" (The glass broke itself). However, in contrast to English, the less agentive constructions in Spanish would be more commonly used. In each case, the same linguistic resources are available to the speaker, but each language has a different typical center of gravity along those continua.

To test whether the differences in how Spanish and English speakers would be inclined to describe events like a glass breaking might affect how they remembered and assessed those events, Fausey and Boroditsky (2008) showed subjects a series of short video vignettes in which someone does something – opens a door, pops a balloon, knocks a doll off a table, puts a sticker on a paper, and so forth. Some of the video clips show acts that appear to be intentional on the part of the actors; others show acts that are more likely interpreted as accidental. Later, the subjects were tested on their memory of the videos and asked what happened in each vignette. In the case of the apparently intentional acts, both the Spanish- and the English-speaking subjects described the episodes using agentive language. However, the English speakers were much more likely to use agentive language in describing the vignettes of accidental actions than either the Spanish speakers or the fully bilingual English–Spanish speakers. Even more strikingly, the English speakers were more likely to remember which agents had acted in those accidental vignettes than the Spanish speakers; though each group performed identically in a control memory test. Fausey and Boroditsky conclude that the contrast in the syntactic preferences between English and Spanish is responsible for the differential recall of agency in the case of accidental actions. This finding raises intriguing questions for law, given the many legal issues that involve causal attribution in accidentally produced harms.

In a second experimental study, Fausey and Boroditsky (2006) tested whether differences in the language of agency between English and Spanish affected subjects' judgment of the culpability of the actors who caused harm. Again, Spanish-speaking and English-speaking subjects were shown video vignettes of acts causing harm or damage. Each subject saw nine vignettes in which the act appears intentional and nine in which the act appears unintentional. Afterward, subjects were asked to rate the blame-worthiness of the actor in the vignettes on a nine-point scale. Both groups – the Spanish speakers and the English speakers – assessed the intentional vignettes identically, using agentive language to describe the acts of the actor and assessing the same degree of culpability. But the results were strikingly different when it came to the vignettes of accidental harm. Here, the English-speaking subjects were considerably more likely than the Spanish-speaking subjects to use agentive language in describing what happened, and assigned blame ratings twice as high as those assessed by Spanish speakers.

Luna Filipovic, another cognitive linguist, has followed up on this research by conducting a similar kind of video clip experiment (2013). She noted that English syntax creates an ambiguity with respect to intentionality even though it emphasizes agency grammatically. That is, in saying "I broke the glass," the hearer does not know whether the speaker did so intentionally or accidentally. Spanish, however, does not express the same facts with this ambiguity. In the case of the intentionally broken glass, the speaker would say "*Rompí el vaso*," meaning "I broke the glass (on purpose)," whereas if the glass were inadvertently broken, say by slipping accidentally from the speaker's hand, the speaker would say instead, "*Se me rompió el vaso*," or "It happened to me that the glass broke." Filipovic identifies a court proceeding (2013: 7) in which the English ambiguity described here caused a disastrous mistranslation:

Q: Okay, you said before that she fell or you dropped her on the steps.

A: Sí, sí, se me cayó. (translation – yes, yes, to-me-it-happened-that-she-fell)
Interpreter: Yes, I dropped her.

Here the witness clearly testified in Spanish that he did not intentionally drop her, but that she fell, but the interpreter picked the intentional, agentive "dropped" as the translation for his unintentional "fell."

Filipovic's 2013 study, like Fausey and Boroditsky's research, also tested the memory of her two linguistic groups of subjects for video vignettes of intentional and unintentionally caused harms. Filipovic, too, found that both the English speakers and Spanish speakers performed identically in recalling and assessing the acts of the intentional actors. When it came to the vignettes of the accidental harms, however, Filipovic found that the Spanish speakers were more likely to recall that the accidental harms were unintentionally caused, whereas the English speakers were more likely to mistakenly attribute intentionality in those cases. She concluded that the ambiguity in English agentive statements – that "I broke the glass" can mean either intentionally or unintentionally – may be the cause of the mis-remembering of the English speakers' in the accidental harm vignettes, while the Spanish speakers linguistic repertoire provided them with a less ambiguous linguistic coding of what they observed. Taken in tandem, the experiments by Filipovic and Fausey and Boroditsky strongly suggest that the syntactic resources of a language can predispose its speakers to differentially notice and remember aspects of agency and culpability. Given the centrality of those issues to the judgments made in courts of law, these findings suggest that courts and lawyers ignore the reality of linguistic relativity at their peril.

Some Recommendations and a Final Consideration

A recognition of the impact of linguistic relativity in law should cause us to reconsider the law's long-standing insistence that court interpreters be limited to verbatim repackaging of a speaker's words into a perfect equivalent in the target language. If we care that legal judgments accurately reflect the full meaning of the testimony of the witnesses out of which those judgments get fashioned, then interpreters must be given the ability to explain their translations in the context of the imperfect linguistic and cultural mapping between the languages in question. Likewise, if the official transcripts of legal proceedings are made solely in one language, there can be no way to determine how much has been gained or lost in translation in the interpreted testimony. Such a practice only buries the problem and makes it invisible; it does not banish it.

Perhaps expecting court interpreters to articulate for monolingual fact-finders the subtleties of interlinguistic relativity in the course of interpreting witness testimony is asking too much. It is difficult enough to try to render the surface sense of testimony from one language to another on the fly; to add to that task the obligation to explain what is gained and lost in translation may well be to expect the impossible. It would not be impractical, however, to provide expert evidence to the court on these matters. Expert testimony by linguists and anthropologists would permit the fact-finders to have a greater appreciation of the issues of linguistic relativity that is essential if the ultimate legal judgments are to be sound reflections of the witnesses' testimony. Legal thought is marked by a deeply entrenched ideology of language that assumes that language is merely a transparent medium for mapping thought onto external reality (Ainsworth 2008); expert evidence on the existence and importance of interlinguistic relativity could serve to challenge that unexamined ideology to the benefit of just and fair legal outcomes.

Finally, one may well wonder whether examples like the ones discussed in this chapter are instances of purely cultural differences rather than language-based differences. Does linguistic variation simply reflect underlying cultural patterns or does a language's structure and characteristics in some way "nudge" thought and cognition in particular ways in its own right? There is some intriguing research that suggests that language does play a role, independent of cultural norms and experiences. Research interviews with fully bilingual and bicultural subjects have shown that the language used in the interview has a pronounced tendency to channel the subjects' responses. For example, fluent Greek–English bilinguals expressed contrasting emotional reactions to identical stories, depending on whether the stories were related in the English or Greek language (Panayiotou 2004). In another study (Ramirez-Esparza et al. 2006), fluent Spanish–English bilinguals asked to describe themselves did so quite differently when asked to do so in Spanish rather than in English, suggesting that the language in which the interview took place "nudged" their expressions of self-identity in contrasting directions. Language has been shown to "prime" subject response even when the interview questions are emotionally neutral. When fluent Mandarin–English subjects living in the United States were asked "Name a statue of someone standing with a raised arm looking into the distance," if they were asked in Chinese, they were likely to respond "Chairman Mao," but if they were asked in English, the response was likely to be "the Statue of Liberty"; being asked to name a famous tourist site in Chinese resulted in answers like the Great Wall or the Forbidden City, while asking the subjects the same question in English prompted answers like the Grand Canyon or the Space Needle (Marian and Kaushanskaya 2007).

Perhaps in the end the question of whether language influences thought directly or only as mediated by culture presupposes a dichotomy between language and culture that is fundamentally misleading. Language is an inseparable part of how cultures instantiate themselves, and language is the medium through which cultural values and perspectives are propagated from generation to generation. Nicholas Evans (2009) calls this process "social cognition in grammar." This is why there is a race against time to preserve dying languages – because we recognize that the loss of a language is a body blow to its originating culture. Separating language and culture, and asking which is in the driver's seat, is not a useful way to think about the relationship between language, thought, and culture. In a multilingual and multicultural world, linguistic relativism challenges law to take seriously the question of how our legal judgment processes and practices can better come to accommodate the multiplicity of real grammars that we make use of in communication and so come closer to fulfilling law's promise of justice in its judgments.

REFERENCES

Aikhenvald, A. Y. (2011). Evidentials. In M. Aronoff (ed.) *Oxford Bibliography Online*. New York: Oxford University Press, 1–45.

Ainsworth, J. (2008). 'You have the right to remain silent . . . ' but only if you ask for it just so: The role of linguistic ideology in American police interrogation. *International Journal of Speech, Language, and the Law* 15: 1–21.

Alford, D. K. H. (1978). The demise of the Whorf hypothesis. In *Proceedings of the 4th Annual Meeting of the Berkeley Linguistics Society*. Berkeley, CA: Berkeley Linguistics Society, 485–499.

Anderson, J. (1995). *An Introduction to Neural Networks*. Cambridge, MA: MIT Press.

Andrews, D. (1994). The Russian color categories *sinij* and *goluboj*: An experimental analysis of their interpretation in the standard and émigré language. *Journal of Slavic Linguistics* 2: 9–28.

Athanasopoulos, P. (2009). Cognitive representation of color in bilinguals: The case of Greek blues. *Bilingualism: Language and Cognition* 12: 83–95.

Barnes, J. (1984). Evidentials in the Tuyuca verb. *International Journal of American Linguistics* 50: 255–271.

Berk-Seligson, S. (1988). The impact of politeness in witness testimony: The influence of the court interpreter. *Multilingua* 7: 411–440.

Berlin, B. and Kay, P. (1969). *Basic Color Terms: Their Universality and Evolution*. Berkeley: University of California Press.

Boroditsky, L. (2001). Does language shape thought?: Mandarin and English speakers' conceptions of time. *Cognitive Psychology* 43: 1–22.

Boroditsky, L., Fausey, C. and Long, B. (2009). The role of language in eyewitness memory: Remembering who did it in English and Japanese. *Proceedings of the Cognitive Science Society*, vol. 31.

Boroditsky, L., Schmidt, L. A. and Phillips, W. (2003). Sex, syntax, and semantics. In D. Gertner and S. Goldin-Meadow (eds.) *Language in Mind: Advances in the Study of Language and Thought*. Cambridge, MA: MIT Press, 61–79.

Chomsky, N. (1965). *Aspects of the Theory of Syntax*. Cambridge, MA: MIT Press.

Chomsky, N. (1981). *Lectures on Government and Binding*. Berlin: Mouton de Gruyter.

Chomsky, N. (1995). *The Minimalist Program*. Cambridge, MA: MIT Press.

Conley, J. M., O'Barr, W. M. and Lind, E. A. (1978). The power of language: Presentation style in the courtroom. *Duke Law Journal* 1978: 1375–1399.

Evans, N. (2009). *Dying Words: Endangered Languages and What They Have to Tell Us*. Malden, MA: Wiley-Blackwell.

Evans, N. and Levinson, S. C. (2009). The myth of language universals: Language diversity and its importance to cognitive science. *Behavioral and Brain Sciences* 32: 429–492.

Faller, M. (2004). The deictic use of non-experiential past in Cuzco Quechua. *Journal of Semantics* 21: 45–85.

Fausey, C. M. and Boroditsky, L. (2006). Linguistic contributions to reasoning about causal agents. *Proceedings of the 28th Annual Meeting of the Cognitive Sciences Society.*

Fausey, C. M. and Boroditsky, L. (2008). English and Spanish speakers remember causal agents differently. *Proceedings of the 30th Annual Meeting of the Cognitive Sciences Society.*

Fausey, C. M. and Boroditsky, L. (2010). Subtle linguistic cues influence perceived blame and financial liability. *Psychonomic Bulletin and Review* 17: 644–650.

Fausey, C. M. and Boroditsky, L. (2011). Who dunnit? Cross-linguistic differences in eye-witness memory. *Psychonomic Bulletin and Review* 18: 150–157.

Filipovic, L. (2007). Language as a witness: Insights from cognitive linguistics. *International Journal of Speech, Language, and the Law* 14: 245–267.

Filipovic, L. (2013). Constructing causation in language and memory: Implications for access to justice in multilingual interactions. *International Journal of Speech, Language, and the Law* 20.1: 1–19.

Fishman, J. A. (1967). Bilingualism with and without diglossia; diglossia with and without bilingualism. *Journal of Social Issues* 23, 29–38.

Fishman, J. A. (1980). The Whorfian hypothesis: Variations of valuation, confirmation, and disconfirmation. *International Journal of the Sociology of Language* 26: 25–40.

Gibbons, J. (2003). *Forensic Linguistics*. Oxford: Blackwell.

Gumperz, J. and Levinson, S. C. (eds.) (1996). *Rethinking Linguistic Relativity*. Cambridge: Cambridge University Press.

Hale, S. and Gibbons, J. (1997). Varying realities: Patterned changes in the interpreter's representation of courtroom and external realities. *Applied Linguistics* 20: 203–220.

Hitchens, J. (1994). Critical implications of Franz Boas' theory and methodology. *Dialectical Anthropology* 19, 237–253.

Johanson, L. and Utas, B. (2000). *Evidentials: Turkic, Iranian and Neighboring Languages*. Berlin: Mouton de Gruyter.

Johnson, D. E. and Lappin, S. (1997). A critique of the minimalist program. *Linguistics and Philosophy* 20: 273–333.

Kornai, A. and Pullum, G. K. (1990). The X-bar theory of phrase structure. *Language* 66: 24–50.

Leavitt, J. (2001). *Linguistic Relativism: Language Diversity and Modern Thought*. Cambridge: Cambridge University Press.

Levinson, S. C. (2000). Yeli Dnye and the theory of basic color terms. *Journal of Linguistic Anthropology* 10: 3–55.

Malotki, E. (1983). *Hopi Time: A Linguistic Analysis of the Temporal Concepts in the Hopi Language*. Berlin: Mouton.

Marian, V. and Kaushanskaya, M. (2007). Language context guides memory content. *Psychonomic Bulletin and Review* 14: 925–933.

Mason, I. and Stewart, M. (2001). Interactional pragmatics, face, and the dialog interpreter. In I. Mason (ed.) *Triadic Exchanges: Studies in Dialogue Interpreting*. New York: Routledge, 51–71.

Mellinkoff, D. (1963). *The Language of the Law*. Boston: Little Brown.

Olschewsky, T. M. (1969). *Problems in the Philosophy of Language*. New York: Holt, Rinehart, and Winston.

Panayiotou, A. (2004). Switching codes, switching code: Bilinguals' emotional responses in English and Greek. *Journal of Multilingual and Multicultural Development* 25: 124–139.

Parkinson, M. (1981). Verbal behavior and courtroom success. *Communication Education* 30: 22–32.

Pavenko, A. (2003). Eyewitness memory in late bilinguals: Evidence for discursive relativity. *International Journal of Bilingualism* 7: 257–281.

Perlovsky, L. (2009). Language and emotions: Emotional Sapir-Whorf hypothesis. *Neural Networks* 22: 518–526.

Postema, G. J. (2012). Custom, normative practice, and the law. *Duke Law Journal* 62: 707–738.

Ramirez-Esparza, N., Gosling, S. D., Benet-Martinez, V., Potter, J. P. and Pennebaker, J. W. (2006). Do bilinguals have two personalities?: A special case of cultural frame shifting. *Journal of Research in Personality* 40: 99–120.

Regier, T. and Kay, P. (2009). Language, thought, and color: Whorf was half right. *Trends in Cognitive Science* 13: 439–446.

Roberson, D., Davies, I. and Davidoff, J. (2000). Color categories are not universal: Replications and new evidence from a stone-age culture. *Journal of Experimental Psychology* 129: 369–398.

Rosch, E. (1979). Human categorization. *Studies in Cross-Cultural Communication* 1: 3–47.

Schlag, P. (1991). Normativity and the politics of form. *University of Pennsylvania Law Review* 139: 801–932.

Schlichter, A. (1986). The origins and deictic nature of Wintu evidentials. In W. Chafe and J. Nichols (eds.) *Evidentiality: The Linguistic Coding of Evidentiality*, vol. 20. Norwood, NJ: Ablex, 46–59.

Sohn, H.-M. (2006). *Korean Language in Culture and Society*. Honolulu: University of Hawaii Press.

Spaak, T. (2003). Legal positivism, law's normativity, and the normative force of legal justification. *Ratio Juris* 16: 469–485.

White, J. B. (1985). *Heracles' Bow: Essays on the Rhetoric and Poetics of the Law.* Madison: University of Wisconsin Press.

Whorf, B. L. (1956). An American Indian model of the universe. In J. B. Carroll (ed.) *Language, Thought, and Reality: Selected Writings of Benjamin Lee Whorf.* Cambridge, MA: MIT Press, 57–64.

Wierzbicka, A. (1994). Semantics and epistemology: The meaning of 'evidential' in cross-linguistic perspective. *Language Sciences* 16, 81–137.

12 Legal Indeterminacy in the Spoken Word*

Lawrence M. Solan and Silvia Dahmen

EDITORS' NOTE TO CHAPTER 12

In western legal traditions, until around the twelfth century legal proceedings mainly took the form of spoken ritual. The gradual transition that then took place in law, from oral to written practice, occurred in parallel with the more general shift from orality to literacy in European societies (for discussion with reference to England, see Clanchy 2012). In key respects, the situation in law resembled that wider change, and indeed contributed to it. But the historical shift was never total; and in the modern period the relationship between speech and writing has continued to be complicated by interaction between ephemeral speech, recorded (and so fixed) audio, and rapidly changing forms of communicative interaction by way of instantly backed-up digital media (including body cameras). Despite the general availability of relevant technologies, in many legal processes spontaneous and semi-scripted speech has continued to be the main way of accomplishing a considerable number of tasks: eliciting information, issuing arrest warnings, cross-examining witnesses, affirming and swearing oaths, and so forth. In many situations, the spoken word has only a transient existence before it is lost forever, or alternatively transcribed or summarized in a written record.

These important aspects of speech have ramifications in law. For example, scholars studying the interface between language and law have devoted a great deal of effort to investigating the contribution made by linguistic indeterminacy (e.g. uncertainty arising from vagueness and ambiguity) to legal indeterminacy; but most of their research starts with legal language in written form. In the following essay, by contrast, Solan and Dahmen show why indeterminacy encountered in spoken language also matters. If spoken communication is not recorded, they point out, confusion about what is said may remain unnoticed, and the source of the misunderstanding in question cannot be traced. Even

* The authors express their gratitude to Geoffrey Harrison, Robert Leonard, Roger Shuy, and Tom Roeper for providing some of the data discussed in this article, and Sandra Disner, Helen Fraser, Michael Jessen, and Douglas Whalen for helpful comments on an earlier draft. We are especially grateful to the editors of this volume for their insightful comments and suggestions.

where communication has been recorded, the quality of the recording may still lead to indeterminacy. And even these two situations do not exhaust the possibilities for linguistic indeterminacy. There are inherent features in how people speak that leave scope for competing interpretations; and speech perception may be skewed by contextual factors and biases based on prior experience and knowledge. In recordings involving multiple participants, apart from problems of exactly what is said and unintelligible moments of overlap of a kind studied in Conversation Analysis, there is sometimes also the apparently basic question of who it was who said whatever was said.

Solan and Dahmen's essay identifies features of speech, and of contexts in which speech is produced and perceived, that contribute to uncertainty in interpreting spoken interaction in legally relevant settings. They observe that loss in meaning during the transmission of spoken words used between law enforcement officers and citizens can have severe consequences: a misinterpretation of recorded speech, for example, could serve as incriminating evidence. Solan and Dahmen review how courts have dealt with disputed transcription and illustrate how linguists can sometimes assist the courts in resolving speech perception difficulties. Although their chapter focuses on the English language, many of Solan and Dahmen's insights are generalizable to spoken communication in other languages.

REFERENCE

Clanchy, M. (2012). *From Memory to Written Record: England 1066–1307* (3rd ed.). London: Wiley-Blackwell.

Legal Indeterminacy in the Spoken Word

Language and Power in Construing Verbal Interactions

The interpretation of legal texts – constitutions, statutes, regulations, and contracts – is a subject of both judicial action and legal scholarship. Judges and scholars read and reread the language, arguing about how to resolve ambiguity, what to do about vagueness, which pragmatic inferences are appropriate to draw from context, how much attention to pay to history, how to characterize the intent of the drafters, and so on (compare, e.g. Scalia and Garner 2012 and Katzmann 2014). Even when the dispute is over language that was originally spoken, if the words are recorded, or remembered because there were only a few, the discussion is a matter of analyzing the actual words that were used.

These interpretive tasks become more problematic when the language in dispute is not a law or contract, but rather involves an encounter between citizens and the police. It is up to the judge to decide whose interpretation prevails, and at least in the United States, the courts appear generally to give the benefit of the doubt to the police. In one seminal case,[1] a car driven by a young Latino man, Mr. Bustamonte, was stopped by a police officer for a minor traffic infraction. The officer said, "Does the trunk open?" Bustamonte opened the trunk. The officer's subsequent search uncovered some stolen checks, for which Bustamonte was prosecuted. Bustamonte argued that the checks should be suppressed because they were illegally seized: The police officer had no right to search the trunk without a warrant or probable cause that a crime was being committed. The officer responded that he had been given permission. The case, which reached the U.S. Supreme Court, boiled down to the meaning of "Does the trunk open." Everyone agreed that the utterance should not be understood as an inquiry about the latch mechanism that holds it shut. Rather, Bustamonte took the position that this was an illegal command to open the trunk; the police took the position that it was merely a request.

The language the officer used was equally susceptible to being understood as a request or a command. The power relationship between the parties determines how it is actually understood (Solan and Tiersma, 2005; Nadler and Trout, 2012). A relatively powerless person will think he must comply. This is often the case when police officers seeking consent to a search are concerned. If, in contrast, Bustamonte had a 5-year-old nephew with him and the child had used those same words, it is very unlikely that Bustamonte would have felt obliged to obey. The Court sided with the police. After all, the utterance took the form of a question.

Once a suspect is taken to the police station, a question may arise as to whether he has adequately asserted his right to be silent or to speak to a lawyer. Indirect speech by a suspect is construed once again in favor of the police. In another important U.S. case,[2] the suspect said in response to having been read his rights, "Maybe I should talk with an attorney." The Court did not accept the argument that people who feel helpless tend to use powerless speech (Conley and O'Barr 2005), and to ask for things indirectly (see Ainsworth 1993). Unless a suspect asserts his rights directly and clearly, his words are construed as merely thinking aloud.

In this chapter, we address an additional context: cases in which there is either a dispute or confusion about what was said in the first place. Language connects sound and meaning. Written language takes most of the uncertainty about the "sound" part of the equation out of the picture. But when the dispute is over what someone actually said aloud, whether in a recorded conversation the transcript of which is murky, or in negotiating a contract, or in interactions with government officials, problems arise that go beyond textual vagueness and

[1] Schneckloth v. Bustamonte, 412 U.S. 218 (1973).
[2] Davis v. United States, 512 U.S. 452 (1994).

ambiguity. Because spoken language consists of a continual flow of sound that does not tell us when one word ends and the next begins, because in spoken English we pronounce a lot of unstressed vowels the same, and because we do not articulate some syllables that the spelling suggests we should, the interpretation of spoken language contains not only the indeterminacies of written language, but also a range of uncertainty triggered by its own character. It should not be surprising that legal systems, as they become more sophisticated and as literacy increases, move always in the direction of more text, less speech, and not the reverse (see Tiersma 1999, 2010).

Moreover, because we must process speech online and very rapidly, we quickly make decisions about what is being said, and then lose our ability to remember the exact words that we heard. The interface between speech and memory, as we will see, also contributes a great deal to legal uncertainty. In this chapter, we look both at recorded encounters in which there is dispute about what was said, and at encounters that were not recorded, where the issue becomes remembering what was said at all. Most of these cases, then, are about how evidence should be analyzed and interpreted. As we will see, the resolution of such disputes also tends to favor the police. Moreover, at times, those who are asked to transcribe recordings are told in advance what police officers or prosecutors believe was said, causing bias to those who create the written record from the spoken word.

Some Linguistic Preliminaries: The Interface between Sound and Syntax

In order for readers not trained in phonetics to understand the problems that arise in disputes over the content of recorded speech, we will need to provide a brief introduction to the relevant linguistic issues. The problems of speech perception that arise in transcript disputes arise in other contexts as well, including the misunderstanding of song lyrics. As we explore the problems later, we illustrate them with examples of misperceived lyrics.

We do not here rely on a detailed picture of how our linguistic capacities are assembled and interact. But we do rely on some general, and, we believe, widely accepted claims about the architecture of our linguistic faculty. During the past half century, linguistic theory has made great progress along many fronts. Though there exist significant disagreements, expressed often through energetic debate, work in such areas as syntax, semantics, phonology, pragmatics, discourse analysis, and psycholinguistics (including both language processing and language acquisition) has borne fruit. One difficult issue that has emerged from this progress is the question of how the various linguistic subsystems fit together ("interface" is used both as a verb and a noun in addressing this problem). The problem is difficult for two reasons. First, in order to know how two subsystems interact, one has to have decided on the proper architecture for the system as a whole (Jackendoff 2002). Second, one has to have developed the subsystems well enough for the interfaces to actually reflect the relationships within a mature theory. We are not really there yet.

Regardless of what is still in contention, some aspects of the relationships among linguistic subsystems seem to be on strong footing. We will specifically assume that the system of sound and the system of syntax are distinct, and must interface. This claim is not controversial, but it is not trivial either. The systems must be separate and distinct in large part because they are composed of entirely different elements. Those who study phonology and phonetics use primitives such as syllables, phonological contrasts (such as voiced/unvoiced, aspirated/unaspirated, sonorant/non-sonorant), and stress contours. The sounds [b] and [v] are distinctive sounds in English, much less so in Spanish, for example. Syllables themselves have structure, and some phonological rules apply only when a sound is in a particular place in the syllable. These features have little or nothing to do with syntax. Whether *pit* is a noun or verb does not depend on whether /p/[3] is its initial sound or /t/ its final sound. In fact, the words "pit" and "tip" are each both nouns and verbs in English. Nor does the sound system tell us a single thing about why "Is the man who is tall happy?"[4] is a good sentence of English, while "Is the man who tall is happy?" is not a good sentence of English. Lining up the sounds with the structure of language is not a simple matter. Later we will show how particular phonological processes, and the phonetic reality of how we speak and hear, interact inadequately with our efforts to form linguistic structures, leading to at least the potential for misunderstanding.

We speak without using a spacebar. Human speech comes in a single flow of sound. Readers unfamiliar with this fact should say the first sentence of this paragraph out loud, first in a normal tone of voice, then pausing as if to hit a spacebar between words. The contrast may surprise you, but we've all experienced it when we try to understand foreign languages. Not only do we not understand the words, until we have gained some proficiency we cannot even judge when one word ends and the next word begins.

Following are two sound spectrograms[5] that Dahmen created of Solan saying "we speak without using a spacebar." The first is spoken naturally. Notice that

[3] We use the ordinary linguistic convention of placing phonemes between forward slashes "/p/." Phonemes are basically the idealized sounds of the language. Thus, we say that both "bottle" and "tub" contain the phoneme /t/ even though they are pronounced entirely differently. When it comes to actual pronunciation, linguist place the sounds between square brackets "[]." In American English, these sounds are represented respectively as $[t^l]$ and $[t^h]$.

[4] This phrase is the title of an animated film, *Is the Man Who Is Tall Happy?* (2013), produced by Michael Gondry and consisting of recorded conversations with Noam Chomsky.

[5] The reader who is aware of the debates over using sound spectrograms as "voice prints" through which an expert can identify a speaker by analyzing the spectrogram alone may mistakenly believe that sound spectrography is in ill repute more generally. It is not. On the contrary, it

there are no columns of pure white going from bottom to top. Such columns would reflect silence. There are, indeed, areas where there is not much sound. These represent such sounds as [s], which we utter by letting air flow between our tongue and our alveolar ridge without using our vocal folds. But no silence.

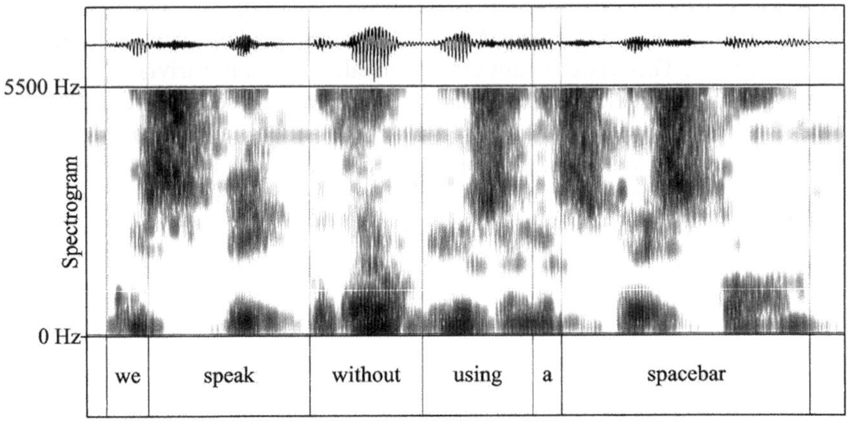

Now consider the second, unnatural way to say the same sentence, pausing between words.

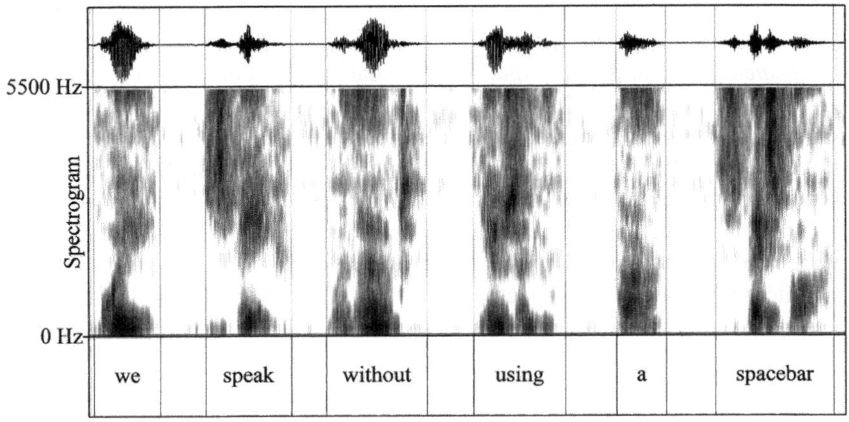

This looks very different, with columns of white reflecting the silence between the words. The first would seem to require more cognitive apparatus to understand as individual words, and it does. The second would seem easier,

is a well-used tool in phonetics. What is in ill repute is the technology's misuse in forensic contexts.

but it also sounds like a robot is speaking. It reflects a style of speech that is simply not how human beings talk.

Thus, we hear language as a single stream. But we do not understand language as a single stream. Our minds locate and tap the spacebar that our voices do not have. We understand speech as consisting of words, phrases, sentences, chunks of discourse. Somehow, we unpack the single flow of sound into its constituent words, and then chunk the words into appropriate syntactic units so that we can understand the relationships among them. And we must do this quickly enough so that the flow of speech does not pass us by while we try to figure it out. Thus, our brains must be equipped to determine where one word ends and the next begins and to then construct some kind of structure so that what we hear makes sense. Later, we will discuss a price that we pay for this rapid processing skill: We cannot remember the precise words that were said (or read) even a few seconds earlier. This itself has legal ramifications to which we return. For now, however, we limit ourselves to difficulties in associating a flow of sound with particular linguistic units.

The best illustrations of these difficulties come from misunderstood lyrics to songs. These are called *mondegreens.* Linguists have found it interesting to identify the contexts in which these errors are likely to happen as a window into our language processing abilities. The most famous is Jimi Hendrix's song Purple Haze, where "'scuse me while I kiss the sky" is misunderstood as "'scuse me while I kiss this guy" (Tang and Nevins 2014; Bond 1999). Others include:[6]

Heard	Sung
"there's a bathroom on the right"	"there's a bad moon on the rise"
"I have my books and I grow a tree to protect me"	". . . and my poetry to protect me"
"steak and a knife, steak and a knife"	"staying alive, staying alive"
"the girl with colitis goes by"	"the girl with kaleidoscope eyes"
"paint the black whiter"	"paperback writer"

We handpicked these examples as ones in which the error included misunderstanding where one word ends and the next begins. In each of them, the hearer got the word boundaries wrong.

Why does this happen in these instances, but not others? There are several reasons. First of all, song lyrics are not predictable from a given situational context; they use a fair amount of figurative speech. Thus, we cannot easily draw inferences about what is being sung from context. The misheard versions

[6] These lyrics are available at www.kissthisguy.com.

contain everyday expressions whereas the original versions have words and expressions that we do not usually use in everyday life. Second, the number of syllables and the rhythmic structure of the misheard and the original versions are alike in all examples (compare "poetry" and "grow a tree"). Third, there are segmental similarities, especially in the vowels, but also in word-initial consonants (e.g. "bathroom on the right – bad moon on the rise"). Fourth, as we described earlier, word boundaries are not audible in connected speech, as there are no acoustic cues for their perception such as pauses between words.

We do not pronounce words the way their spelling suggests. Instead, we reduce unstressed vowels so they sound the same, clip syllables and simplify speech in other ways. In fact, the problem with "'scuse me while I kiss the sky" is a bit more complex. The sounds between the two versions are similar in some very specific ways. We will have to describe the English sound system in a bit more detail to explain why. What we say here will also be relevant to the legal examples discussed in the next section.

First, some consonants are made by allowing air to escape through a slim opening between, say, the tongue and the alveolar ridge (/s/ and /z/). Others, however, require that we stop the air completely and then allow it to burst out. These, appropriately enough, are called stops or plosives. Depending on how we place our lips and tongue, we get different sounds. Some are made with our voices off, others with our voices on. In English, however, the phonologically voiced and voiceless stops (/b, d, g/ and /p, t, k/, respectively) do not mainly differ in the amount of voicing during the stop closure, but in the so called aspiration that accompanies the "voiceless" stops when they are uttered syllable-initially before a vowel, as in *pea, tea, key*. Aspiration means that when the oral closure (e.g. made with both lips in the sound /p/) is released for the vowel, a short explosive noise can be perceived. If you put your hand before your lips and say "pea," you can feel a puff of air after release of the oral closure. Native speakers of English who learn languages such as Spanish or French should be familiar with the fact that aspirating the "p" in *Pedro*, for example, is a sure giveaway of speaking such languages with a foreign accent.

Despite their name, however, "voiced" stops usually do not have the voice turned on during the closure in syllable-initial position, but the vocal folds start vibrating as the vowel sets in and no voiceless aspiration is produced. So the main acoustic cue for perceiving /p, t, k/ instead of /b, d, g/ is the aspiration of the former three. Now, when a voiceless stop is preceded by /s/, as in *sky*, the stop loses its aspiration and becomes very similar to the unaspirated stop that we perceive as /g/. As we do not make pauses between words when we speak, we do not have acoustic cues that tell us where the word boundaries are (compare *a nail* and *an ale* when you say them aloud). So the word boundary in the utterance "the sky" is placed after the /s/, resulting in the misheard utterance "this guy." Most probably this is also motivated by pragmatic intuition that tells us that it is more usual to kiss a person than the sky.

Moreover, the vowels in "this" and "the" do not sound as different as they look in writing. This is because, in English, we tend to pronounce unstressed vowels more or less in the same way, regardless of what the spelling is. This is the well-known "schwa" sound, represented as [ə]. It is the source of many spelling errors in English. If you do not know the spelling in advance, you probably have to guess the middle vowel in words like "histamine," for example. Some mondegreens that do not involve word boundaries are the result of this neutralization of unstressed vowels. Among them are:[7]

Heard	Sung
"ten thousand people making war"	"ten thousand people maybe more"
"you don't need a pinhead"	"you don't need a penny"

In the first, "ing" replaces [i]; in the second, unstressed "head" replaces [i]. There are many more available examples.

Legal Uncertainty and the Human Voice

Most problems of legal interpretation occur whether the language is spoken or written. "Visiting relatives can be annoying" is ambiguous in the same way whether you read it or say it. Similarly, to take an example from U.S. law, whether trading a machine gun for cocaine should count as violating a statute that enhances the sentence for "using a firearm during and in relation to a drug-trafficking crime,"[8] has nothing to do whether the language of the statute is recited aloud or read silently. Of course tone of voice might sometimes matter, but we expect that with most disputes over the meaning of legal texts the words of the text would dominate the analysis. We doubt, for example, that there would be less debate over the scope of the right to keep and bear arms if the U.S. Constitution were committed to memory instead of being committed to parchment.

Occasionally, the written word creates ambiguity not present in the spoken word. This happens when the same spelling is used for two entirely different words. These are called homographs. Among them are "excuse," "wind," "read," "live," and "lead." When read, the two alternatives can only be sorted

[7] Again, lyrics are available on www.kissthisguy.com.
[8] Smith v. United States, 507 U.S. 197 (1993).

out by context. This does not seem to be very difficult – people are excellent contextualizers, especially when the possible meanings are sufficiently distinct (Miller 1996). In many of these examples, the distinctions are made easier by the fact that the two words are not only pronounced differently but are different parts of speech. Moreover, there do not seem to be legal disputes caused by this ambiguity.

For the most part, though, the opposite is true: writing introduces clarity in communication. Writing is what enables law to be so complex, making it possible to think very carefully about the language that was used, and to reread it as necessary. The history of law is in part a history of moving from oral law to written law, often in interesting stages. Peter Tiersma's writings describe a gradual history, driven by increases in both technology and literacy, leading from law as an oral tradition, to one in which writings were not legally binding but constituted evidence of legal commitment, to the predominance of text over speech, and finally, to such obsession with language that statements by judges to resolve specific disputes become "textualized" and are quoted verbatim and analyzed as binding law (Tiersma 1999, 2010). We know of no culture that decided to abandon its system of written law in order to return to an oral tradition.

Confusion: From Music to Law

Some Examples of Murky Recordings Let us move from the realm of recorded music to the realm of recorded speech in legal contexts. As we will see, when recordings are not clear, they provide space for competing interpretations of what was said. Like the interactions between citizens and police described in the beginning of this chapter, prosecutors often offer versions that serve their goals. Though courts do not always accept the prosecutors' version, they are reluctant to throw out the evidence altogether even when there is no consensus as to the content of the recording. The various procedures offered by the courts are generally unsatisfactory if the goal is to get to the truth of what was actually recorded.

Exactly the same confusion that leads to misunderstanding lyrics can lead to misunderstanding the words on recordings of voices from surveillance tapes, wire taps, and the like.[9] Most judicial opinions writing about the resolution of such problems do not mention the actual language in dispute. But occasionally they do. In one such case,[10] the prosecution presented a transcript of a recording containing the following exchange:

[9] See Fraser (2003) for further discussion of how these and other phonetic phenomena are relevant to the production of transcripts of recorded speech.

[10] United States v. Adams, 722 F. 3d 788, 825 (6th Cir. 2013).

MARICLE: Last year... not been around him. His big problem was a conspiracy charge...
KENNON: Right. Conspiracy charges, they could hit him on that, too?

One of the speakers (Maricle) testified at trial that what was really said was:

MARICLE: Last year, I don't remember ever being around him, his big problem was in the state.
KENNON: Stephen Charles represented him on that one too.

The trial judge had admitted the prosecution's transcript into evidence. The appellate court could not tell whether Maricle's version was right, but decided that the recording was not good enough to support the government's version in any event. Consistent with our preceding discussion of phonetics, the appellate court candidly noted:

> We realize that without hearing the recording, readers may wonder just how these two seemingly different interpretations stem from the same portion of the recording. With the benefit of the recording, we too are unsure as to how, but the fact remains that both appear to be accurate when read while listening to the recording.[11]

From what we have seen so far, if the recording is bad enough that only stressed syllables come through, it should not be surprising that "Charles" and "charges" are heard by the different parties, given their conflicting agendas.

Linguists who have testified in such disputes provide some very interesting examples. This literature is important because the linguists more often than the courts describe the details of the disputed language. Roger Shuy (1993: 37–41) reports the case of John Poli, a Nevada farmer who served on the brothel commission (yes, really) of his county. When a woman approached him and his colleague for a license to open a brothel, they suggested that she pay them a bribe. Later they claimed that they were merely trying to ascertain whether she was a legitimate candidate and that they never would have taken money from her. The opportunity to prove this came soon, for the licensure candidate had gone to the FBI in the meantime and returned to Poli and his friend wearing a wire. At the next meeting, which took place in a diner, she raised the question of paying the two commissioners bribes in exchange for favorable treatment in her application for a brothel license, offering them $5,000 right there as a down payment on a $35,000 bribe. The restaurant was noisy, with music, conversation and the sounds of dishes banging as they hit the tables.

Did the commissioners accept the bribe? There was a dispute about what Poli actually said:

[11] *Id.*, at n.30.

Government transcript:	No, I would take a bribe, wouldn't you?
Defendants' transcript:	No, I wouldn't take a bribe, would you?

The case got down to how many syllables occur after the word bribe: two or three? The trial ended in a hung jury. The defendants were retried, this time without the testimony of Shuy, and were then convicted of bribery.

The reason that it is so hard to determine the number of syllables in contracted forms of verbs when they are uttered in connected speech lies in the rhythmic properties of English. Unstressed syllables in English differ from stressed ones in that they are produced with a low level of prominence (reduced intensity or duration), and as we noted earlier, in that they show a great amount of articulatory reduction.

Especially in casual or sloppy speech, sequences of three or more consonants are often reduced by eliding consonants. Very common examples, where consonants are elided regularly from clusters are *handsome* /hænsəm/ or *sandwich* /sænwɪʧ/, where the middle consonant /d/ is not pronounced. The /t/ in the contracted form of *not* is often not pronounced in disyllabic forms followed by another word that begins with a consonant; for example in *wouldn't* [wʊdn] or *mustn't* [məsn] (O'Grady 2013: 52). Disyllabic forms may even become monosyllabic in rapid speech, so that *didn't* can be pronounced like *dint* (Brown 2014). Bad sound quality of the recording and background noise would then add to making it hard to determine the number of syllables in unstressed position. Thus, the fact of this kind of dispute does not surprise us in the least.

In another case, involving a man named Charles Lorraine, who was charged with murder, Shuy (2014: 175–77) discusses the following disputed transcripts over whether Lorraine had waived his Miranda rights:

Government Transcript	Lorraine Transcript
Lorraine: Can't you shut the tape off?	Lorraine: Can't you shut the tape off?
Police: We need it on, Charles. For your benefit as well as ours.	Police: We need it on, Charles. For your benefit as well as ours.
Lorraine: I, I don't wanna talk.	Lorraine: I don wanna talk.
Police: You don't want to talk? I if I turn the tape off, will you tell us?	Police: You don't want to talk? If we turn the tape off will you tell us?
Lorraine: I, I'd wanna talk. Turn the tape off.	Lorraine: Look, I, I duh wanna talk. Turn the tape off.
Police: Okay, okay.	Police: Okay, okay.
	Lorraine: And the TV.
	Police: Alright.

This dispute amounted largely to whether Lorraine said "I'd wanna talk" or "I duh wanna talk," and if the latter, what "duh" means. The spelling suggests that the transcriber was uncertain about what was actually said; otherwise he or she would have spelled out a real word instead of "duh." Shuy describes it as a further reduction of "don't," with a nasal vowel quality still representing the elided nasal [n]. This could be true, but an equally likely explanation for the "duh" could be another segmentation issue. The transcript spells out repetitions like "I, I..." that are typical for people speaking under stress, as in a police examination. It is plausible that Lorraine also produced filler vocalizations typical of disfluent speech (which are very often spelled as "uh"), but they are not accounted for in this transcript. So, Lorraine could have said "I, I'd – uh – wanna talk," and the transcriber (mis)placed a word boundary before the /d/, resulting in the strange form found in the transcript. Shuy's analysis includes other information, most importantly nonverbal information like Lorraine shaking his head repeatedly, which supports his auditory analysis. Lorraine was convicted and sentenced to death. As of December 2015, he remains on Ohio's death row.[12]

Other linguists have been involved in such cases, forensic phoneticians in particular. Peter French (1990) reports a case in the United Kingdom in which a doctor was being investigated for corruptly prescribing narcotics. A private investigator hired an actor to feign being an abuser of certain prescription drugs and to try to get the doctor to prescribe the same drug to him. The doctor refused, but did prescribe a tranquilizer that was less potent. The conversation between them was recorded and turned over to a television producer who used some of the recording in a program on the unethical medical practices of certain doctors. Along with the sound were subtitles to "clarify" what was being said. Among the things discussed was whether one could inject drugs originally made available in tablet form. The subtitle seen on television showed the doctor saying: "you can inject those things," which sounds like the doctor was cooperating in the actor's improper effort to feed his addiction.

The case was turned over to the body responsible for disciplining doctors in Britain. The solicitors representing the doctor retained Peter French, who listened to the remainder of the conversation between the doctor and the actor, and recorded his own lengthy interview with the doctor. French evaluated how the doctor – whose first language was Greek – pronounced both "can" and "can't" in different phonetic contexts. For one thing, French found that the final [t] in "can't" was almost always absent, so its absence in the questioned passage bore no relevance. In addition, both auditory and acoustic analysis[13] showed

12 See www.drc.ohio.gov/public/deathrow.htm.

13 Specifically, the first and second formants of the vowel differed systematically between known instances of "can" and known instances of "can't" in the doctor's speech (French 1990: 211).

that the doctor used slightly different vowels in these words, and that the vowel used in the questioned passage was the same one that the doctor used when he said "can't," and not the same one that the doctor used when he said "can." French concluded that the doctor really said "You can't inject those things, you know." Tom Roeper, a psycholinguist, reports (personal communication) having been involved in a case in which the dispute in a conspiracy case over whether the defendant's voice on a recording said, "Okay, let's kill him," or "Okay, let's kill it." If the former, the defendant conspired to commit a murder. If the latter, he ordered an end to whatever mischief had been contemplated.

It is not easy to hear the difference if the recording is not made under laboratory conditions. Solan recorded his own voice saying, "Okay, let's kill it." Using filters Dahmen created three versions: one with background noise; one with the reverberations that would come from having recorded the sentence in a small room; and the third a clean recording, having filtered out whatever ambient sounds were in Solan's original recording. We later played all three of them, in the order just described, to three different groups of people to whom we presented this work. The first was a group of law professors in New York; the second a group consisting of linguists, philosophers, and lawyers in California; the third a forensic linguistics class in Birmingham, England. There were about 80 people in all hearing the recordings. Every person who responded heard the first two recordings as "Okay, let's kill him," and were surprised to hear that the third recording – the clean one – actually was a recording of the same words as were in the first two recordings. No doubt one would be more likely to expect to hear "him" than "it" when one is waiting for something nefarious. But expectations of violence are not the same as evidence of violence, as our informal experiment illustrates.[14]

Finally, in a well-publicized case,[15] television personality Dr. Phil was sued for defamation. A private investigator had remarked in a surreptitiously recorded interview to an individual suspected of being responsible for the disappearance of a young woman in Aruba, "I'm sure she had sex with all of you." The television report on this interview reported as the answer, "She did. You'd be surprised how simple it was." In the unedited video, however, linguist Robert Leonard proposed that the suspect said, "No, she didn't."[16] Allegations were made that someone involved in the broadcast had doctored the recording before

[14] There are many other instances of linguists reporting informally of their participation in cases involving disputed transcripts. For example, forensic phonetician Sandra Disner reports (personal communication) consulting in a murder case in which the police transcript of a recorded phone call between the defendant and his wife read "Why, the body?" Disner's analysis revealed that the defendant had said, "Why, did that bother you?"

[15] See Jack Hitt, "Words on Trial: Can Linguists Solve Crimes that Stump the Police," *The New Yorker*, July 23, 2012, 24, 27.

[16] See, e.g. http://scrux.com/transcripts/drphilshow/comparison.htm.

airing it. The case, however, was later dismissed for legal reasons unrelated to the linguistic issue.

The Legal Response

The legal system has no satisfactory answer to the problem of how difficult it is to understand what is being said when the signal is degraded, there is noise, and the context is either limited or disputed (see Fishman 2006 for detailed discussion). Some courts hold that the recording is evidence and a transcript of the recording is not evidence – it is just there to aid jurors in figuring out what was actually said in the recording.[17] This makes little sense when there are passages in the recording that are difficult to understand. If the transcript is there only as an aid, and you need the aid because you cannot understand the recording, then, in effect, the transcript is the only evidence to which there is any reason to pay attention. Being told that you should use it but it is not "evidence" in that context is incoherent. Permitting the defense to submit a competing transcript of a recording that no one can understand, as some courts do, has a ring of fairness, but is very unlikely to lead to more accurate decision making.[18]

Other courts accept both the recording and the transcript as evidence, but regard the transcript as opinion evidence, which needs to be demonstrably reliable. When the transcript's contents are disputed, sometimes a court rejects both the recording and the transcripts as unreliable, but at other times the court permits the parties to call as witnesses the experts who produced the conflicting transcripts and allow them to duke it out. Here is how the court in a leading case[19] in which much of the dispute was over who was speaking at various points on the recording:

> We believe that the use of a transcript as a guide is analogous to the use of expert testimony as a device aiding a jury in understanding other types of real evidence. For example, an issue in a case may be whether John Doe's purported signature on a document is actually John Doe's signature. Two handwriting experts may disagree, and if they are asked to testify on each side of the dispute, their divergent testimony creates a jury issue.... Similarly, in the case under discussion, two "experts" [and their respective transcripts] were available to aid the jury in determining the real issue presented, the content and meaning of the tape recordings.
>
> It is therefore incorrect to think of the transcripts as simply an "aid" – as better lighting fixtures in the courtroom would be an "aid" to the jury's vision of witnesses – and not as evidence of any kind. They are evidence and, like other evidence, may be admitted for a

[17] See United States v. Thomas, 553 Fed. Appx. 941 (11th Cir. 2014); United States v. Stone, 960 F.2d 426 (5th Cir. 1992).

[18] See, e.g., United States v. Bell, 651 F.2d 1255 (8th Cir. 1981).

[19] United States v. Onori, 535 F.2d 938 (5th Cir. 1976).

limited purpose only. That purpose here, as the court outlined in its special instruction, was primarily to establish the identity of the speakers at any particular time.[20]

The court went on to consider alternative, acceptable procedures when there is disagreement about what is said on a recording, including the production of a single transcript that contains both versions of the disputed language but is otherwise agreed to by the parties, providing the jury with two separate transcripts and having them listen to the recording twice – once with one transcript as an "aid" and once with the other transcript as an "aid." Rejected was the practice of allowing the judge to resolve the dispute beforehand by accepting one side's version or the other, although when the objections to a transcript are without basis, this certainly is what must happen in any event.

Other courts permit the judge to make such judgments, but only if one of the parties had raised the disagreement. Thus, it was error for a trial judge, listening closely and repeatedly to a recording, to make one thousand changes, 10 per cent of which were substantive, and one of which added the defendant's words, "I think I'm in trouble," even though the government's original transcript had that portion of the recording characterized as inaudible.[21] Still others permit the parties to submit competing transcripts, both of which are considered evidence, and to ask the jury to decide which, if either, is more faithful to the recording, which remains the primary evidence of what was said.[22]

Making accurate transcription more difficult is the fact that we are much better at understanding the words spoken by familiar voices than we are at understanding the words spoken by unfamiliar voices (Nygaard and Pisoni 1998). Virtually all transcriptions used in legal settings are of voices unfamiliar to the transcriber. This leaves transcription open to a very serious problem, which courts sometimes recognize: "priming effects" in producing them. One who listens to a recording is far more likely to hear words if they are primed to hear them by virtue of their appearing in a transcript. Courts that permit competing transcripts to be presented while jurors listen to the recording twice – once with each transcript – appear to recognize this problem, although it is not at all clear to us that they have solved it by employing such an untested procedure.

An interesting case in which the problem was recognized directly occurred in New Zealand.[23] Young David Bain had returned home one day in 1994 from delivering newspapers to find that his entire family had been killed. He was convicted of the murders and sentenced to prison. In 2007, after much publicity,

20 *Id.* at 947.

21 United States v. Adams, 722 F. 3d 788, 825 (6th Cir. 2013). *See also*, United States v. Stone, 2012 U.S. Dist. LEXIS 12272 (E.D. Mich. 2012) (admitting disputed government transcript based on the court's judgment of its accuracy, and not permitting the parties to submit two competing transcripts).

22 United States v. Chaney, 299 Fed. Appx. 447 (5th Cir. 2008).

23 Bain v. The Queen, [2009] NZSC 16.

his conviction was reversed because certain important evidence had not been given to the jury, and a new trial ordered.

When Bain had returned home to find the carnage, he had called the emergency number (the equivalent of U.S. 911). Some of that recording was inaudible. The ambulance officer receiving the call did not hear Bain say anything incriminating, but a police officer who prepared a transcript for use in the retrial, distinctly heard him say, "I shot the prick." A legal battle ensued over the admissibility of the recording and the use of the transcript. In that context, a group of forensic phoneticians,[24] some hired for each side, agreed that the part of the recording that might have contained the relevant language was not audible enough to justify its use at trial. In particular, the experts opined that it was not possible to determine whether the part of the recording at issue consisted only of out-of-breath non-speech sounds, or language. The expert analysis was used in an appeal to the Supreme Court of New Zealand on the question of the recording and transcript. In 2009, that court disallowed the recording based on the opinions of the phoneticians. Bain was acquitted in the second trial and freed.

Using the actual recording from the Bain case, Helen Fraser, Bruce Stevenson, and Tony Marks (2011) set out to investigate experimentally the effects of priming. They played the recording to 190 participants. After hearing it initially, half were given a transcript saying "I shot the prick," while the other half received a transcript saying "he shot them all," referring to the defendant's father. The result, not surprisingly, is that virtually no one heard the incriminating statement without being primed, and, once primed, a majority of those who did hear it thought that the caller should be convicted of the crime. Not so for those who heard the exculpatory statement. Subsequent studies by Fraser and Stevenson (2014), again using a recording taken from an actual murder case, showed that once participants are aware of the reason for the recording and the police transcript in the first place it becomes more difficult to dislodge the priming effect of a police transcript by presenting an alternative one, even with the alternative transcript is, in fact, more accurate.

Of course, technology that filters and enhances speech in order to make it intelligible might reduce the number of cases in which legitimate disputes arise. Our own filtering of speech described earlier in this article is but one demonstration. Nonetheless, technology is not the answer to everything. Courts attempt to require procedures to minimize the effect of our not being able to discern speech sounds accurately when a poor signal or ambient noise compromise the interfaces that allow us in ordinary speech to perceive a continuing flow of sound into words and phrases to which we assign meaning. There is absolutely no reason to believe that jurors are able to come up with the right interpretation

24 They were Peter French, Paul Foulkes, Philip Harrison, and Bronwen Innes.

of recordings when presented with competing transcripts. At the same time, there is no reason to believe that a judge can do it any better in a proceeding in advance of the trial to determine what should subsequently be presented to the jury.

In short, our linguistic competence does not live up to the task of understanding the spoken word under the compromised conditions described here. Making matters worse, if people with no prior expectations are subject to the priming effects of transcription in how they understand recorded speech, then those who transcribe the recordings are all the more likely to succumb to prior expectations, especially if they are employed by one side or the other in a legal case, most typically by the police. The propensity of people to construe information consistent with what they are already committed to believing is called "the confirmation bias" (see Nickerson 1998), and is recognized as a general problem in the forensic sciences (see, e.g. Ellsworth 2012; Kassin, Dror and Kukucka 2013).

Fraser (2014) cites a long history of psycholinguistic research demonstrating that when primed, people understand degraded speech signals consistent with their expectations. For example, Bruce (1958) presented experimental subjects with five sentences, recorded over white noise that made them hard to understand. Prior to hearing a sentence, the participant was primed with a word that was either appropriate or inappropriate for the content of the sentence. For example, one of the experimental sentences was, "I tell you that our team will win the cup next year." When primed with Sport, many people understood it. When primed with Food, however, one subject heard "I tell you that our tea will be something to do with beer." Police transcribers are no less human, and thus no less subject to the confirmation bias than were Bruce's subjects. Fraser recommends that independent laboratories be engaged to prepare transcripts, especially when the parties disagree about what was said.

It is not our position that all cases involving recordings or transcriptions of recordings are resolved unfairly in favor of the police. In many cases the recordings are clear and there is no serious dispute about what was said, whichever side it benefits. However, when there is disagreement, the combination of transcripts being produced by law enforcement agents with a prior commitment to what was said, and a judicial system reluctant to reject evidence that seems probative even when it is very difficult to decipher, creates an advantage for the state and against the accused in many such cases.

Remembering What Was Said

Thus far we have focused on recorded speech. Not all legally relevant speech is recorded, however. Some contracts are verbal, some false statements are verbal, some threats are verbal, statements made in the course of making a deal are spoken, and so on. When it is very important to recover the exact words that were spoken, the legal system is often unable to act, creating a safe harbor for illegal activity, or acts when the evidence is weak (as when it permits jailhouse snitches to testify about the gist of another inmate's admission of guilt), or simply gets it wrong, creating a baseline of injustice. This happens because we are not very good at remembering the exact words we hear.

We noted at the beginning of this chapter that a burden is placed on rule of law values by the way our language faculty interfaces with other cognitive systems, and by how the subsystems of our language faculty interface with each other. The classic example, which Chomsky (1965) used in his early writings to illustrate the difference between competence and performance, is memory. The computational aspects of our linguistic competence can generate infinitely long sentences. ("The man who comes from Brazil but who has lived in the part of Uruguay that the Europeans who tried to settle the part of the mountains that the native population thought were easier to climb in winters that were not as cold as the winters that the northern Europeans believed were more severe than the North Americans would have thought slept.") One comma followed by "and" can start the whole business over, as can recursively inserting more subordinate clauses, relative clauses, and the like.

Memory for verbatim speech typically is just a few seconds (Baddeley 2007; Baddeley, Gathercole and Papagno 1998). After that, we process the speech and remember all or some of its gist. This frees working memory sufficient to continue language processing and to engage in other tasks. From a legal perspective, though, it makes things very difficult when it is important to know exactly what was said. For example, when it comes to such crimes as perjury or the crime of making false statements to a government official, the language that is the subject of the prosecution matters. Of course, we do not remember verbatim what we have read either (test yourself on the first sentence of this paragraph), but you can always go back and reread it – you cannot go back and rehear unrecorded speech.

Consider the following: A law makes it a crime when a person " in any matter within the jurisdiction of the executive, legislative, or judicial branch of the Government of the United States . . . falsifies, conceals, or covers up by any trick, scheme, or device a material fact."[25] People have many interactions with the government in which the communications are verbal, and in which no effort is made to transcribe the interaction. Yet cases in which the false statement was a verbal one are unusual. In one, decided in 1959,[26] a contractor had been negotiating with the government over certain changes that required the government's approval in connection with a construction project. Part of the proof

[25] 18 U.S.C. § 1001(a)(1). See Solan (1993) for additional discussion.
[26] United States v. Coastal Contracting and Engineering Co., Inc., 174 F. Supp. 474 (D. Md. 1959).

of the changes for which the contractor sought additional compensation was a letter that the contractor knew to contain false information. The contractor used that letter during the negotiations and was charged with making false statements to the government not only with respect to the letter, but also with respect to what the contractor said during the meeting when the letter was presented to the government, which, in essence, repeated the false information contained in the letter itself.

In another case, a patient verbally misstated her home address to her doctor in order to get a prescription for a narcotic.[27] And in *Poindexter v. United States*,[28] a case involving members of the Reagan administration lying to Congress about the Iran-Contra scandal, the court rejected claims that unsworn, untranscribed speech was outside the scope of the statute, although it conceded that "[t]he absence of such formal trappings is relevant, of course, to the difficulty of proving beyond a reasonable doubt exactly what the defendant said and whether he intended to deceive his audience as to a material question of fact."

There is no real controversy about this broad characterization of the law. Yet there are few prosecutions for untranscribed verbal false statements. It would be surprising if people have not lied to the U.S. government in their speech over the past fifty years. The better explanation is that our inability to recall exactly what was said creates a safe harbor for liars. This safe harbor is the result of memory limitations causing us to abandon recollection of the stream of speech as we process the words into their syntactic and semantic roles. Without knowing exactly what was said, it is difficult for the government to prove that a lie was told. Even when the government official remembers what was said, there is the distinct possibility that a dispute will arise about the words in question. But it rarely gets that far, because it is so difficult to construct an accusation that is specific enough to put people on adequate notice.

Of course, "rarely" does not mean "never." In 2015, an employee of the U.S. government was indicted in Florida for making a false statement to a government official when she denied having placed a printed copy of the Confederate battle flag on the desk of an African American co-worker.[29] Apparently the statements were sufficiently short and clear for the government to be able to bring a case against her.

The fact that we cannot remember exact words sometimes operates in cases where the police have reported that they have quoted a confession verbatim. In some such cases, linguists have been able to demonstrate that the police have lied, using the phonological loop as a defense weapon. Malcolm Coulthard,

[27] Walker v. United States, 192 F.2d 47 (10th Cir. 1951).

[28] 951 F.2d 369, 388 (D.C. Cir. 1991).

[29] See Indictment in United States v. Susan R. Thompson, available at www.justice.gov/usao-mdfl/file/786516/download.

the British forensic linguist, writes (Coulthard 2002) of a case in which a man was convicted of murder. Part of the evidence was the transcript of an interview in which he confessed to the police having stolen some tires after having lied about his whereabouts that night. The transcript, it turns out, was the police's re-creation of what was said, expanding on notes taken during the conversation. Coulthard found that almost none of the dialogue in the transcript used at the trial was even taken verbatim from the police notes. The fact that people – including members of the police force – could not possibly remember exactly what was said demonstrated that the police fabricated the incriminating dialogue.

In another case that Coulthard (2002) reports, the police claimed that a defendant in a criminal case used precisely the same language – more or less word for word – in a signed confession as he had used in an interview with the police. The defendant claimed on appeal that the transcript of the interview had been fabricated by the police, who then copied it into a confession and browbeat him into signing it. No one is that consistent in the language they use, in part because no one can remember what they actually said earlier. Coulthard's intervention in the appeal was successful.

For the most part, though, police officers testify to the substance of what a witness, suspect, or defendant allegedly said, and the gist that they report is considered adequate to meet evidentiary standards. More troubling, jailhouse snitches do the same, with no real ability to cross-examine on what was said because the witness does not claim to remember precisely what was said (Trott 1996). Again, this is a nod to the need to balance our cognitive limitations against the goal of legal outcomes based on the truth of what actually happened. No doubt, though, it comes at a price.

Knowing Who Said What

A great deal has been written about people's ability to identify the voices of the people they hear. Much of it concerns very interesting debates about how experts, especially forensic phoneticians, should address the task of identifying a questioned voice, or at least reducing the range of plausible identifications (see, e.g. Hollien 2002; Rose 2002; Jessen 2008; Morrison 2009; Foulkes and French 2012). The past two decades have seen considerable progress in this regard, both in terms of developing methodology that takes advantage of new technology, and in terms of the inferential process deemed appropriate to draw conclusions.

The basic issue, though, is the one we address here: If people remembered the voices they heard and if they had the perceptual and analytical skills to identify just whose voice they heard earlier, the legal system would not need forensic phoneticians to serve as experts. We will here make two brief points.

First, we all know that some voices sound alike, others sound very different from one another. If we know what it is that makes each voice sound as it does, like the size and shape of the vocal tract or the length of the vocal folds that influence the pitch of a voice and/or the voice quality (e.g. breathiness or nasality; Jessen 2008: 687, 689), we can come to grips with what kinds of similarities and differences among people lead to mistakes in identifying people from the way they speak.

Second, researchers have now learned the circumstances in which an individual is more likely to find it easy to recognize the voice of another. Of course, people have different levels of skill at this task, as we all know either from our own embarrassing mistakes or from those of others. Recall that in the case of remembering verbatim speech, the problem arises when what is in our working memory must make its way into long-term memory. As that happens, we remember the gist of what we heard, but not the exact words. In the case of voices, the issue is a bit different. The problems are having enough exposure to the voices for them both to be remembered at all and to be accessible.

Among the leading researchers in this area is Canadian psychologist Daniel Yarmey (see Yarmey 2012). Solan and Tiersma (2005) also summarize some of the major research. Not surprisingly, we are better at identifying familiar voices than unfamiliar voices. What makes a voice familiar? The number of exposures, the timing between exposures, the time since the most recent exposure, and how unusual the voice is, are all factors. Stressful situations make identification worse, contrary to the intuitions of many that "I'd recognize that voice anywhere." People are better at recognizing the voices of people in their own ethnic group, just as they are better at identifying the faces of people in their own ethnic group. And people are fairly good at identifying whether someone has a foreign accent, and if so, what that accent is, if it is an accent with which the hearer is familiar.

We merely touch on the research in this area. Our point is a limited one: Just as people cannot remember what was said, they often cannot tell who said it. Thus, the spoken word produces yet another form of legal indeterminacy. This fact, recognized by the law, has motivated advances in forensic phonetics, both with respect to the expert identification of recorded speech, and with respect to the credibility of witnesses who claim to be able to identify a voice under circumstances in which that task would be especially difficult.

Conclusion

Whatever problems in legal interpretation exist must have something to do with our inability to succeed completely in governing ourselves under a rule of law driven so heavily by language. We have attempted here to identify issues concerning our perception and misperception of speech that plague the legal system. Obviously, this chapter is not intended to be a complete account. Rather, it summarizes our perspective and illustrates it generally with respect to some phenomena, in much more detail with respect to others.

The chapter intentionally includes more detail about the workings of our language systems and their interaction with one another than one would typically find in an article addressing problems within the legal system. Part of our goal has been to explore just what it is about these aspects of human cognition that creates gaps in understanding that actors within the system can exploit to their advantage. Many of the examples discussed earlier illustrate prosecutions based on evidence that is unclear at best, whether transcripts of recordings or the testimony of reported speech that cannot be remembered verbatim. Yet we have also seen instances in which people who wish to engage in bad conduct know enough to avoid putting things in writing so that there is no strong evidence of what they actually said. We hope our contribution lies in explaining when and why these things happen.

REFERENCES

Ainsworth, J. E. (1993). In a Different Register: The Pragmatics of Powerlessness in Police Interrogation. *Yale Law Journal* 103: 259–322.

Baddeley, A. (2007). *Working Memory, Thought, and Action*. Oxford: Oxford University Press.

Baddeley, A., Gathercole, S. and Papagno, C. (1998). The Phonological Loop as a Language Learning Device, *Psychological Review* 105: 158–173.

Bond, Z. S. (1999). *Slips of the Ear: Errors in the Perception of Casual Conversation*. San Diego: Academic Press.

Brown, A. (2014). *Pronunciation and Phonetics. A Practical Guide for English Language Teachers*. New York and Oxon: Routledge.

Bruce, D. J. (1958). The Effect of Listeners' Anticipations on the Intelligibility of Heard Speech. *Language and Speech* 1: 79–97.

Chomsky, N. (1965). *Aspects of the Theory of Syntax*. Cambridge, MA: MIT Press.

Conley, J. M. and O'Barr, W. M. (2005). *Just Words: Law, Language, and Power* (2nd ed.). Chicago: University of Chicago Press.

Coulthard, M. (2002). Whose Voice Is It? Invented and Concealed Dialogue in Written Records of Verbal Evidence Produced by the Police. In J. Cotterill (ed.) *Language in the Legal Process*. New York: Palgrave Macmillan, 19–34.

Ellsworth, P. C. (2012). Legal Reasoning and Scientific Reasoning. *Alabama Law Review* 63: 895–918.

Fishman, C. S. (2006). Recordings, Transcripts, and Translations as Evidence, *Washington Law Review* 81: 523–773.

Foulkes, P. and French, P. (2012). Forensic Speaker Comparison: A Linguistic-Acoustic Perspective. In P. M. Tiersma and L. M. Solan (eds.) *The Oxford Handbook of Language and Law*. Oxford: Oxford University Press, 557–572.

Fraser, H. (2003). Issues in Transcription: Factors Affecting the Reliability of Transcripts as Evidence in Legal Cases. *Forensic Linguistics* 10: 203–226.

Fraser, H. (2014). Transcription of Indistinct Forensic Recordings: Problems and Solutions from the Perspective of Phonetic Science. *Language and Law/Linguagem e Direito* 1(2): 5–21.

Fraser, H. and Stevenson, B. (2014). The Power and Persistence of Contextual Priming: More Risks in Using Police Transcripts to Aid Jurors' Perception of Poor Quality Covert Recordings. *International Journal of Evidence & Proof* 18: 205–229.

Fraser, H., Stevenson, B. and Marks, T. (2011). Interpretation of a Crisis Call: Persistence of a Primed Perception of a Disputed Utterance. *International Journal of Speech, Language and the Law* 18: 261–292.

French, P. (1990). Analytic Procedures for the Determination of Disputed Utterances. In H. Kniffka (ed.) *Texte zu Theorie und Praxis forensischer Linguistik*. Tübingen: Max Niemeyer Verlag, 201–213.

Guillemin, B. J. and Watson, C. (2008). Impact of the GSM mobile phone net-work on the speech signal. *International Journal of Speech, Language and the Law* 15: 193–218.

Harrison, P. (2001). GSM interference cancellation for forensic audio: a report on work in progress. *Forensic Linguistics* 8: 9–23.

Hollien, H. (2002). *Forensic Voice Identification*. London: Academic Press.

Jackendoff, R. (2002). *Foundations of Language*. Oxford: Oxford University Press.

Jessen, M. (2008). Forensic Phonetics. *Language and Linguistics Compass* 2: 671–711.

Kassin, S. M., Dror, I. E. and Kukucka, J. (2013). The Forensic Confirmation Bias: Problems, Perspectives, and Proposed Solutions. *Journal of Applied Research in Memory and Cognition* 2: 42–52.

Katzmann, R. A. (2014). *Judging Statutes*. Oxford: Oxford University Press.

Lawrence, S., Nolan, F. and McDougall, K. (2008). Acoustic and perceptual effects of telephone transmission on vowel quality. *International Journal of Speech, Language and the Law* 15: 161–192.

Meyer, A. S. (1992). Investigation of Phonological Encoding through Speech Error Analyses: Achievements, Limitations, and Alternatives. *Cognition* 42: 182–211.

Miller, G. A. (1996). Contextuality. In J. Oakhill and A. Garnham (eds.) *Mental Models in Cognitive Science: Essays in Honour of Phil Johnson-Laird*. East Sussex, England: Psychology Press, 1–18.

Morrison, G. S. (2009). Forensic Voice Comparison and the Paradigm Shift, *Science & Justice* 49: 298–308.

Nadler, J. and Trout, J. D. (2012). The Language of Consent in Police Encounters. In P. M. Tiersma and L. M. Solan (eds.) *The Oxford Handbook of Language and Law*. Oxford: Oxford University Press, 326–339.

Nickerson, R. S. (1998). Confirmation Bias: A Ubiquitous Phenomenon in Many Guises. *Review of General Psychology* 22: 175–220.

Nygaard, L. C. and Pisoni, D. B. (1998). Talker-Specific Learning in Speech Perception. *Perception and Psychophysics* 60: 355–376.

O'Grady, G. (2013). *Key Concepts in Phonetics and Phonology*. New York: Palgrave Macmillan.

Rose, P. (2002). *Forensic Speaker Identification*. London: Taylor & Francis.

Scalia, A. and Garner, B. A. (2012). *Reading Law: The Interpretation of Legal Texts*. St. Paul, MN: Thomson/West.

Shuy, R. W. (1993). *Language Crimes: The Use and Abuse of Language Evidence in the Courtroom*. Cambridge, MA: Blackwell.
Shuy, R. W. (2014). *The Language of Murder Cases: Intentionality, Predisposition, and Voluntariness*. Oxford: Oxford University Press.
Solan, L. (1993). *The Language of Judges*. Chicago: University of Chicago Press.
Solan, L. M. and Tiersma, P. M. (2005). *Speaking of Crime: The Language of Criminal Justice*. Chicago: University of Chicago Press.
Tang, K. and Nevins, A. (2014). Measuring Segmental and Lexical Trends in a Corpus of Naturalistic Speech. In H.-L. Huang, E. Poole and A. Rysling (eds.) Proceedings of the 43rd Meeting of the North East Linguistic Society Vol. 2. GLSA (Graduate Linguistics Student Association), 153–166.
Tiersma, P. (1999). *Legal Language*. Chicago: University of Chicago Press.
Tiersma, P. M. (2010). *Parchment, Paper, Pixels: Law and the Technologies of Communication*. Chicago: University of Chicago Press.
Trott, S. S. (1996). Words of Warning for Prosecutors Using Criminals as Witnesses. *Hastings Law Journal* 47: 1381–1432.
Yarmey, A. D. (2012). Factors Affecting Lay Persons' Identification of Speakers. In P. M. Tiersma and L. M. Solan (eds.) *The Oxford Handbook of Language and Law*. Oxford: Oxford University Press, 547–567.

Afterword

13 The Said of the Unsaid

Peter Goodrich

EDITORS' NOTE TO CHAPTER 13

In the mid-1980s, Peter Goodrich published two highly influential books which presented a major challenge not only to established ways of thinking about language within law but also to the then emergent, descriptive emphasis of studies of legal language derived from linguistics. *Reading the Law* (1986) traced the operation of language, especially writing, through the history of civil law and common law, showing how far legal authority remains caught up in the complexity of rhetorical and hermeneutic thought. *Legal Discourse* (1987) extended such analysis in the direction of critical theories which had been influenced by linguistic models but not subservient to them, paving the way for a great deal of work in the critical legal studies movement. Goodrich's more recent work has continued to focus on symbolic legal representation, highlighting the role played by visual imagery (including architecture, costume, statuary and emblems) in how law achieves its authority and social legitimacy. In this final chapter, Goodrich applies his critical engagement with the languages of law over three decades to the 'unspoken words' trope employed in conceptualization of this book.

Goodrich dissects the intricate relation at various levels between the said and the unsaid, and, instead of seeing the two as a dichotomy, addresses their ontological dependency. The unsaid, he argues, can only be accessed through what is said, but the said can only be understood in context of what remains unsaid. To illustrate the point he is making, Goodrich chooses an example from legal adjudication. The U.S. case *Sandifer v. U.S. Steel Corp.* hinges on the undefined meaning of *work*. Judge Posner, Goodrich explains, sought to fill an acknowledged gap in textual meaning with an image in preference to words. Paradoxically, of course, the image he used to reference reality was itself inevitably not reality but a simulation. So although something unsaid can be made visible, what is seen and said continues to disguise a great deal that remains unseen and unsaid. The meaning and significance of the image may be presented as if it is self-evident, but out-of-context use of the image exposes it to interpretation. Viewed in this light, so Goodrich persuades us using another visual figure, judicial authority may be understood as power to foreground one perspective over another, and so, switching back from visual to verbal communication, through selection and articulation to render an argument either said or unsaid.

REFERENCES

Goodrich, P. (1986). *Reading the Law: A Critical Introduction to Legal Method and Techniques*. Oxford: Blackwell.

Goodrich, P. (1987). *Legal Discourse: Studies in Linguistics, Rhetoric and Legal Analysis*. London: Macmillan.

The Said of the Unsaid

The context is one of stupefaction. The scene takes place in the office of an academic at the University of California at Irvine. It is April 1989, and Jacques Derrida is being interviewed by Michael Sprinker on the topic of the politics of friendship. He, which is to say JD, is retracing his intellectual biography, the troubled trajectory from Algeria to Paris and specifically to that prestigious oxymoron, the Ecole Normale Supérieure (ENS). Moving to the topic of his induction into the French philosophical institution, his relation to Louis Althusser, and to his entourage of acolytes, neophytes and disciples, Derrida embarks upon a description of undecipherable encryptions and paralyzing silences: "Everything took place underground, in the said of the unsaid . . . [in] an intellectual . . . milieu in which the practice of avoidance is stupefying" (Derrida 2002: 158).

The vehemence of the attribution of stupefaction, together with the repeated references to a correlative avoidance, suggest that reconstruction of this particular plurality of the said of the unsaid best begin by addressing the source of the illocutionary force of this nomination. To 'stupefy' is at root to strike, to stun and so to confound, dumbfound and render stupid. It invokes, as Sutherland notes in his bravura digressions on the topic, the process of formation of a pageant of idiots, a chorus of dullards who in this context remain bound to philosophical formalism, to hermetically sealed structures, to the stultifying artifice of unquestioned argot and anserine belonging (Sutherland 2011: 5–6).[1] The stupefied, these 'heroes of their own thought', the *idiotae*, returning here to the level of etymology, reference the uneducated, unlearned and fickle. In the instant context, however, and more candidly, it is philosophers – foolosophers – who wear the face of the untutored, and whose "little shrunken brains", clinging to "modern scientific drivel", desperately avoid any desire, all doubt, any questioning that might humanize them (Lacan 1993: 199).

[1] Longer divagations on the topic, addressed as foolosophy, can be found in van Boxsel (2003).

There are two aspects to stupefying, one active, another passive. First, there is the question of force. The milieu was that of scientific Marxism, a discourse that "seemed to me to give way to a theoreticism or a newfangled scientifism" that ought to have been challenged but whose collective and institutional force left Derrida "paralyzed, silent before something that resembled a sort of theoreticism, a hypostasis of Theory with a capital 'T'" (Derrida 2002: 152).[2] After this, unable to give voice to the paralysis, he admits to finding himself "walled in by a sort of tormented silence . . . coupled with 'an *intellectual*, if not personal, *terrorism*'" (Derrida 2002: 152). There is already a hint of stupefaction in the designation of an impersonal terrorism that forces our author to avoid any sign of questions that might appear "suspicious, backward, idealistic, even reactionary" (Derrida 2002: 153). The result, a lingering aftermath of this intimidation and isolation, was a mode of writing that "was rendered complicated in the extreme, that is, to the point of making them unreadable for those at whom they were directed" (Derrida 2002: 153).

Terror, even and especially intellectual terror and its accompanying institutional intimidation, the intimations of anathematization, stupefy, stun and silence. They undo the subject and render the persona passive. The followers, those that insist upon belonging and who maintain the demarcations, patrol the boundaries, are active only in the passivity of their discipleship, in their choral status and servitude. Derrida, at the furthest extreme of such fellowship, in his uneasy silence, is something of a last instance of fellow-traveling. His passivity may be involuntary, a case of the extreme that proves the rule, but it is still the case that he had to act in part stupefied, silent, enclosed so as to belong, and even years later, reliving the scene of stupefaction, there is a certain caution, a resistance to the candor that will, in Sutherland's depiction, "nominate identities . . . consciously and emphatically" rather than in the more usual mode of "the unconscious or surreptitious" (Sutherland 2011: 3–4). Be that as it may, the second stage of the process is one of a certain inertia that I will designate, in his honor, as traumatic repetition in the rhetorical mode of proleptic prolixity. Inertia is a mode of post-ignition, of rolling on in the wake of an event – a push, a stun, a terror – while remaining within the limits and confines of the timidity that intimidation engendered. Thus the meandering course of a style, the prolixity of diction, the hesitations and deflections that anticipate and defend against reproof and exclusion. It is the latter threat, the specter of denunciation, of exposure and expulsion, that keeps the undertow of the unsaid, precisely so as to remain amongst the said, so as to belong and to institute, even

[2] For another description of the same period and institution, see Lecourt (2001: 11), who remarks on Althusser's lapses into melancholy and long periods of silence that anticipated his later plunge into the night of lethal madness but comments, "my friends and I discerned in it the stamp of genius".

if what is instituted is in effect nothing, an ever present not yet, a thought to come.

The second stage, the degree Nero of stupefaction, and even now I speak from experience, lies precisely in avoidance, in the reigning in of thought so as to guarantee and preserve membership of the *in terrorem* group, the site of institutional reproduction where the said is promulgated – and remains to be promulgated – while the unsaid subsists in its silence, in the nowhere of theory. As the unsaid is by definition as yet unspoken, it has to be tracked through the symptoms exhibited by the said. Here then the confrontation is with a said that says both too much, its prolixity, and too little, its prolepsis. Just as terror abrogates will, the said of the unsaid evacuates the material and the lived, in favor of the apparent safety of formalism and the comfort of abstraction. Theoretical discourse becomes the choral and liturgical rite of the institution, or in this case that part of the academy that constitutes the fashionable in philosophy. Derrida is again close to the mark in depicting a group overtrained in the treatment of problems from an algebraic standpoint, playing abstract philosophical games of decipherment and operating "according to a diplomacy (war by other means)... of avoidance: silence, one doesn't cite or name, everyone distinguishes himself and everything forms a sort of archipelago of discourse without earthly communication, without visible passageway. No one was translated. From time to time, there were, from afar, signals in the night" (Derrida 2002: 158–59).

Waving over the parapet, ships passing in the night, moments of distant interpellation, are all metaphors for the dynamics and politics of friendship, which is of course the context of the particular discussion. *Amicitia* is in its institutional context a Christian concept, a matter of belonging to the brotherhood, of being in the group and so party to the encrypted algebra, the enigmatic or at least undisclosed libidinal economy that drives and inhabits the chimerical archipelago, or what is in effect a conceptual cloud membership. What is important to reproduction of these offices and this habitus of theory is a dual transit of separation and identification. The latter are effectuated through keywords, coded signs, the invention of an esoteric vocabulary and the choral relay of membership criteria and stated positions. Whereas each group in the hierarchy of theory may have its own devices and other heraldic insignia, its own abstract islands, the logic of the group, its banding and bonding *amicitia*, operates according to a well-established pattern of Christian economy, of *philia* and kinship, that precisely defines the shared sense of the unsaid as a facet of all doctrine and discipleship.

The example of Derrida's terror is a paradoxical one. While writing on the politics – the old word – friendship, on 'the immense rumor', on how the brothers malign and curse, he eschews any actual or nominate critique, let alone denunciation.[3] His essays on friends and on the concept of *amicitia* are somewhat spiritual and his 'all out friendship' is reserved for the work of mourning and encomiums of the dead friend.[4] The recognition of the intimidation that he had experienced and the exclusion that he had felt occur while he is interviewed some seven thousand miles away from Paris, in the new world, west of everything. Even there, he expresses ambivalence. He had "very good personal relations" with his theoretical intimidators, even if they never had any philosophical exchanges, even though they forced him into silence, paralysis and isolation. Their non-conversation was 'friendly', and of Althusser he says "we lived in the same 'house', where we were colleagues for twenty years and his students and friends were often, in another context, mine" (Derrida 2002: 152, 158). When the interview really starts to analyze and nominate friends, it is already three-quarters over, and the roll call is in relation to a friendship to come, analyzed through and by way of reference to the prolix prolepsis of the dead, to Aristotle, Montaigne, Kant, Nietzsche, Schmitt, as also Hegel, Marx, Lenin, Blanchot and Heidegger. Here we encounter the said of the 'unsaid to come', the future of democratic expression, the not yet of amity, of politics and law.

It is of course to the said of the unsaid of law that I will direct my attention. But all in good time. The paradox that I wish to stay with is that in recuperating and exposing the intimidation that he experienced, in recounting the stupefying practices at ENS, in revealing a glimpse of the pain and fear that he lived through and which scarred his practices, Derrida nonetheless also repeats the avoidance. The archipelago of the past grouping is left rapidly for the analysis of the specter of a future amicable democracy to come. There is a palpable ambivalence toward these former non-friendly friends, toward this past and prior, institutionally nascent self. Yet the precedent lives on, and the unsaid remains unsaid except insofar as we now know, because of the interview, that the contours of non-saying have been rendered somewhat more precise. The discussion in effect embodies the said of the unsaid while leaving the stupefying practice of avoidance relatively unanalyzed in the past, and I will hazard that it is pretty much unwitting in the present of Derrida's practice, in the displacement of amicable politics into the future, and in the innominate character of its present representation. There is a seeming necessity to the unsaid, an inescapable quality of escape, which Sutherland also and eloquently

[3] Derrida (1997) at 305: "Despite the appearances that this book has multiplied, nothing in it says anything *against* the brother or against fraternity".

[4] Derrida (2001) at 214–15; and equally in Derrida (1997) at 302, "it is *thanks* to death that friendship can be declared".

observes in another context, but which here gains expression in the statement that

> political action is not empirical but constantly strategic. For me, the rule of this strategy would be this 'democracy to come'. But this rule is not that of calculating or calculable knowledge through and through. In this respect, it is not altogether a rule like other rules. Rather it is a law without rule, without obligation – in the sense of obligation to be, obligation to be present. (Derrida 2002: 181)[5]

It can be argued that there is an itinerancy, a non-being, a nowhere to theory, but I suspect that the implicit reference is rather to the incalculability of justice, to invention of decision as the infraction of the rule. The unsaid in this dimension harbors innumerable phantoms, and in its dullard sense, as the untutored, unlearned and dumbfounded daze of the stupefied, it is the unthought of law, the avoidance of materiality, the evacuation of presence, the denial of obligation that lurks spectrally in the shadows of what is not said. Here, in legal discourse, the said of the unsaid echoes both in the choral groupings of the critics, the academic schools in their insecure, follower status, as also in mirror form in the masking of the unthought and unsaid of judgment. It is the latter, the unsaid of judgment, the indetermination of determination that here requires our countertransference. As the celebrated Stanley Fish puts it, judges just judge, that is what they do, it is their group and their game and it is not helped by trying to dissect, but rather that particular unsaid should be appreciated, its aesthetic enjoyed.[6] I beg to differ. I always have. The unheard, the unspoken, the silenced deserve more because the said of the unsaid needs its proper excoriation. That is both an epistemic and an ontological desideratum, without which drive scholarship would be prolixity, bereft of prolepsis and without politics in the very sense that Fish paradoxically desires.

The question is one of access. The definition of the said of the unsaid, or in Fish's terms, of what need not and should not be said, is that of foreclosure. Unable to give voice, precluded from the space of law, from the locus of invention, the intimidated, the silenced is unavailable, and the unsaid remains unsaid. Where Fish offers applause, however, Derrida offers a symptomology, a series of incidental and anecdotal instances, though nothing as direct as nominations or accusations. It is here that the analysis of the figures of diction, the images in thought, can provide a mode of entrance to and exposure of what is not said. The thread that binds together the references to the unsaid at the level of saying, which is that of the symptom, is a certain inarticulacy: the unsaid vanishes

[5] For Sutherland's powerful critique of Derrida's reading of Marx, see Sutherland (2011) at 9–18.

[6] A view most famously put in Fish (1987) arguing at length that theory has no use. My own earlier animadversions on the candid nihilism of Fish's position can be found in Goodrich (2013) chapter 5 (Of Law and Forgetting).

behind emotive references, it evaporates into images. There are walls, enclosures, terror and intimidation, vanishing points formulated algebraically and portentous silences. These are things that cannot or will not be said because of the extremity of emotion and indeed abrogation of emotion that they threaten. The unsaid, the foreclosed thus has a precarious ontological status, a half-life in the said of the unsaid which has an imaginal status. In classical terminology it is the existential *quaestio vexata* of alterity and identity, of ego and alter ego, self and belonging, the vanishing point of the subject being the imaginal scope and presence of the normative in symbolic form. The passage toward the foundation of the social must at a certain point escape reason and encounter the imaginal, the imagistic support that founds the social in its monumental institutional presence and visibility.[7]

The unsaid is a negative formulation of the imaginal, a defensive deflection of the images that invent and inform the normative and juridical representation of the social in its specular foundations. It is the figural that represents the institution, the image that symbolizes and portrays the political, the mode of the many, and the real fiction of the social. Legendre formulates the issue as an historical one: "the monuments of the juridical express, in the radical manner associated with their function as the *writ of power*, the imaginal nature of normativity and its ceaseless quest for the symbolic outcome of an alienation specifically tied to the phenomenon of the image" (1994: 98). In more succinct form, Battista stipulates: "The imaginal is not a world, but it is what makes a world possible in the first place . . . to put it bluntly, the imaginal is a field of possibilities" (2014: 61). The image opens, which is to say founds and also opens up the social, the specular roots of the normative and it is in that opening and unleashing that the unsettling quality of the image is felt. To escape the stupefying effects of foreclosure thus means pursuing the image, opening to the imaginal and exploring the precise form of the unsaid.

In his discussion of a law without rule, Derrida references the incalculable, a knowledge that 'would be' liberated from rule, separated from its prior order and "the objectivity of a presence". Set free from the extant epistemic structure, the 'to come', the proleptic knowledge, the future of being is conceived as democratically disaggregated, no longer ordered around "a theory, a logic or an ontology – perhaps even around an ethical, juridical, or political system" (Derrida 2002: 181). Structure is not given, obligation no longer ordained, and knowledge is spared its invariance and predetermination. Put differently, in a legal context, the image precedes calculation, and the imaginal founds language and the reasoning of juridical deliberation. In specifically juristic terminology,

[7] The most expansive study is that of Legendre (1994). A translation is forthcoming from Routledge. For more recent work on the topic from a political perspective, see Battista (2014) and Legendre (2016).

the *imago decidendi*, the image that finds and founds the decision, precedes and dictates the *ratio decidendi*, the reason for deciding, that subsequent courts must endeavor to follow as precedent, as law.[8] It is time then to be done with avoidance and to broach the said of the unsaid as the imaginal basis of deliberation and determination.

The desire that escapes repression in the form of an image is a sign of invention, a ground of judgment, and I will argue that it is the primary point of access to the limitless domain of the unsaid. There is only the process of coming to consciousness, the emergence in discourse of what defies direct articulation and remains enclosed in the further reaches of the figural, in the specular relay of the imaginal. These lateral intimations, these sense impressions, represent possibilities, glimmerings, slips that momentarily and visibly juxtapose the image and the decision, creativity and rule, desire and law. To pursue the juridical theme further, I will take a recent example, a case, an instance of a decision, in Technicolor, by an academic, a public intellectual, a judge, Richard Posner, in *Sandifer v. U.S. Steel Corp.*[9]

The case went to the U.S. Supreme Court, but the instance of judgment that I will address is the Seventh Circuit Court of Appeals. First the prose. In a class action, the employees of the defendant Steel Corporation sued under the Fair Labor Standards Act for compensation for time spent at work changing into work gear. The Act stipulates a minimum wage for all hours worked but does not define work. The issue was whether the apparel being put on was clothing in the everyday sense, for which compensation was not payable, or whether the items were not clothes, but rather safety equipment, in which case donning the outfit would be encompassed as work, as part of the job and so compensable. As the Act did not define clothes, it was for the Court to determine the propriety of inclusion or exclusion of travel to and from the changing rooms and changing time as work or as being on the workers' own time. As Posner puts it, the failure of the statute to define the meaning of work is "a critical hole that the courts must fill" (592).

A critical hole, a blank space, a lacuna, a gap or breach suggests the figural in its classical sense of *fingo*, forming and making, shaping and fabricating a cover, a screen, an image that will veil the void. Already there is a sense of the hole as a trap – it is critical, dangerous, law threatening – while also inviting invention, creation of an argument, the imaginal depiction of a resolution that will efface the deficit and render the hole whole. The exercise in invention begins with a lexical description: "The alleged clothes consist of flame-retardant pants and jacket, work gloves, metatarsal boots (work boots containing steel or other strong material to protect the toes and instep), a hard hat,

8 On the specifics of the concept of *imago decidendi*, see Goodrich (2017).

9 Sandifer v. U.S. Steel Corp. 678 F.3d 590 (2012).

safety glasses, ear plugs, and a 'snood' (a hood that covers the top of the head, the chin, and the neck)" (592). As the description covers items of apparel that would never be encountered in any non-specialist clothing store, and as two of the items are so unfamiliar as to require parenthetical definition, the impetus of the description would appear to be toward these items being specifically for work and therefore included in the Act. Surprisingly, that is not, however, how it looks to Judge Posner.

The judgment makes a sudden turn, a self-conscious shift in medium and direction of argument with a magnificent apparent non sequitur: since a picture is worth a thousand words, here is a photograph of a man modeling the clothes:

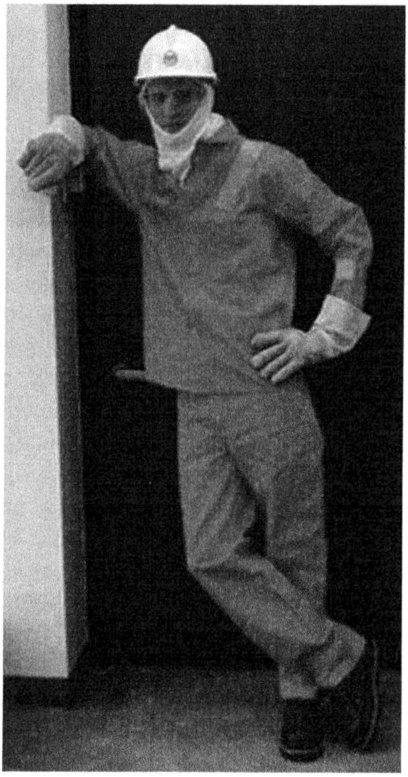

The sudden incursion of an image fills the critical hole in the text and at the very least suggests a screening and veiling of the legal lacuna with a portrait of the real. The image is bright and imposing, taking up over a third of a column and in color but gains little direct discussion, it speaks or more accurately does not speak but obscurely demonstrates for itself. It is literally the said of the unsaid insofar as Posner J. restricts his analysis to stating that, other than the glasses, earplugs and hard hat, "the outfit certainly *seems* to be clothing" (593, italics original). And of the other items, the hat "*might* be regarded as an article of clothing, and in any event putting on the glasses and the hard hat and putting in the ear plugs is a matter of seconds and hence not compensable, because *de minimis*" (593).

The key term, italicized by the Judge, is that it 'seems' to be clothing. The beseeming of the seams is highly suggestive: the outfit has the appearance of clothing, but precisely in seeming to be clothing the Judge is betraying the fact that it is not in reality clothing. The image is a simulation of apparel, a modeling of a costume, but precisely in seeming to be other than it is, in merely representing rather than being clothing, the appearance is deceptive. This quality of simulating is perhaps obvious from the fact that the costume is modeled, that these vestments are presented as fashion and so are advertised as a species of clothing whereas their actual function is quite other to the runway and the *beau monde* of celebrity designers, the in vogue and high style. The Judge gives no consideration to the fact of the costume being modeled, nor does he appear to proffer any attention or weight to the svelte figure and flauntingly seductive pose of the model. This is particularly surprising in that the photograph shown is the product of work of the highest order by a trinitarian concatenation of Judge Posner's law clerks. The photograph proved dispositive and not only withstood appeal to the Supreme Court but merited positive comment from Justice Ginsburg in the course of argument before the Court. It surely deserves mention that the photograph was taken by Timothy Shapiro; the paraphernalia, snood and all, was modeled by Mark Savignac; the conspectus, event and entertainment were assisted, singly and severally, by Daniel Siegfried. They merit condign acknowledgment and proper laudation for an imaginative instance of imaging that early augurs a now expansive trend in the remediation of argument and decision. At the same time, however, the miscognition of the image, the willingness to glance at it and infer without further deliberation that it 'seems', that it appears to be, clothing signally fails to address the fact that precisely in seeming, it dissimulates clothing. The barest rudiments of critical analysis of appearances would hasten caution, at the very least in the sense that seeming is simulating, that the image is staged and that the staging is an unacknowledged part not only of what is shown but also of the hidden driven drive, the desire that opens, and so founds the image as the covert figure of the juridical imagination. There is another scene to this other scene of the image as judgment.

Staying with the 'seeming' to be clothing the image has a dual function. In one aspect it is there to point, to ostensively reference the real. The picture is conjured, judicially inserted, to show that the costume is clothing, to dispense with argument by means of demonstration, by the visible truth of what is modeled for the viewer to apprehend. The picture, somewhat counterintuitively or at least uncritically, is presented as self-evident, or, to borrow from Saint Augustine, as *vera philosophia, non simulationis*. We are supposed to straightforwardly perceive the picture as clothing, in part at least because clothes are what models don, adorn and display, and in other part because that is how the image appears to the Judge, because he says so. The other aspect, however, of this emplotment of a picture in the judgment is that it necessarily traduces the argument by introducing a synecdoche, a picture for a thousand words, as if the picture were simply a substitute, a quicker relay of what the text will bring. In treating the image as self-evident, as seeming to show clothes, the Judge also reduces the image to text, the depiction to language, the portrait to a common sense or putatively uncontested shared perception of common law.

It is in the latter aspect, as a simulation of a common sense of clothes, that the insertion of the image has its greatest effect and moves toward dissimulation – the pretense to not be what it is, an image, a depiction, *veritas falsa*. The depiction is of a model, dressed up as a steel worker, modeling an outfit. It simulates the apparel that the steel worker has to wear in the precise sense that the model is not a steel worker and is nowhere near the agon, the molten pig iron, the sparks, flames, heat and fire of a steel foundry. The simulation, a concept developed by Gilles Deleuze, pretends to something it does not have, a reality that it mirrors whereas, for Deleuze, the simulation "is the phantasm of itself, that is, the effect of the functioning of the simulacrum as machinery.... By rising to the surface, the simulacrum makes the Same and the Similar, the model and the copy, fall under the power of the false (phantasm)" (1990: 263). This is to say that the simulation announces the emergence of the image in the associative domain of the imagination which functions to remove the representation from any immediate connection with the source or apparent subject of the representation. It takes flight and represents in its own right. The image of the model wearing the workers' gear is thus thrust into an associative chain of images that have no actual reference in the empirical domain in which the disputed apparel is used. The dress that is modeled has no relation to the worker, nor is the image related juristically or otherwise to the archive of images upon which it is itself modeled.

For the Judge, the image appears to be extracted *ex nihilo*, as an autonomous, freestanding, undiluted and direct representation of what it is that the workers wear. The inserted depiction, however, proffers the precise opposite of such denotation. It rather channels attention away from the litigating subjects and into an entirely different domain of costume, of 'painted cloth', of livery and coat armor in the classically heraldic terms in which apparel encountered law, and images contested sumptuary rule. Dress has always generated anxiety, in that it expresses spirit and can be variously idiosyncratic, being treated juristically as either excessive, properly restrained or mutedly fashionable.[10] For the purposes of viewing Posner's image, however, it is the fact that the clothes are being modeled that is most striking and significant. In the world of fashion, *Project Runway*, *Top Model* and the like, fashion dominates the domain of dress and it is clothes that are the primary object of modeling. The association of modeling is consistently with fashion and the fashionable, and by extension with the flimsy and evanescent, with changing winds and transient trends expressed in lissome and often emaciated forms. A model is a 'fashionista', a devil wearing Prada, and so to show an outfit being worn by a model is to set up an image that appears to be concerned with clothes, but carries with it an undertow, a vast domain of the unspecified and unsaid lusts and desires, carnal and venal, curatorial and status driven, that fashion imposes.

In *Sandifer* the meaning of such seeming dress, the composition of clothes is deflected by way of the image of the clothes, and specifically by virtue of the absence of the persons who wear them and the context in which they are worn. The model is rather a pretty substitute, a false person, an actor pretending, simulating a worker. But the actor is not a steel worker, nor is the protective gear as modeled, the same as the protective gear worn by workers in the dangerous context of production. The picture used does not represent the subjects under discussion nor does it depict the garments *in situ* or *in actu*. The image rather simulates in the strongest of senses because what it represents is itself a simulation, a modeling of a significantly absent worker. The image hides as much or more than it reveals in that it is a copy of a copy. The point, the *punctum*, in semiotic terms is that "far from being an image without signification, the simulacrum is at the center of an intensification, namely a more sophisticated play of sense, which interpretation should not ignore" (Bertetto 2015: 27). The Judge, however, precisely chooses to ignore, to extract and abstract, to avoid and to stupefy. After all, the model explicitly shows a modeling of clothes. Standing in a doorway, in a nondescript environment, the contexts in which the protective gear would be used, the furnaces, the fires, the smelting, the intense heat and danger that the gear protects against is entirely absent, as are the workers and the smoke and grime, the burns and wounds, that attend such industrial activity. Nothing could be less threatening than the context of the modeling, nor further removed from actual use, and thus distracted by the simulation, the Judge can move to ignore the fact that what is modeled is not clothing that would ever be worn outside a dangerous work environment. He refuses to admit that the items

[10] Watt (2013: xix) arguing for the homonymy of law and dress based upon a territorial similarity between the jurisdiction of law and the jurisdiction of dress. The older heraldic law on clothes, on livery, coat armor and vexillological depictions is referenced in Goodrich (2014).

are protective in function and specific to the work being done, thus falling into the statutory requirement that work time be compensated.

There is a long history of legal intervention in what can be worn, in how different ranks and genders dress, and that history is the subject of sumptuary law, concerned as it is with the social divisions and statuses, the dignities and honors, uniforms and rites that dress models and expresses. Industrial dress is not entirely distinctive, but being primarily functional it is generally governed by the Factories Acts and by health and safety codes, or by military and paramilitary or police regulations. The police officer in the United States and elsewhere may wear a gun, but it is not dress. By extension it can at least be argued associatively, by way of images, that insofar as what is put on is for protection, be it from crime, or fire or industrial hazards, it is probably not 'clothing' in its accepted contemporary senses. Protection may look like clothes when worn by a model or seen out of context, but such modeling and such images are highly deceptive, or in the old language of such debates they are more idols than icons, simulations rather than replications. The image of the protective gear, if uncritically viewed, if judged simply by what the picture seems to show, is a lure, a seduction to fashions and scenes that are not simply non-probative but likely misleading. The picture is in essence here a manner of unsaying, it is the unsaid of the said.

It would have been perfectly possible for the Judge to insert a picture of workers, single or several, of the steel plant, of furnaces, but he chose not to do this. Posner ignores the subjects and their context, the reality of the dispute. The unsaid here gains expression in the unseen. In political terms it is the *who* of the case, the actions and relations that form the subject matter of dispute that are obscured by the non sequitur of the image selected. This is judicially, to borrow a phrase, a reckless unsaid, a refusal to address the dress, to engage with the actors, with who it is that is in this juridical context precluded from appearing and so remains as the said of the unsaid.

The plethora of tropes and metaphors of exclusion, of the silenced, of the unspoken and of the unsaid may add a certain content to critique, but my focus here has been somewhat different. It is upon the unsaid of judgment and specifically the unsaid of the judicial determination. The insertion of a singular image of a singular actor wearing pristine vestments in an anodyne and aseptic context is a way of stating the unsaid, of proffering an imaginal representation of invention that both conceals and reveals. The two coalesce in the image, which is only ever a reference, an association, part of the *iconomus* or law of the visible. Viewed from this more visiocratic perspective, the judgment is part of a scopic regime and law. The image prompts decision against the unseen and unsaid, against the means of production, the workers, the site and space of fabricating steel. As a *soi-disant* economist, Posner the academic is interested in what arrives and circulates on the market, and not with how it gets there or who makes it. They are simply costs and must be subordinated to benefits. Product trumps producers. To legitimate such a judgment, the logic of excision and abstraction removes the issue from the bodies and places of production, the site of the conflict, and redraws it in the form of a model and the seduction of dress.

The latter element of desire deserves a final annotation. Viewing is different to reading. The gaze wanders, it moves and jumps, ignores and focuses upon aspects of the image, it apprehends in sensual form. Reading by contrast scans in linear fashion, is normative and controlled. Bartolus insists, in his early treatise on signs, that it is the law that the eye move from left to right across the page (1994). There is, to borrow from Deleuze, a 'crowned anarchy' to the nomadic distribution of the image, a floating element of chance, of lust, of the law of desire (1990: 280).[11] The figure that Posner chooses to insert belongs within an archive of images, a lexicon, an iconic law of images that advertise, lure, seduce and virtually control. Anticipating orange is the new black, Posner reproduces what is in Barthesian terms a mythology, an advertising message which is paid for by the owner of the product so as to praise and sell the items depicted. In this sense, it is Posner who 'gets sold' in that he selects and uses the image to cover over and escape from the events and the practices that he is purporting to judge. It allows him to render, to paint, an injustice. The image lacks denotation but is suffused with connotation, with the sense and nomadism of desire. The unsaid of this said is precisely the moment of judicial invention, his seduction, the choice of this affectively alluring pose: the model leaning, legs crossed, relaxed, available, desirable. You want this, I want this, the Judge can almost be heard to say. In wanting this, in showing the image, the decision also proffers an elusion, a vanishing point, the unsaid, the stupefaction of judicial desire.

REFERENCES

Bartolus of Saxoferrato ([1358] 1994). *Tractatus de insigniis et armis*. Berkeley, CA: Robbins Collection.

Battista, C. (2014). *Imaginal Politics: Images beyond imagination and the imaginary*. New York: Columbia University Press.

Bertetto, P. (2015). *Le Miroir et le simulacra*. Rennes: Presses Universitaires de Rennes.

Deleuze, G. ([1969] 1990). *The Logic of Sense*. London: Atholone Press.

Derrida, J. (1997). *The Politics of Friendship*. London: Verso.

Derrida, J. (2001). *The Work of Mourning*. Chicago: University of Chicago Press.

Derrida, J. (2002). *Negotiations*. Stanford, CA: Stanford University Press.

Fish, S. (1987). Denis Martinez and the Uses of Theory. *Yale Law Journal* 96: 1773.

[11] For a crucial study of the distinction between reading and viewing, scanning and looking, and on the *ambulatio* of the eye, see Laurence Moinereau, *Le générique du film: de la lettre à la figure* (Rennes: PUF, 2009).

Goodrich, P. (2013). *Law in the Courts of Love*. London: Routledge.
Goodrich, P. (2014). *Legal Emblems and the Art of Law*. Cambridge: Cambridge University Press.
Goodrich, P. (2017). Pictures as Precedents. In E. Anker and B. Meyler (eds.), *New Directions in Law and Literature*. Oxford: Oxford University Press, 176–192.
Lacan, J. (1993). *The Psychoses*. New York: Norton.
Lecourt, D. (2001). *The Mediocracy: French Philosophy since the Mid-1970s*. London: Verso.
Legendre, P. (1994). *Dieu au mirroir: Etude sur l'institution des images*. Paris: Fayard.
Legendre, P. (2016). *L'Animal humain et les suites de sa blessure*. Paris: Fayard.
Moinereau, L. (2009). *Le générique de film: de la lettre à la figure*. Rennes: PUF.
Sutherland, K. (2011). *Stupefaction: A Radical Anatomy of Phantoms*. London: Seagull Books.
van Boxsel, M. (2003). *The Encyclopedia of Stupidity*. London: Reaktion.
Watt, G. (2013). *Dress, Law and the Naked Truth*. London: Bloomsbury.

Index